W9-BXN-499

Independent Feature
Film Production

Independent Feature Film Production

REVISED EDITION

A Complete Guide from
Concept Through Distribution

Gregory Goodell

St. Martin's Griffin ⚲ New York

INDEPENDENT FEATURE FILM PRODUCTION: REVISED EDITION. Copyright © 1982, 1998 by Gregory Goodell. All rights reserved. Printed in the United States of America. No part of this book may be used or reproduced in any manner whatsoever without written permission except in the case of brief quotations embodied in critical articles or reviews. For information, address St. Martin's Press, 175 Fifth Avenue, New York, N.Y. 10010.

Library of Congress Cataloging in Publication Data

Goodell, Gregory.
  Independent feature film production.

  1. Moving-pictures—Production and direction—Hand-
books, manuals, etc.   I. Title.
PN1995.9.P7G64   791.43'068   82-5746
ISBN 0-312-18117-5   AACR2

Revised Edition: June 1998

10

For
Jennifer, Alexandra, and Vanessa

Contents

PART THREE

Production

PART FOUR

Postproduction

PART FIVE

Distribution and Marketing

Acknowledgments

IN ORDER TO THANK ALL OF THE PEOPLE WHO HAVE CONTRIBUTED to this book I would have to name everyone in the film industry with whom I have had the pleasure of working. I have learned from each of them and a part of each one can be found on these pages.

I stand in particular debt to my father, John Goodell, for his careful reading of the manuscript, his insightful comments and suggestions, and for reminding me on several occasions, when I was struggling to phrase something clearly, that "Words are no damn good."

I am especially grateful to Michael Donaldson whose encouragement, support, and invaluable contributions made this edition possible.

Others to whom I am indebted include: Jim Chory for his insights into production, budgeting, and scheduling; Christein Goldstein for her careful reading of the chapters on digital postproduction; John Muto for his perceptive thoughts on production design; Ron Ramin for his contributions to the sections on film music; John Shafer for his input on the material dealing with laboratories; Martin Shapiro for teaching me more than he probably realizes; and Bill Varney for contributing his technical expertise to the sections on postproduction sound.

I would also like to acknowledge contributions from Wendol Jarvis, Gary Kaufman, Sydney Levine, Gary Marsh, Andy Pratt, Dan Satorius, Dov Simons, and Lori Slomka.

Finally, I wish to express my sincere gratitude to Gordon Van Gelder at St. Martin's Press for his careful and meticulous handling of the manuscript, and for his patient understanding of its author.

Preface to the New Edition

AMERICAN DREAM, ANTONIA'S LINE, THE APOSTLE, BIG NIGHT, The Blair Witch Project, Boogie Nights, Braveheart, Brother's Keeper, The Brothers McMullen, Chasing Amy, Clerks, Cop Land, Crumb, Dances With Wolves, Dead Man Walking, El Mariachi, The English Patient, Everyone Says I Love You, Fargo, Four Weddings and a Funeral, Fresh, The Full Monty, Go Fish, Heavy, Hoop Dreams, I Shot Andy Warhol, The Ice Storm, Killing Zoe, Laws of Gravity, Leaving Las Vegas, The Living End, Lone Star, Looking for Richard, Lost Highway, Menace II Society, Mortal Kombat, Night on Earth, Once Were Warriors, Paradise Lost, The Piano, The Player, Private Parts, Public Access, Pulp Fiction, Roger & Me, Scream, Se7en, Shine, The Silence of the Lambs, Slacker, Sling Blade, Smoke, Soul Food, Spanking the Monkey, The Spitfire Grill, Swimming With Sharks, Totally F***ed Up, Tremors, The Wedding Banquet, Welcome to the Dollhouse, Working Girls, Year of the Horse, Zebrahead.

These titles form an eclectic list. Some are theatrical films, others are documentaries. Some are intense, personal statements; others are simply commercial ventures designed to turn a profit. Some have broken box office records and garnered fortunes for their makers; others have received widespread critical acclaim and have won numerous awards. A few have achieved both. But all these films share a common bond: They are all independent features.

The term "feature" refers to the principal attraction playing in a movie theater, usually ninety minutes or more in length. The term "independent" is not so easily defined. Some define a film as independent if the filmmaker is financially at risk for the cost of production; others by the degree to which the filmmaker maintains creative control over the project. Still others argue that if a major movie studio—Disney, MGM, Paramount, Sony (Columbia and Tri-Star are divisions of Sony), Twentieth Century–Fox, Universal, or Warner Bros.—is involved on any level, a film cannot be called independent.

For the purposes of this book, I am defining as independent any film that is *developed* without ties to a major studio, regardless of where the subsequent production and/or distribution financing comes from. The *development* phase, which will be discussed at length in this book, refers to the creation and packaging of the elements necessary to obtain production financing. These elements may include a script, commitments from actors and a director, and a legal structure for the purpose of raising the money to make the picture. Whether production financing comes from friends and relatives, foreign presales, a studio, or some combination of such sources, the most crucial creative decisions that define what the movie will become will be made during development. Consequently, this book addresses not just the struggling independent making a first film on a shoestring budget, but also those who wish to make films on a larger scale, and even independent producers who wish to approach studios for financing and/or distribution.

The stories behind the making of every independent feature are as diverse as the films themselves.

Filmmaker Edward Burns was twenty-six years old, living on peanut butter sandwiches, and working as a van driver in New York when he had a unique idea for a film. "I don't remember ever seeing a film that looked at the Irish-American experience today, and that's what I wanted to do." His parents had encouraged him to write ever since he won a poetry contest in the sixth grade, so he wrote the screenplay for *The Brothers McMullen*. He directed the film in collaboration with cinematographer, Dick Fisher who functioned as photographer, editor, and coproducer. They shot the picture in twenty-two days, on weekends, over the course of several months. The 108-minute film, which was shot in 16mm color, was brought in for less than $20,000. Burns's highly personal, multilayered comedy about three Irish Catholic brothers (one of whom is played by Burns) on Long Island trying to cope with women, relationships, sex, and their religious upbringing won the Grand Jury Prize in the dramatic category at the Sundance International Film Festival, and an Independent Spirit Award for Best First Feature. This remarkable little film was picked up for distribution by Fox Searchlight Pictures, a division of Twentieth Century–Fox, and has grossed over $10 million.

Writer-director James Mangold made his feature debut with a film called *Heavy*. The title describes the main character's 250-pound bulk and the psychic load he carries: guilt, self-loathing, and loneliness. Everybody loved the script, but nobody wanted to make the film because it was about a fat guy. Mangold began with seed money and started shooting without enough to get his film in the can. During production there was a constant scramble for funding. Eventually he succeeded in raising the $1 million necessary to complete the film, which starred Liv Tyler, Shelley Winters, Deborah Harry, and Pruitt Taylor

Vince. *Heavy* received a Special Jury Award for direction at the Sundance International Film Festival, and Mangold was tapped to direct another independent feature from his original screenplay, *Cop Land.* The $15 million film, starring Sylvester Stallone and Robert DeNiro, earned over $45 million at the domestic box office in its first three months of release and established Mangold as a serious player in Hollywood.

Filmmaker Terry Zwigoff believed that investors would rush to fund a documentary feature about the legendary underground comic artist R. Crumb. All he needed, he felt, was some sample footage of Crumb and his brother, Charles. He shot the sample, took it to Hollywood, and spent the next nine years shooting the film and piecing together the money to complete it. Thirty days of that nine years were actually spent filming; the rest was spent raising money from private investors. "It was horrible. I'd be in this situation with great stuff happening, and I'd have to allot myself two rolls of film instead of ten." The 16mm color film cost $300,000. It won top documentary honors at the Sundance International Film Festival, and was bought by Sony Pictures Classics. Zwigoff received an advance of $195,000, out of which he had to pay for the blowup to 35mm. But the gamble paid off. *Crumb* was a critical and box office success, grossing over $3 million in the United States alone. Roger Ebert called it "one of the most remarkable and haunting documentaries ever made."

Dutch-born feminist filmmaker Marleen Gorris wrote a script about a ninety-year-old woman who wakes up one morning and decides that it is time for her to die. "Unlike some," the narrator tells us, "Antonia knew when enough was enough." The film *Antonia's Line,* flashes back thirty-five years to the moment Antonia returns to her hometown after World War II and mothers a matriarchy of illegitimate, strong-minded females. Several producers tried, and failed, to raise financing for the film. Finally, producer Hans de Weers thought to make it a European co-production. De Weers brought in Antonino Lombardo, head of Belgium's Prime Time production concern, and arranged to film part of the picture in Belgium. De Weers and Lombardo put together a consortium of Dutch and Belgian backers. The London-based European Co-Production Fund joined the funding, making it a British-Belgian-Dutch film. A statement describing this complex arrangement was included in the press kit: "Produced by Hans de Weers for Bergen Films and Co-produced by Antonino Lombardo for Prime Time, and Judy Counihan for Bard Entertainment in association with The Dutch Film Fund, The Flemish Community Fund, The European-Co-Production Fund, Investco S.A., NPS/Dutch Cultural Broadcasting Promotion Fund, the Dutch Co-Production Fund & The EURIMAGES Fund." Gorris was given the $2.7 million needed to make her film in later summer, and began shooting in September on locations in Belgium, France, and Holland, with a Dutch cast. When the film was completed, London-based Sales Company, which handled international sales, set up an all-female screening at the Cannes Film Market, explicitly underlining the film's target audience. Even the film's male producers were excluded from the screening. The 200 women who attended responded with such enthusiasm that art house distributor First Look Pictures immediately acquired all North American rights in all media. The film, which earned nearly $5 million in domestic box office grosses, and has been shown in more than twenty countries, won the Audience Award for Best Picture at the Toronto Film Festival, Best Screenplay at the Chicago International Film Festival, and Best Director at the Hamptons International Film Festival. But most significant, it won the Academy Award for Best Foreign Language Film. "An Oscar was as far away from my mind as the North Pole," said Gorris. "You just don't think like that, and now it so happens that *Antonia's Line* has become a commercial film."

Billy Bob Thornton, a self-described hillbilly, spent his early days at his grandmother's house in Alpine, Arkansas, with no indoor plumbing and no electricity; his grandfather was a forest ranger who trapped much of the family food. Thornton became a rock-and-roll singer and drummer before moving to California to pursue an acting career. While performing a minor role as a railroad conductor in the film *The Man Who Broke 1,000 Chains,* he came up with the idea for the title character in his film *Sling Blade.* The story tells of Karl Childers, a man who is released from an asylum after committing a horrible crime twenty-five years earlier. Returning to his hometown, Karl strikes up an unlikely friendship with a young boy and his mother. As Thornton recalls, "I went into my trailer at lunchtime, sat in front of the makeup mirror and started making faces at myself. . . . I started talking like Karl, and his whole story—the entire monologue at the beginning of the film—just came out of me right there." He initially performed the monologue as a one-man stage show called *Swine Before Pearls,* then collaborated with director George Hickenlooper to expand it into a short film titled *Some Folks Call It a Sling Blade.* Hickenlooper and several friends raised $55,000 from several investors and shot a twenty-nine-minute black-and-white film in an abandoned hospital in three days. It debuted at the Sundance International Film Festival, received favorable notices, and became the basis for the feature version. It took Thornton seven days, spread out over a period of two months, to complete the screenplay. He made his directorial debut and starred in the two-hour-and-thirteen-minute film with a remarkable supporting cast that included Robert Duvall, John Ritter, J. T. Walsh, and Dwight Yoakam. The $1.2 million film was shot entirely on location in and around Benton, Arkansas. Although it was shot in color, Thornton wanted it to have a black-and-white feel, to give it a mood and a sense of timelessness. The productions designer, costume designer, and set decorators were instructed to avoid bright colors. They limited themselves mostly to gray and brown tones. Costumes were washed over and over to fade them. Karl's wardrobe was limited to one costume: a gray shirt, gray pants, and clunky black shoes. Interestingly, his clothing remains remarkably pristine and pressed throughout the story. As Thornton describes the title character, "Karl is an angel, even if he's not a very conventional angel. He never sleeps, doesn't sweat, and his clothes never, never get wrinkled or dirty." Immediately after acquisition screenings in New York and Los Angeles, Miramax bought worldwide distribution rights for $10 million. The film has grossed over $24 million at the box office, and earned for Thornton Academy Awards for Best Screenplay Based on Material from Another Medium and Best Actor. *Sling Blade* also won the Independent Spirit Award for Best First Feature, and a Special Jury Prize at the Chicago International Film Festival. Thornton parlayed his success with *Sling Blade* into a multimillion-dollar multipicture deal with Miramax that calls for him to write, direct, and perhaps act in at least three films. According to an article in *The Hollywood Reporter,* he will receive a minimum of $2 million per picture plus a share of the films' gross revenues.

New Jersey filmmaker Kevin Smith set out to make a comedy, originally titled *Inconvenience,* about clerks in a convenience store and a video store. He shot the film in 16mm black and white in twenty-one straight days for a budget of $27,000. Smith and his producer, Scott Mosier, took their film to the Independent Feature Film market in New York. The screening was scheduled for Sunday morning at ten o'clock. There were eleven people in the audience and ten of them were members of Smith's film crew, but the eleventh was a distribution scout whose solitary word of mouth started *Clerks* on its way to the New Directors/New Film series at the Museum of Modern Art and the Sundance International Film Festival. Miramax picked up distribution rights, then spent an additional $200,000 to complete the picture in 35mm and remix the sound track. They spent another $1.7 million in advertising, and attached trailers for the film to 800 prints of *Pulp Fiction* during its initial release, thereby capitalizing on the wide release of that enormously successful picture. *Clerks* grossed over $3 million in domestic release, another $1 million in overseas revenue, and sold 60,000 videocassettes. Smith followed *Clerks* with *Mallrats,* a $6.1 million disappointment for Gramercy Pictures, then rebounded by returning to his low-budget roots with *Chasing Amy,* a comedy about a regular guy from New Jersey who falls in love with a lesbian. *Chasing Amy* was completed for less than $1 million and has earned over $12 million at the domestic box office alone.

John O'Brien's novel, *Leaving Las Vegas,* sold fewer than 2,000 copies. After reading a copy given to him by a friend, art dealer-turned-producer Stuart Regen tracked down O'Brien, who was working odd jobs at the time, and optioned the novel for $2,000. Regen teamed with Lila Cazès and Annie Stewart to produce, and Mike Figgis to write and direct. The completed screenplay was shown to Nicolas Cage, who agreed to star in the film. The package was then offered to several major U.S. studios and all of the significant independent companies, all of whom turned it down. The quote was, "We think it will make a wonderful film, but we wouldn't know how to market it." A French company, Lumiere Pictures, put up the entire $3.6 million budget. The film was shot on location in Los Angeles, Las Vegas, and Laughlin, Nevada, in twenty-eight days using 16mm color film. In addition to writing and directing the film, Figgis, whose roots are in experimental theater, composed the music and played trumpet during the recording session. MGM/UA acquired distribution rights to *Leaving Las Vegas* for $1.5 million and spent less than $2 million on advertising. The film opened initially in a handful of theaters in major cities, and quickly expanded to 200 screens. Among the many accolades bestowed on the film and its makers are:

- Academy Award for Best Actor
- Golden Globe Award for Best Performance by an Actor
- Independent Spirit Awards for Best Feature, Best Director, Best Actor, and Best Cinematography
- Chicago Film Critics Association awards for Best Actor and Best Actress
- Screen Actors Guild Award for Best Lead Male Actor
- National Society of Film Critics awards for Best Director, Best Actor, and Best Actress
- National Board of Review award for Best Actor
- Los Angeles Film Critics Association awards for Best Picture, Best Actor, and Best Actress
- New York Film Critics awards for Best Picture and Best Actor
- Boston Society of Film Critics award for Best Actor
- Society of Texas Film Critics award for Best Actor
- San Sebastion Film Festival Silver Shell awards for Best Director and Best Actor

Leaving Las Vegas, the film that nobody wanted, has grossed in excess of $35 million, sold not by an expensive advertising campaign but by the positive word of mouth generated by enthusiastic audiences.

Twenty-three-year-old Mexican filmmaker Robert Rodriguez won prizes on the festival circuit with an eight-minute short titled *Bedhead,* starring four of his nine siblings, and fully expected that someday he would be offered an opportunity to direct a feature. For practice, he made an eighty-one-minute film intended for the Spanish direct-to-video market on a budget of $7,225. His plan was to use the profits from that film to make another independent feature "for practice." Rodriguez earned $3,000 of the budget by checking himself into a medical research facility that was seeking people to test a cholesterol-lowering drug. During his thirty days in the hospital, for which he was paid $100 a day, he wrote the script for *El Mariachi.* Carlos Gallardo, Rodriguez's longtime friend and star of the film, sold part of his land to help finance the film, and the balance came from Rodriguez's savings. The story is set in a Mexican border town. It tells of a mariachi musician who comes to town and is mistaken for a hit man who arrives on the same day; both are dressed in black and both carry guitar cases. Rodriguez wrote the script with very little dialogue so that he could shoot most of the film without recording sound. "Where I really saved was in shooting the movie silent. A lot of takes would have been blown due to unexpected drive-bys, noises, and all the things that usually blow a sound take." Rodriguez shot as little film as possible, partly because his borrowed Arri 16S camera was so old, he was worried that it might break down. For food, he and his small entourage went to Gallardo's house for home-cooked meals. On some days Rodriguez saved even more by letting the cast go before lunch. He kept his shooting ratio down by shooting everything in one take. Initially he intended to film for three or four weeks, but after the first ten days he was asked to return his borrowed camera because it had been sold. He condensed the rest of the shooting into four days. He cut the picture in two-and-a-half weeks, editing initially on one-half-inch video; he then transferred it to three-quarter-inch for the final cut. A local cable company allowed him to use a character generator with which he subtitled the entire film. Rodriguez's credits on the film include writer, director, film editor, sound effects editor, music editor, camera operator, still photographer, and special effects. The film won the Audience Award at the Sundance International Film Festival and was picked up by Columbia Pictures for distribution. The studio spent an additional $1 million to complete the picture, which included blowing it up to 35mm and creating a new sound track. *El Mariachi* grossed over $2 million and sold over 20,000 videocassettes. Columbia was so impressed with Rodriguez that they gave him $7 million to make a sequel, called *Desperado,* which starred Antonio Banderas. Rodriguez is credited on that film as writer, director, editor, and steadicam operator. *Desperado,* which won the Golden Palm at the Cannes International Film Festival, has grossed over $50 million.

Mary Harron was so intrigued by the author of the SCUM Manifesto (Society for Cutting Up Men), Valerie Solanas, who also shot and nearly killed Andy Warhol, that she decided to make a film about her. Harron spent two years researching and compiling information about Solanas before cowriting the screenplay with Daniel Minahan. New York producer Christine Vachon first heard about the script from Harron's friend, casting director Dan Haughey. She met with Harron and coproducer Tom Kalin, and the process began. Lindsay Law, having recently been named president of Fox Searchlight Pictures, and Anthony Wall came aboard as the film's executive producers. The $1.7 million film, titled *I Shot Andy Warhol,* was writer-director Harron's first feature. The cast included Lili Taylor, Stephen Dorff, and Jared Harris. Ms. Taylor won Special Jury Recognition at the Sundance International Film Festival for her role as the film's star. Total foreign and domestic box office grosses, plus video revenues from 100,000 units, for Harron's first feature topped $10 million.

The Sacred Heart League, a Mississippi-based Catholic charity, conducted a research study to determine how best to increase its financial strength in keeping with the principals of the organization. The study suggested that they produce an independent feature film. Roger Courts, the league's head fund-raiser, formed a for-profit production company called Gregory Productions, Inc., with the intention of making a film that would "present the values of the Judeo-Christian tradition." After considering several projects, he hired writer-director Lee David Zlotoff (creator of ABC's "MacGyver") to write and direct a "character-driven drama about the human spirit." Zotloff wrote *The Spitfire Grill,* a story about a girl on release from prison who finds work and friends in a small town in Maine. The film was shot in thirty-six days in Vermont for a budget of $6.1 million. It premiered at the Sundance International Film Festival, where it received standing ovations, won the coveted Audience Award, and was purchased by Castle Rock for $10 million, triple the amount ever paid for an independent film at Sundance.

Filmmaker Barbara Kopple first chronicled the struggle of American working people in her now classic documentary *Harlan County, U.S.A.,* which won the Academy Award for Best Documentary Feature. Nearly ten years later she and producer Arthur Cohn traveled to Worthington,

Minnesota, to make a film about how the harsh economic realities of plant closings and wage concessions were affecting workers in the heartland. While in Worthington, Kopple saw a story on the news about the Hormel meat-packing plant, located 100 miles away in Austin, Minnesota. The company was declaring a $29 million profit while announcing plans to cut the paychecks of their 1,500 employees by nearly 25 percent—and the employees were prepared to fight back. Kopple went to Austin, where she shot footage of a union rally, thus beginning a five-year odyssey to complete *American Dream.* She immersed herself in the Austin community, lived with its people, and gained a trust that made it possible for proud, strong union men to sit in front of her camera and weep when talking about their inability to provide for their families. She endured wind chills of sixty below, carried and operated her own sound gear, and was continually struggling to raise money to finish the project. In addition to private investors, she received contributions from foundations and church groups. Kopple recalls one point when "my New York office called and said, 'We have two hundred and seventy-five dollars left in the bank. What are you going to do?' I thought, What am I going to do about it? I can't even get warm. Later on, they phoned back, saying, 'We just got twenty-five thousand dollars from Bruce Springsteen.' And I burst into tears from exhaustion and relief." Springsteen's contribution was especially fitting because the local meat-packers' slogan was the same as the title of one of his hit songs, "No Retreat, No Surrender." The 100-minute film, shot in 16mm color for a cost of nearly $1 million, won Ms. Kopple her second Academy Award for Best Feature Documentary, as well as the Grand Jury Prize, the Audience Award, and the Filmmaker's Trophy at the Sundance International Film Festival. Kopple achieved what she set out to do. Janet Maslin said in *The New York Times* that "Ms. Kopple's stirring, forthright film captures an American town, the strength of its traditions and the deep and permanent ways in which those traditions can be destroyed. Her work is as important as it is good."

Bryan Singer teamed with Christopher McQuarrie and Michael Feit Dougan to write a film about an evil stranger who arrives one day in the small town of Brewster. The stranger starts a local public-access cable TV show called "Our Town," and invites people to call in with their responses to one simple question: What's wrong with Brewster? Singer made his directorial debut with this study of the malaise lurking beneath the tranquil surface of a typical small American town. The film, titled *Public Access,* was shot in eighteen days, almost entirely in Los Angeles, for $250,000. At the Sundance International Film Festival it shared

the Grand Jury Prize with Victor Nuñez's *Ruby in Paradise.* Singer and
McQuarrie teamed again when Singer directed McQuarrie's original
screenplay for *The Usual Suspects,* a $5.5 million independent feature
for Gramercy Pictures. The film won Academy Awards for Best Screenplay and Best Supporting Actor, and has earned over $45 million in do-
mestic and foreign box office grosses, and another $11 million from the
sale of 185,000 video units.

Filmmaker Paul Bucknor discussed an idea for a gender-reversal film
titled *Satisfaction* with Uberto Pasolini at the Cannes Film Festival.
Bucknor's idea was "to explore friendships and sexual relationships between the different races in modern Britain." When they met again a
year later in London, Pasolini suggested a deal to make the film with
Bucknor as coproducer. Simon Beaufoy was commissioned to write the
script, his first feature credit, about six laid-off Sheffield steel workers
who regain their dignity by forming a strip troupe. Pasolini secured financing to develop the script from Britain's Channel Four, but when the
script was completed Channel Four turned down the project for production financing. Pasolini signed director Peter Cattaneo, who planned to
take his seventy-minute film, *Loved Up,* to Sundance that year. Pasolini
brought his package, which included Beaufoy's script and Cattaneo, to
sell at the same festival. When Fox Searchlight executives saw *Loved
Up* at Sundance, and Pasolini's package, they agreed to finance the
movie, now titled *The Full Monty,* for a budget of $3 million. The film
was shot in seven weeks. Before shooting the final scene, in which the
film's heroes bare all before a crowd of 400 screaming women from
northern England, shots of whiskey were passed around to the cast. Cattaneo further bolstered the actors' confidence by promising a "one-take
deal." Sundance officials saw the ninety-minute film twelve months
after Pasolini made his deal with Fox Searchlight. Even though the
deadline had passed for it to be included officially in the festival, they
arranged a screening for it in the town library. Following the Sundance
premier, Fox Searchlight held Monday-night test screenings in ten cities
across the country during July and early August in advance of the film's
official opening on August 13. A teaser ad tied to the test screenings
asked, What is the Full Monty? Following the screenings, word of
mouth spread quickly. When the film opened officially on six screens in
Los Angeles, New York, and San Francisco, *The Full Monty* grossed
$244,375 in the first weekend, boasting the highest per-screen average
of any movie released that year. The film expanded to 387 screens
across the country, played to sellout audiences, and in five weeks rose to
number three in the box office charts. The buzz was so hot that talk-
show hosts, and the general public, began using the expression "the full

monty" to mean "going all the way." The takings for each screen were the highest in America, exceeding even those of Hollywood's biggest concurrent releases. In its first month in the United Kingdom *The Full Monty* took in nearly $13 million, topping the box office charts for three straight weeks, and becoming the most successful film in British history. Worldwide box office for this $3 million film exceeded $150 million. Nobody predicted this extraordinary success. According to Cattaneo, "The joke on the set was that the film would probably go straight to video."

AN ENTIRE BOOK could be written about each of these films on its way to eventual success. The purpose of this book, however, is to guide others in the making of successful independent feature films. Each film travels essentially the same path from concept through distribution. This book examines, in depth, each step along the way. The contents have been divided into five sections:

1. Legal Structuring and Financing
2. The Preproduction Package
3. The Production Process
4. Postproduction
5. Distribution and Marketing

The book is organized to complement all areas of filmmaking and will prove useful for everyone from interested students to seasoned professionals. Some portions address themselves specifically to the independent producer; other sections are written for the director. Certain technical aspects of filmmaking are examined from both points of view. These technical discussions are not intended as how-to-do-it sections; they are meant to explain what everyone on the production team does and how *they* do it. Part 5 explains how to position a completed, or partially completed, film in the marketplace. Every venue for motion picture marketing (domestic, international, video, and so on) has distribution companies seeking product, and every distribution company has at least one acquisition executive whose job is to find and acquire films. The initial market for an independent film seeking distribution is not the movie-going public; it is the acquisition executives at distribution companies. This section will tell you how to attract their attention so that *they* will come to *you.*

I refer often in this book to low-budget and medium-budget features. When I say low budget I am talking about films that cost a few thousand dollars to $2 million; a medium budget is between $2 and $10 million. I have been cautious not to mention specific salaries and prices (except in sample production budgets), since these are subject to change. I have, however, included all of the information necessary to find current prices for everything necessary to complete a motion picture.

For the newcomer, this book may at first appear complicated and difficult. I am not claiming to make the process easy; independent feature film production requires tenacity, creativity, and just plain hard work on the part of everyone involved. But the more you understand, the less complicated and difficult it becomes. The real complexities come when you approach production without a thorough understanding of the process. Those more experienced in motion picture production will already be familiar with the information in some portions of this book. But there is always the possibility that even in these areas you will find a useful new detail or a new slant that makes reading the entire book worthwhile.

Legal Structuring
and Financing

An Overview
of Independent Financing

IN THE YEARS SINCE THIS BOOK WAS FIRST WRITTEN, THERE HAVE been extensive changes in the financing options available to producers of independent feature films. All of the methods discussed in the original version of this book have been updated, and many new approaches have been added. These revisions were written in consultation with Michael C. Donaldson, an entertainment attorney in Beverly Hills, California, with an emphasis on independent producers of feature films and television productions. The following discussion should not be construed as legal counsel or advice; keep in mind that before making a commitment to any specific format for handling these matters, it is important to obtain professional legal counsel.

One way to locate an appropriate attorney for your needs is through word-of-mouth reputation within the film community. Another way is through local bar associations that have referral systems for various types of legal services. If you are seeking an entertainment attorney in Los Angeles County, you can telephone the referral service at the Los Angeles County Bar Association or the Beverly Hills Bar Association. Both services will locate an appropriate attorney in Los Angeles County and arrange an appointment for you. Attorneys who are listed with this referral service are those who meet certain bar association requirements, pay a nominal fee for the listing, and agree to provide a free initial consultation to potential clients. You will pay a small fee to the bar association to help defray their expenses. In Los Angeles, the initial consultation with an attorney is limited to half an hour; anything beyond the initial half hour will be billed by the attorney at an hourly rate. Since legal opinions vary, it is best to interview several experienced attorneys before choosing one. When you have selected one who is knowledgeable, whom you trust, and with whom you are comfortable, stick closely to that person's advice.

Obtaining financing is often the most difficult part of making a film. Regardless of how you go about raising money, be certain that you are fully prepared to convince investors of the merits of your project before you walk in the door. This preparation often requires as much creativity as making the film itself, and it is extremely important, because if you are turned down you will almost never get a second chance. You will probably experience a string of rejections before you succeed in funding a motion picture. Remember that no matter who turns you down, if their reason for saying no is because they don't like your project, they are expressing nothing more than their *opinion*. The rejections may have nothing to do with the merits of the project, but they will certainly test whether or not you are passionately committed to the film you intend to make.

The Studios

The principal source of motion picture financing comes from the major studios: Disney, MGM, Paramount, Sony (Columbia and Tri-Star are divisions of Sony), Twentieth Century–Fox, Universal, and Warner Bros. They finance films costing between $10 million and $200 million apiece, and produce approximately 25 percent of the total number of films made each year. They each spend between $400 million and $500 million a year on film production, and they make a profit. Unlike the odds in gambling casinos, where, if you play long enough, you will lose, the more films a company makes, the greater are its odds for success. A study by Paul Kagan and Associates of movies costing over $4 million produced the following results: A random slate of five pictures was not profitable, a random slate of ten pictures was not profitable, but a random slate of twenty-five pictures *was* profitable. The study indicated that one out of twenty pictures garnered a profit, and that profit was enough to offset the losses incurred by the others. It should be noted that this study was done at the beginning of the blockbuster era (the *Batman* era) and would probably be less true during times when the studios lean toward producing smaller pictures.

There is even speculation that the *Batman* era was a concerted effort on the part of the major studios to buy all the box office and drive out the middle-level competition. Midsize companies like Castle Rock and Imagine Films, who simply supplied product to the majors for distribution, survived the era quite nicely. Small companies, such as October Films and Strand Releasing, weren't hurt because their films compete for a select audience that doesn't threaten the box office of major studio releases. But it was difficult for midsize companies, such as Orion and Weintraub, to survive because they were attempting to distribute their films in direct competition with the majors, and they simply didn't have the cash to produce an equal number of films. Such a company might be lucky initially and produce one or more successful films, but the danger in doing so is the same danger faced by a person who goes to Atlantic City and wins on the first throw of the dice. It is easy to lose sight of the fact that you are playing a game of odds, and regardless of how the odds are stacked in the long run, the fact is that nobody can consistently pick winners. In his book *Adventures in the Screen Trade,* William Goldman wrote what has become one of the most quoted lines in the industry. He says that a basic truth of the movie business is "Nobody knows anything." But in a separate interview he went on to say why: "No one has the least idea because you're guessing public taste three years down the line. No one knows what will work and that's why it's all a crap shoot."

When independent films began to earn significant dollars—close to 15 percent (nearly $750 million) of the annual box office sales in North America—the studio blockbusters couldn't drive them out because the public was ravenous for alternatives to mainstream studio blockbusters. *Pulp Fiction* was made for $8 million and earned in excess of $210 million worldwide. *Four Weddings and a Funeral* was made for $6 million and grossed $250 million worldwide. *Dead Man Walking* cost $12 million and grossed $100 million worldwide. So what did the studios do? They began gobbling up the independents, either by acquiring successful independent companies or by establishing divisions for the purpose of financing and/or acquiring for distribution lower-budget, edgier films made outside the studio system. Examples include Disney's purchase of Miramax; New Line went to Time Warner; Gramercy is a division of Polygram; October was bought by Universal; Sony uses Sony Classics to handle lower-budget, edgier movies; and Fox created Searchlight for the same purpose. According to Robert Redford, "The majors have always been predatory. They'll scoop up anything they can if they think they can make money with it." Studio ownership didn't spell the demise of these sources for financing and/or distribution, and by all accounts they are left alone to make films as they see fit, but they are not entirely free from the influence of their parent companies. For example, films with an NC-17 rating (which bars anyone under the age of seventeen from purchasing a ticket) are shunned by the studios because video chains and theaters often refuse to carry them. In the old days, Miramax wouldn't have hesitated to take on a film with an NC-17 rating, but since Disney bought the company that is no longer the case. Miramax has established a subsidiary company, Dimension Films, to handle such material.

Because of the size of their bank accounts, facilities, and organizations, major studios have the most clout in terms of financing, distribution, and the availability of "name" talent; and the majority of box office income is generated by studio-affiliated projects. For these reasons, many filmmakers ultimately seek studio affiliation, either directly or in association with an independent company with a studio deal. One consideration is that the studio will insist on creative control over the picture, including final cut of the film, with power to override the producer whenever there is a difference of opinion. An experienced producer with an excellent track record, as well as a handful of stars and directors, may negotiate for some of this power. The most notable example is Woody Allen, a thoroughly independent filmmaker who maintains complete creative control over his films while working within the studio system. In a recent interview, he said, "I can't imagine that the business should be run any other way than that the director has complete control of his films. My situation may be unique, but that doesn't speak well for the business—it shouldn't be unique."

Relinquishing creative control to the studios means that the filmmaker is encumbered with, and often frustrated by, notes from a variety of executives, many of whom remain faceless and nameless. These begin with script suggestions and continue throughout production with comments on everything from lighting to camera placement to actors' performances, and on into postproduction with notes on every version of the film through the final cut, at which point the project is often taken over completely by the studio.

Henry Jaglom (*Always, Can She Bake a Cherry Pie?, Eating, New Years Day*), who makes his films for under $1 million, was once offered a budget of nearly $20 million to make a studio film, with $1.5 million for him as director. He agreed, with one stipulation: that the studio give him authority over the final cut. This would have allowed him to join the studio system yet remain independent. The studio refused and the deal fell apart. Referring to his independence, Jaglom said, "If you want to be a serious artist in film, you have to get your financing away from Hollywood. I get mine from the Europeans. My films do very well in Europe." Jim Jarmusch (*Down by Law, Mystery Train, Night on Earth, Permanent Vacation, Stranger Than Paradise*) shares this insistence for creative control: "The only thing that matters to me is to protect my ability to be the navigator of the ship. I decide how the film is cut, how long it is, what music is used, who the cast is. I make films by hand." In order to maintain that control, he pieces together his financing almost entirely from European and Japanese sources. It would be simpler for him to finance his films domestically, but in doing so he would be forced to give up some of his coveted creative control. John Sayles shares this sentiment and offers this advice about raising money: "It's like hitchhiking: It can be the third car that stops, or it can be the three-thousandth one that gives you the ride. But you also have to know when not to get in the car."

Studios periodically take risks with independent filmmakers, either with financing or distribution, or both, especially if they feel that those filmmakers have their finger on the pulse of the country's youth. But for these filmmakers to remain fully independent, the financing must come from some other source. That isn't to say that a film loses its heart or its uniqueness simply because it is financed by a major studio. Studio films that exhibit a commitment to artistic integrity include *Edward Scissorhands, The People Vs. Larry Flynt, Quiz Show,* and *Searching for Bobby Fischer.* What studio affiliation means, simply, is that if there are disagreements between the filmmaker and the studio, the studio has the final say.

For most independent producers seeking studio affiliation, there are a number of stumbling blocks that stand in the way. In the first place, it is rare for a studio to commit itself to production financing without a substantially developed package. The term "package" defines a combination of elements that may include a script, stars, director, and budget. Studios will sometimes agree to fund an independent producer who is *developing* a property such as a book, an idea, or a story line into a screenplay. In such cases the studio will provide funds for optioning the source material (a book, magazine article, rights to a true story, and the like), if any, and writing the script. This is called getting the studio "pregnant," and the deeper their commitment is, the better. If a producer approaches a studio with a completed script, the studio may option the script or buy it outright with the intention of packaging it for production.

An independent producer who enters what is commonly referred to as "development hell" is no longer making a truly independent film. The fundamental decisions that define what the movie will become, including the direction and tone of the story and screenplay, and the selection of the screenwriter, cast, and director, will be subject to committee approval at the studio. Nonetheless, many independent producers seek such affiliation, and for that reason a brief discussion of the studio development process is appropriate.

A development deal is made official when the parties involved sign a letter (called a *deal memo*) outlining the basic terms of the agreement such as salary, time schedule, credit on screen and in advertising material, percentage participation in the film's profits, and "turnaround" rights. The turnaround provisions cover such things as which party controls the property, how the studio's costs will be repaid if the project is successfully set up elsewhere, interest on the studio's costs, and lingering profit participation on the part of the studio that initially developed the material. A formal contract containing the details of the agreement in appropriate legal language is negotiated and prepared by agents and attorneys while the project is in active development. The total payment a producer agrees to accept (if and when the picture is produced) may involve impressive sums of money, but the majority of it is speculative. The contract usually allows for only a small portion of a producer's income (often 10 percent or less) to be paid during development. The important payments come only if the film is subsequently financed for production.

Generally, a development deal is a *step deal* in which the studio pays the persons who are contributing to the property's development (such as a writer or producer) in increments as the project is developed. The writer is the one who fares best financially if a project is aborted during the development stage, for often the writer is the only one who receives any significant payment. Step one in the deal might be the story outline for the screenplay, a first-draft script would follow as step two, and so on. The studio will retain the right to stop the process at any step along the way, though it will be liable for payments guaranteed in the development deal; for example, if the writer is guaranteed payment for a story, a first draft, a rewrite, and a polish, the studio will pay for each of these steps even if the project is aborted at an early point.

Most commonly, producers seeking a development deal approach studios through an agent or entertainment attorney who submits the property, often a completed script, to the studio on behalf of the producer. In other instances the agent or attorney will arrange a meeting between the producer and a creative development executive at the studio, during which the producer will verbally "pitch" the idea or story in the hope of convincing the executive to fund the development of the project.

If you pitch to the studios, be sure that you have done your homework. You must not only be the expert on your project, able to answer any questions that might come up, but you must be knowledgeable about the studio you're pitching to. Some studios like to be involved in the packaging process, others like producers to come in with elements that are attractive to that studio. Unless you are fully familiar with the studios' policies, it is best to approach them with no packaging. An actor or director might sell at one studio but not at another. Studios have different relationships with different actors, and attaching your project to any actor, with the exception of the few bankable stars, may limit your financing opportunities. Another consideration—and it's one of the most "iffy" things about packaging a film independently—is the question of whether you can successfully hold on to your cast while you get the money. If you raise your money based on an actor's commitment and availability and that actor becomes unavailable by the time you raise your money, you may have to start over. Before even *suggesting* actors, it is important to find out which actors have deals at which studios. Your best source of information will be agents and entertainment attorneys familiar with the various studios. Another resource is the *Hollywood Creative Directory* (see Appendix E). This publication lists, among other things, actors with studio deals, independent companies with studio deals, and includes cross-referenced indexes with names, companies, and contact information.

When pitching to a studio, stay focused on one or two projects that you believe in, rather than presenting ten projects in the hope that one sparks an interest. This is crucial: Your passionate commitment to a project will do more to convince an executive of its worth than almost anything else you can do. Be succinct, but take as long as you need to tell your story. Also, be able to identify the film's target audience. Demonstrate that you have an understanding of the business as well as a creative approach to your project. In most cases you won't be pitching to the committee that makes the final decision, so you must give the executive some business ammunition to present to that committee.

When seeking studio affiliation for production, it is unwise to present a budget because they will have their own approach to budgeting. If and when you do get into discussion about the budget, the worst thing you can do is minimize the costs. They might say yes, and you won't be able to deliver the film.

Unfortunately, a great many pictures are partly or completely developed but never produced, and in such cases the producer, even with an adequate contract, often encounters problems in regaining ownership of the original property. It is therefore extremely important to negotiate *in advance* what will happen to a property should the studio elect to abandon it during the development process and put it into turnaround.

Studios are often loathe to put even a partially developed property into turnaround because of the subsequent embarrassment if and when the producer sets the project up elsewhere and turns it into a major success. Examples include *E.T.,* which was in turnaround at Columbia when it went to Universal. *Se7en* was put into turnaround at Warner Bros. because they had a thematically similar movie called *Copycat.* Paramount purchased for very little money a novel that was in turnaround called *Forrest Gump. Home Alone* was ready to begin shooting when Warner Bros. put it into turnaround because they didn't feel that Macaulay Culkin could carry the film. Even *Gone With the Wind* was in turnaround. When this sort of thing happens, heads roll at the studios.

A deal with a major studio is almost always a production/distribution (P/D) deal in which the studio ties up worldwide distribution rights from the beginning. When a studio is financing the production, it is in a powerful position to negotiate a distribution deal that weighs heavily in its favor. Given the sophisticated accounting techniques for which the major distributors have gained a formidable reputation, the independent producer is generally advised to negotiate a large advance and not to expect much additional income from net profit participation in the picture. Even if a picture is extremely successful, an independent producer's participation might not be meaningful.

By the time *Batman* had earned $285 million worldwide, it had garnered for the distributor a fee of nearly $89 million (31 percent), but the net participants received nothing. Even many in the Hollywood community were startled when financial statements surfaced showing that the blockbuster was wallowing in red ink. Two of the film's executive producers, Benjamin Melniker and Michael Uslan, sued for $8 million in damages. The lawsuit alleged that, based on Warner's accounting formula, "*Batman* will never earn net profits." Warners Bros. issued a statement saying that "the monies were paid strictly in accordance with the signed contracts between the various parties." Table 1 is a copy of the studio accounting sheet as filed by Warner Bros. in Los Angeles Superior Court.

It doesn't always work out that way but, as you can see, even an extremely successful film may have a difficult time digging its way out of the studio's accounting hole. Entertainment lawyers in Los Angeles commonly recommend that clients audit any picture that has any likelihood of going into profits. An audit of studio books for U.S. and Canadian expenditures costs about $15,000. However, these audits routinely uncover millions of dollars in "errors," almost all of which were made in the studio's favor. There are no stories circulating in Hollywood of studio accountants getting rapidly promoted by calling close ones in the producer's favor. It is interesting to note that the final true accounting will usually be slightly different for various participants because of differing definitions in their contracts.

Clearly the best deal for a producer is a gross deal, since there is less room to manipulate what that means. Even with a gross deal, however, studios often find ways to define their obligations favorably. The principal reason for this is the labyrinth of contract terms and unending pages of accounting definitions in a net participation deal. That is why there is

TABLE 1

'Batman' Breakdown

Gross Receipts:
Domestic
    Theatrical $148,207,352
    Nontheatrical 1,998,812
    Television 0
Foreign
    Theatrical/Nontheatrical 64,197,049
    Television 2,620,000
Pay TV 24,320,501
Videocassette 34,328,942
Music 460,863
Records 461,993
Merchandising 8,806,000
TOTAL GROSS RECEIPTS 285,401,512
Less: Accounts Receivable 137,241

Reportable Gross Receipts **285,264,271**

Distribution Fee **88,962,584**

Net Receipts After Distribution Fee **196,301,687**

Expenses:
Prints 8,877,399
Preprint, Dubbing, Subtitles, Editing, etc. 1,229,135
Advertising and Publicity (includes 10% override) 59,989,121
Taxes, Duties, Customs, and Fees 3,691,826
Trade Associations 2,124,109
Freight, Cartage, Handling, and Insurance 1,442,246
Miscellaneous, Checking, and Collection Costs, etc. 1,588,324
Guild, Union, and Residual Payments 2,494,740
TOTAL EXPENSES 81,436,900

Net Receipts (Loss) After
    Distribution Fee and Expenses **114,864,787**

Investment and Other Deductions
Negative Cost and/or Advance 120,895,652
Interest 14,141,373
Gross Participation 0
Deferments 0
TOTAL INVESTMENT AND OTHER DEDUCTIONS 135,037,025

Net Receipts (Deficit)
    Unrecouped ....(20,172,238)

Net Receipts (Deficit) ....**(20,172,238)**

Source: Warner Bros. financial statement in L.A. Superior Court.

such emphasis placed on involving experienced legal and accounting counsel in distribution negotiations who will know early on what the distribution agreement will mean in *practice.*

The following quote from *Legal and Business Problems of Financing Motion Pictures* illustrates this disparity: "The beginning of wisdom in understanding distribution agreements is to recognize that the terms 'net profits' and 'gross receipts,' when incorporated in a distribution agreement, take on meanings totally different than those associated with these terms by accountants or the general financial community." In other words, these terms are *redefined* in distribution agreements. Judge Harvey A. Schneider, who presided over the Art Buchwald versus Paramount breach-of-contract trial, concluded that the studio's net profit formula is essentially unfair and branded certain portions of it "unconscionable." At an earlier phase of the trial, star Eddie Murphy commented that net profits have long been scoffed at in the industry as meaningless "monkey points." In order to protect themselves from the repercussions of the Buchwald trial, some studios changed the language in their contracts that refers to gross and net profits to such phrases as "participation points," "net proceeds," "formula break-even points," and "contingent payments."

Ronald Bass, entertainment-attorney-turned-screenwriter (*Dangerous Minds, The Joy Luck Club, My Best Friend's Wedding, Rain Man, Sleeping With the Enemy, Waiting to Exhale*), has a different view of studio contracts: "My perspective as a lawyer, having negotiated a million of them, is that while it's very, very hard under those definitions for a picture to reach net profits the way those definitions are calculated—there isn't anything surreptitious or secretive going on. There's nothing underhanded in the definition—the studios say this is the way they want to do business."

One factor that contributes to the difficulty of a film ever reaching net profits is that gross participants are paid first. These are usually the film's stars, though sometimes others, such as a star director or star producer, can command gross participation. By the time *Rain Man* had returned $228 million in gross receipts to United Artists, the film was still in the hole for more than $30 million, largely because of the gross participants (principally Tom Cruise and Dustin Hoffman). Of the $228 million in gross receipts, United Artists took $79 million (35 percent) as a distribution fee plus $55 million to cover distribution expenses (prints, advertising, residual payments, and taxes), which left $94 million. If there had been no gross participants, the film would have paid back its $46 million production costs and been into healthy net profits. But the gross players received $77 million of that $94 million, which left only $17 million to cover the $46 million production cost. Add to the remaining production debt of $29 million the $750,000 still owed in deferred payments, and you have a deficit of nearly $30 million. Finally, if and when a film reaches net profits, the studio usually keeps 50 percent of net profits for itself. There are usually so many gross participants ahead of any net participants that it is hard for anyone to reach net profits but, as Ronald Bass says, "there isn't anything secretive or unfair about it."

Another disadvantage to the studio deal, at least for the beginning producer with a low- or medium-budget picture, is that the studios are not generally interested in low- and medium-budget films. When I say low budget I am talking about films that cost a few thousand dollars to $2 million; a medium budget is between $2 million and $10 million.

The average negative cost (the cost to produce a movie) of studio films has risen dramatically over the years. According to the MPAA (Motion Picture Association of America), in 1960 the figure was $1 million. The average cost today is nearly $40 million. Add to that an average of $20 million for marketing costs and you have an investment of $60 million per picture. The combined production and marketing costs for major summer releases average well over $100 million per picture. It has even come to the point where studios today are telling established independent producers not to bother them with a project unless they think it can make $100 million. Jack Valenti, president of the MPAA, said in reference to the film industry's desire to lower production costs that within the studio system "it's going to be a difficult journey because there is no virtue so universally unpopular as frugality."

An exception to this is when the studios court a hot new independent filmmaker in the hopes of getting a blockbuster for a price (the next *Pulp Fiction* or *Shine*). According to Lauren Zalanick, one of the producers of *Kids,* the silent prayer of a studio executive courting a new director is "Maybe they will make me a beautiful, brilliant $8 million film . . . that will gross $100 million." Remember that we're talking here about financing the *making* of a film, not picking up a film for distribution once it's completed. The latter issue will be discussed in Chapter 23.

There are several reasons that studio films cost as much as they do. First, the studios have contracts with the unions, which add considerably to a film's budget. Teamsters alone can cost over a million dollars. Second, a producer will usually be required to utilize the studio's production facilities (phone system, sound stages, prop shop, wardrobe department, studio drivers, and so on), all of which will be provided to the producer at nonnegotiable top-of-the-market prices. The studio will tack on overhead and surcharges for the use of its facilities and equipment. This means that the studio is paying *itself,* and this money is referred to in the budget as "soft dollars." They do this because, when the film is distributed, all costs of production, including "soft dollars," are paid back to the studio before any money is shared among net profit participants. This explains why studios often make money even when their pictures don't.

Third, there are hefty built-in overhead expenses involved in running a studio facility that can boost production budgets by as much as 25 percent. Lastly, because production and distribution costs for most studio films are so inherently high, the studios find it necessary to hedge their bets with expensive name stars, name producers, and name directors. Within the studio system, executives say that the high cost of making films is the result of several things: the increasing importance of the overseas market, which favors action and high-tech blockbusters; the desire among studios to make franchise films that they can merchandise at stores or exploit in sequels and in theme parks; and the fact that actors and crew involved in a studio picture expect to be paid top dollar and are unwilling to cut their fees (as many do willingly when making independent films). There is also the fear among these executives that if they make more risky films and they fail at the box office, they will lose their jobs. So they "green light" megabudget, star-driven derivative action films like *Daylight, Eraser,* and *Speed 2: Cruise Control.*

Independent Production Companies with Studio Deals

Of the approximately 150 films released by the major studios each year, roughly half come from independent production companies such as Castle Rock, Imagine, and Mandalay. Stars very often have their own production companies with similar studio deals, and they are constantly on the lookout for good scripts. These companies are generally affiliated with a studio for both production and distribution, so deals with them often offer pros and cons similar to the direct studio deal. A development deal with a nonstudio production company has an advantage over a studio deal, since independent companies generally produce a much higher percentage of the pictures they develop. As mentioned earlier with respect to studios, your best source of information about these companies will be agents and entertainment attorneys who deal with them on a regular basis. Another valuable resource when approaching companies with studio deals is the *Hollywood Creative Directory* (see Appendix E).

For the beginning independent producer, there are substantial road-blocks and downside considerations to direct or indirect affiliation with the studios, and often one must find an alternate source of financing.

The Specialists

Specialists in motion picture financing are usually tax attorneys or investment counselors. They have clients with high-risk capital who wish to invest in motion pictures. They will generally "pool" motion picture investment capital from a number of clients and invest in several films simultaneously, thereby cross-collateralizing the investment and minimizing the risks. These are usually studio films.

For the independent beginning producer, the problems with the specialists are similar to the problems with major studios. They are not generally interested in small films but prefer substantially packaged major star properties or movies that are sold on the basis of spectacular special effects, in which the star is the elaborate special effects and the carnival-ride nature of the movie itself (*Twister, Independence Day, Jurassic Park*), rather than an actor. The reason is simply because *every* producer, from the most well established to the struggling beginner, has a tin cup out; rarely will a producer dip into his or her own pocket to produce a film. This means that the specialists have their pick of experienced producers with strong track records, which reduces the risk of cost overruns and increases the likelihood of attracting, and obtaining commitments from, major stars. It is best to approach the specialists through an entertainment law firm accustomed to moving in these circles.

One kind of specialist, known as a producer's rep, is increasingly interested in supporting independent filmmakers. The term "producer's rep" refers most commonly to individuals who assist in setting up distribution for films once they are completed, and sometimes when they are only partially completed; in some cases they will fund independent filmmakers who have completed principal photography and are seeking completion money in exchange for an equity participation in the film. There is a growing subculture of these individuals, among them John Pierson, who has represented and/or financed over twenty first features since 1985, including *Clerks, Crumb, Go Fish, Roger & Me, She's Gotta Have It, Slacker, The Thin Blue Line,* and *Working Girls*. The role of the producer's rep is discussed in more detail in Part 5 of this book, "Distribution and Marketing."

Bank Loans

Lending production money to a producer is a highly sophisticated and specialized banking activity. Relatively few banks are involved in this kind of lending, and those that are generally restrict their business to the major studios or producers closely associated with the majors or with established foreign sales companies. The most active lending institutions for independent producers include City National Bank, Mercantile National, Tokai Bank, World Bank, Lincoln Bank, and Imperial Bank.

It is important to remember that banks loan money on *assets*. A producer's dream of a finished film is *not* a bankable asset, nor is a completed script. No bank, anywhere in the world, will loan production monies based on a script regardless of its potential commercial appeal. A script can be effective in securing commitments from stars and a director, and certainly for putting together an accurate budget, but from a bank's point of view the only purpose for having a script is to identify the project for which you are seeking financing. As often as not, the project will be described to the bank merely by its title and author. Not even a finished film is considered a bankable asset. A bankable asset is a contract from a strong distributor or studio unconditionally promising to pay a certain amount of money to the producer on a fixed date. Therefore, in order to obtain production financing from a bank or private lending institution, it is necessary to obtain a *distribution guarantee* or a *negative pickup deal* from a reputable distributor. Exceptions to the above are the one or two European banks that will lend money based on the projections of reputable foreign sales agents; this is more fully discussed in Chapter 24, "Foreign Distribution."

A *distribution guarantee* is a contractual agreement whereby a distributor is licensed by the producer to distribute a film over a specified time, generally not less than seven years, since that is the minimum time it takes for a film to run a complete cycle that includes theatrical distribution, video sales, television sales, etc. This time frame can be double or even triple the seven-year cycle (usually written into contracts as seven, fifteen, or twenty-one years). The distributor obtains this license in return for a guaranteed minimum payment to the producer, usually within two years of the time the license begins. The licensed time period begins with the initial release of the film, usually within six months after delivery of the negative and other materials listed in the agreement. Thus, the first payment to the producer may not take place for two and a half years or more after the distribution agreement is signed.

The portion of the guaranteed amount that the producer will be able to borrow, and the interest on the loan, depend largely on the bank's perception of the distributor's ability to pay the producer whether or not the film performs well at the box office. The distributor's credit standing is a serious consideration. If a major distributor makes this guarantee, the producer will probably be able to borrow a very high percentage of the budget. If the guarantor is a small independent distributor whose credit rating is not sufficient to assure payment of the guarantee, the bank may require a pledge of assets such as stocks, bonds, and interest in other films before loaning the money. In addition to the interest on the loan, lending institutions will sometimes require participation in the film's profits. In most cases the bank will also insist that the producer pay the bank's legal fees for preparing and reviewing documents.

An acceptable distribution guarantee, which is extremely difficult for an independent producer to secure, will not by itself ensure that the bank will loan the money. The bank will also require and carefully scrutinize a great deal of additional documentation and information, including:

- a synopsis of the project
- a copy of the script
- biographies of all persons attached to the project
- proof of your right to film the literary property under consideration (called the "chain of title" documents)
- a copy of the distribution guarantee
- a copy of the distribution agreement (see Chapter 22)
- a copy of any foreign sales contracts
- a copy of the completion guarantee (discussed later in this chapter)
- a detailed budget
- a cash flow chart that includes a drawdown schedule showing when the money will be needed
- a complete financial statement of any other investors involved in the project
- a security agreement that puts the bank in a first lien position with respect to the film, the literary property upon which the film will be based, and the producer's share of receipts from all sources (this means that the bank has the first legal claim to these assets)
- an agreement between the bank and the distributor in which the distributor agrees to pay the producer's share of receipts directly to the bank until the loan plus interest is repaid; should the fin-

ished film perform poorly at the box office, the distributor will still be contractually required to make payments to the bank.

If the bank approves the loan, it will advance money during production, usually on a weekly basis, according to the drawdown schedule set forth in the documents listed above. A producer should be conscientious when working out this cash flow with the bank because it is very different to change once a picture is underway. Each advance must be preceded by a detailed cost report of monies spent to date. This procedure continues until the film is completed. Although repayment of the loan is in no way contingent upon distribution, the bank will receive monthly distribution reports that include release dates, advertising budgets, an itemization of gross film rental, distribution fees, distribution expenses, and the producer's payments as agreed to in the loan documents.

In all lending situations, regardless of the size of the loan, a great deal of paperwork is required in the negotiating process and even more in generating the detailed reports of progress required by the lender. The advent of computers and associated software programs have simplified this work and at the same time encouraged the use of longer and more explicit documentation. In all legal aspects of filmmaking, it has become practical to create agreements and contracts that include all sorts of protections against obscure, but not impossible, problems. Previously a great deal of this would have been regarded as not warranting the legal time and money required. With computers, the writing of such material is largely a matter of pushing the correct buttons and overseeing the reams of paper that spill out of the printer. It does reduce the possibility of future squabbles and expensive court actions, but while the writing is easy, the reading is time consuming.

Negative pickup is a very broad term that usually refers to a distribution agreement negotiated prior to a film's completion. Upon completion, the distributor actually "picks up" the original negative and other material listed in the agreement. The principal difference between a distribution guarantee and a negative pickup deal is that in the latter case the distributor is contracting to *buy* the original negative *and* the right to distribute the picture, if and when the picture is completed. The producer receives a payment that usually exceeds the actual negative cost (the cost of producing the film), to cover such things as interest on the bank loan and the producer's fee plus overhead. Quite often the distributor will also agree to pay the producer an advance against the film's profits. This may be paid upon delivery of the completed picture, but more commonly it will not be paid until the end of the first year of distribution, by which time the distributor has hopefully recouped at least the lion's share of expenses.

Any overbudget costs in a negative pickup deal are solely the responsibility of the producer, who must arrange for a completion bond (discussed later in this chapter) that will guarantee delivery of a finished film. In this way there is little or no risk for the distributor if for any reason the film is not finished or if the finished film in any way fails to meet the requirements set forth in the negative pickup agreement.

A negative pickup deal may be used by a producer as collateral for a bank loan for production financing, especially if the agreement provides for a large distribution advance, such as the entire cost of making the film. In some cases the distributor will put the agreed-upon sum into an escrow account for release upon delivery of the negative. However, keep in mind that the larger the advance, the smaller will be the producer's percentage participation in the film's profits.

Like a distribution guarantee, a negative pickup deal is difficult to secure. One of the problems is defining the motion picture that the producer will deliver. The script must be mutually agreed upon and adhered to during production. Deviations from the script may render the film unacceptable, or may give the studio a legal argument not to accept it if it doesn't appear to them to have commercial potential. An agreement must be drawn up that lists, and guarantees the involvement of, certain key people in the production, such as the director and principal cast members. As stated earlier, holding on to these individuals, especially actors, while attempting to raise financing is often a difficult problem for independent producers. The agreement must also define acceptable standards of technical quality; disputes regarding the technical quality of the finished film can sometimes be resolved by a competent laboratory. But standards vary throughout the world; if you clear in Germany, for example, where standards are currently the toughest, you will generally clear in all other countries. The agreement will also include a copy of the film's budget in order to ensure that the producer plans to spend enough to produce a quality product.

The negative pickup agreement is subject to many complications and should include contingency plans for which the producer can negotiate. For example, what happens if a principal cast member becomes ill and the insurance company finds it more economical to replace that cast member rather than wait for his or her recovery? Ideally, contingency plans will be spelled out in the negative pickup agreement to cover all complications that it is reasonable to anticipate.

Upon completion of the film, assuming that all the terms of the contract have been adhered to by the producer, a laboratory or other mutually agreed-upon third party will issue a letter stating that the finished film is of acceptable technical quality, that the script was substantially adhered to, that the agreed-upon cast members appeared in their proper roles, and so forth. This third-party opinion letter is one of the items that must be delivered to the distributor before any funds are released to the producer (or lending institution) to help pay back the loan. This is not to be confused with the *laboratory access letter,* generally called the "lab letter," which defines who has access to the negative and sound tracks at any given point in time (see Chapter 23).

While some films are successfully financed in this way, obtaining a negative pickup deal is complex and time consuming. For a producer without a substantially packaged property, a distribution guarantee or a negative pickup deal is virtually impossible to obtain, and without either of these, a bank loan for production financing is usually out of the question.

None of what has been stated thus far should be confused with a scenario in which the distributor actually *guarantees the loan.* From a bank's point of view, this has the obvious advantage of opening an additional source of repayment in the event that the borrower (e.g., the producer) defaults on the loan. In addition, the distributor's guarantee is a strong statement to the bank that the distributor has the utmost faith in your project. Loan guarantees from a distributor are rare put have been known to occur. One of the principal reasons they are less attractive to distributors than distribution guarantees and negative pickups is because the distributor is directly on the hook to the bank, regardless of whether or not the producer meets the contractual obligations. Distributors who find themselves in dire financial straits will commonly work out compromise arrangements with producers (like paying back eighty cents on the dollar) or will accuse the producer of some sort of breach of contract in order to avoid their financial obligations. But banks will demand full payment of the loan and will aggressively initiate legal action to collect it.

An equally important reason why loan guarantees are unattractive to distributors has to do with how they appear on the distributor's balance sheet. In order to appear financially strong to bankers, creditors, and vendors, it is important for a distributor to maintain a clean balance sheet. The heavier the distributor's contingent liabilities, the less financially secure it appears to the bank. Under "generally accepted accounting practices," a direct loan guarantee must appear immediately on the distributor's balance sheet as a contingent liability in the full amount of the loan guaranteed—even though the money goes directly from the bank to the producer and is never seen by the distributor. This amount remains on the distributor's (guarantor's) balance sheet as a contingent liability until it is repaid to the bank by the producer. A distribution guarantee or negative pickup, on the other hand, is "off balance sheet" until the producer delivers the film to the distributor; at that point the distributor is obligated to pay the producer, and the amount paid must appear on the distributor's balance sheet.

The reason why a distribution guarantee or negative pickup does not appear on a distributor's balance sheet is because the guarantee is speculative: It is based on the producer's delivery of the film and attendant material defined in the contract—and producers don't always deliver. The term "delivery" is complex and means not only delivery of the film itself, but also delivery of additional material called for in the contract, such as publicity items, legal documentation, and insurance policies (see Appendix F). Until the distributor agrees that all required delivery items are complete and acceptable, "delivery" has not legally taken place and the obligation to the producer will not appear on the distributor's balance sheet.

Banks require distributors to disclose the number of distribution guarantees and negative pickup deals they are committed to, but there is no reliable way to check on this. The difficulty of ascertaining how heavily committed distributors are is one reason why so few banks are actively involved in the business of lending money to producers based on distribution guarantees and negative pickup deals.

Completion Bond (Completion Guarantee)

When a producer has a script, a budget, and other elements necessary for a distributor to commit to a distribution guarantee or a negative pickup deal, the producer will approach a bank. If the bank agrees to loan the money to the producer, it will generally require the producer to provide protection against overbudget expenses by securing a *completion bond.* This bond is supplied by a third party called a *completion guarantor,* which acts as an underwriter for the project. The bond guarantees to cover overbudget expenses, thereby insuring that the film will not go unfinished for lack of funds.

When seeking a completion bond, a producer must convince the completion guarantor that the movie will be completed within its budget. Documentation the completion guarantor will require includes:

- script
- budget (with a 10 percent contingency)

- schedules for production and postproduction
- depending on the script, they may ask to see detailed budgets and contracts for certain areas, like special visual effects
- contracts with producers, director, and actors
- any special contracts you may have, e.g., if your picture is based on an aircraft carrier they will need to know that the navy has signed a contract allowing you to film on one of their carriers

In addition to this documentation, the completion guarantor will request to meet with the producers and director whose reputations are crucial to the bond company. Completion bond companies simply will not insure a film to be produced or directed by someone who has given them problems in the past. Following those discussions, they will go over the budget carefully to ensure that the movie can be made for its anticipated budget. They will want approval rights over certain crew members, in particular the production manager and production accountant. Once you secure the completion bond, the bank will release the money and you can make the picture.

During production, the bond company requires the producer to supply extensive reporting so that if the picture begins to climb over budget, the guarantor knows about it almost immediately. These include call sheets, production reports, and "hot costs" on a daily basis, as well as weekly cost reports. Hot costs are costs for major variables such as labor, film stock, extras, overtime, bumps in pay, etc., and indicate how much of what was budgeted for these items was actually used. Hot cost reports are not appropriate for low-budget films, where all expenses need to be tracked as closely as hot costs are on a major feature.

The guarantor will examine not only production costs but, even more important, cost *projections*. The single most significant concern the guarantor will have is whether or not the company is making its shooting day, meaning whether the production is on schedule. The fact that a filmmaker completes the scheduled number of scenes at the end of each shooting day doesn't necessarily mean the picture is on budget. The two most telling factors, aside from the schedule, are the amount of time spent each day in order to complete the scenes, and the amount of film stock that is being used. Overtime payments and the expenditure of an excessive amount of film stock are indicators that a film is in trouble. A representative from the completion guarantor will probably visit the set to ensure that you have spent your money the way the budget indicates. This individual might, for example, check to ensure that your lighting package is consistent with the one indicated in your budget.

If the production is having difficulties, one of the most unnerving moments for a producer is when the completion guarantor arrives on the set. This is usually a production manager who works for the completion bond company and who has come for the purpose of auditing the books or simply observing the production with an eye to discerning why things are going awry. This person may begin to intervene in the production, questioning the producer and/or director's reasons for shooting a particular scene in a certain way or even questioning whether it is necessary to shoot the scene at all. Remember that artistic considerations are not what's most important to the guarantor; what matters is the money. If things are not proceeding on schedule and on budget, the completion guarantor has certain rights of intervention. If it is apparent that the producer is not in financial control of the picture, these rights can be enforced even before any of the contingency money is spent. This intervention may take the form of discussions and suggestions from the completion guarantor or the mandating of wholesale changes in the production team. If the picture is going over budget, the completion guarantor has the right to insist on replacing any crew members who are causing problems. The completion guarantor may suggest that the director of photography be replaced with someone who works more quickly. Most crew members are hired on a daily basis and can be dismissed at the whim of the producer, but in some cases a dismissal may require honoring a minimum contractual guarantee; for instance, a director of photography who is contractually guaranteed ten weeks of work but is replaced after the fourth week must be paid for the remaining six weeks. The completion guarantor also has the right to mandate replacing the director (this becomes more problematic when you are dealing with an A-list director, partly because it is difficult to find an A-list director who is willing to replace another A-list director). Once you're over budget, the bond company decides if and when to take over. If the bond company feels that the picture is seriously out of control, the company can replace the producers, production manager, and accountant, and can even execute a complete legal takeover of the picture.

It is rare for a bond company to take over a film, but it does happen. Film Finances took over the $25 million film *The Adventures of Baron Munchausen* when the budget had reached $31 million; the company spent an additional $15 million to complete it. *Malcolm X* was reportedly taken over by Completion Bond Company of Century City when the costs climbed $5 million over budget (from $28 million to $33 million) by the end of principal photography.

In most cases the guarantor will have prenegotiated a desirable relationship with the distributor in the event that the guarantor takes over a picture. In such cases, the producer loses any entitlement to additional revenues, and often will be held liable for any losses incurred by the studio as a result of the guarantor taking over. The guarantor is typically in first position to recoup any money spent. On a P/D financed film, for example, the guarantor recoups any overbudget expenses first; the distributor then recoups all of the budgeted costs of production.

Bear in mind that the completion guarantor has no desire to take over a picture. Unlike a studio, where the executives may be so pleased with the direction an overbudget film is taking that they are willing to support it, a bond company has no incentive to do so. This is because the bond company is not a profit participant in the film. They would much rather work with you and for you to help complete the film on time and on budget. It is therefore wise, when entering into a relationship with a completion guarantor, to view them has a helping hand, not as an ogre standing in the wings waiting to pounce if something goes wrong.

The reason studios have the flexibility to go over budget at will is because the studio is its own bank and acts as its own completion guarantor. The exception is Buena Vista, which distributes Disney, Miramax, and Touchstone films; almost all of their films, regardless of the size of the budget, use a bond company. The studio executive who works closely with the writer and director is called the creative executive, but the studio executive who deals with the physical production of the movie is called the production executive. This person functions on behalf of the studio, much like a representative from a bond company. The production executive will closely examine the budget, meet with the producer and director, and visit the set regularly during production to monitor expenses.

Producers making films that require a completion bond generally pay 5 to 6 percent of the budget to the guarantor, with a negotiable rebate that may reduce that figure to 3 percent of the budget if the completion money is not used. The size of the rebate depends on the risk involved for the guarantor. With a first-time producer the risk is relatively high, and the guarantor might only be willing to offer a small rebate if the money is not used; in such a case the completion bond might end up costing the producer 5 percent instead of 6 percent. On the other hand, a producer with a strong on-budget track record who works regularly with the guarantor can usually negotiate for a rebate that reduces the cost of the bond to 3 percent of the budget if the completion money is not used.

Completion bond companies are included in several of the reference texts listed in Appendix E, and additional information about them can be found on the Internet.

Foreign Equity Investment

There is an abundance of production investment money (or investment in the form of goods and services) available in foreign countries such as Australia, Canada, Hong Kong, Hungary, Japan, Romania, and Western Europe. During the next several years, we will probably see increasing coproductions with countries of the European Economic Community, a flurry of activity in the Eastern Bloc countries until their economies catch up with the West, and a subsequent exploration in Asia as their film industries mature while the gap between the American dollar and their economies remains wide.

The best route to foreign production money is through entertainment law firms that are knowledgeable in financing motion pictures in the country that best fits the producer's needs. For example, an entertainment law firm knowledgeable in Canadian production financing will have connections with Canadian specialists (Canadian law firms or Canadian investment counselors who represent Canadian film investors). However, the beginning independent producer must have something more to offer than just an idea. Given a solid package, an experienced entertainment law firm will often succeed in financing productions with foreign money. An attorney experienced in financing motion pictures in this way may be found either through word of mouth within the film community or through local bar associations, as described in the beginning of this chapter.

Another resource for independent producers is the International Film Financing Conference (IFFCON), held each year in San Francisco. The purpose of the three-day event (which includes private meetings, roundtables, panels, and social events) is to provide independent producers with an opportunity to establish business relationships with, and share information with, foreign financiers, buyers, and coproducers from around the world. See Appendix E for information on how to contact IFFCON.

A significant incentive for a producer to film outside the United States is that the cost of crews and technical services goes down almost in direct proportion to the country's distance from the United States (exceptions include London and Paris, which are more costly than Los Angeles). Filming in less industrialized nations can be especially difficult. There are inherent frustrations in dealing with foreign languages and customs, and bad plumbing goes from exotic to annoying very quickly.

In several countries, the government has offered significant tax advantages for film investments; in some cases, the government itself will help subsidize productions. Their incentive for doing so is to stimulate their country's economy by offering production jobs to their people. In order to qualify for these subsidies, the majority of the film must be shot in their country using native talent, technicians, and facilities. Often there is a point system that allows producers to import key elements, such as writer, director, and stars, from outside the country in which the film is being financed. In Canada, for example, you cannot achieve the minimum point plateau without at least the producer, writer, or director being a Canadian citizen. In Australia the point system is similar, but no matter how the points are allocated, in order for a project to qualify for support from the Australian film office, there must be an Australian producer who controls the project. The reason for this is that the Australian government wishes to have more of their citizens trained to produce films. Canada is especially appealing to producers because meeting that country's requirement to film all or most of the project in Canada is relatively easy. Vancouver is just a few hours away from Los Angeles by plane and is in the same time zone; the same can be said for New York with respect to Toronto and Montreal. An additional incentive is added when the monetary exchange rate favors the producer. When filming in these countries, it is important to play by the rules. Canada recently rescinded the tax break for investors in a film in which an American writer used a pseudonym in order to qualify as a Canadian under the point system. This is not only unethical, it contributes to an atmosphere of mistrust, making shooting films in foreign countries more difficult for people working legitimately within the host country's guidelines.

Countries as diverse as Hungary, India, and Zimbabwe unintentionally create an incentive for film financing through their law controlling the export of capital from their countries. These are generally described as "blocked-funds" countries. Their governments have passed laws restricting their citizens' ability to take cash out of their countries. Film investments, therefore, present wealthy persons within those countries who would like to have cash reserves outside the country with totally legal, moral, and ethical investment opportunities. Every country with blocked-funds laws has a large number of such individuals, and often the governments involved will help put these deals together. Such deals certainly are not discouraged, and they work like this: The producer brings in as many production people and actors as he or she likes. The investor pays for all services, technicians, food, and lodging purchased in the country. The investor's money is then repaid with proceeds from the film. What makes this investment highly attractive is that such repayment takes place within the country in which it was *earned,* thereby creating wealth for the investor outside his or her homeland. The investor's government is happy with the money that has been spent inside its borders, with the employment of its people during the making of the film, and with the potential ancillary benefits of a feature film having been shot in their country. Such benefits might include a heightened awareness of the country as a tourist attraction, as was certainly the case with Australia and *Crocodile Dundee.*

Blocked-funds financing arrangements are similar to the below-the-line deals that were once carried to a fine extreme in Communist countries and are still available in some Eastern Communist countries where the governments have not yet divested themselves of government-owned assets such as studio facilities, airlines, and hotels. In these countries, goods and services, as opposed to the cash to buy them, are sometimes provided in exchange for an equity position in the film. The film industry in many of these countries is highly advanced; however, personal inspection by experienced production personnel is necessary in order to ascertain what is usable within the country and what must be imported. For example, in some countries the phone systems are woefully inadequate, fax machines may be unavailable, and often small items that we take for granted are not available at the corner drugstore. A producer has no way of evaluating these things without actually visiting the country. Usually such inspection trips are wholly or partially underwritten by the country's investors or the government itself.

Foreign tax advantages and foreign government subsidies for motion pictures are constantly changing. Various tax and legal considerations abound, including such pitfalls as double taxation and control of the property and cash flow. A producer entering into such financing arrangements must become thoroughly familiar with the foreign regulations governing the project. Much of this information is readily available through the country's embassy, but it is important that these deals be carefully reviewed with competent legal counsel.

Closely tied to the above discussion are international coproduction deals. In its purest form, a multinational coproduction deal is the result of a treaty signed by two countries that affords their nationals reciprocal benefits in the event that they join together to produce a film or films. Because so-called intellectual properties (films, music, software, trademarks) are among our nation's healthiest export items, the United States has never had an incentive to enter into such bilateral coproduction treaties.

In a looser sense, the phrase "foreign coproduction" in this country refers to any situation in which an American producer enters into a partnership with a foreign producer or production company to produce a film for whatever motivation applies. The most common reason for entering into such coproduction deals is that they make it far easier for an American producer to qualify for production incentives offered by the other nation, such as tax incentives in Canada and government grants in Australia and Germany.

There is another foreign financing option called the debt-equity swap, a method commonly used to finance a wide variety of enterprises. For a while this was popular with film producers, and it may surface again in the future. It is a tripartite (three-party) situation in which a producer approaches an American bank holding extensive hard-to-collect debts from a foreign country. The producer agrees to pay a portion of the debt, usually 50 percent, from the net proceeds of the film, and the bank forgives the remaining portion of the original loan. The debtor nation, happy to be relieved of the obligation to the bank, provides the producer with below-the-line goods and services within its country's borders in an amount equal to its original cash debt to the bank. Obviously, this approach will appear attractive to a bank only if it feels there is a better shot at collecting from the film's net proceeds than from the debtor nation.

Producers filming abroad should be aware that many countries have censorship laws requiring that scripts be reviewed prior to granting permission for filming within those countries. Members of the former Communist Bloc come most quickly to mind, but the same holds true for nations as diverse as Japan and Mexico. In Mexico, for example, Catholic and antigovernment sensibilities run unusually high, so producers should be alert to these issues in their scripts. While it is clearly not ethical to do so, some producers skirt this concern by submitting a "tempered" version of their script to the government but include the potentially offensive material when they are shooting the movie. This approach is not advisable, not only because it is unethical, but also because it puts the production at obvious risk if the falsification is discovered. This usually happens when a government representative visits the set or when a local crew member is offended by the material being shot and reports it.

If you utilize a foreign investment that requires you to shoot your picture abroad, or if you choose to shoot abroad for any reason, be sure to obtain a copy of a local government weather guide and check to ensure that the season you intend to shoot is favorable for your production.

Foreign Presales

The term "foreign presales" refers to selling the right to distribute a film in one or more foreign territories prior to the commencement of principal photography or prior to the film's completion. Today most independent film financing comes from international "sales agents" (sometimes called a producer's reps or, erroneously, distributors). A producer seeking production financing will approach these agents with a package that includes a script, a director, a cast, and a budget.

There are two types of sales agents. The first will give the producer a contract that guarantees the budget, or a portion of the budget, that is considered bankable based on the net worth of the agent's company. This sales agent typically receives between 20 and 30 percent of foreign sales and an equity position in the film's back-end profits. The agent will be somewhat involved creatively, especially with respect to casting, since the cast is what drives most foreign sales deals, but not nearly as much as with a studio. This is a major difference between studio and presale financing.

The second, and more common, type of international sales agent generally cannot afford to guarantee a film's budget. This person will take your package to film markets and will raise production money through foreign presales contracts. The largest film markets are AFM (the American Film Market), held in Santa Monica, California, in February; MIF (Marché International du Film), held in Cannes, France, in May, concurrently with the Cannes International Film Festival; and MIFED (Mercato Internazionale Filme e Documentario), held in Milan, Italy, in October. A presale contract guarantees distribution rights in a particular territory for a fixed period of time in exchange for a certain amount of money. There is no formula for the key element(s) in a sales package. Most commonly the key element will be an actor, but sometimes it will be a producer or director with a strong track record, or an internationally known writer such as Stephen King.

As with many forms of production financing, successful foreign presales require the assembly of a complete package. The sales agent will take the package into the field and presell one or more territories, collect an advance, and pass that on to the producer under a stringent intraparty agreement signed by everyone involved. This type of financing generally involves a license agreement with the foreign buyer similar to a distribution guarantee, but it does not include an equity participation for the buyer. There are a few foreign sales agents who may put up a portion of the production money for a film, perhaps 50 percent, without actually preselling the film to foreign buyers; in such cases the sales agent will generally seek some equity participation in the project.

A handful of foreign sales agents even have a sufficient track record to allow producers to borrow on their sales *projections*. In such cases the sales agent will make a confidential projection (seen only by the producer and the bank), which represents all the territories in the world. The sales agent will then attempt to presell several, usually four, territories, as a demonstration of the accuracy of the remainder of the projections. The agent must bring to the bank contracts completed by established lawyers that reflect unconditional obligations to pay an amount reasonably close to the agent's projections for those territories upon delivery of the film. Let's say, for example, that the total foreign sales projections are $1 million, and that the contracts for the four "sample" territories come in at 90 percent of the projections. Based on this sample and depending on the strength of the buyers, the bank may rewrite the total projections to reflect the 10 percent difference, that is, to reflect a more accurate overall projection of $900,000. The bank may elect to loan only $600,000 based upon those projections. The amount of the loan will depend on the risk of incomplete foreign sales, the risk inherent in the film business, and the percentage of the amount projected from the four territories that is actually committed by foreign buyers. The bank will discount the amount of the loan in order to build in a profit margin for itself, and in order to allow for the anticipated rate of inflation since they are loaning the money today but getting repaid at some point in the future. Only a few foreign sales agents have the strength to make this kind of arrangement, and only a few banks make this kind of loan.

With any of these bank financing arrangements, you will not only need to pay your own attorney, you will generally be called upon to pay the bank's legal fees for creating and processing the documents; this can run as high as $25,000. Producers often negotiate a "not to exceed" figure, but this figure most often magically and almost automatically becomes the precise figure for these services. Unfortunately, the "not to exceed" figure is typically set slightly above market rates "so that no one gets hurt"—except the producer.

If the film is already finished, a foreign sales agent will act as a middleman, representing the producer's film and negotiating the sales with foreign buyers around the world (this is discussed more fully in Chapter 24). For a film that has not yet begun principal photography, a typical foreign presale deal would be structured as follows:

- 10 percent upon signing the contract
- 10 percent upon commencement of principal photography
- 10 percent upon completion of principal photography
- the balance upon delivery of the items stipulated in the contract (see Chapter 24)

One variation is for the buyer to pay nothing until completion of the answer print. At that point, the buyer pays 20 percent. The balance of 80 percent is paid when the producer delivers the items stipulated in the contract. In this way the buyer does not take any risk with respect to the film's completion, only with respect to how it will turn out. Clearly the less the buyer risks, the less the buyer will get for the money.

The sales agent will need about three months to prepare, so if you want an agent to take your film to the film market in Cannes in May, you should finalize a deal with that agent in February.

Grants for Independent Feature Production

Independent motion picture projects are sometimes funded in part or in whole by grants from federal and local government agencies, private foundations, special interest groups, academic scholarships, educational research funds, and media organizations. Examples of independent features that have been successfully financed, either partially or completely, by such grants include *The Living End, Spanking the Monkey,* and *Working Girls.*

Because grant programs are subject to continuous modification, it is important to conduct a thorough search in an effort to learn which organizations might be interested in funding a particular project, and to learn as much as possible about those organizations. Each funding source has unique requirements and restrictions. Some will fund only individuals, some offer grants only to those working in a limited field of interest, some will restrict funding to persons living in a particular region such as the state in which the funding organization is located, and all of them have set limits on the amount of money they will award for any given project. This may range anywhere from $100 to $600,000 or more, depending on the nature of the project and the policy of the organization. Some organizations offer grants only to nonprofit organizations. In such cases it is often possible for a filmmaker to obtain sponsorship from a nonprofit organization, thereby rendering the project eligible for such grants. The IDA (International Documentary Association), an organization founded in 1982 and comprised of 1,600 members in 26 countries, offers its nonprofit status to members who apply for, and are approved for, a relationship of this kind for documentary films in exchange for 5 percent of the money received from the grant. See Appendix E for information about how to contact the IDA.

There are hundreds of organizations in the United States offering grant money and other types of support for motion picture production.

No single reference book lists them all, but libraries generally carry several volumes on this subject. One worthwhile source is *Money for Film and Video Artists,* a book from the American Council for the Arts. It lists over a hundred organizations that support filmmakers and videographers with grants, awards, fellowships, artists' residencies, equipment access, legal assistance, loan programs, emergency assistance, and technical and support services. Information about each organization includes its name, address, and telephone number; the type of award and/or scope of service it offers; eligibility requirements; and the organization's application, selection, and notification process. The book also tells how many applications are received by each organization, how many awards are given, and the dollar range of those awards. Funding sources are listed alphabetically, geographically, and by medium (film or video) and format (35mm, 16mm, 8mm, one-inch, three-quarter-inch, Beta production, etc.).

The American Council for the Arts in New York operates a Web site and hot line, funded by ACA and a consortium of supporters, that provides a nationwide information and referral service for visual artists. The library staff will match the specific needs of the callers with a database of information for visual artists, including where to go and whom to contact regarding such issues as funding, insurance, health, and law. An artist may also inquire about a specific funding organization. Included in the database are foundations and government programs funding visual artists, programs of various arts councils, arts service organizations, Volunteer Lawyers for the Arts, and others who provide information, technical assistance, and/or services to visual artists.

Another resource is a single-volume directory titled *Free Money for People in the Arts* by Laurie Blum. It lists organizations that provide grants, prizes, residency programs, and other funding to individual artists. Each entry includes the name and address of the funding organization, a description of the grant program, eligibility requirements, the dollar amount of the awards, the number of awards given, and the application procedures. The book also includes sample grant applications and guidelines for writing them successfully.

Magazines devoted to independent film and video production often include notices about available grant money. The information generally includes the name of the funding source, the amounts of money involved, application procedure, submission deadline, and contact information. A great deal of information about motion picture grants can be found on the Internet. A search of key words will result in a list of organizations, books, and other resources, along with additional hyperlinks, for this type of funding.

In addition to funding sources that award grants specifically for motion picture and video production, it may be worthwhile to approach organizations that award grants in a particular field of interest. For example, if you are making a documentary feature that revolves around life in the sea, it may be worthwhile to approach organizations that fund oceanographic research projects. One advantage to this approach is that you will probably not be competing with other filmmakers for money. It is often helpful to obtain the support of a well-recognized specialist in your project's particular area of interest. For example, in the case of the oceanographic project, the support of a leading oceanographer, perhaps as technical adviser, might go a long way toward strengthening the credibility of the project.

It is important to apply for a grant appropriate to your project. Don't submit a proposal for a feature-length film to an organization that states clearly their intention exclusively to fund short films. No matter how compelling your project, if it doesn't fit the intention of the sponsor, you will not be considered for funding.

Once you determine which funding sources appear most likely to support your project, write to them requesting information about their organization and, specifically, about their grant program. Also request an application form. This information may help you to narrow down the list of potential funding sources. The next step is to send a letter briefly describing your proposed project. If the funding organization responds positively, you will be asked to provide more information or, possibly, to submit a formal application.

An application for a motion picture grant usually requires a complete description of the proposed project, a detailed budget and timetable, biographical sketches of the principal people involved, the specific objectives of the film, and the reasons why it is significant and worthwhile. The application must be a persuasive document, one that clearly articulates what you are hoping to accomplish and how you intend to do it, but hyping your project with an obvious sales pitch will likely turn off any grant reader. Bear in mind that this document is a statement not only about your project, but about the way you think and work. If the application is carefully organized, well written, concise, and thorough, it will speak volumes for how well you communicate, which, after all, is what filmmaking is all about.

There is an overwhelming number of applications for motion picture grants submitted to funding organizations each year. Only a small fraction actually receive grants, so the chances for any one project obtaining such funds are slim. However, if one conducts a careful search to determine the most likely sources and organizes the project information with care, the likelihood of acceptance is greatly improved. If a grant is denied, you may always write an appeal letter reemphasizing the significance of the project and requesting specific information about why it was rejected. Based on the organization's response, you may wish to approach them a second time with a modified proposal.

Other Sources

Cable companies are an increasingly viable source of financing for independent films. Many of these companies, including HBO, Showtime, Lifetime, and even Encore, can be thought of as ministudios that happen to have cable outlets. The deals these companies make with producers have more in common with traditional studio deals than with television deals. The films will sometimes receive an initial theatrical release before they appear in video stores or on cable television. The companies control the theatrical release of these films and often move them quickly into video stores in order to take full advantage of the theatrical exposure. This differs from more conventional theatrical distribution deals, which contain a holdback provision that keeps films out of video stores, usually for six months, in order to maximize the films' theatrical potential.

The home video boom has diminished over the years, but this is still a major source of motion picture financing. Every major studio has a video arm that finances between twelve and twenty-four films a year. Independent video companies, such as Live, finance films for the home video market, but some of these titles receive their initial distribution theatrically. The video companies have discovered that if they intend to spend $250,000 promoting a video release, it may be more cost effective to spend that money on a limited theatrical run rather than simply promoting the title as a video.

There are many additional sources of financing for motion pictures. Members of the National Association of Theater Owners (NATO), such as General Cinema, United Artists Theaters, AMC Theaters, and Mann Theaters, will sometimes sponsor productions; several independent distributors allocate funds for production; wealthy entrepreneurs have financed films independently; and the list goes on. But how does the independent producer tap into these sources? The answer is that in every situation mentioned thus far, the financing entity (be it a major studio or an independent source) rarely commits to production financing without a substantially developed package. At the very least, this means a completed screenplay or the rights to an existing literary property, and at most it means commitments from stars, director, and perhaps a portion of the financing already in place, as from a foreign presale.

All of these doors can be opened if you have the right script at the right time, and have the right agent or lawyer working on your behalf to market the property. But even without a script, it is entirely possible for an independent producer to make a development step deal with many of these sources. Bear in mind, however, that with the exception of the granting organizations and perhaps some of the independent distributors, there will generally be considerable reluctance to develop a property with a new producer making a first feature. That isn't to say it doesn't happen, because it does, and these sources are worth pursuing, but unless funds are available to develop and package a property, all of the above doors are pretty tough to open.

Creative Financing and Self-Financing

Producers who have approached the financing sources discussed thus far and who have come up empty handed do have additional options. The same is true for independent producers who lack accessibility to these financing sources. Clearly the simplest route to nonstudio financing is to be born rich. But even filmmakers with little money have financed their films, in part or in whole, with savings, often with added support from friends and relatives. Richard Linklater partially financed the film *Slacker* by getting from his mother the same amount she contributed to his sister's wedding on the theory that he wouldn't be getting married. John Sayles used the income from his screenwriting career to help fund his early films, and more recently put up $1 million of his own money to begin his Spanish-language film, *Hombres Armados.* By now nearly everyone knows the story of Robert Rodriguez selling his body to medical science to help fund *El Mariachi.*

One drawback to funding your film personally is that it creates a potential conflict of interest. Your objectivity, when choosing between what's best for the film and what will cost the least amount of money, will undoubtedly be skewed when it's your own money at risk. Another approach that does not create this conflict is to fund a picture, at least in part, by obtaining the equivalent of cash by bartering for special deals with cast and crew members, equipment houses, and facilities. Saving money in this way is often easier than raising an equivalent amount from lenders or investors. Some filmmakers offer nothing more to the cast and crew than a featured credit in the finished film. A credit on a feature can be a valuable asset to a struggling actor's or crew member's career, and this is often a fair trade. One producer, probably inspired by Tom Sawyer whitewashing his Aunt Polly's fence, took this notion a step farther: He *charged* actors for the opportunity to appear in, and receive a credit on, his film. Actors lined up for the opportunity. He chose six for the key roles, charged them $1,300 apiece, and raised the $8,000 necessary to begin production. This was not done under the jurisdiction of the Screen Actors Guild, since SAG members, while permitted to invest in a film, may not work on a film in which employment is conditional upon such an investment.

The Hollywood Stock Exchange, which began as a game on the Internet, markets imaginary shares in future movies and profiles its investors. It then sells this information to major production and distribution companies that use it to help determine the demographics of potential audiences, marketing campaigns, and box office projections for their films. The company's owners took this concept a step farther when they decided to make their own film and sell real shares to the public. This approach constitutes a public offering, for which there are many SEC requirements.

These kinds of creative financing efforts are the hallmark of independent filmmakers, and I applaud them. There are other, more dubious, approaches that deserve mention in the hopes of discouraging filmmakers from using them. Some are blatantly illegal. Others have the potential to lead filmmakers into bankruptcy and loss of credit. Examples of illegal funding include "borrowing" money and/or equipment without permission and crashing your car in order to collect the insurance. Both have been done in an effort to finance an independent film. A more common scenario is the penchant on the part of some filmmakers to spend money they don't have, maxing out their personal line of credit, in order to make a film. These are filmmakers who fall into the trap of believing so completely in the eventual success of their projects that they go into serious personal debt in order to raise financing. Many of these individuals have been inspired by the handful of stories about filmmakers who raised money, in whole or in part, by mortgaging their homes or using credit cards to make their first film. Examples include *The Brothers Mc-Mullen, Brother's Keeper, Clerks,* and *Hollywood Shuffle.* It worked for those filmmakers. That sort of gambling is a statement about your belief in your project, but it is not very different from the handful of people who become so caught up in the euphoric hope of winning the lottery that they mortgage their homes and max out their credit cards in order to buy lottery tickets. There are stories of creditors who enter these people's homes and find the occupants surrounded by stacks of worthless lottery tickets. There are also stories about creditors who enter the homes of filmmakers and find them surrounded by celluloid. Even if you manage to make your film in this way, remember that it will take time to market and sell it (if it is sold at all), and interest charges and penalties on mortgage payments and credit card charges mount up so quickly that they may easily exceed the cost of the film. Believing in your film is crucial, but no matter how much you believe, no matter how desperate you are for financing, it's not worth risking years of debt, bankruptcy, and the loss of your credit rating. And, as this book will demonstrate, going into this kind of debt is *not necessary.*

Private Domestic Investment

Many independent feature films are successfully financed every year by people who are not rich and who do not go out on a limb with mortgages and credit cards, using a variety of funding sources and legal structures. These producers often turn to private domestic investors, convince them that a project has commercial potential, that it is a desirable investment, and that the producer is capable of delivering a quality picture on schedule and within budget. This takes time and requires legal consultation, but it can be done by anyone with a serious commitment to making a film.

When financing a motion picture in this way, there are several legal structures to consider: partnerships (limited and general, public and private), limited liability companies, corporations (public and private), investment trusts, and sole proprietorships. Regardless of which entity you select, when you are raising money from other people, you are entering the field of *securities.* Securities can be stock in a corporation, units in a limited partnership, or any other means by which one person gives another person money or property in exchange for an interest in the future of that other person's business venture. Though people commonly attempt to circumvent this definition in order to avoid dealing with the highly regulated world of securities, it is foolish to do so; the federal government, as well as each state, has an agency charged with the aggressive enforcement of federal and state securities laws.

Regulations for public offerings are commonly known as "blue sky" laws; they are designed to prevent someone from "selling a patch of blue sky" to unsophisticated investors. But not all investors need the same protection. Preexisting business associates and well-informed, sophisticated investors need less protection than individuals whose lack of knowledge and experience makes them more prone to deception. If a producer limits the solicitation of funds to this group and fulfills some additional requirements, the investment will qualify as a private offering. The producer will still be responsible for full disclosure to the investors but may be able to avoid the cumbersome and costly SEC (Securities and Exchange Commission) registration provisions required for public offerings.

From a legal and accounting point of view, a private offering is far simpler to construct than a public offering. Public corporations and public limited partnerships allow one to solicit and receive investments from a large number of people. Unlike a private offering, which limits the investors you can approach to friends and business associates, a public offering allows you to take out an ad in the paper and speak about your project at conventions or public forums. Public offerings also, however, require registration with the Securities and Exchange Commission (SEC). This is difficult, costly, and time consuming. A complete formal prospectus must be assembled, and an underwriter must be found to market the stock. There are instances in which going public has proven successful for financing independent films, but for many independent producers the cost and difficulty far outweigh the advantages. A private study conducted by the entertainment law firm of Berton & Donaldson concludes that "while this approach has been successful for production entities financing *several* films, usually cross-collateralizing them in an effort to minimize the investment risk, no *single-film* public offering over the past ten years has been successfully financed."

One of the disadvantages of a standard corporation is that corporate profits are taxable income to the corporation. When the remaining profit is distributed to the stockholders, it is taxed again as income to the individual investors, resulting in double taxation. A subchapter "S" corporation eliminates this double taxation, but the restrictions and limitations make this structure unworkable for the financing of most motion pictures. In the case of a sole proprietorship, such as a film production company entirely owned and financed by one individual, the profit flows directly to that person and is taxable only as personal income; the sole proprietor is liable for all debts and liabilities of the company. In a general partnership between two or more people, the profits are divided between them on the basis of agreed percentages and taxed once, as income to the individuals. A principal danger in a general partnership is that all of the members are responsible for the debts of the partnership and each of them has the authority to create such debts. Since a general partnership creates unlimited liability for each partner, it is usually formed by only two or three people who know each other well.

Another financing entity that is becoming increasingly popular is a limited liability company (LLC). To be properly structured, an LLC must have no more than two of the four attributes that the Internal Revenue Service has characterized as essentially corporate. These four corporate attributes are identified as limited liability, centralized management, continuity of life, and free transferability of interests. Since everyone wants limited liability, you can choose one of the remaining three; for motion picture projects, the most common choice is centralized management. This structure is taxed like a partnership, with all net income and losses flowing through to the individual partners, but is treated legally like a corporation, which means that the liability for each member, including those governing the company's affairs, is limited to the individual's investment in the production.

Historically, one of the most common and successful structures for financing motion pictures has been the *limited partnership*. This provides the investor (the limited partner) with the same limited liability as a stockholder in a corporation, but also allows the profits to flow to the investors without being first taxed at the company level. Control of the partnership business, as well as all liabilities for the partnership, rest with the general partner.

The Limited Partnership

Limited partnerships have been and continue to be used successfully by producers throughout the film industry, from the struggling independent with a single low-budget feature to the major studio funding multipicture packages. However, because of the many funding sources available to filmmakers in today's marketplace, they are being used less commonly than in the past. In a sense, limited partnerships have become the fallback for producers for whom other sources are unavailable.

A limited partnership may be used for financing an entire production, or a series of productions, or for financing the development and/or packaging of one or more productions. Almost every kind of picture imaginable, from small independent films like *Crumb* to large studio pictures like *Beauty and the Beast,* has been financed using this structure. The members of the partnership are divided into two classes: *general partners* and *limited partners.* Quite commonly, the producer, or producers, are the general partner(s); the investors are the limited partners. The profit, if any, flows to both the general and limited partners with no intermediate taxation.

The general partner has complete control over the operation of the partnership. In the case of a motion picture, this includes both financial and creative control over the making of the film. With this authority comes the responsibility for all debts and obligations of the partnership (under certain limited circumstances, the general partner may become a corporation and thereby obtain some degree of protection from these obligations). The limited partners have no control over the operation of the partnership, but they are fully protected against liability for all debts and obligations incurred by the general partner.

The restrictions and responsibilities for both the general partner and the limited partners are detailed in the sample limited partnership agreement in Appendix A. This is a typical California limited partnership agreement and is included as a reference guide, not as a do-it-yourself, fill-in-the-blanks document. No matter how small the budget, it is essential to invest whatever money is necessary to put the financing structure together properly. Every project is different and requires modification of the basic forms. Also, the laws governing limited partnerships vary from state to state and are subject to periodic change. If you do not have the money to pay an attorney, you may be able to pay for these legal services on a deferral basis, or by offering the attorney an equity position in your film.

A producer who fails to comply with the law, for whatever reason, and comes under investigation by the attorney general's office, risks being charged with fraud. Even if the error was inadvertent (perhaps a copy of the budget was left out of the investment memorandum), the fact remains that the producer failed to disclose fully and properly the required details of the investment offering, and a disgruntled investor may seek legal action. The producer may demonstrate to the attorney general's office that a sincere effort had been made to comply with the law, perhaps by submitting copies of legal bills for setting up the limited partnership, but an honest intention is not enough; the producer must comply literally with the law. In such cases the attorney general will probably offer the producer a choice between a settlement and a court case. A settlement with the attorney general's office usually involves repayment of the investor's money plus a fine to cover the state's legal costs.

When a limited partnership draws investors from more than one state, the complexities and costs increase because the partnership must not be in conflict with the laws of any state involved. As stated earlier, the term "blue sky" refers to laws designed to protect investors from improper offerings; "long arm" statutes have to do with the point at which an offering comes under scrutiny and/or jurisdiction in states other than the one in which the partnership originates. It is crucial that the legal counsel for a multistate partnership be fully familiar with these policies.

In most states the law defines the legal number of investors allowed to participate in a limited partnership and still have the partnership considered private. In California the maximum number is restricted to thirty-five. The general partner (usually the producer) is allowed to *solicit* investments directly from any number of potential investors but must not advertise or otherwise seek investments publicly (in some states there are restrictions not only on the number of investors, but also on the number of solicitations allowed). In California, if a picture is budgeted at $500,000, the average investment (assuming the maximum of thirty-five investors) will be $14,285.71.

In most states there are laws restricting a group of investors from pooling their money and entering a partnership under a single name. In California, for example, each individual investing in a limited partnership, through any channel, counts as one of the thirty-five investors. A producer cannot gather together ten aunts and uncles who wish to invest $2,000 each and bring them in as a single $20,000 investment. There are some exceptions, such as investment groups that are preexisting and that fulfill other state requirements, but in most cases each individual counts against the thirty-five-investor limit. Governments are adamant about this restriction, and there is no legal way to circumvent the intent of the law. The best scam artists in the country have tried and have only succeeded in teaching the government which methods are most likely to be attempted.

At first glance it may appear that this creates an enormous roadblock to financing an independent picture. After all, how many doors will you have to knock on before you find thirty-five investors willing to fund your entire budget? Fifty? A hundred? Two hundred? It's hard to say. But no matter how frustrating the process becomes, don't be tempted to make what is clearly a public offering. If, for example, you are invited to speak to a convention of doctors in Las Vegas on the subject of motion picture investments and at the end of the talk you say, "By the way, if any of you are interested in investing in films, come up and see me at the end of the day and I'll tell you about my latest project," you are clearly making a public offering that will probably get you in trouble with the state attorney general and the SEC. Even closing with "I'm not legally allowed to tell you about my latest project" is a dangerous statement in a public forum.

It is not uncommon for a producer who has funded 50 percent of a film with private investments to obtain the balance from a distributor in exchange for domestic or foreign distribution rights. This is because, in most cases, the more money you raise, the easier it is to find the rest. Each investor who comes on board is expressing faith in your project and the willingness to gamble on your success.

Chapters 2 through 6 are devoted to a detailed analysis of motion picture financing through private domestic investment, specifically in relation to low- and medium-budget pictures, using a limited partnership structure and a limited partnership investment memorandum. Regardless of the funding source you approach, the information that follows will be a useful aid in selling the investment.

2

Selling the Investment

The Investment Memorandum

THIS INFORMATION IS INTENDED TO GUIDE THE INDEPENDENT PRO-
ducer in drafting an *investment memorandum* for financing a motion
picture using a limited partnership structure. While professional legal
counsel is essential in these matters, you may do a great deal of the
work on your own. In doing so, you will save a substantial amount of
money and learn something in the process.

The investment memorandum is the most important document for
selling your motion picture to potential investors. The memorandum
should contain all of the information necessary for an investor to make
an intelligent decision about your project, and any information that the
investor's legal and accounting counsel may need in order to evaluate
the investment from their special points of view.

The general partner is required by law to present a complete picture
of the investment, including negative as well as positive factors. It is
therefore important to include in the memorandum a statement describing motion pictures as an inherently high-risk venture. Unless this is
clearly stated, an investor may subsequently sue the general partner for
falsifying the level of rise or, at the very least, giving an incomplete picture of the investment. It is customary to make a "risks" statement
twice, presented first in general terms on the first page prior to the table
of contents, usually in bold letters. It isn't necessary to go into the negative statistics on independent production, but a clear statement about
the nature of the investment is crucial. A sample opening page in a typical memorandum reads as follows:

This memorandum describes the formation and operation of a
limited partnership to engage in the business of the production and
exploitation of a motion picture.

The contents of this memorandum are confidential and are dis-
closed pursuant to a confidential relationship and may not be
reproduced or otherwise used except for the purpose intended
herein.

The partnership interests described in this memorandum will not be registered under the Securities and Exchange Act of 1933 or any local securities law and are described for investment only and not with a view to resale or distribution.

The purchase of partnership interests described herein entails a high degree of risk and is suitable for purchase only by those who can afford a total loss of their investment. Further, risk factors as contained in this memorandum (which does not include all possible factors) should be carefully evaluated by each prospective purchaser of a limited partnership interest herein.

The contents of this memorandum are not to be construed by any prospective purchaser of a limited partnership interest as business, legal, or tax advice, and each such prospective purchaser will be required to demonstrate that he or she has the ability to evaluate the purchase of the limited partnership interest described herein or has retained the services of a representative who has such knowledge and expertise as may be necessary to evaluate said purchase.

This memorandum is neither an offer to sell nor a prospectus, but is informational in nature.

The second "risks" statement will fall within the body of the memorandum and will contain a more detailed description of the risks involved.

Following the opening statement will be a table of contents for the memorandum, which generally covers the following:

- the business of the partnership
- distribution of revenues and allocation of profits and losses
- sales of the partnership interests
- sale of the film
- tax consequences
- depreciation
- the general partner
- rights and obligations of the limited partners
- rights and obligations of the general partner
- conflict of interest
- the motion picture
- legal and accounting services
- distribution
- budget
- timetable

• risk factors
• additional information

The material in the memorandum is a combination of legal and accounting data and specific information about the motion picture to which it refers. The following sections will describe the type of information customarily included under each item in the table of contents.

THE BUSINESS OF THE PARTNERSHIP

This section describes in brief the following elements:

1. The intention of the partnership to finance, produce, and cause the distribution of a feature-length, 35mm color motion picture tentatively titled, _____.

2. The anticipated rating for the motion picture from the Motion Picture Association of America. There are five MPAA ratings: G, PG, PG-13, R, and NC-17 (see Chapter 26).

3. The anticipated date for completion of the picture.

4. The total capital required from the limited partners. For the sake of this discussion, we will assume a production budget of $500,000 (in the case of a mini-maxi offering, discussed later in this chapter, two budgets would necessarily be included).

5. The stages of production through which the partnership investment will finance the film. In this case, we will say that the investment ($500,000) will finance the making of the motion picture through a final composite answer print. In other words, through the making of the film, but not the film's distribution. The costs of distribution will be borne later by the distributor. *Note:* This is by far the most common approach, but it is important to include in the budget funds for promoting the film once it's finished (see Chapter 9).

6. The number of years the partnership will run.

7. The distribution of net profits. This may be divided in any way the general partner decides. Obviously it must be acceptable to the proposed limited partners or they will not invest. It is customary to divide profits 50 percent to the limited partners and 50 percent to the general partner. This will be discussed further in the next section, "Distribution of Revenues and Allocation of Profits and Losses."

8. A description of the partnership interests, i.e., the number of limited partnership interests that will be offered and the cost for each interest. In our example, 100 partnership interests will be offered at a cost of $5,000 each (1 percent of the budget). We will request a minimum

purchase of three limited partnership interests (or units) per limited partner. If you sell half of the investment ($250,000) to a single investor, the average investment for the other $250,000, assuming you utilize the maximum of thirty-four more investors, will be $250,000 divided by 34 = $7,352.94. It is unwise to start with investments of less than 1/35 of your budget in the hope of finding large investors farther down the road. If you sell only one unit ($5,000) to each of your first twenty investors, you will have raised $100,000, but the average investment for the remaining fifteen signatures goes up to $400,000 divided by 15 = $26,666.67, and your job becomes all the more difficult. Wait until you've got the large investors committed, *then* lower your minimum.

9. A description of what happens to the investors' money prior to production: Generally, it will be placed in a third-party escrow account for release to the general partner upon completion of financing. The general partner must establish a reasonable date by which financing will be completed or the escrow money must be returned to the investors. This date may be revised by mutual consent of the general partner and the limited partners. If, for example, a deadline of eighteen months has been set for financing and by that time only 90 percent of the budget has been raised, the producer may request an extension of the escrow closing date. There are also variations to this procedure, which are discussed in Chapter 5.

10. A recommendation that prospective limited partners carefully consider the risk factors described in the memorandum.

11. The mailing address for the general partner.

12. A statement that defines the investment memorandum as *informational in nature* and *not* as an offering to sell, or a solicitation. This is important, especially in states that define the maximum number of investors that the general partner may *solicit*. The inclusion of this statement may make it possible for the general partner to circulate more memoranda than the maximum number of solicitations allowed by those laws. In other words, by defining the investment memorandum as *informational in nature* and not as a solicitation, the general partner avoids a *gross* violation of the law. However, if the general partner uses this as an excuse to print 500 memoranda and sends them to the Fortune 500 mailing list, the action will be interpreted as a public offering and will probably result in serious legal trouble.

It is advisable to number and keep a log of the memoranda. Keep track of to whom they are given and the date. Not only is this a sound organizational approach, it also offers some degree of protection if, for example, someone copies the document and makes it available in an amount or manner that would make the offering public.

DISTRIBUTION OF REVENUES
AND ALLOCATION OF PROFITS AND LOSSES

Revenues from the motion picture may be derived from domestic and foreign theatrical distribution, sales to television and video markets, as well as any money-making ancillary and merchandising rights (see Chapter 25). *Box office gross* refers to the amount of money taken in at the box offices of all the theaters that are playing the film; it is also the amount that people tend to quote when referring to how well or how poorly a picture is performing. Between 40 and 50 percent of the box office gross is received by the distributor and is referred to as *gross film rental* or *gross receipts*. This section of the memorandum describes how gross receipts are filtered down from the distributor to the partnership and into the hands of the investors. The following is typical of the manner in which revenues are distributed.

The *order* in which the percentages are calculated is established by the contractual relationship with the distributor, and it is crucial. The customary arrangement is for the distributor's percentage to be deducted from gross film rental (gross receipts), and distribution costs (prints and advertising) deducted from the balance. In this case the distributor's portion will be considerably larger, and the portion allocated to the partnership quite a lot smaller, than if the distribution costs were deducted first, and the balance divided between the distributor and the partnership. It is important to bear this kind of arithmetic in mind when setting up the details of the distribution contract.

After the foregoing deductions, the proceeds are further reduced by payment of production costs that exceeded the capital contributed by the limited partners—loans, extended credit, deferred payments to talent and technical facilities, and partnership overhead expense. Finally, the balance constitutes partnership distributable cash (profit), which is usually divided equally, half going to the general partner and the other half to the limited partners. It is common to pay deferred salaries to actors and production personnel *after* the investors have recouped their investment but *before* they receive profits. In the previous example, deferred salaries are paid *before* the limited partners are paid, as is typical with major stars.

It is customary for the general partner to retain a certain number of percentage participation points (shares in the film's potential profits) for major talent such as writer, director, stars, and composer. These are generally deducted off the top from net film rental, thereby being shared by both the general partner and the limited partners. Occasionally, they will be deducted solely from the general partner's share of the partnership distributable cash. In the latter case, if the partnership distributable cash is divided 50/50 between the general partner and the limited partners, the percentage points for major talent will be worth exactly half as much as if they were deducted off the top from net film rental.

Everyone invests with an eye to profits, but of far greater importance to every investor is recoupment—getting back the initial investment. Consequently, as an additional incentive for investors, the general partner may offer an accelerated rate of payback. From the investor's point of view, the ideal situation is a distribution of partnership distributable case as follows: 100 percent to the limited partners until recoupment of their total capital contribution; 0 percent to the general partner during recoupment. Thereafter, partnership distributable cash will be distributed 50 percent to the limited partners and 50 percent to the general partner. In this way, money goes back to money first. However, if the general partner is unable to afford a zero income during recoupment, an alternative rate of payback may be offered, such as 90/10 in favor of the limited partners, or 80/20. An even greater incentive for investors is an accelerated rate of payment *beyond* recoupment. In other words, the general partner might offer the investors a 90/10 split until the investors receive 125 percent of their investment. At that point, the split becomes 50/50.

As you can see, the figures and their positioning may be adjusted in a variety of ways. Ultimately, the distribution of revenues should be structured in such a way as to make the investment as attractive as possible for the limited partners while maintaining a palatable and potentially lucrative position for the general partner.

Profits and losses are generally allocated in the same relative percentage relationships as partnership distributable cash. They may, in some cases, differ. It is advisable to consult an experienced accountant before finalizing such allocation.

SALE OF THE PARTNERSHIP INTERESTS

This section describes a partnership interest as a capital asset and defines the manner in which gains and losses will be taxed. Consult an experienced accountant for the specific wording of this section, as it may vary from project to project.

SALE OF THE FILM

This section describes the film as a depreciable asset and defines the manner in which income or loss will be treated if the film is sold. Again, an experienced accountant should be consulted for the specific wording of this section for each project.

TAX CONSEQUENCES

This is a statement by the general partnership saying that tax consequences of an investment in the partnership may vary depending on the investor's personal tax status, and that the general partner is not in a position to give tax advice or evaluate the tax consequence of this investment for any of the limited partners. According to the IRS, a "partnership" is any venture in which two or more parties combine to carry on a trade, profession, or business, and in which the parties share the profits and/or losses from that venture. This section recommends that all prospective limited partners consult their personal tax advisers regarding the projected tax consequences of the investment.

DEPRECIATION

This section describes the method that the partnership will use to determine depreciation of the film for federal income tax purposes. One such method that has been approved by the revenue rulings is the income forecast method. This provides for depreciation of the film over the period of time during which the film is expected to generate profits. The forecast is based on conditions known to exist when the forecast is made. At the end of each year, as more information becomes available regarding the remaining life of the film, the forecast may be revised upward or downward.

It is advisable for the general partner to consult an experienced accountant for the method of depreciation best suited for each project, and for the specific wording for this section of the memorandum.

THE GENERAL PARTNER

This is a biographical sketch of the person(s) who will make up the general partner side of the limited partnership. Background information substantiating the general partner's ability to deliver a professional motion picture within the parameters outlined in the memorandum should be included. If the general partner has produced previous pictures, such credits should be also noted.

This is an area where it is easy to run into trouble. The law requires that a private offering memorandum be scrupulously accurate. If you exaggerate your credits, perhaps claiming to have produced a film that you merely invested in, or developed but didn't produce, you open yourself up to subsequent attack. To be safe, include only credits that you have actually received on screen. Investors have successfully testified in court that they invest not in projects but in people, and that they based their investment decision on the biographical data included in the memorandum. In some such instances the courts have ruled that the investor was defrauded under the federal and state securities laws.

RIGHTS AND OBLIGATIONS OF THE GENERAL PARTNER

Limited partners are advised to consult the limited partnership agreement for a complete understanding of the rights and obligations of the general partner. In addition, this section should briefly summarize these rights and obligations as described in Appendix A.

Also included should be:

- the fee, if any, that the general partner will take in addition to the general partner's share of partnership distributable cash.
- a statement describing the accounting and bookkeeping procedures that the general partner intends to use in running the partnership business.
- the availability of partnership records. It is customary to offer the limited partners access to partnership records upon request.
- the frequency with which statements of partnership operations will be sent to the limited partners.

CONFLICT OF INTEREST

This is a protective statement for the general partner that defines the general partner's services to the partnership as nonexclusive. The general partner retains the right to be involved with other projects, even similar projects that may be in competition with the activities of the partnership.

THE MOTION PICTURE

This is a description of the type of film that the partnership intends to produce. It often takes the form of a brief, two- or three-page story synopsis describing the characters and principal events in the film. This section is one of the most important sales tools in the memorandum. In addition to communicating basic information about the picture, the synopsis should be written in such a way as to capture the "feeling" of the film, whether it's comedy, action, suspense, or drama. This isn't easy to do in two or three pages, but it's worth spending some time on. It's better to capture the mood and feeling of the film than to outline the story points technically. The synopsis should whet the appetite of the investors but should not include phrases like "a hilarious film" or "thoughtfully written." Those conclusions should be left to the reader.

The format of the synopsis depends on the subject matter. It may take the form of a short story, or it may be presented more formally with an introductory paragraph, a paragraph on each of the principal characters, and a couple of pages describing the story, perhaps highlighting some specific scenes.

At this stage in the development of your project, you may have nothing more than an idea on which to base your synopsis. If your project is based on an existing literary property or if you have a completed screenplay, indicate at the end of the synopsis that the completed screenplay or literary property is available upon request.

LEGAL AND ACCOUNTING SERVICES

This is a list of the legal and accounting firms that will represent and advise the partnership. Include their addresses and phone numbers.

DISTRIBUTION

If you have a prearranged distribution agreement, perhaps a cofinancing deal with a distributor, the details of such an agreement should be described in this section. Include a synopsis of pertinent information, such as territories covered, advances, guarantees, definition of profits, and commitments to prints and advertising. It may be to your advantage to include a copy of the distribution agreement; in any case this document should be made available to the limited partners upon request.

If you do not have a prearranged distribution agreement, this section may take the form of a "best efforts" clause stating that the general partner will use its best efforts to obtain a distribution deal for the film that, in the opinion of the general partner, will be in the best interests of the partnership. It is wise to include a description of the *minimum* distribution deal that the general partner would like, but never make a flat agreement that a lesser deal will not be accepted. Should the general partner be locked into a minimum distribution deal but unable to negotiate such a deal, the limited partners could technically be approached with a request that this section of the agreement be modified. This can create problems. The limited partners might not agree to the lesser distribution deal. Also, if they become too deeply involved in decision-making, they run the risk of crossing the line between limited and general partners, and thereby losing their limited partner protection against lawsuits. Furthermore, the limited partners could accuse the general partner of "bait and switch," meaning that the general partner baited them into the investment with a guarantee of certain minimum distribution terms, knowing that those terms might well be switched for lesser terms at a later date.

BUDGET

This should be a brief synopsis of how the money will be spent. You may utilize a standard budget summary form as shown in Table 2, or you may simply wish to ballpark the budget as follows:

*Cost of financing (4%)	$ 20,000
Preproduction	30,000
Production	275,000
Postproduction	125,000
Subtotal	450,000
Contingency (11%)	50,000
Total	$500,000

*The cost of financing covers direct costs incurred in raising money. This may include a finder's fee, generally between 2 and 5 percent (of money raised by outside parties) as payment for financing efforts.

Any budget should include qualifications to allow for later modification, but one of the risks of ballparking a budget is that no matter how many caveats you include in the memorandum, this budget will be considered one of the representations in the offering; any significant differences between this and the final budget will have to be explained to the limited partners.

If you have a detailed budget breakdown (see Appendix B), it should be available to the investors upon request. Most investors will never ask for it. Detailed motion picture budgets are almost impossible for an inexperienced person to evaluate, and the budget summary derived from a detailed budget, such as the one that follows, usually includes all of the information an investor requires.

TABLE 2   **Sample Budget Top Sheet**

Title _____ Production company _____

Above-the-line

100 Screenplay	$16,000	
200 Producer	17,000	
300 Director	12,500	
400 Cast	55,000	$100,500

Below-the-line
Production

500 Production staff	20,700	
600 Extras	6,000	
700 Set operations	34,800	
800 Sets	17,000	
900 Props	10,600	
1000 Costumes	6,900	
1100 Makeup and hairdressing	7,000	
1200 Production equipment	21,000	
1300 Locations/studio	12,800	
1400 Laboratory and film	39,000	
1500 Tests	500	
1600 Production miscellaneous	16,500	192,800

Postproduction

1700 Editing	46,000	
1800 Sound	14,500	
1900 Music	26,000	
2000 Titles and opticals	5,000	
2100 Laboratory	12,800	
2200 Sound mix	11,800	116,100

Other costs

2300 Insurance	$20,000	
2400 Miscellaneous	25,100	45,100
Total		454,500
10% Contingency		45,500
Grand total		$500,000

Note: Every film budget is unique and must be written for the specific requirements of each project. This budget is for a film using SAG actors. Fringes and taxes are included in the totals. There is no allowance for a completion bond because bond companies generally will not bond a film costing less than $1 million.

It is often possible to estimate a production budget based solely on an idea prior to writing a screenplay, and sometimes even before writing a story. This is discussed in Chapter 3, "Starting from Scratch."

THE MINI-MAXI OFFERING

There is considerable flexibility in the way a motion picture budget can be written (see Chapter 9). The budget for an independent feature based on the adaptation of a novel might be $3 million, but for an additional half million the producer could hire a bigger star, shoot for a few extra days, or film in a more exotic location. This is why it is common for a motion picture offering to include *two different budgets.* In this way a producer may attempt to raise an ideal (maxi) budget but may go forward with the project as long as the lesser (mini) budget is raised. The producer must explain to the investors exactly what the additional money in the higher budget will buy and in what way it is expected to pay off at the box office. Based on statistical box office data available from sources such as *Art Murphy's Box Office Register, The Hollywood Reporter, Variety,* Paul Kagan Associates, and others listed in Appendix E, a producer may have reason to believe that the lower budget will double the investor's money, while the addition of a bigger star for the higher budget has a reasonable possibility of tripling the investment. In all cases the producer must be very careful about what kinds of representations are made to investors and potential investors, but if the producer has intelligently gone about determining the two budgets, the investors should recognize that the larger budget, with its additional money, will provide insurance against losses rather than being an added risk, even though the smaller budget is adequate to make the film.

TIMETABLE

The length of time that investment capital will be tied up is of paramount importance to every investor. As this is directly related to the completion date of the film, the investor will be interested in the schedule for production. A timetable should include principal phases of the production process and should speak in terms of *anticipated* time periods rather than firm commitments. Further, since the financing of a film is the most unpredictable aspect of the entire process (second only to the weather), it is a mistake to include dates—even approximate ones—in the timetable. Instead, speak in terms of *blocks of time,* as shown in Table 3. From an investor's standpoint, the more you can do to minimize the time between completion of financing and commencement of

TABLE 3	**Timetable**

1st week	Begin preproduction
	Casting
	Crew allocation
	Location scouting
	Lock production schedule
	Allocate equipment, props, costumes
	Begin set construction
6th week	Casting completed
	Crew allocation completed
	Locations secured
	Equipment, props, costumes secured
	Begin rehearsal
8th week	Begin principal photography
	Begin postproduction editing
12th week	End principal photography
13th week	Editor's cut completed
23rd week	Director's cut completed
27th week	Final cut completed
	Begin sound editing
	Spot sound effects
	Spot music
	Order titles & opticals
32nd week	Score music
33rd week	Sound editing completed
	Mix sound
	Transfer sound to optical track
	Begin negative cutting
34th week	Negative cutting completed
	Color timing
35th week	Screen first trial composite
	answer print

principal photography the better. For one thing, it makes the timetable easier to read; for another, it means that the money will be tied up for a shorter period of time. That said, don't make the mistake of rushing into principal photography without taking time to prepare adequately. The more time you spend efficiently planning your production, the better and less expensive your film will be.

In most cases, when you are seeking production financing, the script will already be written. If not, you will need to add a writing schedule to the beginning of the following timetable. This is difficult, since writing a script can, and often does, take years. Steven Hicks spent four years researching and writing the script for *Shine;* it took Anthony Minghella two years to adapt *The English Patient.* If you are hiring a writer as part of a development deal, it is important to spell out contractually when the writer will deliver the material. You might, for example, allow eight weeks for delivery of the treatment, twelve weeks for delivery of the first draft, and four weeks for a rewrite, with two weeks between each phase for the producer to study the material and suggest changes. This adds up to a total of seven months from the time the writer begins to the time the producer has in hand a second-draft script. The script may need additional work, but hopefully it will be far enough along so that the producer can ballpark a budget and begin to raise production financing.

For the sake of simplicity I am assuming that you will raise all of the money before beginning preproduction. As a practical matter, much of the preproduction work, including casting, location scouting, and assembling the crew, is often done as the money is being raised.

RISK FACTORS

From the general partner's point of view, this section is a most unfortunate necessity. Motion picture investment is an extremely high-risk proposition, and the general partner is legally bound to present a complete picture of this aspect of the investment. Of the total number of MPAA-rated independent films produced annually (between 300 and 500), approximately 17 percent are released by the majors, 29 percent are released by nonmajor distributors, 15 percent go directly to video or cable, and 39 percent find no domestic distribution whatsoever. Many independent films don't seek an MPAA rating until they have a distribution deal, so the number of MPAA-rated films is only a fraction of the total number of independent films produced. Of the MPAA-rated films that receive distribution, only a fraction achieve profitability.

This section should include a statement titled "The General Unprofitability of Motion Pictures" that states that motion picture investment entails a high degree of risk even when the picture is substantially packaged prior to financing. Recoupment of the investment and additional profits are largely a function of the film's cost of production and distribution in relation to its public appeal. The extent to which a picture will appeal to the public is largely dependent upon unpredictable critical reviews and public taste. Unless otherwise stated, the investors in an unsuccessful picture will have no opportunity to recoup their investment by any investment in, or cross-collateralization with, any other picture. A substantial portion of motion pictures do not achieve profitability.

Fortunately, investors are used to reading such dire predictions and are seldom dissuaded from investing in an otherwise attractive project.

ADDITIONAL INFORMATION

Given the bleak nature of the "Risk Factors" section, it is helpful to shore up the memorandum with positive information about film investments. Include any information that will substantiate your project in the eyes of the investor. Copies of magazine articles that speak favorably about independent production, or about motion picture investments in general, are helpful. It's worth watching financial publications like *BusinessWeek* and *Forbes* and industry trade papers like *Variety* and *The Hollywood Reporter* for favorable articles about film investment. Paul Kagan Associates provides the most sophisticated (and expensive) data on the subject of film investments. It might also be worth including articles or publications that show the topicality of your subject matter. If, for example, your story deals with saving the whales, you might include articles highlighting recent controversies on the subject.

If you have made arrangements with a writer for your screenplay, or with a director or actors, include an accurate list of their credits. These credits will help solidify your project in the eyes of the investor. Overstatement is tempting, but the same cautionary note applies here as in the section on the general partner. It is dangerous to be anything but scrupulously accurate when describing the screenwriter and other elements of the package. If any statement is false, it could lead to serious charges down the road.

It's also helpful to include artwork. This may range from a simple home-art sketch or title treatment to a four-color printing of an original painting. The fact is that people don't like to read; they like to look at pictures. If you have a completed screenplay or story outline, you might consider making a brief storyboard (see Chapter 15). Strive for a *visual representation of the mood of your film.* A mock newspaper ad might well serve this purpose and at the same time give the investor a feeling for how you intend to sell the finished picture.

These are just a few thoughts on how best to shore up your investment memorandum. Anything of this nature that you add to your presentation will be helpful in selling the investment. Remember, however, that you are bound by the way the magazine clippings, artwork, and any other suggested advertising material represent the investment, and you will be held liable if they are not reasonable representations.

3

Starting from Scratch

Step One: Defining the Concept

THE CONVENTIONAL APPROACH TO PRODUCING A MOTION PICTURE begins with a story, a book, a magazine article, or an idea that is developed into a screenplay. Based on the screenplay, a producer formulates a production budget and shooting schedule, assembles the necessary people and facilities, and guides the making of the film through production and postproduction. Based on the completed picture, an advertising campaign is developed. The distributor then uses the campaign to market the picture.

But what if the picture is not marketable? One publicist at a major film festival, who wished to remain anonymous, said of a particular year's crop of independent films, "I'm representing a lot of good, interesting films, but if I were a distributor, I honestly wouldn't know what to do with them." If distributors are unable to see a way to market your film, then you have to tell them how. That requires that you think about your market in advance. Answer the tough question: Who will pay to see my film and why? Remember that if you can't figure out how to sell your film, there is a high probability that no one else will, either.

An alternative approach that is well worth considering, especially for the producer with a low- or medium-budget picture, *begins with the campaign:* a marketing concept that defines the specific audience toward which the film will be targeted. This is a common practice with producers of large-budget films attempting to finance them with foreign presales. Every year in Cannes huge posters for pictures not yet shot are displayed along the Coissette; some films have been completely financed in this way. Companies will sometimes take this to the extreme of creating the *illusion* that a picture has already been shot. For example, if there is a star attached to the property, producers will sometimes use stills of that star from another movie in the poster for the movie they are attempting to finance. This is clearly misleading and is not recommended, but it happens.

When using this approach, it is easiest to stay within a commercially proven genre such as action, adventure, comedy, horror, mystery, thriller, science fiction, or romance. Since producers of low-budget films cannot afford name stars or lavish special effects, it is important that their pictures contain some theatrically exploitable element that will draw audiences into the theater. The producer must think in terms of something that isn't available on television or cable. This usually involves violence, sex, or some shock value that extends beyond the censorship limitations of those media. Exploitation pictures are obvious examples, but others include *Kids, Leaving Las Vegas,* and *Trainspotting.* These are extraordinarily well-made pictures, and part of their appeal is the extent to which they shock their audiences. This is not the only way, however, for a low- or medium-budget picture to become successful. *The Brothers McMullen, Lone Star, Shine, Sling Blade,* and *Welcome to the Dollhouse* succeeded because they had compelling stories with powerful characters who dealt with issues that transcend the traditional fare available in other media. And they succeeded despite the fact that they have no clearly defined built-in marketing hook. They won awards and received critical acclaim in the media.

It is extremely difficult to achieve the level of excellence found in these pictures within the limitations of a small budget and tight shooting schedule, and it is impossible to predict awards and critical acclaim. Consequently, if you want to hedge your bet commercially, it is important at this point to determine which elements in your film may be utilized to develop a powerful advertising campaign. How do you intend to sell your picture to the public? Why will people choose your picture over all the others? You are after concepts, or hooks, to draw people in. You don't need a finished newspaper ad, but mock-up ideas for title treatments, artwork, and lead lines are important. A *lead line* is a descriptive phrase or sentence that elaborates on the title. The lead line for *Anaconda* was "When you can't breath, you can't scream." The campaign may change drastically before your picture is ready for distribution, but at least you know going in that you've got a marketable concept.

Consider a producer who wishes to make a medium-budget independent feature within the horror film genre. There are subspecies within that genre, such as monster films, supernatural films, and crazed-killer films. Perhaps the producer develops a film idea about subterranean creatures who depend on oil for their survival, much as we depend on water. The creatures' life source is rapidly vanishing as more and more oil is pumped out of the earth to run factories, homes, and automobiles. One night a group of "oil people" burrow out of the ground to seek revenge. They wreak havoc on a small town in oil-rich Texas. This is a variation on the standard monster theme. It has room for all of the terrifying, gruesome moments that horror-film audiences enjoy. It also has the potential for transcending a simple horror film by becoming a metaphor for the repercussions of greed, and perhaps widening its audience appeal. Finally, it has some unique marketing hooks for the advertising campaign. At this point, this is just an idea. But there is enough information to formulate a sales approach, including a title, artwork, and lead lines.

Step Two: Researching the Market

Once you have defined your approach to advertising, you may determine a budget for production. Obviously, without a screenplay it isn't possible to write a detailed budget. However, by conducting a market research study of box office grosses for similar films over the past several years, a producer may get a pretty good idea of the grosses to expect from a film in that genre. And those anticipated grosses make it possible to determine a sensible maximum budget.

As stated earlier, this data is available from sources such as *Art Murphy's Box Office Register,* industry trade papers, and databases on the Internet. An excellent fee-based source of information is available through PK (Paul Kagan) Baseline, an on-line system that you can access using their dial-up software (Baseline Classic) and for which you will be charged on a per-minute basics; or you can access their Internet site (Baseline on the Web) and obtain information on a per-document basis. If you don't have a computer and modem, you can make use of their telephone-research service or their print reports. Their telephone-research-service charges are based on the type and volume of information you request. Another fee-based source of domestic and international box office information is Entertainment Data, Inc. This organization collects data from approximately 24,000 screens in the United States, Canada, the United Kingdom, and Germany on a daily basis. Their reports include weekly updates of distributor-reported box office for roughly eighty current films, as well as historical data for films dating back to 1982. This information is available both as a hard-copy service and on-line. Information on how to contact these services is included in Appendix E.

The producer must carefully select which films to include in the market research. It is easy to be deceived by grosses for pictures that happened to break out of a conventional run to become box office hits. Those films are the exception, and it is foolish to begin a motion picture project expecting such a lucky break. The "hit" figure may be used to sell the investor on the notion that your picture has a *chance* to become a hit. This will be discussed further in Chapter 4, "Selling the Investor" but for now the producer must look to similar films that simply ran a standard circuit for low-budget horror films and never broke out, never became hits. This research will indicate a box office gross that is relatively safe for the producer to expect from a film of this genre. You should also factor in what you can expect from your film from other sources, including video sales, TV sales, and foreign sales in the event that you don't get a domestic theatrical release.

A standard industry rule of thumb says that a picture must gross between three and four times its negative cost to break even. For planning purposes, a multiple of four is safest. This takes into account the theater's cut, the distributor's cut, and the cost of promoting the film. Once the anticipated gross is determined, based on the market research, the producer divides by four to determine a *maximum* production budget. This is one-quarter of the amount the film may reasonably be expected to earn. If the producer then budgets the film for less than this amount, the difference will be the anticipated profit.

The following is an example using fictitious horror films for the market research study:

Title	Worldwide Grosses
Swamp Menace	$ 2,525,000
Attic Killers	3,300,000
Death by Design	1,825,000
The Closed Room	2,900,000
Vengeance Is Mine	3,850,000
Fear for Me	3,600,000
Total	$18,000,000

The average worldwide gross for the six films is $18,000,000 divided by 6 = $3,000,000. Dividing this by a conservative figure of four results in a sensible maximum budget for this genre of $750,000. If the producer budgets the film for less, say $500,000, the balance of $250,000 will be the expected net profit to the partnership. Obviously, if you can produce a competitive picture for even less, say $300,000, your profit potential will be that much greater.

Even with this cautious approach to budgeting, there is no guarantee that a film will be successful. Success depends on the quality of the completed picture, on a reasonable distribution deal, and on the public's reaction to the film, the advertising campaign, and unpredictable critical reviews. However, investors will be greatly comforted by this market research knowing that you have hedged your bet, carefully weighed the downside, and budgeted the picture with maximum protection for the investment.

Step Three: Determining the Budget

After completing the foregoing research study to determine the maximum sensible budget for your chosen genre, you must list your potential investors to determine how much money you might realistically raise. This is difficult since you won't know how real your potential investors are until they've actually invested and their checks have cleared the bank. However, it's a worthwhile exercise and may save you a great deal of trouble. There is nothing worse than going to all the effort of *partially* financing a picture and then having to give the money back because you couldn't raise the balance of the budget. This list of investors will be combined with your market research to determine your final budget. Ultimately, you must settle on a figure that is both large enough to produce a competitive film within your chosen genre and small enough to afford reasonable protection and profit potential for the investor. Above all, it must be an amount that you can realistically expect to raise.

Every aspect of production will be designed to fit within the parameters of the final budget. Budgeting is further discussed in Chapter 10, but for now all we need to understand is the process for arriving at this figure.

4

Selling the Investor

A PRODUCER WHO HAS FOLLOWED THE PROCEDURE OUTLINED IN the previous chapters has all of the information necessary to assemble an investment memorandum with which to approach potential investors. Before doing so, it is important to understand why people invest in motion pictures.

Many years ago, when the tax-shelter laws provided tremendous leverage for motion picture investments, the answer to this question was obvious: Motion pictures were a good investment. Today, however, the statistical reality is that motion pictures are dangerously high-risk, "long shot" investments. Yet people still invest, and independently financed films do get made.

One reason for this apparent contradiction is similar to the reason people buy lottery tickets. In the lottery, the statistical odds are against ticket buyers, but there is a *chance* they'll hit a winner, and if they do, they'll win big. Motion pictures are a similar high-risk gamble. Nobody invests in films to beat bank interest; the risks are simply too great. But people do invest if they believe the film stands a chance of becoming a hit. With all of the marketing venues available, a successful picture today is more successful than ever, and a winning film, like a lucky number in a state lottery, can return far greater profits to the investor than the so-called safe investments.

Most films don't make money, but that dismal statistical reality can be restated in a brighter light. Some pictures *do* make money, and of the ones that do, some make a hell of a lot. The history of the industry clearly demonstrates that everyone starting out to make a picture, from the established entrepreneur with the multimillion-dollar studio spectacular to the first-time producer with a low-budget film, stands a chance of having a hit. A computer study that researched the success-to-failure ratio of producers and directors over a period of twenty-five years, examining some 300 pictures, both majors and independents, arrived at the "absolutely inescapable conclusion that the ratio of success to failure is the same for any producer or director over a given span of time, regardless of reputation." No combination of producer, writer, director, stars, or story concept will guarantee a success. Alternately, it is *possi-*

ble for an unknown producer with a no-name, low-budget picture to produce a hit. Therein lies the key to selling any independent motion picture investment.

Another market-research study of films in your genre will be helpful when communicating this concept to investors. This time, however, you must look to the pictures in your genre and your budget range that *did* break out to become box office hits. Such a survey might look like this (again, using fictitious titles and grosses):

Title	Worldwide Gross
The Blood Bank	$29,000,000
Kill Joy	$15,750,000
Mask of Doom	$18,000,000
The Open Tomb	$13,500,000

Such exceptional box office grosses are nothing to count on, but they demonstrate that it's *possible* for your picture to generate similar grosses.

When talking with investors, talk about the hit. Talk about what's *possible*. A multimillion-dollar return on a $500,000 investment is possible, as your market research will indicate. In addition, you've hedged your bet by establishing a budget that will be relatively easy to recoup. You can make no guarantees to your investors, but viewed in this light, you will be offering them an attractive business proposal in spite of the statistical odds against your film's eventual success.

Another reason, possibly the main reason, why people invest in films today is a strictly human one. It has nothing to do with facts and figures. People invest in movies because it's exciting. Nobody goes to a cocktail party talking about their commodity investments, but people love to talk about their movie investments. There is a certain glamour attached to it. Consider the people who invest in films: They are not generally film people, for whom the magic and glamour of the movies is part of their daily lives. Film people invest in real estate, mutual funds, and biotechnology. The sort of people who invest in films are real estate developers, doctors, and lawyers. They are generally professionals with high-risk gambling money—venture capital looking for an exciting investment. Offer them an opportunity to visit the set, to watch the filming and meet the actors. Even if they don't visit the set, the idea of an involvement in the entertainment world, especially movies, has a very special appeal. Robert Redford followed his statement about the studios gobbling up successful independent companies that fund filmmakers by saying

"There are still plenty of outlets out there and I think the outlets will increase, because there's always the independent financial source that gets off on being able to finance a movie."

You'll find, incidentally, that there is a downside to the glamour of the movies. As I said before, people love to talk about film investments. Consequently, you will find many people who will talk forever about the possibility of investing, but will never come through with a check. Don't let this discourage you. It's a reflection of the nature of the investment, not of your project or your ability to sell. Also, people may be deterred from investing by friends who deride them for putting money into an independent film. It may be helpful to caution investors about this before it happens.

The bottom line in seeking an investment is getting the check. Many filmmakers have learned from bitter experience and from countless expectations and disappointments that nothing is real but the check. Don't count on the promises and verbal commitments of prospective investors until you've actually got the check and it has cleared through their bank.

Variations on the
Escrow Account

AS STATED EARLIER, THE INVESTOR'S MONEY IS USUALLY PLACED IN a third-party escrow account until a certain total is reached, often the entire budget (or, in the case of a mini-maxi offering, when the minimum budget has been raised). Only then is the money released to the general partner. This is to prevent the general partner from spending any of the invested money until the entire budget has been raised. Should the general partner spend the first $70,000 that comes in and then be unable to raise the balance of the budget, the picture will never be made and the first investors will have lost their money. The investors are risking their money on the *film,* not on the producer's ability to *finance* the film.

There are, however, variations on this basic theme. In most states, any of the limited partners may agree to release their portion of the escrow account before the entire budget is raised. This requires written authorization and generally carries an extra benefit for the investor(s) who takes this added risk. For example, if a budget of $500,000 is broken down, as in the "Budget" section of the investment memorandum as follows

Cost of financing (4%)	$ 20,000
Preproduction	30,000
Production	275,000
Postproduction	125,000
Subtotal	450,000
Contingency (11%)	50,000
Total	$500,000

a producer might argue that the money be released when the escrow account contains enough to cover costs through principal photography—the production phase. This amount would be $30,000 for the preproduction, plus $275,000 for production, plus $14,200 for the 4 percent cost of financing, plus $35,000 for the 11 percent contingency, rounded off equals $350,000.

The producer's case may be based on the fact that the most difficult money to raise is the preproduction and production money. These first phases entail the highest degree of risk. What if the production is delayed due to unexpected weather, or what if the director is ill for two weeks during production? What if the film for an expensive day's shooting is damaged in the laboratory, or lost? These are potential risks, and often a medium-budget film cannot afford elaborate insurance policies and completion guarantees to cover these risks. Once the film is in the can, the risk for investors is greatly reduced. The balance of $150,000 may be easier to raise once principal photography is completed, either from additional investors or perhaps from a distribution advance.

For the producer who has attempted unsuccessfully to raise the entire production budget, or who knows that he or she cannot reasonably expect to raise the entire budget, it is advisable to enter into the process with the intention of raising initially only that portion of the budget that will carry the project through a predefined phase, such as the shooting of sample scenes, or completion of principal photography, at which time the producer will attempt to raise the money for the next phase. An example is the independent film *Suture,* cowritten and codirected by Scott McGehee and David Siegel. They raised money from nonindustry sources using a limited partnership, but they didn't raise enough to finish the film. Their plan was to raise enough so that they could complete filming and assemble a rough cut to show distributors and/or additional investors. They did not reveal this to the cast or crew during filming. Completion money was provided in exchange for European distribution rights, and when the film was finished, Goldwyn picked up distribution for the rest of the world. This approach is common for documentaries for which events must be shot as they occur, and for which much of the writing is done during postproduction.

According to John Pierson, "It's become a world of piecemeal, ad hoc, stop-and-start financing. More low-budget features are started with partial budgets intended to get it in the can, or maybe only shoot sample scenes, than full ones." Going into a project with the intention of raising only a portion of the total budget to begin with is far preferable to attempting to raise the entire amount, failing, and being forced to switch the game plan on the investors partway through.

When the escrow account is scheduled to be released prior to completion of financing, the initial investors (class A investors) are taking a greater risk than the class B investors, who come on board later. It is therefore reasonable, though not always practical, to offer class A investors a favored payback position to compensate for their additional level of risk. For example, class A partners might be allowed to recoup their entire investment prior to the class B partners receiving anything. Each class of investors must sign separate documents acknowledging the differences in risk and payback positions.

By structuring the escrow account in this way, a producer can begin making the picture with partial financing and raise the balance of the budget during production and postproduction. It is rarely easy to raise money, but the job becomes less difficult when you can invite potential investors to the set during production, or into the cutting room to view dailies. At these stages, the project is no longer just words on paper. It's a concrete reality. It will be evident to the potential class B partners that you're going to make the film whether they invest or not. You're not depending on their investment to make your first move.

What a producer will need to offer to class B investors is directly proportional to the perceived marketability of the film at the point when the class B investors enter the picture. If they are entering at the beginning of the postproduction phase and it is apparent from the dailies that the finished picture will far exceed the producer's initial expectations, the producer will be in a position to bargain from strength. It's easier to raise money when you're not desperate for money. As with finding a job, it's easy to find a job when you've got a job, but much more difficult when you're unemployed. If the shot footage is disappointing, the class B investors, if any, will probably sense that the producer is desperate and will drive a very hard bargain. They may insist on being "last in, first out." If you must offer a favored payback position to class B investors, it is important to present the investment opportunity initially to your class A investors. If they pass, chances are that they will agree to the terms for other investors because it is in their interest that the film be completed.

This approach can be broken down even farther into class C partners, class D partners, and so forth. But it's best to keep the structure as simple as possible, ideally with one class of investors supplying the entire budget.

The Development Company

AFTER CONDUCTING A MARKET-RESEARCH SURVEY TO DETERMINE the maximum sensible budget for your picture, and after listing all of your sources for investment to determine how much money you might realistically raise, you may find that you don't have enough contacts to raise enough money to produce a competitive film within your chosen genre.

Your project doesn't have to die simply because you don't have an obvious route to complete or even partial production financing. You have the option of forming a development company to develop and package your project in such a way as to make production financing possible. In other words, if you don't have enough financing available through immediate sources, based solely on the material you have assembled (possibly just an idea at this point), you may use the limited partnership structure to form a development company for the purpose of assembling whatever elements, in your opinion, will make it possible to raise production financing.

Perhaps you'll need to raise enough money to finance the writing of the screenplay, obtain commitments from a director, engage the services of a casting director and lock in principal cast members, hire a production manager to complete a detailed budget and shooting schedule, and determine final locations for shooting. With this package under your belt, a whole new world of financing opportunities will open up to you. You're no longer limited to people you know personally and who will invest simply because of an idea and your good word. You will have a substantially developed package that may be offered not only to private investors but to studios, distributors, foreign sales agents, and all other sources of motion picture financing.

Development company investment is an extremely high-risk proposition, far more so than production financing, since many more pictures are developed than are produced. The consolation for the development company investor is that the partnership is usually structured so that development costs are built in to the production budget and are paid back to the development company investors upon completion of production financing. In other words, the development company investors are risking their investment capital not on the success of the picture but on the producer's ability to assemble a package of elements that will result in successful production financing.

In addition to recoupment of capital upon completion of production financing, the limited partners in a limited-partnership development company will also have a profit participation in the film. This will generally be defined as a percentage of the general partner's share of profits. If the finished picture is successful, the development company investors will see profits along with everyone else. But even if the picture is a total failure, as long as it's financed, they will get their money back.

The limited partners in a limited-partnership development company may require the general partner to guarantee a minimum participation in the production financing structure in order to ensure that they don't wind up with an insignificant percentage of the film's profits. As an example, a producer might offer the development company limited partners recoupment of their capital investment upon completion of production financing, 25 percent of all profits that the general partner receives from the film, and a guarantee that the general partner will offer no more than 50 percent profit participation in the film in return for production financing. In this way, the development company investors are assured a minimum 12.5 percent profit participation in the film, according to the following formula: 100 percent of the partnership distributable cash for the production financing limited partnership will be divided 50 percent to the general partner, 50 percent to the production-financing limited partners. The general partner's 50 percent share equals 100 percent of the partnership distributable cash for the development company limited partnership and will be divided 75 percent to the general partner, 25 percent to the development-company limited partners. The development-company limited partners' 25 percent share of the development company's partnership distributable cash is equal to 12.5 percent of the total partnership distributable cash for the production-financing limited partnership. What the general partner offers the limited partners in a development company and what restriction the limited partners place on the general partner's production financing negotiations both depend on the specifics of each project.

Ultimately, throughout the process of financing, the producer must offer whatever is necessary in order to raise the money while at the same time maintaining ownership of a reasonable share of the film's profits; otherwise the project may no longer be worth the producer's while. In some cases a person making a first feature may feel that it is worth giving up every form of remuneration simply because of the inherent value in completing a film and receiving the recognition. But remember two things: First, if the film is not received as well as you hope, you will be left with nothing; and second, if you don't place a reasonable value on yourself and the services you have to offer, the investors probably won't either.

Preproduction

Introduction

PREPRODUCTION INVOLVES THE ASSEMBLY OF ALL THE ELEMENTS necessary to begin principal photography. At a minimum this requires four to six weeks. Studio films generally prep for twelve to sixteen weeks. A picture that requires extensive preparation, such as one that relies heavily on special effects, might prep for as long as a year.

The previous section pointed out that the more time you spend planning your picture during preproduction, the better and more economical the process of making the picture will be. That said, there may be times when an actor's availability or the release date of your film will drive your preproduction schedule faster than you would like. An actor may only be willing to commit to a specific time slot, which may mean that your preproduction time must be cut in half. A distributor might sign a distribution agreement only if you commit to delivering your film by a date that requires shortening your schedule. Often it will be in your best interest to make the effort and the compromises required to meet such demands.

The order in which preproduction elements are assembled varies from project to project. In some cases, complete production financing will be secured prior to beginning this phase. In other cases, development funding will finance elements like writing the script and preparing a budget. Perhaps a producer will borrow from a bank, or use personal savings, to begin the process. There are several permutations, and the information contained in this part applies to all of them.

For the sake of simplicity we will assume two things: First, that the producer has completed production financing and is no longer concerned with legal structures and raising money but can devote full time to producing the picture; second, that the producer has raised the financing based only on an *idea* for a film, or perhaps a simple story line. Consequently, this section will examine the preproduction process, beginning with an idea for a film and following its development and packaging up to the first day of principal photography.

A general philosophy to apply during preproduction of a low- or medium-budget picture is, "Shoot for the moon, then compromise to fit the budget." Don't restrict yourself to actors, crew members, locations, and other elements that you're certain will be available within your budget. Try for more. In doing so, you'll get many rejections but you'll also get a few yeses. In approaching preproduction in this way, you will know, when you've completed packaging your picture, that you have assembled the finest elements available within your budget. And you will have set the highest standards possible for your picture. You will find that this attitude is contagious. It will spark the enthusiasm of everyone around you. People on all levels of production respond to a filmmaker who is sincerely trying to make the best film possible within the limitations of the budget.

The Screenplay

IT IS IMPOSSIBLE TO OVERSTATE THE IMPORTANCE OF THE STORY structure and screenplay for a film. There is a saying in the business: "If it ain't on the page, it ain't on the stage." The screenplay is the foundation for a picture, and it had better be good, or everything else will crumble around it. The reason most beginning independent filmmakers fail is because they have little or no experience judging the quality of a screenplay and often have no seasoned producer who can offer an objective and thoughtful evaluation. Ironically, the screenplay is also the one significant area in which independent filmmakers can have a significant edge over their counterparts at the studios.

Because of the size of their budgets, studios often homogenize their pictures and play it safe, remaking previously successful films like *Sabrina,* or recycling hit TV shows like "The Brady Bunch" and "Leave It to Beaver." Sometimes studio films depend less on the script than on special effects, action, and the carnival-ride nature of the film. The basis for the script *Speed II: Cruise Control* was not compelling characters or an intriguing plot; it was born out of a dream that director Jan De Bont had in which an out-of-control cruise ship ran into a Caribbean village. The entire script was written to accommodate that $83,000-per-second five-minute stunt, the most expensive single stunt in motion picture history. Robert Redford said about the trend of increasing budgets in Hollywood, "You could see the handwriting on the wall. There were going to be fewer and fewer chances for diversity and for real writing and real screenplays." Independents can take risks the studios will never take. And they can offer the viewing public something new and fresh. A tightly woven story that does not depend on expensive special effects is an entirely feasible project for an independent filmmaker working with a modest budget. In fact, over the past few years more screenwriters of independent films have won an Academy Award for screenwriting than those writing studio pictures. Michael De Luca, president of production at New Line Cinema, has said, "With independent film, it's all script driven because you're not selling big-star casting. So it's got to be about the script."

Producer Laura Ziskin (*Pretty Woman, What About Bob?, Old*

Friends), who heads her own division at Fox, says that when you're spending $60 million or more to make a movie, "you become very, very careful not to do anything that's going to turn off any segment of the audience." In other words, you play it very safe. One result of this fear-driven approach is that studios bring in more and more writers to "fix" scripts, whether they are broken or not. There were seven writers on *The Rock,* seven on *Eraser,* and thirty-two on *The Flintstones.*

Complicating this further is the willingness of some screenwriters to become doctors on material that is clearly beneath their talents. Steven Zaillian (*Searching for Bobby Fischer, Schindler's List*) is one of the great writing talents in Hollywood today, but his name surfaced as one of the writers on both *Mission: Impossible* and *Twister.* Finally, there is the screenwriter's willingness to compromise his or her own material. Hollywood's highest-paid writer, Joe Eszterhas (*Basic Instinct, Evil Empire, Showgirls*), says, "Screenwriters are their own worst enemies. . . . To get the credit, to get the money, they make changes that they know are destroying the material." The difficulty for a writer is to walk the fine line between fighting for what he or she thinks is right and remaining open to the possibility that someone's alternative suggestion is valid and will improve the work.

Many top screenwriters in Hollywood are paid huge salaries as "script doctors" by studio executives, partly because scripts are often in trouble, and partly as a self-preservation technique on the part of the executive. If the movie fails, the executive can always say, "But I hired William Goldman or Alvin Sargent" or "I hired William Goldman *and* Alvin Sargent!" It isn't just studio executives and producers who have caused this contemporary thrashing of a screenwriter's work. A-list actors often demand script approval as part of their deal, which means they will bring in one or more of their favorite writers to revise the script. Some of these same actors have arrived on the set having rewritten their own lines, often to the detriment of the script, and they've gotten away with it. This attitude is quite different from one expressed by Katharine Hepburn in a 1981 interview in *Time* magazine: "You do what the script tells you. Deliver the goods without comment. Live it—do it—or shut up. After all, the writer is what's important."

Directors are no less prone to picking up a pen and tinkering with a writer's vision. But most directors, while defending the right to a possessory credit ("A Film by . . ."), will admit that unless they also wrote the script, they are not truly the author of the film. One exception is John Carpenter, who said in an interview in *DGA* magazine, "As a director, I am the author of my movies. I know that's not a popular view with writers, but I'm sorry. If the writer thinks he's an auteur, then let him thread up his screenplay in a projector and we'll take a look at it." *Webster's New World Dictionary* defines the term "auteur" as the "primary creator of a film, especially the director." But "creation" implies generating something new rather than working from something that already exists. Screenwriters don't claim to be filmmakers, but they rightfully claim credit for the initial creation of the film's story line, structure, and characters. William Goldman once said that the real pleasure for the screenwriter is that he or she gets to make the movie first. A director can cover flaws in the script, perhaps finding innovative ways to make tedious dialogue interesting to watch, but if the director is working with a weak script, the finished picture will probably be just as weak. Some directors, including Sidney Lumet, are opposed to the possessory credit and stipulate in their contracts that the credit not be allowed on their movies or in the advertising and publicity for those movies.

One important reason for placing such strong emphasis on the quality of the screenplay, especially for independent filmmakers, is that given two scripts with essentially the same characters and production values, the better script *will cost less to produce.* There is an abundance of mediocre material floating around. Consequently, actors and even technicians will often take a sizable cut in salary for the opportunity to work on an independent film with a good script. Examples include Robert De Niro and Sylvester Stallone in *Cop Land*; Nicolas Cage and Elisabeth Shue in *Leaving Las Vegas*; and Bruce Willis and John Travolta in *Pulp Fiction.* If an independent producer settles for a routine story with shallow characters, depending solely on exploitation value to sell the picture, the production will struggle with mediocre talent and little enthusiasm all the way down the line. But if the producer goes through the necessary struggle to develop or acquire the rights to a good script with a solid story structure and compelling characters, a whole world of otherwise unavailable talent will open up.

In general, the process for writing a screenplay follows these stages:

1. *Treatment:* An essay-style description of the story and characters. There is no specific length, but a treatment generally runs twenty-five to thirty pages.
2. *First Draft:* Complete screenplay in standard form (see Table 4). Usually longer than the final draft.
3. *Second Draft:* A rewrite of the first draft incorporating significant changes in plot, story line, or the interrelationship of the characters.
4. *Polish:* Revisions of specific dialogue, action, settings, etc. Not a complete rewrite.

TABLE 4   **Screenplay Page in Standard Form**

EXT—BLAKE'S HOUSE—NIGHT

Roxanne trots through slush and snow toward Blake's pickup; it is parked
in shadow, engine purring. She hops in the passenger seat, throws her head
back.

>   BLAKE
>   You get it?

Roxanne opens her knapsack, reaches in for the jewels: diamonds, emer-
alds, rubies, and sapphires sparkle in the lamp-lit glare.

>   BLAKE
>   God bless America.

He touches them tentatively, as though they were alive, then plunges his
hand into the knapsack and pulls out a fistful of wealth.

>   ROXANNE
>   Trust me now?

Blake's grin shows yellow teeth; he kisses her like an animal, then jams
the truck into gear and pops the clutch. Rubber squeals against asphalt.

EXT—COUNTRY ROAD—NIGHT

The pickup flashes through darkness.

EXT—MOTEL—NIGHT

The pickup rumbles to a stop beneath a "vacancy" sign that buzzes pink.
There is no light on in the office.

Blake kills the engine, climbs out, then reconsiders and takes the keys.
Roxanne unrolls her window; a nighttime breeze cools her face. Blake circles the truck, mud sucking at his boots as he approaches the office.

>   ROXANNE
>   Maybe we shouldn't stop so
>   close to town.
>   BLAKE
>   You think they're gonna come
>   after us?

Roxanne looks away, nervous. Blake senses her concern, returns to the
truck.

A script in standard form runs approximately one page per minute of screen time. This means that a script for a 110-minute film will be approximately 110 pages long. When you get into the editing room, however, you will want room to trim and tighten various scenes, and possibly eliminate some altogether. In order to allow for such pacing options during editing, the final script will generally be longer, often 10 percent longer, than the final running time of the film.

A screenplay may undergo any number of treatments, drafts, and polishes before being either abandoned or completed. Generally, a producer will negotiate for a specific number of writing phases, paying a predetermined portion of the total writer's fee at the beginning of each phase, with a bonus and net profit participation for the writer if the picture goes into production *and* if the writer receives screen credit (writers are sometimes replaced and so extensively rewritten that they receive no credit on the finished film). It is fairly standard for a writer to receive 5 percent of net profits for a solo credit, and 2½ percent of net profits if the credit is shared. A large production bonus and hefty profit participation are obvious incentives for the writer, but the more the producer arranges to defer, the more will be the total cost of the script. The writer will reasonably demand a larger fee if a portion of that fee is contingent upon successful production financing, which is almost always the case in feature films.

There are some exceptions to the conventional approach to formulating a screenplay. Mike Leigh (*Career Girls, High Hopes, Life Is Sweet, Naked, Secrets & Lies*) has, for twenty-five years, begun films and plays without a script, with nothing more than an intuitive sense for a time, a place, and a predicament. He rehearses with his actors for months, defining characters and situations, but never revealing to them his overall strategy. In other words, the actors don't know entirely what the film is about until they see the finished product on the screen. However—and this is an important point—during the rehearsal process the film defines itself in Leigh's mind so completely, and the individual scenes are worked out with the actors in such detail, that by the time filming begins there is no improvisation. Everything is set. "What we shoot is completely precise. The literary qualities, the literary considerations, the writing qualities are very, very important, and I deal with those in as writerly a way as I can. But always on the floor, working with them [the actors], and writing through directing." What this means is that the screenplay is written as a collaborative effort among Leigh and his actors, and exists fully (although perhaps not on paper) before filming begins. "For me, the writing process and the directing process are the same thing. As far as I'm concerned, the script is the film. The film is the script." Leigh sees this as not very different from what conventional writers do. "What I do is what everybody does, really. Which is to say, to write a script, you sit down, you start improvising, and discover what it is by writing it. And that's all I do, really! The only difference is . . . that I don't do it in isolation and then have the problem of finding the actors. It all meshes together." This approach is unconventional, but for Leigh's particular genius it works.

If one is seeking a development deal in order to obtain money to *finance* the writing of a script, it is sometimes possible to present a film idea with a "verbal pitch." This is usually done by an experienced independent producer and writer. It involves arranging a meeting with a development executive at a studio or production company, usually through an agent, and outlining the story and characters in so compelling a manner that the executive's company will finance the writing of the screenplay. The company will also pay to acquire whatever rights, if any, are necessary, such as the rights to a book, a magazine article, or a person's life story.

Submitting a finished script to a studio or production company in the hopes of selling it outright or obtaining production financing is generally done through an agent. Most of these scripts are submitted not to executives who make decisions, but to readers who write an analysis of the script. This is called "coverage," and it will include a synopsis of the story as well as information about the setting, time period, genre, and whether it is a low-, medium-, or high-budget project. It may also include a checklist that rates elements such as characterization, dialogue, structure, story line, and production values as excellent, good, fair, or poor. According to veteran producer David Brown (*The Saint, The Player, Driving Miss Daisy, Jaws*), "You'd be amazed to know—although writers wouldn't—how few producers and studio executives actually read. They delegate that to the 'coverage' brigade or 'story analysts' who are extraordinarily influential in forming the studio 'take' on scripts and books." This is true to a lesser degree when working with executives and producers at independent production companies.

When the money for the purchase and/or development of a property is coming from a studio or other production entity, that company will own the material. A producer's right to reacquire the material if it is abandoned at some point (which most projects are) is something for serious negotiation. These are the turnaround provisions (see Chapter 1).

If you are a filmmaker interested in writing an original screenplay, or an adaptation, either on spec or as part of a development deal, it is important to understand the fundamentals of the craft. The many courses offered by colleges and universities are worth consideration, as well as those offered by organizations such as The American Film Institute and The Sundance Institute. Sundance offers a Screenwriters Lab, a five-day workshop that takes place in January and June during which aspiring screenwriters bring completed scripts and are given the opportunity for one-on-one problem-solving story sessions with seasoned screenwriters. Only a small handful of slots is available for the many hundreds of screenplays submitted for consideration. There are also a number of excellent books on the market, available at most bookstores, in particular those specializing in books on cinema.

What to Look for in a Screenplay

The simplest and most helpful question you can ask yourself when reading a completed screenplay, assuming the subject matter appeals to you, is "Did it hold my interest?" If it was so compelling that you were unable to put it down until you finished reading, you might have a winner. Another quality of a well-crafted screenplay is its ability to convey the movie before it is shot. In other words, the reader should be able to see and hear and feel the experience of the movie simply by reading the words on the page. Beyond that, if you are hoping to make a commercially successful film, there are eight checklist elements to look for that are based on research conducted a few years ago by a major Hollywood studio in an effort to determine common denominators that are true of all blockbuster movies. The criteria are subjective, and these qualities don't hold true for many successful films, but the list nonetheless provides a useful yardstick for judging the commercial potential of a screenplay.

1. *Energy.* This refers to dramatic tension, not action or special effects.
2. *Pace.* All of the films in the study set a swift pace at the outset and maintained it throughout the film.
3. *Three acts.* Each film had a linear three-act story structure, plus opening and closing sequences that bookended the films.
4. *Characters the audience cares about.* A crucial element in any successful film.
5. *Strong visceral response.* The audience viewing the films experienced a strong emotional reaction, as opposed to an interesting cerebral exercise.
6. *Unique.* There are many ways to define this, but essentially it means that the stories and characters were not derivative; they were original.

7. *Accessible.* No matter how outlandish the setting, each film in the study had characters and stories that the audience could strongly identify with and relate to.

8. *One genre.* Genre refers to an artistic category such as action, comedy, drama, or suspense. You may be able to mix genres, such as comedy and suspense, and create a successful movie, but none of the films in the study did so. They each stuck to a clearly defined genre.

There are two fascinating things about this study. The first is that each of these qualities was almost certainly evident in the screenplay, before even the first frame of the film was shot. Second, none of these qualities common to movies in the study has anything to do with budget, action, special effects, stars, or directors. A small independent film can address each of these qualities successfully, and many do. Obviously, meeting this criteria is no guarantee that a film will be a success, and certainly filmmakers should not feel artistically constrained by such a list, but it does provide a useful yardstick for measuring the potential commercial success of a film.

The Writers Guild

Most experienced film and television writers belong to the Writers Guild of America (WGA), an organization that began in 1942 with a five-page contract between the guild and signatory producers. Today the contract is over 400 pages long and covers virtually every aspect of film and television writing. For theatrical features, the contract establishes two sets of minimum fees: one for low-budget productions (under $2.5 million) and another for high-budget productions (over $2.5 million). Some producers split their companies into two separate entities, one that is a signatory to the WGA, allowing them to purchase material and work with WGA writers, and another company that is not a signatory to the guild and therefore not bound by the guild's regulations. For more information about the guild contract, you may call or write to the Writers Guild of America at the address and phone number listed in Appendix E.

For the struggling independent producer, one disadvantage to signing with the Writers Guild is that you must pay the writer at least guild minimum for each step in the writing process (story, draft, revisions, and polish). A script may undergo any number of revisions before it is ready to go before the cameras, and guild minimums for these revisions may be prohibitive. One solution is to find a nonguild writer who is willing to stick with you through the entire process, and who is willing to take at least partial compensation in the form of deferred payments and/or a share of the film's profits.

Producers who hire guild writers must fill out a simple form that lists *all* writers who worked on the project and includes the producer's tentative wording for the writing credit(s) on the film. The form will be reviewed by the guild and by each writer who worked on the project. It is prudent to err on the side of overinclusion when compiling the list of all persons who contributed to the script, but the producer does not need to include all of those writers in the tentative credit. It may be that two people wrote the script, then a third writer was hired to make minor dialogue changes. The producer may not feel that the third writer's contribution warrants inclusion in the credits, but the third writer should nonetheless be included in the complete list of contributing writers. The tentative credit will be considered final if neither the guild nor one or more of the writers disputes it.

In the event of a credit dispute, the determination of the guild's Credit Arbitration Committee, comprised of member writers, will determine the final writing credits. About 300 cases a year come before the guild's arbitration committee. Producers should be aware that writing credits within the guild are taken seriously and should be meticulous about abiding by the guild's final determination. If a producer fails to follow precisely the credit as determined by the guild, the producer or production company may be fined. In one such dispute an independent arbiter was brought in and awarded a team of writers $10,000 apiece in damages and an additional $10,000 in damages to the guild. The film was *A Case of Honor,* and it was released with the following writing credit: Screenplay by John Trayne and William Hellinger. The credit should have read, "Written by" (the most prestigious writing credit, since it indicates that the writers wrote both the original story and the screenplay), and there should have been an ampersand (&) between their names, which indicates a writing *team,* as opposed to the word "and" between their names, which indicates two separate writers. These may seem like trivial issues, but credits often determine a writer's worth, and they are taken seriously by the guild. Most contracts between producers and non-WGA writers adopt the guild guidelines for the wording, placement, and size of writing credits.

GUILD REGISTRATION

If you have written an original treatment or screenplay, it is wise to register it with the Writers Guild before showing it to anyone. The purpose of the registration, which is available to both members and nonmembers, is to protect the property (which can include material written for theatrical and television motion pictures, radio programs, video formats, and interactive media) from theft by establishing a date of authorship. As demonstrated by the $900,000 judgment Art Buchwald and Alain Bernheim received when they sued Paramount for using their two-and-a-half-page treatment titled "King for a Day" as the basis for the Eddie Murphy film *Coming to America,* ideas in the form of treatments and screenplays can be worth a great deal of money (attorneys in the case were initially seeking $6.2 million, which is the amount paid to John Landis for directing the film).

The guild registers approximately one hundred scripts and treatments a day; they come from all over the world but mostly from writers in the United States. Approximately two-thirds of the film and television registrations are for treatments and summaries of stories for film and television productions: the rest are completed scripts. The registration office also accepts novels and other books, stage plays, short stories, poems, commercials, lyrics, and drawings. Each registration is valid for five years and may be renewed for an additional five years. It is wise to reregister material if substantial changes have been made to its content.

In order to register a property you must submit one 8½-by-11 unbound copy of the work (no brads, staples, or folders), a cover sheet with the author's full legal name(s), the social security number of one writer, and the registration fee of $10.00 for members and $20.00 for nonmembers. Registration can also be done electronically over the Internet. Contact information for the Writers Guild Registration Service is included in Appendix E.

COPYRIGHT

Whether or not you register your property with the guild, you are still protected under copyright laws. These laws protect three basic rights. The most obvious is the literal inversion of the term, i.e., the right to copy. The second is the right to publish the work so that it becomes available to the general public. The third right covers the right to make derivative works. These are variations on the work: condensations, language translations, and the use of written material as the basis for a motion picture.

All of these rights belong automatically to the author of the property the moment the material exists in observable form, such as on paper or in the memory of a computer. Themes, ideas, or plots expressed merely as spoken words or thoughts are not, and cannot be copyrighted. The author of a work for hire, such as a commissioned screenplay, is defined for copyright purposes not as the person who creates the material, but as the employer. In other words, if you are hired to write a script, the employer is considered the author and will own the copyright. The copyright for a script written on spec is initially owned by the screenwriter, but when the script is sold, the production company or studio will invariably require that the copyright be transferred to that company. This is an ongoing bone of contention between production companies and certain members of the Writers Guild, but the issue is not simple and is not limited to the specifics of copyrights; it blends into some arcane and complicated labor laws that deal with the question of whether writers can simultaneously be authors and owners of their properties and still be considered employees (a requirement if they are to be represented as a group, the WGA, in a collective bargaining agreement). In Canada and most other foreign countries, writers can be both authors and owners of their work, and therefore may retain the copyright.

Properties said to be in the public domain, meaning that these works are the property of the public, include material for which the copyright has expired, material created by employees of the United States government as part of their jobs, and material such as facts and events that are otherwise not governed by copyright laws.

A writer's work is protected by copyright laws whether or not it is *registered* with the U.S. Copyright Office. Since failing to register in no way diminishes your rights, many writers (and most screenwriters) don't bother to file. The principal reasons to register with the copyright office are:

1. To establish a public record of ownership.
2. Because registration is usually a requirement in the event of an infringement lawsuit.
3. Because copyright holders who register before an infringement action, and who win the lawsuit, may collect attorney's fees and be eligible for statutory damages.

Registering material with the copyright office is simple. Begin by contacting the U.S. Copyright Office, which is listed in Appendix E, and requesting form PA (which stands for "performing arts").

A copyright is legally effective for fifty years after the death of the author or, in the case of a work for hire, one hundred years from the date the material was created. Any and all unauthorized use of copyrighted material should be considered with great care. Curiously, the very act of asking permission, as a matter of courtesy, may mitigate against you, for it may be viewed as evidence that you knew the material was protected under the copyright laws.

Titles for motion pictures cannot be copyrighted. You can, however, volunteer to sign a subscription agreement and register a title with the Motion Picture Association of America. This binds you to the arbitration system of the MPAA. The system is of questionable value for independent filmmakers because the factors that the arbitration committee considers when resolving title disputes are weighted in favor of the studios. Contact information for the MPAA is included in Appendix E. For more information on copyright issues see *Clearance & Copyright* by Michael C. Donaldson, also listed in Appendix E.

Screenwriting Software

There are some excellent screenwriters who use typewriters, and even a few who work with paper and pencil. But as with all aspects of the film industry, screenwriting has been enormously influenced by computers and software designed to aid writers with everything from the conception and organization of stories and characters to the printing of the final script in standard screenplay format.

The simplest programs do nothing but format a conventional word processor's document in standard screenplay form, creating proper page breaks, adding scene numbers, etc. More sophisticated programs are dedicated word processors that format and paginate your screenplay as you write. These programs are able to handle changes made after the scene and page numbers are locked for production, including the ability to create A & B scenes, A & B pages, omitted scenes, and X-changes (see Chapter 17). Some include additional tools such as index card systems and the ability to generate lists of cast, locations, and so on. Some are capable of exporting their files into software designed for budgeting and scheduling productions. They all allow you to modify the formatting options to fit your needs.

Story development software runs the gamut from programs that help organize ideas to programs that help create them. Many have a form of "artificial intelligence," meaning that once you input the necessary data about your story and characters, the program guides you through the writing process by asking questions and making suggestions that relate specifically to your screenplay. Some of these programs include additional options, such as icons that give you a visual reference to each character and tools that will help analyze your story as you write and after it's finished.

It is beyond the scope of this book to list or review these programs, but the most comprehensive resource for additional information is the Writers' Computer Store listed in Appendix E. This company has been in existence since 1982 and has developed a reputation as the most knowledgeable and complete source of products and information for screenwriters who use computers.

Acquiring an Existing Screenplay

Screenwriters, both aspiring newcomers and established professionals, often work on speculative projects in the hopes of marketing their completed scripts. The largest fees paid to writers are paid for these spec scripts, especially those that end up in bidding wars among the studios. As of this writing, the highest fee ever paid for a spec script has gone to screenwriter Joe Eszterhas ($4.5 million for *Evil Empire*). Thousands of other spec scripts are completed each year that languish on writers' shelves. Most belong there, but some are brilliant and deserve to be produced.

A producer who wishes to obtain the rights to a completed screenplay may purchase the property outright, in which case it will be owned by the producer. More often, however, the property will be optioned for substantially less money than an outright purchase, which gives the producer the exclusive right to purchase the property within a specified period of time. The purpose of the option is to allow the producer to tie up the rights to the property for a given period of time, during which the producer will seek development and/or production financing, secure in the knowledge that, if successful, he or she has the exclusive right to purchase the property.

The price of an option is negotiable and is paid against the eventual total purchase price of the property. For example, if the total purchase price is $75,000 and the option costs $5,000, the balance due the author, assuming the producer chooses to exercise the option and purchase the property, is $70,000. The time limit on an option is also negotiable. It can run anywhere from a few months to several years. Commonly, an option period runs twelve or eighteen months, with two renewal provisions. The price of the option will often increase with each renewal, and the renewal option money is generally not applicable against the purchase price. A producer may purchase the property at any time during the option period. When the option period(s) expires, the producer may purchase the property, negotiate for an additional renewal, or lose both the rights to the property and the money paid for the option. The Writers

Guild contract permits a signatory company to option literary material from guild members for a period of up to eighteen months for 10 percent of the guild minimum; each renewal period of up to eighteen months requires an additional 10 percent of guild minimum.

An option agreement functions as an entire contract between a producer and a screenwriter, including provisions for the eventual success of the completed film. Such provisions include the total purchase price of the property, the screenwriter's percentage participation in the film's profits, the size and placement of the writer's credit both on the picture and in paid advertising and promotional materials, and the author's rights in the event that a sequel, remake, television or cable movie, and/or television series is produced based on the original screenplay.

A producer wishing to purchase or option a completed screenplay must first contact the screenwriter or the screenwriter's agent to determine the availability of the property. Contact information for the writer or the agent will probably be included on the title page of the screenplay. If not, a producer can usually find the information by contacting the Writers Guild of America, which is listed in Appendix E.

If the property is available, the producer or the producer's representative, often an entertainment attorney, will negotiate for the appropriate rights, including:

- all motion picture rights, including sequel and remake rights
- all television and cable rights, including television and cable serial rights
- all video, laser disc, compact disc, and electronic rights
- all merchandising rights associated with the motion picture and television rights (see Chapter 22)
- publishing rights, including novelization of the screenplay

A producer inexperienced in such negotiations should obtain the services of an appropriate attorney or agent. Such representatives may be found either through word-of-mouth reputation within the film community or, in the case of an attorney, by following the procedure outlined in Chapter 1. A list of literary agencies may be found in several of the publications listed in Appendix E.

If a producer engages the services of an attorney to negotiate the acquisition, the attorney will most likely charge the producer on an hourly basis. It is difficult, however, for a beginning independent producer to find an established entertainment attorney willing to provide this kind of service. If a producer engages an agent to handle the negotiations, the agent will not charge the producer for services rendered, nor will the agent take a percentage of whatever money changes hands. However, the agent will insist on the exclusive right to negotiate the producer's development and/or production deal for the property. If such a deal transpires, the agent will take the standard 10 percent commission on the producer's development and/or production fee.

Acquiring a Published Work

A producer wishing to acquire the motion picture and television rights to a published work such as a novel, short story, magazine article, or stage play should avoid dealing with the publisher and make every effort to speak directly with the author or playwright. This may take a little detective work. Good places to start looking for contact information are the Internet and the library. If you are going after the rights to a new book, the process will be more straightforward than if you are seeking the rights to something older, say, an Agatha Christie novel, in which case the rights will often be controlled by the author's heirs or estate.

Ownership of these rights is subject to negotiation between the author and the publisher, but they are usually retained by the author. Sometimes they are shared between the publisher and the author, in which case the publishing contract will stipulate which party is empowered to negotiate the sale of these rights. If you contact the publisher but the author controls the rights, the publisher will invariably attempt to keep you away from the author and to negotiate a deal that benefits both the author and the publisher.

Once you make contact with the person or entity that controls the rights, discussions and negotiations begin. Again, it is imperative that the producer either be skilled in this type of negotiation or that the services of an appropriate representative, either an attorney or an agent, be obtained to negotiate on behalf of the producer. Negotiating for the rights to a published work is a specialized area, so it is important that the producer take time to select an experienced representative carefully. If a producer fails to do so, certain rights which otherwise would be included may be left out of the contract, thereby reducing the value of the option and, consequently, reducing the producer's negotiating strength with potential financiers.

In the case of a published work, the rights for which one must negotiate are similar to those for a completed screenplay. Publication rights are obviously excluded, since they are already tied in to a publisher. However, the producer should obtain the right to publish a synopsis of the material (usually limited to between 7,500 and 10,000 words) to be used in promotional materials such as pamphlets, brochures, and press releases.

As with a completed screenplay, a producer will sometimes pay an outright purchase price for ownership of the motion picture, television, cable, video, and disc rights to a published work, but it is far more common to purchase an option on the material against an eventual purchase price. Optioning a published work serves the same purpose as optioning a completed screenplay: It allows the producer to tie up the rights to a property for a specified period of time, during which development and/or production financing can be pursued.

The amount of money paid for an option on a published work varies enormously depending on the material in question. A highly commercial short story by an established author appearing in a current issue of a major magazine will be considerably more difficult and more expensive to option than a story that appeared twenty years ago in a lesser publication. The time limit on such an option also varies and is open to negotiation. The important thing is to allow plenty of time to develop the property and raise production financing to cover the purchase price of the source material. This generally takes several years.

Once a producer has secured the option, the property can be developed. This often means simply hiring someone to write a screenplay based on the optioned material but can also include seeking commitments from a director and principal cast members, and hiring a production manager to assemble a production budget and shooting schedule. In many cases independent producers will finance this development with personal money. In other cases development funding will be sought from a third-party source, such as private investments, an established production company, or even a studio, based solely on the optioned material. If a development deal is struck, the financier will pick up the cost of the option and pay for the development of the property. A producer may receive a fee for supervising the development of the material, but more often the deal will include nothing for the producer but money to cover out-of-pocket expenses until the property is picked up for production.

Acquiring the Rights to a True Story

Stories for screenplays can often be found in our own lives, in the lives of our family and friends, and in the lives we hear about secondhand, as in the news. *Brother's Keeper, Crumb, I Shot Andy Warhol, Not Without My Daughter, Rain Man, Roger & Me,* and *Shine* fall into this category.

True stories are often the basis for television movies. These are generally stories that have made national news, and they are usually bid on by several producers simultaneously. The cost of a person's rights, whether for a feature or a television movie, varies greatly, so it is dangerous to quote figures. In some cases, a producer will be able to negotiate for a free option, often in exchange for a more significant purchase price if the film gets produced. If the person whose rights you seek is deceased, you or your attorney may negotiate with that person's family or estate, or in some cases you may not have to purchase any rights at all. Nonetheless, it may be worthwhile to negotiate for the rights to the person's family in order to obtain their cooperation in telling the story.

Persons whose true stories appear in magazines and newspapers can sometimes be contacted through the reporter who wrote the article that sparked your interest. Writers for magazines are apt to want remuneration for their story since they have generally spent several months researching an article and establishing a point of view for the story. The rights to a story written for a magazine belong to the writer, not to the magazine. Sometimes magazine writers make formal or informal arrangements with the people about whom they are writing, for an involvement in any film or television sale of the story. Often this person can be very helpful in obtaining the rights to the people about whom the story was written. Unlike magazine writers, newspaper journalists generally report the facts of a story without establishing a specific point of view and are therefore less likely to claim ownership of their stories.

A producer, having secured the rights to a property, and having obtained development financing, is then faced with the critical task of selecting an appropriate person to write the screenplay.

Selecting a Writer

The most important skill to look for in a writer, regardless of genre, is that person's ability to tell a compelling story with well-defined characters whom the audience cares about. Beyond that, if you have an original idea for a film, or if you have acquired the rights to a published work or a true story, you most likely have in mind a *style* in which you would like to see your project executed. Look for a writer who exhibits a style and a sensitivity for the kind of picture you're making (action, comedy, drama, suspense, romance, and so on). To go with an untried writer in any given area is dangerous. A myth common to many beginning producers is that a good writer can write anything. Someone who has written several comedies may also be able to write suspense, but unless you see an example of it, you can't be sure. Even within a stylistic category you must be highly selective. Each category covers a broad spectrum of styles. *City Slickers, The Nutty Professor, Private Parts,* and *Austin Powers* are examples of different comedic styles. Someone who writes suspense may not write with a style that fits your image of how a particular suspense story should be treated. I am using terms like "style" and "sensitivity" because there is no concrete formula or guideline for selecting a writer.

The way to begin selecting an appropriate writer for your film is to watch films. When you have selected a few pictures that exhibit the writing style you're after, *read the screenplays* for those films. You will learn a great deal more about potential writers by reading their screenplays than by watching finished films. Read at least two samples of each writer's work. It is important that the writer be consistently competent, and the only way to judge this is to read several scripts. The Writers Guild of America maintains a credits department that will give you a complete list of a member writer's credits.

If you are a beginning producer without much experience judging screenplays, it is easy to throw up your hands and take a shot in the dark. This is riskier than betting your entire development financing on a state lottery. If you are in this position, you can hedge your bet significantly if you do one simple thing before reading sample script submissions from potential writers: Go to a film library and read several critically acclaimed screenplays in the genre for which you are seeking a writer. This will give you a sense of what to expect in a screenplay and will establish a benchmark against which to judge sample submissions. Hopefully you will find a writer for your project who lives up to the standards of excellence and professionalism that you find in these scripts.

Screenplays are available from writers' agents or from film libraries, university cinema departments, and for purchase from commercial outlets such as Hollywood Collectables and Script City (see Appendix E). There is also a publication called *Scenario, The Magazine of Screenwriting Art* (see Appendix E) that publishes four complete screenplays (in each case it's the writer's favorite draft) plus interviews with the screenwriters in four quarterly issues; the only drawback is that the material, while faithful to the writer's words, is not published in standard screenplay format.

The Academy of Motion Picture Arts and Sciences' Margaret Herrick Library has compiled a cross-referenced journal called *The Union List of Motion Picture Scripts.* This volume is a compilation of script holdings at the following major repositories in Southern California: The Academy of Motion Picture Arts and Sciences; The American Film Institute; The Frances Howard Goldwyn Hollywood Regional Library; Sherwood Experimental College; University of California, Los Angeles; University of Southern California; and the Writers Guild of America, West. Highlights include over 23,000 titles alphabetized with the year of release and distributor, expanded cross-referencing of working/alternate titles, contact information for all libraries, and separate motion picture treatments indexed by year. This publication is available for purchase from the Academy of Motion Picture Arts and Sciences, which is listed in Appendix E.

Once you have selected potential writers, contact their agents. The Writers Guild has an agency department that will tell you the name, address, and phone number of a member writer's agent. This information is offered as a service to producers and may be obtained by phoning the guild. If you contact agents and discover that your chosen writers are unavailable either because of prior commitments, lack of interest in the material, or because you can't afford them, their agents will undoubtedly recommend other writers within their agencies. Having gone to agents requesting a particular writer, you will have communicated to them in the most specific way possible the kind of writer you're after. You will also have set a standard of excellence for your project that will inevitably affect the attitude of the agents.

You can also contact literary agents without having a particular writer in mind. When discussing your project with the agent, be clear about your budget limitations and the style of writer you're after. Be as specific as possible; use examples from well-known films to communicate what you're seeking. They will recommend clients they feel are most appropriate and, assuming the writer is not a well-known commodity, will send you one or more sample screenplays to read. Remember, it is the agent's job to find work for their clients. Remember also that if you're a producer with money to spend, every agency door will be wide open—the only thing in your path will be a welcome mat. Even the most powerful agencies have clients whose careers are just beginning and whom the agency is in the process of nurturing. A list of literary agents can be found in many of the reference sources listed in Appendix E.

If you are unable to afford the Writer's Guild minimum wage for your writer, you will have to go outside this standard system to locate an unrepresented, generally unpublished, unproduced writer. Good ones exist but are hard to find. The best way to find them is by word of mouth. Talk to as many people as you can about what you're looking for and eventually it will come your way. If you have no direct contacts within the film community, you might contact screenwriting professors at colleges and universities with strong cinema departments. They may be able to put you in touch with a brilliant new talent who will develop your story into a script that the studios would kill to own. Literary agents may have received script submissions from beginning writers and may recommend some.

Once you have narrowed down your selection of appropriate candidates, meet with them to discuss the project. It is imperative that you and the writer (or, in the case of a team, writers) feel comfortable with each other. It is also important that the person you choose to structure the story and develop the characters has a passion for the material. Ideally a writer will have some personal connection, however distant, to the material in question. Writers interviewing for work do far better if they can find a personal connection to the material rather than simply reiterating what the producer already knows: that the material is wonderful and will make a sensational film.

Working with the Writer (Script versus Budget)

If a fixed budget is established prior to starting the script (as described in Chapter 3), the producer must guide the writer in such a way as to ensure that the finished script is molded to fit the budget. The producer must roughly budget each treatment, draft, and revision along the way, working with the writer to juggle both artistic and financial considerations so as to arrive at an optimum screenplay within the predetermined budget. However, if your only consideration when cutting or modifying a scene is the budget, you are not acting as a true *producer,* but as a *line producer* (see Chapter 12); of at least equal importance is the impact of the modification on the *story.* Always search for solutions that address the budget concerns without compromising the strength of the script.

Any scene that you cannot afford to execute at the level of excellence you set for your entire project must be discarded or modified. This often means racking your brain to combine scenes or to come up with an equally effective but less expensive scene. The time to make these decisions is during the writing. Many ideas with great merit will be discarded because of the budget. However, compromising in this way, beginning at the concept level, you won't run the risk of compromising during production and having an awkward scene in the finished film simply because you really couldn't afford to shoot it in the first place. If you wait until you're on the set, the compromises you will be forced to make will drag down the quality and effectiveness of the finished picture.

A constant juggling and rejuggling of script versus budget goes on at every level of film production, regardless of the size of the budget. It is not the ideal way to write the best possible screenplay, but if you're working within a small budget it is the *only* way to produce a first-rate picture. This kind of careful, detailed planning will clearly evidence itself in a consistent standard of excellence throughout your finished film.

Script Timing

When you arrive at a draft of your screenplay that seems relatively close to what you're after, have it timed. The standard rule of thumb, one minute of screen time for each page written in standard screenplay form, is a useful guide, but its accuracy will vary depending on the style of the writer, the nature of the material, and the director. A more accurate timing may be obtained from a competent script supervisor. This will cost a few hundred dollars, but if it saves you from shooting more scenes than you need or from writing more material when you have enough, it's worth the expense. Actually, it's worth it just to *know* how long your film will run.

Script supervisors use a variety of methods to time scripts. Some simply lock themselves in a room with the script and a stopwatch and act out every scene in the film. After many years of experience timing shots and sequences on the set (a routine responsibility for a script supervisor) and subsequently comparing notes with the running time of the finished film, script supervisors develop a remarkably accurate sense for timing scenes from a screenplay. This is especially true when the script supervisor has worked previously with the person who will direct the film and, ideally, with the writer of the screenplay. This combination is not usually the case, but if you can find a script supervisor who has at least worked with the director, you will obtain a more reliable timing.

Table 5 offers an example of the kind of information to expect from a detailed script timing. Note that it is standard to define a scene's length by the number of whole pages and eighths-of-a-page the scene covers, i.e., a scene that is one and a half pages long is referred to as "one and four-eighths" pages.

In lieu of a script supervisor, an experienced first AD (assistant director) or UPM (unit production manager), especially if they are familiar with the film's director, will be able to provide a fairly accurate estimate of the film's overall running time.

Ideally, the length of the finished film will be determined by whatever length most effectively tells the story. Feature films commonly run

TABLE 5 **Sample Page from Script Timing**

Title________________________ **Page**________________________

Scene numbers	***Sets and action***	***Pages***	***Time***
104	*Interior Richard's Castle* Richard tells Alexis how he lost his kingdom.	3 4/8	3:05
105–106	*Interior Richard's Castle* Alexis follows Richard down stone steps.	3/8	0:27
107	*Interior Subterranean Chamber* Alexis is introduced to the knowledge of the kings.	6/8	1:06
108–110	*Montage: Interior Chamber* Alexis reads the scrolls as Richard looks on.	4/8	0:45
111	*Exterior Woodland Pool* Richard admonishes Alexis, calls for the test.	1 7/8	2:20
112–114	*Exterior Forest* Alexis rescues Jeremy and learns of the reward.	1 3/8	1:58
115	*Exterior Forest* Alexis sends Jeremy on his way.	1 2/8	1:24
116	*Exterior Richard's Castle* Alexis enters the castle.	1/8	0:12
117	*Interior Castle* Alexis sees herself in the mirror, slightly aged.	3/8	0:40
118	*Interior Castle* Alexis and Richard discuss the future.	1 1/8	1:04
119–124	*Exterior Forest* Richard hands Alexis a flower and she rides off.	1 1/8	1:44
125,127,129, 131	*Exterior Encampment* Alexis says she has come to assist Jeremy.	3	4:05

between ninety and 110 minutes. There are films that run as short as seventy-five minutes (short running times are generally limited to direct-to-video releases), and others that run in excess of three hours. From the distributor's and theater owner's points of view, 100 minutes is ideal. This allows time to schedule showings every two hours with twenty minutes in between to sell tickets and popcorn and run previews of coming attractions. From a producer's point of view, a film that runs considerably longer is hard to sell, so it is important to weed out any scenes that will not be needed in the finished picture. If you shoot too much material, you are not only wasting money, you are potentially compromising the story. If you need to cut out sections of the film in order to get it down to a reasonable length, you may be forced to cut out an important piece of the plot.

Selecting the Director, the Unit Production Manager, and the First Assistant Director

The Guild Question

THE DIRECTORS GUILD OF AMERICA (DGA) IS A UNION WHOSE membership includes directors, unit production managers, and assistant directors. Its contract covers minimum wages, standards for working conditions, and creative rights. A producer who signs a DGA contract must hire guild personnel in all of these categories and abide by all of the rules of the contract. Before signing with the guild, take particular note of the provisions for working conditions because they have an enormous financial impact on a production. First-time producers often make assumptions about salaries based on DGA minimums without considering such things as meal penalties and turnaround limits.

Unless you are working with an extremely low budget, it is worth exploring a relationship with the guild. The organization has made a sincere effort to address the needs of producers making low- and medium-budget pictures, and the experience of the membership can sometimes more than pay for itself in the added efficiency of your production. In an effort to make DGA personnel available to a variety of productions, the guild has broken down its contract minimums into three budget categories: low-budget (up to $500,000), medium budget (between $500,000 and $1.5 million), and high budget (over $1.5 million). In New York the guild has negotiated special agreements for films with budgets up to $6 million. For producers working with low budgets or whose productions have special needs, the guild will attempt to negotiate individual contracts tailored to those needs. The contract can be extremely flexible with respect to salaries and working conditions, but the production company must honor the guild's pension, health, and welfare requirements. Even with the flexibility the guild offers, for a producer making an ultra-low-budget film, a relationship with the guild is out of the question. The only choice is guerrilla filmmaking (no guilds, no unions, no permits, and no insurance).

The Director

The screenplay is the foundation upon which a film is built, but it is the director who must translate the words on paper into the images and sounds of a film. This includes directing the activities of the cast and crew during preproduction, production, and postproduction. On many independent films the director wears more than one hat, often that of writer, producer, and/or actor, and sometimes even cinematographer, editor, composer, and stunt coordinator.

If you are producing a picture that was not written by the director, it is best to bring the director into the project as early as possible. The director will make contributions to the screenplay at one stage or another, and if these thoughts can be incorporated during the early writing process, so much the better. If you can bring together a writer and director who work well together, the director may make contributions to the script right from the start. This will help the entire filmmaking process because the director will fully understand the structure of the story and the nature of the characters involved.

When selecting a director, a producer must look for finished work that exhibits a style consistent with the producer's vision of the film. Don't limit yourself to looking only at feature films; a director's style might be evident in television programs, commercials, music videos, or student films. The producer must also consider the director's experience and reputation for working within the schedule and budget limitations anticipated for the project. It is generally safer to hire a director who has experience working on films smaller than yours rather than larger. When exploring a director's reputation for respecting budget and schedule limitations, it is often helpful to talk with the producers and/or production managers with whom the director has worked on previous films. These individuals can usually be contacted through the production offices that made the films or through the distribution companies that released them.

If you are considering directors who are members of the DGA, you will find them listed alphabetically in the *Directors Guild of America Membership Directory*. This directory is updated and published annually, and it is available from the guild for a nominal charge. It lists all members throughout the country, their agency or other contact information, membership category (director, production manager, etc.), and

many of their credits. If you are seeking information about a few specific individuals, you can request it over the phone by calling the guild
office in Los Angeles, New York, or Chicago. Contact information for
the DGA is included in Appendix E.

If none of your selected directors is available for your project, their
agents will undoubtedly recommend others. As with writers, you can go
directly to agents for recommendations without having a particular director in mind. Describe your picture and your budget limitations to the
agent, and if there are any appropriate people available within the
agency they will be recommended.

If you select a director who is not represented by an agent or an attorney but who is a member of the Directors Guild, you can write to that
person, or leave a message, in care of the guild. If you have a potential
director in mind who is not a guild member, you can often make contact
through the production company or the distributor of the film upon
which you based your selection.

At the top end of the spectrum are star directors. This isn't a term for
directors who work with stars; it is a term for directors who *are* stars.
These are people like Alan Parker, Barry Levinson, Martin Scorcese,
Steven Spielberg, and Ridley Scott. If you have a strong script and a reasonable budget, these individuals are not to be ruled out, but there are
downside considerations worth knowing in advance. Unlike an experienced producer of major motion pictures, who walks hand in hand with
the director throughout preproduction, production, and postproduction,
a fledgling producer who has succeeded in developing a property to
which a star director becomes attached should be prepared for the director to take over the project completely. It is not uncommon for a star director to have the producer fired, banned from the set, or otherwise
driven out of the production process. These directors commonly have
their own producers who come along as part of the director's deal, and
they function on behalf of the director. The advantage for the director,
and possibly for the film, is that this results in a single voice of authority. The advantage for the producer who has nurtured the project along
until the director became involved is that the project suddenly becomes
a high-profile major motion picture; the disadvantage is that the producer will very likely be left in the dust. There is no right or wrong
about hiring a director of this stature, but it's important to be aware of
the potential repercussions.

The Unit Production Manager and the First Assistant Director

One of the most important members of your team during preproduction and production will be the unit production manager (UPM). The UPM is responsible for the logistics of production through completion of principal photography. In the old studio days, each studio had a production manager who oversaw several films simultaneously, each of which was referred to as a production unit, and each of which had its own *unit* production manager. Today the studio overseer is called the "vice president in charge of production," but the nomenclature for the person managing a specific production is still *unit* production manager. On films that are split up into several units, for instance, into a first unit, a second unit, and a special effects unit, each unit may require its own UPM. If you are producing a picture under the DGA contract, you are required to consult with the director before hiring a UPM.

Together with the producer, the UPM will finalize a detailed production budget and will monitor and juggle the figures in that budget throughout the making of the film. Though much of a production manager's time is spent in the office, a good UPM will visit the set often enough to maintain a good relationship with the director and key crew members, and to keep tabs on how the production is proceeding. If there are problems, the UPM will want to know about them as early as possible.

The UPM is usually empowered to negotiate deals for crew, equipment, locations, catering, etc., on behalf of the producer. This position requires a highly skilled, experienced individual with an in-depth nuts-and-bolts knowledge of motion picture production; it also requires someone skilled in interpersonal relationships. The production manager must walk the fine line between caring for the needs of the cast and crew (from supplying adequate film stock to ensuring that there are enough honey wagons on the set), letting each individual involved in the production know that his or her needs are being well looked after, while at the same time maintaining the producer's budget and schedule.

Part of the production manager's job is to supply the director with whatever tools the director feels are necessary for the picture. If the director has a shot in mind that calls for a Titan crane, a good UPM will make every effort to furnish the crane. What UPMs can't tolerate is a director who requests a Titan crane because it "might be needed." The UPM can't be expected to fight for items in the budget that may never be used.

Because of the pressures, both self-imposed and external, placed on the artistic team assembled to make a film, including not only the director but the director of photography, production designer, and costume designer, the UPM will be under constant pressure to spend more money than is available. A typical scenario:

COSTUME DESIGNER: I need an additional $30,000 for the extras in the school auditorium because the students are supposed to wear uniforms.

UPM: The two hundred kids in the background can show up in white shirts and black pants and nobody will know the difference.

COSTUME DESIGNER: No, I have to dress everyone. I'm responsible for the look of the picture and I insist.

How does a UPM appease the artistic concerns of the costume designer and at the same time take into consideration the budgetary concerns? This is a constant battle, backwards and forwards, between the UPM and the artistic department heads. The question most often asked by a UPM is, "How much is enough?" A costume designer can dress everyone in the scene, or dress only the principal actors; costumes can be purchased at secondhand stores or manufactured from scratch. A production designer can build every set from the ground up, or work with existing walls on practical locations, perhaps changing nothing but the paint. All of these choices must be monitored by the UPM without unduly inhibiting the artistic contributions of the personalities involved. It is the producer's job to oversee these negotiations because the producer will often become the arbiter.

The production manager's work is closely coupled with that of the first assistant director (first AD), and both should be involved in preproduction as early as possible. You can think of the first AD as a foreman in a shop and the UPM as the manager who sits in the office. The function of the first AD is discussed further in Chapter 17, but for now it is important to understand that this person is responsible for running the production *on the set,* ensuring that everything remains on schedule. It is the first AD who sets the tone and tempo on the set and who is responsible for creating an optimum environment in which the director can work.

If a conflict arises between the planned shooting schedule and the director's wishes, the first AD will make every effort to juggle the schedule in an attempt to accommodate the director. If this can't be done within the budget, if, for instance, the schedule change requires paying for an extra day in a particular location, the first AD must then work with, and in some instances fight with, the production manager on behalf of the director. If the production manager cannot find a way to accommodate the director, it is up to the production manager, not the first AD, to enforce the planned schedule.

On large-budget productions, the first AD is hired very early in the preproduction phase and is responsible for organizing the shooting schedule. On smaller-budget pictures, this is rarely affordable, and the schedule is initially assembled by the UPM. The director normally chooses the first AD; this is a contractual requirement if you sign with the DGA. Most experienced production managers and assistant directors are members of the DGA, but if you choose not to sign with the guild it is still possible to find qualified people for these positions. Since there is no structured organization for nonguild production managers and assistant directors, one way to find them is by word-of-mouth reputation. Let your needs be known to as many people as possible within your film community and eventually the right people will come your way. Another approach is to contact trade publications such as *Variety* and *The Hollywood Reporter* with information about your project. These papers routinely publish announcements about upcoming productions. Production personnel watch the trades for this information and often contact producers and directors to offer their services. You can also take out paid advertisements in trade publications announcing your production plans.

Because of the profound influence the UPM and first AD will have on your picture, it is important that they be accustomed to working within the budget and schedule parameters of your film. A production manager or first assistant director who works regularly on multimillion-dollar major studio productions may be ill suited for a medium-budget independent project. Alternately, a production manager or first assistant director experienced only in low-budget films is usually a poor choice for an epic period piece.

Finally, it is important to hire a production manager and a first assistant director who believe in your project and are dedicated to its successful completion. Their attitudes will greatly influence the morale of everyone else involved.

The Budget

THIS CHAPTER WAS PRECEDED BY DISCUSSIONS ABOUT THE DIREC-
tor, UPM, and first AD in order to stress the importance of selecting
these people prior to finalizing a detailed budget and schedule for your
film. A truly accurate budget and schedule are almost impossible to assemble without their input. At the studio level, the director is a part of
this process and will be asked to sign off on the final budget.

One hears all the time about pictures going over budget and over
schedule. The production company blames the producer, who passes
blame on to the director, or the star, or the cinematographer. Without
question, there are cases in which these individuals contribute to the
problem, but that doesn't come close to explaining why so many pictures go over budget and over schedule. The fact is that pictures are
often *under* budgeted and *under* scheduled to begin with. This is easily
understood by anyone who has tried to get a picture off the ground. If
you can convince investors or a production company that you can make
a picture for less money in less time, it will be that much easier to finance. Consequently, producers often find themselves in the uncomfortable position of whittling their budgets unrealistically, or rationalizing
that they can really do it for less, in order to make their project more appealing to potential sources of financing. But they suffer for it in the
long run. Once production begins, a different attitude sets in.

The producer who has made those budget compromises on paper will
do everything possible to make the production as good as possible but
will end up torn between two unpleasant alternatives. Either the project
goes over budget or the quality deteriorates below the level of excellence that was advertised to the investors. The difficulty of financing
films is the principal cause of this painful dilemma.

Remember that every single element in the production hinges on the
budget. If you rationalize too optimistically when writing the final budget, the problems you create will haunt you throughout the making of
your film. This is especially true on a low- or medium-budget independent picture with little protection for overbudget costs.

If you have what should be a $500,000 project that you've managed
to squeeze into a $450,000 budget and everyone involved does their ut-

most to stay within budget, even making some painful compromises, your project may still be $25,000 over budget when you enter the post-production phase. If the production phase of the budget is any indication of how tightly postproduction is budgeted, you're in real trouble. Where does the money come from? Do you cut an already meager sound effects budget in half? Do you cut the music budget by a third? Do you eliminate ADR? Do you go to a second-rate mixing facility? Or a third-rate effects house? You may do all of the above and still not fall within your $450,000 budget. Chances are that you will ultimately spend $500,000 on the picture and will have created an enormous headache for yourself—and compromised the quality of your picture—by not facing that reality in the first place.

Often you will be in the position of "backing into" a budget. This means that the financing is fixed, possibly because the production company is willing to spend only a fixed amount on the film, and you have to find a way to make the picture for whatever that number is. If you are raising your budget with presales, the amount you are able to presell will define your budget. If you are raising money independently, you must realistically ask yourself how much you can raise, and base your budget on that figure. Studio pictures are budgeted based on what the studio is willing to spend on the picture, and consequently studio producers are often backing into a budget, though neither the producers nor the studios acknowledge this openly. If you find yourself in the position of backing into a budget that is less than a reasonable figure, *change the script*.

Nick Gomez had 80 percent of the budget in place before he began writing his script for *Laws of Gravity,* and he wrote the script to fit the budget ($38,000). He set most of the film outdoors, using areas of his Brooklyn neighborhood that he knew he could use for free. Robert Rodriguez wrote *El Mariachi* not only for his anticipated budget, but around elements he had at his disposal. These included a motorcycle, a school bus, two bars, a jail, a ranch, and a pit bull. He also wrote the script with minimal dialogue (a worthwhile exercise for any filmmaker), so that the majority of the film could be shot without having to record sound.

Roger Corman, who believes that adversity in the form of low budgets spawns creativity, routinely modified scripts so they would fit the budget. He faced this problem when making a film called *The Nest,* about man-eating cockroaches: The heroes were supposed to fight the roaches on a beach, then climb into a boat and row away. There wasn't enough money in the budget to pay for an insect wrangler, so the script was changed. A single giant cockroach, built by the special effects team, would attack the heroes. The special effects team built the giant roach but didn't have the money to make it mobile; all it could move was its jaw. Again, the script was changed. The giant cockroach was placed inside a tunnel through which the heroes had to pass in order to get to the beach. They battled their way around the giant cockroach, made it to the beach, and rowed away. And the film stayed on budget.

Some independent production companies make films in the $500,000-to-$2-million budget range for direct-to-video distribution. The most successful of these are always backing into a budget based on the worst-case scenario. They ask distributors what will be the *least* they can be certain of recouping if they deliver a movie in a certain genre with certain elements attached. The distributor's estimated worst-case scenario becomes the budget for the film. This gives the production company the greatest financial protection, but not necessarily the highest return on the investment.

Many successful independent films were started with enough funding to complete the picture only partially, but clearly there are dangers in doing this. If you consider the statistical odds against the success of an independent film, it is naive to begin one unless you have adequate funds to complete it. One can argue in favor of naiveté, citing great accomplishments by people too inexperienced to know that what they were doing "couldn't be done." In a sense, it is naive for anyone to believe they can make a successful independent film. Yet people do it all the time, and those most likely to succeed are the ones who possess both an unshakable conviction in their projects (which is not the same thing as naiveté) and a firm grasp on the realities of the business.

There are people in the industry who claim that any film can be made for any amount of money. In theory, perhaps, that's true. I suppose they could have made *Gone With the Wind* in one location, using a backyard, a stucco house, and friends from the neighborhood, but chances are it wouldn't have been very successful. For any screenplay, there is a bottom-line budget, a minimum amount of money necessary to produce a film that meets the standards of quality *for that film's anticipated marketplace.* If your available financing is less than that minimum budget figure, change the script and rebudget until you've got a picture you can afford to make.

If you refuse to modify your script and stick adamantly to an unrealistic budget, you will be forced to make severe compromises and cutbacks in the quality of any portion of your film will drag down the quality of everything else in the film. You must strive for the highest level of quality attainable within your budget *throughout every aspect of production.* Everything in your film depends on everything else. You may go over budget during principal photography in order to attain a certain level of quality, but if you get into postproduction and can't afford to maintain that level, your extra effort and expense during production will go right down the drain.

You may be unable to raise enough money to meet even the minimum budgetary needs no matter how you modify the script. Some filmmakers in this position set out to raise only enough money to complete principal photography, convinced that they will find the rest of the money once the film is in the can. Others raise enough to shoot a few sample scenes in the hope that these scenes will be enough to convince investors or a distributor to pick up the balance of the financing. The important thing is to define your goal, whether it's a completed screenplay, a completed film, or a partially completed film, and to budget for it accurately.

When assembling the budget, it is important to give equal emphasis to every step in the process of making the film. Production managers often make the mistake of carefully budgeting the principal photography stage, but only casually budgeting for postproduction. This is because, first, the principal photography stage is the most exciting aspect of production and, second, because production managers are not involved in postproduction and consequently they often know little about it. It is important for the production manager to consult with the producer, the director, and the editor in order to budget postproduction accurately. If the principal photography stage turns out to be exceptional, there is often room to expand the postproduction budget, but this is not something to count on. All stages of production must be budgeted with equal care and accuracy right from the start.

Bear in mind that even with a carefully planned budget, the producer and production manager must remain flexible enough to change the budget, if necessary, to accommodate unanticipated problems. I'm referring here to juggling within the budget, for example, paying for a greater number of extras by sacrificing a day's crane rental. Such changes should be made only if they improve the overall result, not simply with an eye to solving an immediate problem.

The Ideal Budget

The average budget for a studio-affiliated feature is around $40 million; fifty years ago that figure was $400,000. The upper end of studio pictures is currently pushing the $200 million mark. *Waterworld* cost Universal $175 million. *Titanic,* at *over* $200 million, was so expensive that it was financed by two studios, Fox and Paramount; the film will have to earn half a billion dollars just to break even. Independent feature motion-picture budgets can range anywhere from a few thousand dollars to tens of millions. Two extremes are *Clerks,* made for $27,000, and *Stargate,* made for $55 million.

The optimum figure, the budget for which producers strive, is that magic figure that will result in a maximum return on the invested dollar. This is not necessarily the minimum, bottom-line figure. For example, given three different production budgets for the same screenplay, the box office grosses might look like this:

Budget	$ 500,000	$ 1,200,000	$ 7,000,000
Box Office Gross:	3,500,000	19,100,000	29,000,000
Budget X 4 = Break-even Point	− 2,000,000	− 4,800,000	− 28,000,000
Box Office Gross after Breakeven:	= $1,500,000	= $14,300,000	= $1,000,000

The box office gross is divided among theater owners, domestic distributors, foreign sales agents, foreign distributors, the producer, and the investors. This figure becomes the break-even point when it reaches approximately four times the film's budget. In each of the three cases, there is a profit beyond the break-even point for the investors. The $500,000 investors will realize a reasonable profit per dollar invested. The $7 million investors will realize very little profit, but the $1.2 million investors will realize an enormous return on their investment. The $500,000 project was sensible, the $7 million project was not, but the $1.2 million figure was the closest to an optimum budget.

When a producer has the flexibility to develop an ideal budget as opposed to backing into a budget, it is difficult to determine what that figure should be. It requires, first, writing an optimum screenplay without significant compromises for the budget and, second, basing the production budget on three things: the script, the potential market, and the producer's ability to package elements with the script that will appeal to a maximum number of people within that market. Costs for these elements must be balanced with the projected income they will generate. The important thing is that the costs of these added elements are not so great as to reduce the return on the invested dollar. For example, a series of elaborate special effects may increase the box office gross to such an extent that investors realize an additional $1 million return. But if the cost for these special effects exceeded $12 million, the additional expense will decrease the overall return per invested dollar.

The optimum, ideal budget is rarely achieved in motion picture production. It is an extremely difficult thing to gauge, and it becomes increasingly difficult with the complexity of the project and the various media available in which to market it. A producer, in attempting to determine an optimum budget, must depend on the counsel of many specialists, from stunt coordinators to sound engineers, but eventually a decision must be made, fingers crossed, and the producer must move on.

Independent producers generally agree that it is best to avoid a budget area referred to in the industry as "no-man's-land." This is a budget that is too low to attract stars, but too high to expect the film to turn a profit. There is disagreement as to what this figure is. Some feel that the magic figure is between $5 million and $10 million; others think it starts at $4 million. Producer and president of Fox Searchlight, Lindsay Law, who has been involved in an impressive list of independent films, including *Angels & Insects, Brother's Keeper, El Norte, I Shot Andy Warhol, Longtime Companion, Ethan Frome, Stand and Deliver, Testament,* and *The Thin Blue Line,* believes that the perfect budget for an independent feature lies somewhere between $500,000 and $2.5 million. A movie made for less than $2 million will probably, at the very least, break even if there are reasonable sales to foreign countries, to video outlets, and to television.

The Standard Budget

A motion picture budget is generally broken down into *above-the-line* costs and *below-the-line* costs. Above-the-line includes producer, director, story rights, screenwriter, and principal cast. These are usually fixed fees. Below-the-line is everything else, including atmosphere talent, technicians, equipment, location costs, and film stock.

The ratio between above-the-line and below-the-line costs varies from picture to picture, but since most films are cast driven, the tendency is to weigh the budget heavily toward above-the-line costs. A film made for $1 million, for example, might budget $300,000 for the cast. A reasonable balance for a studio feature film is one-third of the budget above-the-line and two-thirds below-the-line, but on pictures that employ one or more A-list actors that ratio is often reversed. In those cases the producers may be making a megabudget movie, but have no more than $12 million to $15 million for the cost of the physical production. The cost for below-the-line *personnel* is generally between 11 and 15 percent of the total budget regardless of the size of the budget. These costs may be as low as 8 percent or as high as 25 percent, depending on the nature of the picture.

The breakdown of a standard studio budget, based on statistical averages from hundreds of film budgets, is 5 percent for the story and screenplay; 5 percent for the producer and director; 20 percent for the cast; 20 percent for studio overhead; 35 percent for crew, sets, costumes, equipment, film stock, etc.; 5 percent for taxes; and 10 percent for contingencies. As a general rule, the lower the budget, the greater will be the percentage of the budget spent below-the-line. In other words, the *relative* costs for producer, director, screenplay, and cast are less for small-budget pictures. An A-list actor might receive $15 million or more for work on a single picture, whereas on an ultra-low-budget film the entire cast might work for nothing more than free lunches and possibly a share in the film's profits.

A production manager writing a budget for a film is faced with an enormously sophisticated task. Cost estimates will be based primarily on the production manager's past experience with other films, but in some cases the production manager will rely on other UPMs for counsel, often exchanging budgets and comparing figures. This is especially true if the picture being budgeted is to be shot in a location with which the production manager is not fully familiar. Experienced production managers know whom to call for assistance when budgeting costs for specialty areas such as stunts, animal wrangling, and special effects. They will obtain input from specialists in these areas whose estimates for the costs in their particular departments will be incorporated into the final budget.

There are a number of excellent computer programs that UPMs use to budget films. They come with a variety of budget forms, databases of union and guild rates, databases that can be customized to include negotiable and nonunion rates, tools for calculating fringe benefits, and the ability to store and retrieve a variety of budgets for the same project. You may wish to compare a budget for shooting domestically with another for shooting in Australia. Or one for shooting in a studio with another for shooting on location. Computing programs have enormous flexibility for making global changes. If you add an extra day, a special effect, a new location, or change your camera package, by pushing a few keys everything (the entire structure) will change to include the information and the way it affects costs. Change it back, juggle it around, examine how the change in one sequence affects costs down the road, press a key to convert dollars to the currency of any other country, and it will all be accomplished in seconds.

While these programs speed the process and relieve much of the drudgery of budgeting, they don't supply the estimates. Those must be supplied by an experienced UPM. A mistake many novice producers make is to assume that because they have the software, they can budget a picture. This is an area where producers can get into serious trouble. You can't budget a picture from books or software; you must budget from experience. That's why it is vitally important to hire an experienced professional to do the job.

As with other software programs, it is beyond the scope of this book to list or review them. Anyone interested in additional information can contact the Writers' Computer Store listed in Appendix E. Additional reference sources that production managers find helpful when budgeting a picture are also included in Appendix E.

Depending on the complexity of the picture, it is possible for a thoroughly experienced UPM to complete a reasonably accurate preliminary budget for a feature film in one or two days. Here, too, I must stress the word *experienced,* because there are a number of people who advertise the ability to produce budgets and production boards, often for a cut rate, who are not competent to do so. These individuals often have the software to print out professional-looking budgets and boards but have had little or no experience on a film set. No matter what tools are used, it is crucial that an experienced individual do the job. Ideally, this will be a person accustomed to working in your film's budget category and who is familiar with the geographic area in which you intend to shoot your film.

Because of the complexity of this task and the number of variables involved, production managers commonly request a production accountant to verify their figures, often using a portion of their fee to pay for this service. A production accountant is the person who sets up and maintains the books and payroll system throughout the making of a film and is therefore in a knowledgeable position to verify a production manager's cost estimates.

It is standard to add a contingency figure of 10 percent to the budget for an independent film. One of the major differences between studio financing and independent or bank financing is that there is no contingency figure built into a studio budget. If the picture goes over budget, the studio absorbs the costs. In some cases the studio will build this in themselves, putting an $18 million budget on paper but knowing the film will cost $20 million. Producers of studio-financed films are sometimes induced to control the budget and schedule by means of a penalty formula. For example, if a production goes over budget, the producer's profit participation is decreased by a predetermined formula. The standard formula for a large studio film is 1 point (or percent) of the producer's participation for every 1 percent that the picture goes over budget. Alert producers try to negotiate a similarly structured bonus provision should the picture be brought in on time and/or under budget; the danger here is that the producer will be influenced by personal monetary gains at the expense of the picture.

Although it is less common, there are situations when a picture goes over budget and the producer, in lieu of being fired, offers to pay for the overbudget costs out of his or her fee. Typically, this is viewed as a penalty, not a deferral, because the producer will not be allowed to recoup the loss. In rare instances, a distributor may negotiate for a contractual clause authorizing the withholding of a portion of the producer's fee until the picture is completed; if the costs exceed the budget, this money will be used to cover, or at least help to cover, the overbudget expenses. It is highly unusual for a producer to accept such terms, primarily because overbudget problems during production are often perceived, from the producer's point of view, as the responsibility of the director. This is especially true on pictures helmed by A-list directors; on those pictures the producer often works for the director and has little or no control over the director's behavior.

The Low-Budget Budget

There are many systems for "ballparking" budgets, but the lower the budget, the more dangerous this becomes. This is largely because for low-budget films, any small change is a large percentage of the total. A multimillion-dollar film can afford a few days' leeway, but that same few days for a low-budget film may have a disastrous effect. For many low-budget films there is little or no protection for overbudget costs.

The lower the budget, the more heavily weighted will be the below-the-line nonfixed fee costs. Extremely low-budget, nonguild, non-union films in which the producer, writer, director, and actors work for nothing, other than (hopefully) a share in the film's profits, will have a zero above-the-line budget.

Since the making of a film is dependent upon so many unpredictable variables, not the least of which is the weather, one solution to budgeting is to raise the contingency from a standard 10 percent to 20 percent. The latter is probably more realistic for most low-budget films. Begin by budgeting every aspect of your film down to the minutest detail, from the number of rolls of gaffer's tape you'll use to the number of days you'll need to rent editing space several months down the road. A good production manager will be able to help estimate many of these costs quite accurately. Once you've listed every conceivable expense for your entire production, add 10 percent for the things you forgot. Then add another 10 percent for contingencies. Investors understand that a reasonable contingency figure is an essential part of budgeting. However, problems arise when an investor, unfamiliar with the nature of low-budget film production, sees a contingency as high as 20 percent and assumes that the producer doesn't have a tight rein on spending.

One solution for this is to budget each category of production with a built-in, hidden contingency of 10 percent, then add an additional overall 10 percent contingency to the top sheet of your budget. This will give you a 10 percent contingency on paper but an actual 20 percent contingency for the film. In order for this to work, you must realistically budget your picture for 80 percent of the total budget and do your utmost to stay within that figure. Don't fall into the trap of borrowing from the 20 percent. Consider it unavailable, spent money. It will invariably find a way of disappearing on its own with no help from you. People budgeting studio features always find ways to pad the budget, and if the studio discovers this, which they usually do, they will often allow all or part of the padding to be kept.

When making a low-budget film you will undoubtedly be offering deferred payments and possibly profit participation to certain members of the cast and crew. There is no rule of thumb for determining individual figures, but a film that costs $300,000 will probably incur deferments of $30,000, or 10 percent of the budget.

The Ultra-Low-Budget Budget

A question often asked by beginning producers is, "What is the least possible amount it will cost to make a ninety-minute thirty-five-millimeter feature film?" The minimum figure necessary to obtain a 35mm answer print for commercial release in theaters is between $100,000 and $150,000 (an exception was *White Trash,* which was shot on Hi-8 video and released in 35mm for a total budget of $46,000). When shooting on film, even when making an ultra-low-budget picture, say for $20,000, by the time you have all the elements in place for distribution—which will probably include remixing the sound, obtaining insurance, paying for music rights, and contractual lab elements such as the music and effects track for foreign dubbing—and the blowup from 16mm to 35mm—the costs will have risen to between $100,000 and $150,000.

That doesn't mean you need that much in cash, and you certainly don't need that much to start or even to complete a preliminary, and possibly saleable, version of your film. If you include the process of fund-raising as a part of the filmmaking process, you will probably start with nothing but the change in your pocket. If you consider the time you begin preproduction as the start of the process, you will need only a small portion of the $100,000 to begin making your film. If you choose to shoot your film in some medium other than 35mm, such as Super 16mm, you may complete your film for considerably less than $100,000, and convince a distributor to finance the blowup to 35mm and possibly to remix the sound track. *Clerks* was initially completed in 16mm for $27,000, *The Brothers McMullen* for $20,000, *El Mariachi* for only $7,000, *Laws of Gravity* $38,000, and *Slacker* for $23,000. Or you may complete a portion of the film, as was the case with *Go Fish,* which was partially completed in 16mm for $10,000 and, based on that material, obtained financing for the balance of its $63,000 budget. So the amount you will need to begin—write your script and commence financing—is zero. By the time you have completed a ninety-minute 35mm film, the minimum amount that will have been spent is $100,000.

Some ways you can keep the budget low include: buying film stock in short ends or by shooting in video (see Chapter 14); avoiding children and animals since they are often unpredictable and require special considerations; avoiding weather references in the script that are hard to control, such as snow when you're shooting in July; arranging for actors to supply their own makeup, and wardrobe; find locations that you can use for free; ignoring permits, insurance, unions, and guilds; paying cast and crew members with deferred payments, meals, and snacks (feed them well). Last, avoid complex camera setups that require elaborate lighting and extensive preparation for the crew on the day you are shooting. If you keep it simple, you can shoot as many as fifty setups a day. Another approach is to work out each scene thoroughly in rehearsal, then let the camera follow the actors in long, single-setup masters. This worked extremely well for Nick Gomez when he made *Laws of Gravity.* Determine what your average shooting ratio will be, then ration your film judiciously, based on the complexity and importance of each scene. If you can afford an average shooting ratio of 3 to 1, you may wish to shoot some scenes in one take with one setup, for a ratio of 1 to 1, so that you can shoot a higher ratio, say 5 to 1, on more complex or important scenes.

In a popular two-day seminar offered by The Hollywood Film Institute (listed in Appendix E), instructor Dov S-S Simens describes the simplest ultra-low-budget film imaginable. You take a cluster of friends who are bright, witty, and fun to watch into a single room. You turn on your camera and ask them to talk for ninety minutes. You shoot everything with a wide-angle lens, stopping only to reload your camera. At the end of ninety minutes you will have shot 8,100 feet of film, for a ratio of 1 to 1. You will have virtually no picture editing costs. Your dialogue, music, and sound effects will be minimal. Your sound mix will be simple. And you might have a wonderful little film. If you beg, borrow, and steal everything you need, you might be able to make this film without spending a penny. This is for a 35mm ninety-minute color feature film. More realistically, the above-mentioned film will probably cost a minimum of $12,000 in cash and considerably more in deferred payments.

The more no-cost deals you make, the more you will give away in deferred payments and profit participation. Since a picture that costs nothing will necessarily defer everything, you may be forced to give away your entire share of the film's profits. It may be worth it to you, simply in order to make your film, but this kind of no-budget approach is usually more trouble, more time consuming, and in the long run more expensive than raising a small amount of financing.

Motion Picture Insurance

Insurance requirements vary from picture to picture, and their cost is negotiable. A film with many dangerous stunts will be more costly to insure than a drawing room mystery. Film insurance is priced based on a film's budget on a cost-per-thousand basis. Depending on the film, insurance will cost between 2 and 4 percent of the total budget, plus the cost of workers' compensation, which is required by state law. One reason insurance costs vary is because the amount of the deductible is negotiable. Another reason is that producers don't necessarily need to insure everything in the budget. You can exclude certain things. For example, you might exclude the costs of the script, the music, and other items that won't be affected if your star gets sick for a few days. The best way to approach this is to go through the budget with a reputable insurance agent, exclude what you can reasonably exclude, and then negotiate the cost.

The rates you pay for errors and omissions (E & O) insurance (see below), time limits, and deductibility are the result of subjective evaluation, not only by the insurance company underwriters but by outside counsel. Your application for E & O will be signed by your attorney, and the reputation he or she has for obtaining and checking all necessary clearances for this insurance will affect what you are ultimately asked to pay. This aspect of setting charges is rarely discussed or admitted to by the insurance companies, but it exists.

The following information regarding various types of insurance coverages for motion picture and television productions is included as a courtesy of Truman Van Dyke Company, insurance brokers to the entertainment industry. For additional information, contact Truman Van Dyke Company, which is listed in Appendix E.

MOTION PICTURE AND TELEVISION INSURANCE COVERAGES LIST

The following brief descriptions are general in nature and are not a complete explanation of the policy terms.

Cast Insurance: Reimburses the production company for any extra expense necessary to complete principal photography of an insured production due to the death, injury, or sickness of any insured performer or director. Insured performers (or director) must take a physical examination prior to being covered by this insurance. Physical examination cost to be paid by production company. Coverage usually begins two to four weeks prior to the beginning of principal photography. Extended-term preproduction cast insurance is available.

Negative Film and Videotape: Covers against all risks of direct physical loss, damage, or destruction of raw film or tape stock, exposed film (developed or undeveloped), recorded videotape, sound tracks, and tapes, up to the amount of insured production cost.

Coverage does not include loss caused by fogging; faulty camera or sound equipment; faulty developing, editing, processing, or manipulation by the cameraman; exposure to light, dampness, or temperature changes; or errors in judgment in exposure, lighting, or sound recording, or from the use of incorrect type of raw film stock or tape.

Faulty Stock, Camera, and Processing: Covers loss, damage, or destruction of raw film or tape stock, exposed film (developed or undeveloped), recorded videotape, sound tracks, and tapes caused by or resulting from fogging or the use of faulty materials (including cameras and videotape recorders), faulty sound equipment, faulty developing; faulty editing or faulty processing, and accidental erasure of videotape recordings.

Coverage does not include loss caused by errors of judgment in exposure, lighting, or sound recording, from use of incorrect type of raw stock, or faulty manipulation by the cameraman. This coverage can only be purchased with negative film and videotape coverage.

Props, Sets, and Wardrobe: Provides coverage on props, sets, scenery, costumes, wardrobe, and similar theatrical property against all risks of direct physical loss, damage, or destruction occurring during the production.

Extra Expense: Reimburses the production company for any extra expenses necessary to complete principal photography of an insured production due to the damage of destruction of property of facilities (props, sets or equipment) used in connection with the production. Coverage includes losses due to faulty generator operation.

Miscellaneous Equipment: Covers against all risks of direct physical loss, damage, or destruction to cameras, camera equipment, sound, lighting (including breakage of globes), and grip equipment, owned by or rented to production company. Coverage can be extended to cover mobile equipment vans, studio location units, or similar units upon payment of an additional premium.

Property Damage Liability: Pays for damage or destruction of property of others (including loss of the property) while the property is in the care, custody, or control of the production company and is used or to be used in an insured production.

Coverage does not apply to liability for destruction of property caused by operation of motor vehicle, aircraft, or watercraft, including damage to the foregoing. Liability for damage to any property rented or leased that may be covered under "Props, Sets, and Wardrobe," or "Miscellaneous Equipment" insurance (except that loss of use of any such equipment is covered).

This insurance is not covered under comprehensive liability policy. Property damage coverage written as part of a comprehensive liability policy excludes damage to any property in the production company's care, custody, or control.

Errors and Omissions: Covers legal liability and defense for the production company against lawsuits alleging unauthorized use of titles, format, ideas, characters, plots, plagiarism, unfair competition, or breach of contract. Also protects for alleged libel, slander, defamation of character, or invasion of privacy. This coverage will usually be required by a distributor prior to release of any theatrical or television production.

Workers' Compensation: This coverage is required to be carried by state law and applies to all temporary or permanent cast or production crew members. Coverage provides medical, disability, or death benefits to any cast or crew member who becomes injured in the course of their employment. Coverage applies on a twenty-four-hour-per-day basis whenever employees are on location away from their homes.

Individuals who call themselves independent contractors will usually be held to be employees as far as workers' compensation is concerned, and failure to carry this insurance can result in having to pay any benefits required under the law plus penalty rewards.

Comprehensive Liability: Protects the production company against claims for bodily injury or property damage liability arising out of filming the picture. Coverage includes use of all non-owned vehicles (both on and off camera), including physical damage to such vehicles. This coverage will be required prior to filming on any city or state roadways, or any location sites requiring film permits.

Coverage does not apply to use of any aircraft or watercraft, which must be separately insured before any coverage will apply.

Guild/Union Flight Accident: Provides motion picture/television (LATSE/NABET/SAG/DGA) guild or union contract requirements for aircraft accidental death insurance for all production company cast or crew members. Coverage is blanket and the limits or liability meet all signatory requirements.

Completion Guaranty Bond: Completion guaranty bonds are available for feature motion picture productions that meet certain minimum budget requirements. The completion guaranty will provide completion funds for up to 100 percent of the total picture budget.

These brief descriptions provide a simplified explanation of the various types of insurance protection available to motion picture and television production companies. Most of these coverages will have deductibles of varying amounts, depending upon the limits of insurance coverage required.

It is wise to obtain bids from several reputable insurance companies and negotiate among them for the lowest price. Members of certain filmmaking organizations may be eligible for discounted insurance plans. For example, the insurance supplier for the Association of Independent Video & Filmmakers (AIVF) offers reduced rates to members for both personal and production insurance; this includes a wide range of health insurance options as well as special liability, E & O, and production insurance tailored for the needs of low-budget mediamakers (filmmakers, videomakers, etc.). Commercial and documentary production companies can obtain annual producers insurance policies (PIPs) incorporating various combinations of film insurance coverages. The International Documentary Association (see Appendix E) is an excellent source of information about insurance and other issues for documentary filmmakers.

PRODUCERS' ERRORS AND OMISSION LIABILITY INSURANCE CLEARANCE PROCEDURES

The following information is provided to assist an applicant's attorney in making certain that all necessary clearance procedures have been taken before applying for an errors and omissions insurance policy. Issuance of this type of insurance is contingent upon approval by the insurance carrier of a completed application and a representation that all clearance procedures have been accomplished.

1. The script must be reviewed by the applicant's attorney prior to commencement of any production to eliminate matter that may be defamatory, invades privacy, or is otherwise potentially actionable.

2. Unless the work is an unpublished original not based on any other work, a copyright report must be obtained and submitted with the application. Both domestic and foreign copyrights and renewal rights should be checked. If a completed film is being acquired, a similar review should be made on copyright and renewals on any copyrighted underlying property.

3. If the script or story is an unpublished original, the origins of the work should be determined—basic idea, sequence of events, and characters. It should be ascertained if submissions of any similar properties have been received by the applicant, and if so, the circumstances as to why the submitting party may not claim theft or infringement should be described in detail.

4. Prior to final title selection, a title clearance should be obtained from one of the title clearance firms shown below. The title of any production is excluded from coverage until a satisfactory title report has been obtained. We recommend you contact the following firms for information on their services and fees:

Thomson & Thomson
Copyright Research Group
500 E Street, S.W. Suite 970
Washington, D.C. 20024-2710

Customer Service Department
Telephone: 1-800-356-8630
Fax: (202) 728-0744
Fax: 1-800-822-8823

Law Offices of
Dennis Angel
1075 Central Avenue, Suite 414
Scarsdale, New York 10583

Telephone: (914) 472-0820
         (212) 239-4225
Fax: (914) 472-0826

5. Whether the production is fictional (and locations are identifiable) or factual, it should be made certain that no names, faces, or likenesses of any recognizable living persons are used unless written releases have been obtained. Release is unnecessary if a person is part of a crowd scene or shown in a fleeting background. The term "living persons" includes thinly disguised versions of living persons who are readily identifiable because of identity of other characters or because of the factual, historical, or geographic setting.

6. Releases are not required of persons who are members of Screen Actors Guild (SAG), American Federation of Television and Radio Artists (AFTRA), or Screen Extras Guild (SEG), as they were compensated for their performances/appearances as members of such guilds. Releases obtained from living persons referred to in 5, above, should conform to the language used on the enclosed sample personal release.

7. If music is used, the applicant must obtain all necessary synchronization and performance licenses.

8. Written agreements must exist between the applicant and all creators, authors, writers, performers, and any other persons providing material (including quotations from copyrighted works) or on-screen services.

9. If distinctive locations, buildings, businesses, personal property, or products are filmed, written release should be secured.

This is not necessary if nondistinctive background use is made of real property.

10. If the production involves actual events, it should be ascertained that the author's sources are independent and primary (contemporaneous newspaper reports, court transcripts, interviews with witnesses, etc.) and not secondary (another author's copyrighted work, autobiographies, copyrighted magazine articles, etc.).

11. If not previously submitted, a final shooting script must be submitted with the completed application. If the production is a documentary-type production, then the shooting outline or treatment should be submitted.

12. Coverage for errors and omissions insurance cannot be bound before the completed application has been approved by the insurance carrier's clearance attorney.

This information is submitted as a guide for proper clearance procedures to be accomplished prior to obtaining producers' errors and omissions insurance for motion picture or television productions.

TABLE 6 **Sample Personal Release**

To: _____
(Production Company)

From: _____
(Releasing Party)

Re: _____
(Title of Production)

In consideration of your filming me, or otherwise recording me, my performance, or voice in the above production, I hereby grant to you, which term shall include not only yourself, but your employees, agents, successors, licensees, and assigns, the irrevocable right and license to use, simulate, and impersonate forever my name, face, likeness, voice, appearance, actions, activities, career, and experiences either actually or fictionally, under my name as undersigned, or under any other name in, and/or in connection with, the production, distribution, exhibition, advertising, and other exploitation of the above production in perpetuity throughout the world. The rights herein granted to you shall include the right to depict and/or portray me to such extent and in such manner as you in your discretion may determine, and to edit any of my statements or comments and/or to juxtapose my face, likeness, appearance, actions, activities, career, experiences, and/or statements or comments, or any simulation and/or impersonation thereof, with any film clips and/or other material. I acknowledge that any editing of my statements or comments and of all portions of the above production and/or juxtapositions of film clips and/or other material shall be at your sole discretion.

Further, you shall have the right to distribute, exhibit, or otherwise exploit any such production, in whole or in part, by any method and in any medium, including theatrically, nontheatrically, and by means of television or otherwise in connection with the above production or separate and apart from the above production.

In granting this release, I understand you have relied hereon in making the above production and will incur substantial expense based upon such reliance. I warrant that I have not been induced to execute this release by any agreements or statements made by your representative as to the nature or extent of your proposed exercise of any of the rights hereby granted, and I understand that you are under no obligation to exercise any of your rights, licenses, and privileges herein granted to you.

I hereby release and discharge you from any and all liability arising out of any injury of any kind that may be sustained by me from participation in or in connection with the making or utilization of the above production or by reason of the exercise by you of any of the rights granted to you hereunder.

Name: _____
(Sign)

_____
(Print)

Address: _____

_____

_____

Dated: _____

To be completed if participant is under twenty-one years of age:

I represent that I am the parent or guardian of the minor who has signed the above release, and I hereby agree that I and said minor will be bound thereby.

Parent/Guardian: _____
                              (Signature)

_____
(Print)

_____
(Address)

_____

Before closing this chapter on budgets, I would like to mention a crucial budget item for independent filmmakers producing a picture with no guaranteed distribution. This is the cost of promotion. Many filmmakers complete their films but have no funds left with which to market and/or sell them. Depending on how you intend to promote your finished product (something you should think about carefully before beginning production), promotional expenses can range anywhere from festival entry fees and shipping costs to personal appearances and paid publicists in a variety of countries. The important thing is to plan for reasonable promotional expenses and to protect that money throughout the making of your film. Investors will be grateful.

The Shooting Schedule
and Continuity Breakdown

The Production Board

ONE OF THE PRIMARY RESPONSIBILITIES OF THE FIRST ASSISTANT DI-rector, in consultation with the director and subject to approval by the producer, is to organize the final shooting schedule for production. If a preliminary schedule was assembled by the production manager for budgeting purposes, it will be modified and refined by the first assistant director. The schedule is laid out on a multipanel production board, a portion of which is shown in Table 7.

The left-hand column lists and numbers each cast member, starting with the most significant player. The vertical strips across the remainder of the board represent all of the scenes in the film and contain the following information:

- whether the scenes are day or night, exterior or interior
- the number of script pages these scenes cover (partial pages are counted in "eighths," so that 1½ pages is referred to as 1⅛ pages)
- the scene numbers that the particular strip represents
- a brief description of the scenes represented by that strip
- which cast members are involved in the scenes; characters are listed by numbers opposite the character's name in the left-hand column of the production board

These strips are available in a variety of colors the AD may use to indicate information about the day's shooting. Blue strips might be used for exteriors, green for interiors, white for scenes requiring snow, and orange for rest days. How these colors are used depends on the requirements of the script and the preference of the AD. Each vertical strip is removable so that the entire board can be easily rearranged to accommodate changes in the schedule. In the sample production-board section, the black strips are used to separate shooting days.

TABLE 7 **Sample Panel from Production Board**

Date															
DAY OR NIGHT			D	D	D	D	D	D	N		D	D	D	D/N	N
PAGE COUNT			1 4/8	1 4/8	1 4/8	1 4/8	3	3 4/8	1 2/8		1 6/8	6/8	2		3
SCENE NUMBERS			8A	8B	178	87 88	104	105 106	110 116		2, 3 61	62 63	219		62 85
								107 108	308			218	287		
Title THE WAND PRODUCER DIRECTOR PRODUCTION MANAGER ASSISTANT DIRECTOR **Script dated**			EXT. TELIMAN'S FORT	EXT. TELIMAN'S FORT	EXT. TELIMAN'S FORT	INT. TELIMAN'S FORT	INT. TELIMAN'S FORT	INT. TELIMAN'S FORT	INT. RICHARD'S CASTLE	REST DAY	INT. RICHARD'S CASTLE	INT. RICHARD'S CASTLE	INT. SUBTERRANEAN CHAMBER	COMPLETE ALL CASTLE INTS.	KING NELLIS'S ENCAMPMENT
Character	**Artist**	**No.**													
ALEXIS		**1**			1	1	1	1				1	1		
JEREMY		**2**					2	2	2		2	2			
MONROE		**3**					3								
JAGG		**4**													
TESSIE		**5**	5	5											5
LADIA		**6**	6												6
ILLANA		**7**	7												7
KING NELLIS		**8**													8
QUEEN JULIA		**9**													9
TELIMAN		**10**	10	10	10						10				
RICHARD		**11**				11	11	11	11			11			
AKNAR		**12**													
CYRIL		**13**													
LEYMAN		**14**													
HORSE THIEF		**15**													
SOLDIER #1		**16**													16
SOLDIER #2		**17**													17
LUTE PLAYER		**18**										18			
MAGICIAN		**19**	19										19		
FISHERMAN		**20**													
		21													
		22													
		23													
		24													
		25													
		26													
		27													
		28													
		29													
		30													
		31													
		32													
EXTRAS (#)		**33**	(6)	(10)	(10)			(8)	(20)		(4)				(35)
SPECIAL EFFECTS		**34**	X										X		
		35													

Studio schedules are defined by the budget, which dictates how many shooting days the production can afford. In the days of *Taxi Driver* and *The French Connection,* the average production schedule was forty days. Today the average studio production schedule is sixty days. This means that a director of a two-hour 120-page studio feature will shoot an average of two pages per day. *Leaving Las Vegas* was shot in thirty days. The running time of *Leaving Las Vegas* is 112 minutes, so the director shot nearly four pages a day. Movies made for television are shot in eighteen to twenty days, usually on a schedule of three 6-day weeks or four 5-day weeks. Scripts for television movies are approximately 105 pages long, so the director will shoot an average of five to six pages per day.

Action takes the longest to shoot and is on the screen for the least amount of time. You may spend a day or more shooting an action sequence that is no longer than an eighth of a page, but you can make up the time by shooting several walk-and-talk dialogue scenes the next day. "Walk-and-talk" refers to a dialogue scene in which people are speaking while walking, usually outdoors; this is often more interesting visually than the same two people sitting at a picnic table or on a park bench.

Studio features are in production for several consecutive months, while low-budget independent films are often shot in a matter of weeks. The production schedule for an independent film might also be spread out sporadically over a period of months as the money trickles in. Writer/director Gregg Araki filmed *The Living End* off and on over a period of four months. Other pictures are filmed in a short period under intense pressure. Writer/director Albert Pyun shot *Adrenaline* in sixteen days and *Omega Doom* in ten days (he allows no chairs on the set and claims a staggering 90 to 100 setups a day).

While pictures often go over schedule, they rarely come in under schedule. That is because the team making the film, in an effort to do the best possible job, will invariably use every last second available to them, and still press for more. In so doing, directors and other artists involved in the filmmaking process sometimes lose sight of the fact that filmmaking is a business. The reason people invest money in a film project is in the hopes of reaping a profit, not furthering someone's career. Yet there is no director or cinematographer who wouldn't like a few extra days or weeks added to the schedule. On a small picture, with little room for overages, this is rarely possible. Since the director, more than anyone, has the power to keep the picture on schedule, one solution is to make a portion of his or her salary contingent upon that schedule being adhered to strictly. In this way the director has something personal at stake. There is also the advantage of a certain feverish energy on a movie set where people are working under pressure that often brings out the best in everyone.

The scenes of a film are almost never shot in sequence, from beginning to end. From an economic standpoint, it would be extremely inefficient to do this. Consequently, the first AD juggles all of the production elements—cast, crew, locations, equipment, and so on—reordering scenes in the film for the most economically efficient shooting schedule. If there are several scenes in the film that take place in a single location, the AD will arrange to shoot them back to back, regardless of when they will appear in the finished film.

In addition, the AD must consider the availability of cast members, allow adequate time for moving from location to location, allow time for set construction and set decorating, and consider endless other details when making a schedule. If the picture is being made under the jurisdiction of unions and/or guilds, the AD must be fully familiar with their working rules, including such things as meal penalties, special provisions for minors, forced calls, and turnaround time (how quickly an actor or crew member who completes a day's work can be asked to "turn around" and return to work without the production paying a penalty), all of which may affect the way the shooting schedule is organized.

A good AD will always have a backup "What if . . . ?" plan. What if it rains? What if the lead actor gets sick? What if the equipment fails? ADs will try to schedule exteriors early in the schedule, so if it rains, they will have an alternate interior location, called a "cover set," at their fingertips. If they leave the exteriors until last and it rains when the script calls for sunshine, the producer will either have to wait out the rain or have the script modified to fit the weather.

The problems facing an assistant director when scheduling a picture may be best understood by using a simple example. It will be a worthwhile exercise to cut up strips of paper and mock up a rough production board for the following scenario.

Consider a film with two characters, Simon and Roxanne. The film will be shot in two locations, A and B, with a four-week shooting schedule, two weeks at each location. Roxanne will appear in all of the scenes at location A and will therefore work for both weeks at location A, but will be needed for only one week at location B. Simon will work only for one week at location A, but for both weeks at location B. If Simon begins work before the second week at location A, there will be some nonworking holding days for which, according to standard Screen Actors Guild (SAG) regulations, he must be paid.

The standard SAG contract, called the Codified Basic Agreement, requires payment for any holding time between workdays if that holding time is less than ten consecutive days when shooting within the United States and its territories, and fourteen consecutive days when shooting in any other country. Additional regulations must be considered when filming on distant location within the United States; in Los Angeles a distant location is defined as anything beyond the *studio zone.* The studio zone encompasses everything within a thirty-mile radius of the intersection of Beverly Boulevard and La Cienega Boulevard.

If Roxanne's scenes aren't scheduled for the first week at location B, she will have nonworking holding days as well. It would appear best to schedule Roxanne alone for the first week at location A, with Roxanne and Simon together for the second week at location A. However, the first scene in the script involves Roxanne and Simon traveling in Roxanne's 1946 classic Rolls-Royce. They are in an accident. No one is hurt, but the car is badly dented and Roxanne will be driving it that way throughout the film.

If the first week involves Roxanne alone, driving the damaged Rolls-Royce, the AD will either have to arrange to have the Rolls repaired for the accident scene scheduled for the second week when Roxanne and Simon will be together (which will require some down time to repair the car), or the AD will have to consult with the production manager about buying or renting a second 1946 classic Rolls for the accident sequence in the second week. If Simon is an extremely expensive actor, it may be less expensive for the production manager to buy or rent the second Rolls-Royce than to hold Simon over for an extra week at location A.

But suppose all of Simon and Roxanne's scenes together at location A are exterior? Is it worth risking bad weather during the second week at location A with no interior backups? If bad weather sets in and there are no cover sets, it could cause a day or more of holding time, not just for Simon but for the entire production.

Perhaps the production manager will swallow the added expense of holding Simon for an extra week, saving the cost of the second Rolls and maintaining a flexibility to accommodate bad weather. In making this decision, the assistant director and production manager must weigh not just the cost for each element but also the weather forecast and the area's reputation for predictable or unpredictable weather. There may not be an obvious good decision, in which case the AD will have to throw in a bit of educated guessing based on past experience.

Now, if you consider a picture with ten locations, fifteen cast members, production variables including set construction time, expensive special effects, an enlarged crew for particularly difficult sequences, makeup changes for aging or modifying the "look" of an actor partway through the story, and unusual weather requirements such as snow, and continue to list all of the elements that an assistant director must juggle in a typical screenplay, you will begin to get an understanding of the difficulties involved in scheduling a picture.

Having taken all of the above into consideration and developed the most economically efficient shooting schedule possible—with a maximum number of backup plans—the assistant director is faced with still another problem. In scheduling a production, artistic considerations must be taken into account. It may be that the most economically efficient schedule dictates shooting a particular scene, say scene number 86, on the first day of production. But suppose the director refuses to shoot scene number 86 on the first day on the grounds that it's a difficult, intensely emotional scene for the actors, and the director wants the cast to become familiar with one another, and wants also for the operation of the crew to become well oiled, before attempting to shoot scene number 86. The director might suggest shooting it during the fourth or fifth week of production. This is a valid consideration and one that the assistant director must respect. Moving scene number 86 to the fourth or fifth week, however, might throw off every other sequence in the schedule and the AD may have to reconstruct the entire schedule from scratch.

This section is not an attempt to teach the reader how to schedule a production. Rather, its purpose is to convey a profound respect for the complexity and sophistication of the tasks that face production managers and assistant directors, and to encourage filmmakers to weigh their choices carefully when hiring them.

Today most productions are scheduled using computer programs designed for this purpose. These programs are often capable of sharing and exchanging information with the software program used for budgeting the film. The programs print production board strips on white paper, which are slid into plastic sleeves that come in a variety of colors, and these plastic sleeves are then inserted into the production board. The programs include additional functions such as the ability to format and print production calendars, call sheets, and elements lists (props, extras, wardrobe, and the like), and the flexibility to customize databases for cast, crew, props, costumes, locations, and more. You can create, save, and compare a variety of scheduling options, and make global changes in a matter of seconds. It is beyond the scope of this book to list or review scheduling software programs, but a valuable resource for anyone interested in additional information is the Writers' Computer Store listed in Appendix E. Other sources that production managers and ADs find helpful when scheduling a picture are also listed in Appendix E.

As with budgeting software, beginning producers sometimes think that these scheduling programs make it possible for anyone to schedule a picture. They don't. The programs make the process faster and easier, but they don't eliminate the need for an experienced individual to input and manipulate the data. The process involves a kind of thinking that cannot be handled by existing "artificial intelligence" systems.

Continuity Breakdown

A film is made up of a number of sequences, each consisting of one or more shots (camera setups and/or takes). Continuity refers to the consistency of the look and sound of each shot in the film. If an actor changes the action or dialogue from one take to another within a given sequence, the continuity among the shots is compromised. For example, if an actress picks up a glass with her right hand in a medium shot, then picks it up with her left hand in a closer shot, the continuity between the two shots is broken and they will not cut together in the editing room. Among the responsibilities of the script supervisor is the policing of continuity discrepancies in the action and dialogue, and to bring these to the attention of the director.

Various department personnel contribute to maintaining continuity on the set. If actors are filmed entering a restaurant in a light rain and are later filmed walking to their table inside the restaurant on a sound stage, their clothes and hair need to be dampened in order to maintain the continuity between the interior shot and the previously filmed exterior shot. The people responsible for this are the on-set wardrobe and hair personnel. If there is a calendar or clock in the shot, it must reflect the correct date and time for that moment in the film; the clock must also be reset to the same time at the beginning of each shot. The on-set dressers are responsible for this. Another continuity issue has to do with the camera's point of view. This includes such things as the direction and speed with which the camera moves during a shot, which side of the camera actors enter and exit from, and where they are looking during a take. The continuity of an actor's eyeline is critical, especially when it needs to be matched with the eyeline of another actor in another shot. The camera operator and script supervisor assist the actors in maintaining this aspect of the film's continuity. Each of the departments mentioned in this paragraph, as well as the script supervisor, takes meticulous written and mental notes during production, supplemented with extensive Polaroid snapshots, which serve as accurate continuity references. It is an expected courtesy on the set that the person taking the Polaroid picture announce it with the word "Flashing!" This lets everyone know that a strobe is about to be fired so that they can glance away from the flash.

A useful tool for establishing and maintaining continuity throughout a film are continuity breakdown sheets. These sheets contain all pertinent information regarding the visual and audio requirements of each scene in the film, such as costumes, special effects, stunts, vehicles, props, extras, and special sound equipment (e.g., wireless microphones). These breakdown sheets are an important reference for production personnel who are concerned with the continuity of the film, such as the property master, special effects coordinator, stunt coordinator, transportation captain, and wardrobe supervisor. They are also useful for the first AD when constructing the production board, since the scheduling of particular sequences may be dictated by information contained on the breakdown sheets. Many computer programs designed for motion picture scheduling also have tools for generating continuity breakdowns.

A sample breakdown sheet is featured in Table 8.

TABLE 8 **Sample Page Continuity Breakdown**

Title _____ Producer _____ Breakdown
                                                       page_____
Set/location_____ Director _____ Script pages:___
Scene nos. <u>18, 18A, 37</u> Day or night D_____ 15, 34
Synopsis: POV shot from office building, down the street to the ware-
               house.
               Camera zooms in on warehouse as car stops in front.
               McGuff steps slowly from the car, passes "No Trespassing"
               sign.
               Yellow cab is parked in alley.
               Montage: Coroner's station wagon being loaded with bodies
               of *McGuff's family.* VO of *prosecutor.*

Cast	Costume no.	Atmosphere	Props
McGuff	6	Coroner Attendants Sheriff Cab driver	"No Trespass- ing" sign Stretchers (4) Body bags
Bits	**Special effects**		**Vehicles and animals**

McGuff's family
  or shapes to match
  in body bags
			McGuff's car
			Coroner's
			  station wagon
			Yellow cab
			Sheriff's car

Stunts	**Sound**		**Special notes**

11

Casting

ONCE A DETAILED BUDGET AND BOARD ARE COMPLETED, A PRO-
ducer knows how much money is available to spend on the actors and
for how many days or weeks each will be needed (one exception is
when a producer attaches a star to a project; the star will often be in
place before the budget is finalized because the attachment of the star
will impact the cost of the film so heavily). By this time the script
should be close to finished, with perhaps an additional polish or two left
to go. This, along with a tentative date for the commencement of principal photography, is everything a producer needs to begin casting. If a
studio or production company is involved in the financing of the picture,
the release of production financing may be dependent on the producer
securing the services of an actor approved by the studio or production
company. In other cases the producer may be free to cast the picture
without limitation.

The producer and director will usually work closely together during
the casting process. Ideally, the writer will be involved in the process as
well; the writer understands more thoroughly than anyone the characters in the script and can often play a crucial role in the selection of actors who will bring them to life. How the relationship among the
producer, director, and writer works is as much a matter of personal
chemistry as anything else. There will be disagreements and discussions
during casting, but since it is the director who will guide the actors and
their performances throughout the making of the picture, it is crucial
that the selection be consistent with the director's overall vision of the
film. Many directors believe that their job is half over if the picture is
well cast. Steven Spielberg once said that 80 percent of what the director contributes to a film is the selection of the actors. Paul Mazursky
feels that it's more like 90 percent. And George Cukor, when asked how
he managed to draw such wonderful performances from his cast,
replied, "I hire wonderful actors." Taking care to cast a picture properly
will save time and money all the way down the line. On the set, a poorly
chosen actor might cost the production substantial time and money in
retakes; and if the scene never quite works, even more time will be spent
in postproduction attempting to cut around the awkward performance.

The Casting Director

A casting director is someone who specializes in finding and recommending the most appropriate actors for each speaking role (or, in special cases, principal nonspeaking roles) in the film. The casting director does not make any final decisions with respect to hiring actors whom he or she recommends. Casting directors will commonly assist producers, often for very little money, in attaching principal actors to a film so that the producer can use the actors' names to help raise financing. The producer will then be obligated to hire the same casting director to cast the entire picture if and when it is successfully financed for production.

An experienced casting director has accumulated a vast file of actors and actresses in memory, in file cabinets, or in computer data banks; devotes a tremendous amount of time to studying actors' abilities; constantly has feelers out for fresh new talent; has a rough idea of how much certain actors cost; may have inside information about which types of roles certain actors are looking for; may know about various actors' schedules and availability; has a thorough working knowledge of SAG rules and regulations; has a great deal of experience dealing with actors' agents and has established a working rapport with many of them.

Casting directors commonly handle negotiations on behalf of the producer with agents regarding actors' contracts, including salary and screen credit. Some casting directors will break down a total budget figure for an entire cast into detailed allotments for each character in the script. Since all agents are concerned with protecting their clientele, an unknown producer cannot call up an agency like CAA or William Morris and expect the same reception a respected casting director will receive. Such a person adds credibility to a project and limits the possibility that the agent will falsify information; the casting director probably has enough connections to verify the agent's statement about what a particular actor received for his or her last picture.

In some cases an aggressive casting director might initially bypass the agent altogether and give your script directly to an actor. Good scripts attract actors, but some agents are interested only in the money. If you have a low- or medium-budget project, such an agent may tell you that the actor has read and turned down your script when the agent didn't even forward it for consideration in the first place.

Casting directors have no union that establishes their working standards or minimum wages. Their fees vary depending on the casting director's reputation, the film's budget, the number of speaking parts, and the complexity of those parts. There is, however, a nationwide organization comprised of nearly 250 casting directors called the Casting Society of America (CSA). Each member is elected to its roster based on his or her experience and demonstrated standards of professionalism. The majority of professional casting directors belong to this organization; there are also a number of excellent casting directors who choose not to belong.

The most efficient way to locate a casting director is through Breakdown Services, Ltd. (see Appendix E), a company that since 1971 has provided services to virtually every agent, manager, producer, and casting director in the business. In addition to offering several casting services, which will be discussed later in this chapter, they publish in conjunction with the CSA an annual directory titled *Casting By . . .* that lists every CSA member in the country. Members are listed alphabetically with their credits, geographically by state, and cross-referenced in an alphabetical listing of credits. There is a small roster of members who choose not to include their credits.

Breakdown Services, Ltd., also publishes a booklet called the *C/D Directory* that lists both CSA and non-CSA casting directors, their associates, and their assistants who cast for motion picture and television productions in the Los Angeles area. The directory lists names, titles, addresses, and phone numbers, but not credits. A new directory is published every three months, and it's updated every two weeks; this is because there is a 10 percent turnover of information in the directory per week (mostly address changes). One can purchase a year's subscription, which includes all updates, or a single issue. There is a separate *New York C/D Directory* that lists names, telephone numbers, addresses, and studio or network affiliations of New York casting personnel. It is published quarterly and updated monthly; this is because New York casting personnel move around much less frequently than their counterparts in Los Angeles. The *New York C/D Directory* is sold only on a single-issue basis.

Other ways for a producer to find an appropriate casting director are through word of mouth within the film community, by watching films and noting the casting directors on those films that seem particularly well cast, and by seeking recommendations from actors' agents. These agents work closely with casting directors and will often recommend three or four actors they feel are right for the project. A producer may also phone Breakdown Services, Ltd., discuss with them the budget and the type of picture being made, and the company will recommend casting directors they feel are appropriate.

Once a producer has selected a potential casting director, a meeting should be arranged with the producer, director, and the casting director to discuss the project, schedule, and budget. If all three feel comfortable with the prospect of working together, they will begin casting the picture.

In some cases a producer will decide to cast a film without the aid of a casting director. This is commonly done on low-budget films for which the producer has more time and energy than money. For the following discussion on the casting process, we will assume that this is the case. The process is the same whether a casting director is employed or not. The difference lies in who does the work: an experienced, knowledgeable casting director or a struggling producer whose budget simply cannot accommodate the cost.

Academy Players Directory

An important tool for anyone casting a film is a four-volume publication put out every year since 1937 by the Academy of Motion Picture Arts and Sciences titled the *Academy Players Directory.* Each of the four volumes is the size of a large telephone book, and together they contain a photographic listing of virtually every actor and actress (over 15,000) in the business. In addition to actors' names and photographs, there is descriptive information, a list of special talents and skills (sports. accents, languages, etc.), credits, agency information, and guild affiliation.

The four volumes, updated four times a year, are broken down as follows:

Volume One: Leading Women/Ingenues
Volume Two: Leading Men/Younger Leading Men
Volume Three: Characters and Comediennes/Comedians
Volume Four: Children/Master Index

Special features include indexes for African-American, Hispanic, Asian Pacific, and Native American performers, as well as for artists with disabilities. A reference supplement listing agents, casting directors, and radio and television stations is issued with each new edition. These books are particularly useful when you are looking for recognizable faces and names for certain roles in your film. When thumbing through the photographs, you will inevitably find a number of potential actors for your film whom you might have overlooked if you had relied solely on your memory.

The *Academy Players Directory* can be found in many public library systems, or it can be purchased from the academy at the address and phone number listed in Appendix E. The directory is also available on CD-Rom and may be accessed via the Internet and through a joint venture called "The Link" between the Academy of Motion Picture Arts and Sciences and Breakdown Services, Ltd. Using the Link, producers and casting directors who have the proper equipment are able to download the information contained in the *Academy Players Directory,* including photographs, descriptions, special talents, credits, agency representation, and guild affiliation. Actor information can be searched by name or by using a variety of attributes. For example, a casting director or producer could download text and picture information for all actors in the *Players Directory* who are female, African-American, ingenues, skilled in archery and horseback riding, and have the ability to speak with a French accent.

Another electronic casting service is offered by Star Caster Network. This service provides a continuously updated private electronic link between casting directors and agents. Participating casting directors store all of the information, including photos, of participating agents' clients on a hard disk in their office. When a casting director is ready to begin casting, he or she will send profiles of the characters to be cast to participating agents, who will then select appropriate clients for the roles. The agents send coded information to the casting director's computer, instructing it to pull up and display data on the selected actors. Because the data is already on the hard disk in the casting director's office, retrieving it is nearly instantaneous. Also, because the system uses a private link, it is more secure than systems that communicate via the Internet. Star Caster Network charges agencies and their clients for participation in this service.

The future will undoubtedly bring us the ability to search for and review live-action video clips of actors in much the same way. Beyond that, it may be possible for computers to interpret an actor's performance in one situation and apply it to an entirely different scene, so that you might be able to view an actor reading *your* script in *your* "virtual" location without the actor ever knowing such a "reading" took place. These are issues that the Screen Actors Guild is monitoring closely.

Breakdown Services, Ltd.

Breakdown Services, Ltd., specializes in the dissemination of casting information for feature films, television programs, and plays to actors' agents and personal managers (this should not be confused with continuity breakdowns mentioned in Chapter 10, which are unrelated). When a project is submitted to Breakdown Services, Ltd., they write a synopsis of the story and a descriptive breakdown of each character in the film along with any additional information the producer feels is pertinent to the project (for example, a request that the breakdown sheets not reveal any confidential story point in the script, or that agents submit only name actors for certain roles). The breakdown sheets are sent to the casting director for approval (or to the producer if no casting director is attached to the project) and then distributed to clients, who are comprised of actors' agents and personal managers, throughout the United States, Canada, and England (or to a limited area such as New York if the producer so requests). Distribution is either in the form of a hard copy delivered to clients or from the company's Web site. Agents and managers will review the breakdowns and submit actors for various roles. Submissions are made either in the form of hard-copy photos and résumés or, if the agent and casting director are connected to the Internet, using "The Link." The submission will include the picture and text the actor is using in the *Players Directory* (which includes credits, talents, description, agency representation, and guild affiliation), plus any comments the agent may wish to add, such as the actor's availability or most recent credits. There is also a feature for including a cover letter if the agent chooses to do so. Agents can also use the system to submit clients who are not included in the *Players Directory,* but those submissions will not include a photograph. When submissions are received by casting directors, they can be organized and prioritized within the computer, and printed for use by the producer, director, and casting director during casting sessions. Agencies and casting directors are increasingly communicating in this way, and, eventually, this will expand to include the transmission of full-motion video and sound.

The value of using contemporary technology is that breakdowns can be delivered several times a day, alerting agents and managers almost instantly to new projects as they come up, and, conversely, agents and managers in both Los Angeles and New York can submit instantly to casting directors on either coast.

This service is available at no charge to producers and casting directors of all funded dramatic films. Breakdown Services does not want to put its reputation on the line by disseminating information about projects that are not financed. If a film has not been financed, for a modest fee Breakdown Services will complete a written breakdown that the producer may use as a quick-reference synopsis of the story and characters. Such information may help prospective investors better understand the project; it may also be useful when approaching casting directors. Once the project is funded, Breakdown Services, Ltd., will refund the producer's money and begin circulating casting information to agents and managers. In this way, the company protects its reputation within the casting community by limiting the breakdowns they send out to projects that are funded and ready to begin casting.

If a project has a known casting director attached, it is assumed that the picture is funded and ready for casting. If there isn't a known casting director attached, Breakdown Services will require verification that the project is funded before proceeding beyond the above-mentioned breakdown-for-fee service. If, for example, an independent film is being produced with SAG actors, Breakdown Services may contact SAG to ensure that the production's paperwork is in order with SAG before proceeding with the dissemination of casting information. In the case of a student film or other film in which the actors will not be paid, Breakdown Services requires the filmmaker to provide the written breakdown and to pay for the cost of paper necessary to make copies; Breakdown Services will copy and distribute the information to agents and managers.

Aside from a project's funding status, the only requirements are that sync sound is utilized in the film, and that the producer is willing to receive written submissions (photos and résumés) from agents for potential actors and is willing to make individual appointments with them (as opposed to "cattle calls," which will be discussed later in this chapter). A producer using this service must be prepared to have the project represented honestly on the breakdown sheets. If the film is non-SAG, the agents receiving the sheets must know this. If there is nudity, sex, violence, or excessive gore, this information must be included. The purpose of this system is to disseminate information quickly and accurately. If a project is misrepresented or incompletely described, the producer, agent, and actors will waste a great deal of time with useless submissions and interviews.

Breakdown Services carefully checks out agents and managers who wish to subscribe to their service and accepts subscriptions only from those who have established themselves as reputable representatives of actors. Consequently, producers will not be hounded by unprofessional or disreputable agents. They will, however, be inundated with mail-in submissions that will include a photograph and résumé of each potential actor. There may be hundreds of submissions for a single role, and the only way to handle them is to sort through them, select the most likely candidates, and arrange to interview them.

A producer who wishes to use this service should not send in a script "cold." Contact should be made initially by phone to Breakdown Services, Ltd., at one of their locations listed in Appendix E. If a casting director is involved with the project, a field representative will come out to discuss the project and pick up a copy of the script. If a casting director is not attached, the producer will be asked to send the script by mail. A feature film will usually be broken down within twenty-four hours of the time the script is received. The Los Angeles office employs several full-time writers and completes breakdowns for fifty to seventy scripts per week.

Table 9 is an example of the kind of information commonly included on breakdown sheets. These sheets were prepared prior to casting *Fargo* and are included with permission from Breakdown Services, Ltd. Frances McDormand was cast to play "Marge" before the breakdown sheets were written, so a description of her character is not included.

TABLE 9   **Script Breakdown for *Fargo***

The information contained in this document is the exclusive property of Breakdown Services, Ltd. Any unauthorized reproduction, duplication, copying or use of the information contained herein, without prior written consent of Breakdown Services, Ltd., is strictly prohibited.

"FARGO"	Producers: Ethan Coen
POLYGRAM PICTURES	Writers: Joel & Ethan Coen
FEATURE FILM	Director: Joel Coen
	Casting Director: John Lyons
	Casting Associates:
	Jane Brody (Minneapolis/Chicago)
	Christine Sheaks (LA)
	Kathleen Chopin (NY)
	Shoot: Mid January for 10 weeks
	Location: Minneapolis

ALL WRITTEN SUBMISSIONS TO:	JOHN LYONS CASTING
	C/O "CITY HALL" PRODUCTIONS
	10 COLUMBUS CIRCLE
	17TH FLOOR
	NYC 10019

NOTE: ALL ACTORS MUST BE ABLE TO SPEAK IN A MINNESOTA DIALECT.

STORY LINE: Jerry Lundegaard, in his early 40's and working in his father-in-law's car dealership in Minnesota, has always played fast and loose with other people's money, whether he is tacking on unwanted options to a car order or borrowing against imaginary inventory. In need of $40,000, quickly, Jerry hatches a scheme to have his wife Jean kidnapped, to have her father pay the ransom and to walk away with half the cash. However, the amateur kidnappers he lures, Carl Rolvaag and Gaear Grimsrud, fold under pressure, using a gun where a cool head is needed. A trail of blood and bodies results.

JERRY LUNDEGAARD: 39–44; slightly dull, foggy guy who never gets the big picture; he is starting to paunch, not in good shape, an indoor kind of guy. Jerry is a wheeler/dealer, a loser with a fantasy of himself as a schemer, a perpetual font of off-center money making ideas which range from ill-conceived to illegal. He's not half as smart as he thinks he is and is desperately resentful of his successful father-in-law, who is his boss. There is an air of sweaty desperation about him. In trying to extort money from his father-in-law through the planned kidnapping of his wife, he initiates a tragic, bloody series of violent events . . . LEAD

WADE GUSTAFSON: 62–68; Wade is virile, vigorous, powerful and possessed of a booming voice. He has a barrel chest and a full head of gray hair; he clearly has those Scandinavian genes which age very well, and is in strapping physical condition. Hale and hearty, used to being in charge, he is a bit of a bully and the antithesis of Jerry. He is also Jerry's father-in-law and owner of the car dealership where Jerry works. A shrewd businessman, he has capital to work with and that is the vein of gold Jerry is trying to tap. When his daughter is kidnapped, Gustafson's first impulse is to call the authorities. He is dissuaded by Jerry and by his financial advisor, Stan Grossman. When the penultimate moment arrives, Wade cannot bear to sit on the sidelines. He decides to deliver the ransom himself with disastrous consequences . . . LEAD

NORM GUNDERSON: 38–43, tall, gentle, sweet-spirited, he is large (not fat) but pot-bellied. His wife Marge is Chief of the Brainerd Police Department while Norm, who looks more like a police chief than his pregnant wife, is a wildlife artist/painter who is presently competing to have one of his mallard paintings chosen by the Postal Service for a stamp. Laconic and steady, he is his wife's caretaker, making sure she eats a good breakfast and worrying that she's dressed warmly enough. They truly love each other . . . FEATURED

JEAN LUNDEGAARD: 36–40. Jerry's wife, she is the quintessential Midwest mom, suburban and middle class to the extreme. As Scotty's mother, she has the usual concerns about grades, unrealized academic potential and too many extracurricular activities. She is a devoted daughter to Wade and is reasonably content with her home life with Jerry . . . FEATURED

STAN GROSSMAN: 39–45. Probably from one of the two or three Jewish families in Fargo, he is Wade Gustafson's financial advisor and investment partner. Also far more savvy than Jerry in business. He is very clear-thinking when dealing with Jean's kidnapping, worrying about Scotty who has been completely forgotten by his own father . . . 3 SCENES

LOU: 26–45, very large, lumbering and Scandinavian, he is a uniformed officer with the Brainerd Police Department and Marge's right-hand man. Helps Marge with the initial investigation of the triple homicide out on the highway. Is respectful of his boss who is a more acute investigator than he . . . 4 SCENES

SCOTTY LUNDEGAARD: 12 years old; Jean and Jerry's son. A typical teenager. Very upset and teary when his mother is kidnapped . . . 2 SCENES

SHEP PROUDFOOT: 33–48; Native American, a very large, threatening and physically imposing guy. He is a parolee on robbery charges and works as a mechanic in the car dealership and is Jerry's connection with Carl, the kid-napper. Shep is a man of few words, has a terse way of phrasing things and is a very intense individual . . . 2 SCENES

GLEN YONAGITA: 37–43; sweet and forlorn, the same age as Marge Gun-derson, the Brainerd Chief of Police. Japanese American, he is going slightly paunchy and speaks with a heavy Minnesotan accent. Glen gradu-ated from high school with Marge and after seeing an article about her suc-cess in the Police Department is re-establishing old school ties. He is recently widowed, very sad, very lonely and feeling very much like a loser. He tries to kindle a romantic relationship with Marge . . . 2 SCENES

IRATE SEALANT CUSTOMER: 35–50; an ex–drill sergeant type, an explo-sive Marine personality, an irate customer of Jerry's who has come to pick up his new car and found that he has been charged for a coat of sealant which he did not order. He can really bellow at the top of his lungs. He is particularly furious with Jerry because the sealant was discussed at the purchase and re-jected as an option. Clearly Jerry has chosen to ignore him and is now trying to get him to pay for something he specifically didn't want . . . 1 SCENE

GARY: 30's, another uniformed Brainerd policeman helping in the homicide investigation. Very Scandinavian, a little slow, very low energy . . . 1 SCENE

Another offering from Breakdown Services, Ltd., which can be found on their Web site, is called "Actor Access." This makes available directly to actors the breakdown sheets for projects that casting direc-tors or producers have authorized for release. These casting directors and producers are willing to accept open submissions, meaning submissions directly from actors. These are generally for projects that are not affiliated with SAG, and will pay very little to the actor (if anything). Consequently, there is little motivation for agents to submit clients, but there is great motivation for up-and-coming actors to respond. There is no charge to the actor for using this service.

The Casting Process

Casting for most films can be broken down into three categories: principal players (major speaking parts), secondary players (nonmajor speaking parts), and extras (nonspeaking atmosphere talent). There are similarities in the way one goes about casting for each category, but there are also differences.

PRINCIPAL PLAYERS

Many actors are cast in principal roles based on readings from the producer's script. These auditions will tell you a great deal about the actors' suitability for particular roles, but the only way you will ever know how someone will appear on film is to see that person on film. Videotape will tell you a great deal, but nothing will tell you as much as the big screen. Usually, when casting principals, you will base your choices on actors you've seen in other films. If you are considering someone for a principal role who's never been in a film, by all means shoot a screen test.

The difference between a screen test and an audition is that in a screen test the actor performs a scene from the producer's script *on film,* often in full costume and makeup, and usually with the star they are to play opposite. Prior to shooting the test, the actor's entire deal with respect to the picture will be negotiated as though he or she were set to perform in the film. The deal is then contingent upon satisfactory completion of the test. SAG actors are not paid for the test if they are subsequently hired for the part; if they are not hired they must be paid a minimum of one-half of a day's pay. Non-SAG actors are not generally paid for a screen test, but they will usually receive a copy of the completed test to use as a sample of their work. If you can't afford to shoot a test on film, use video equipment. The principal players can make or break your picture, so it's well worth the effort to test their talent thoroughly before hiring them.

Assuming you select actors for your principal roles based on their performances in other films, your first step will be to contact their agents. Agency information can be found either in the *Academy Players*

Directory or by contacting the Screen Actors Guild. The function of the agents is to counsel their clients, to negotiate on their behalf, and to protect their interests. The agent will ask to read the script; if the material is of interest it will be forwarded to the agent's client. This is assuming that the agent feels you can afford to pay the client's fee, or that the material will enhance the client's career, and that the client has no prior commitment that conflicts with your schedule. If you have a flexible production schedule, it might be helpful to ask the agent when it will be a good time for the actor to be in your film. If you have a personal connection to a potential actor for your film, it's often best to bypass the agent. The worst the actor will say is "Call my agent."

It is the agent's job to negotiate on behalf of the client for the best deal possible. This is often based on the last deal negotiated for that client (referred to as the client's "quote"), with each deal setting something of a precedent for the future. However, a good agent will also look to the long-range implications of a project. If the role you're offering could launch the actor into a whole new area of opportunity, the agent will take that into consideration when negotiating the deal and will perhaps bend a bit to accommodate your budget. When lowering the price, the deal is sometimes called a "no quote," meaning that the price negotiated will remain confidential and will not set a precedent for the actor's future deals. Don't hesitate to stress the strength of the role you have to offer. This is worth a great deal and is often a more powerful inducement than money. Certainly money wasn't foremost on the minds of Bruce Willis and John Travolta when they agreed to star in *Pulp Fiction,* nor was it on the minds of Sylvester Stallone and Robert De Niro when they accepted starring roles in *Cop Land.* Many A-list actors are open to doing small films if they are attracted to the material. The worst that can happen is that the agent turns you down and recommends another client better suited, in the agent's opinion, to your project. As a producer, take the attitude that a good deal is good for everyone involved and often offers rewards beyond the immediate dollar.

In discussing the screenplay, I said that the most important consideration for an actor is the screenplay. All actors are on the lookout for vehicles that will best serve their talents and expand their horizons. This is true for the top-paid superstar as well as the struggling newcomer. An actor who has become well known for comedy may wish to expand into drama or action, and will almost certainly be willing to take a cut in salary for the opportunity to play such a role. But since the actor is known only for comedic work, dramatic roles will be offered first to actors who have proven themselves in that genre. Rarely will a comedic actor get first crack at those roles. The reason Michael Madsen accepted the role of the father in *Free Willy* wasn't because it was a terribly challenging piece of material; it was because it gave him an opportunity to play a character entirely different from the sadistic heavy (*Reservoir Dogs, Kill Me Again, Donnie Brasco*) for which he has become so well known.

If you can find the right person at the right time, with the right script, you'll not only negotiate a reasonable price, you'll have an energetic, enthusiastic performer. An actor who takes on a role because of moderate, routine interest in the script, or purely for the money, will be limited to a competent, professional performance. Chances are that you will not get that added magical energy that's sparked by a genuine enthusiasm for the project.

The higher up the talent ladder you go, the more elements you will need to have in place in order to attract actors. Those who are in constant demand, and certainly those who are considered bankable stars, will hesitate, with good reason, to commit to a project unless they know in advance who will be directing them. Often they will insist on approval of the director. They may want to have the script rewritten by a writer of their choice. Their agent may insist on a pay-or-play deal, which means that if an actor reads the script and agrees to perform in your film, you are contractually obligated to pay the actor's fee whether you make the film or not. Dealing with actors at this level may be impractical for your production, in which case you should drop back a notch and seek the finest actors with the strongest name values that you can comfortably work with.

Finding a well-known actor whose enthusiasm will be sparked by a role in your film isn't easy. Occasionally, word of mouth will advertise what sort of role a particular actor is seeking, but this is often thirdhand rumor information. The answer to this dilemma is to expose your project to whichever actors you consider right for your project. Don't limit yourself to the ones you know for certain you can afford, the ones who'll take the part simply because you can pay their fee. As with seeking your writer and director, always go for the best, at least a cut above what is safe.

Approaching your casting in this way, you will suffer many rejections, but expecting the rejections will make them easier to take. And, occasionally, you'll get a yes. With some roles, you will have to compromise, falling back on actors who fit more easily within your budget. Following this pattern—shooting for the moon, then compromising to fit your budget—you will be setting the highest standards for your picture and you will know that you have assembled the best possible cast within your budget.

A film may be exceptionally well cast with actors who work for SAG minimum or with non-SAG actors who are happy to work for nothing more than a screen credit. However, if you are seeking actors with substantial experience performing before the camera and several screen credits to back them up, they will undoubtedly be members of SAG and will almost certainly expect overscale salaries. A related consideration is that an expensive actor implies a certain budget level, whether in fact the budget is at that level or not, and everyone else in the cast and crew may expect to be paid accordingly. This is an issue that should be clarified up front with everyone involved.

When you are casting unknown actors, take your time. See as many people as it takes to find the ideal candidates for your film. Take the attitude that it's better not to make the film than to make it with the wrong actors. You may find them quickly, but if not, and you keep at it, eventually you will succeed.

SCREEN ACTORS GUILD

A producer who wishes to hire SAG actors must sign a guild agreement, thereby giving SAG jurisdiction over all actors, stuntpersons, and a minimum number of extras in the film. The agreement provides for minimum contract requirements, including salaries, the number of working hours in a day, meal penalties, turnaround times, nonworking holding days, insurance requirements, and overtime provisions. Much of this will vary depending on which of three agreements you sign. The standard agreement covers pictures budgeted over $2 million; for these films, all principal actors and a minimum of thirty extras and five stand-ins (persons who observe rehearsals on the set and "stand in" for actors during the lighting setup) must be members of SAG. The low-budget agreement covers films with budgets ranging from $500,000 to $2 million (the affirmative action low-budget agreement has a ceiling of $2,750,000); the number of extras required by SAG under this agreement is negotiable. The modified low-budget agreement covers films made for less than $500,000. This agreement waives entirely the requirement to utilize a minimum number of SAG extras. These budgets refer to the total cost of production, including above-the-line, below-the-line, and deferred salaries.

There is a variation on the modified low-budget agreement called the limited exhibition agreement, which covers independent films made for under $200,000, and a further variation that covers art or experimental features made for less than $75,000. Under the limited exhibition agreement, a producer may utilize both SAG and non-SAG actors in the same film. Two films that have been made in this way are Michael Corrente's *Federal Hill* and Charles Lane's black-and-white silent film, *Sidewalk*

Stories. SAG determines whether a film falls into one of these categories on a case-by-case basis, but essentially this provides a way for a filmmaker to utilize sag talent for a film that is being produced without the intention of a national theatrical distribution, direct-to-video distribution, or airings on commercial TV or cable. These films can be released nontheatrically for nonpaying audiences, semitheatrically for film societies and film festivals, on public television, on noncommercial basic cable, and for runs of up to two weeks in art houses and small audience theaters specializing in new creative films. A filmmaker who violates the terms of the limited exhibition agreement, by increasing the budget beyond the parameters of the agreement or by distributing the film commercially, for example, must renegotiate with SAG and compensate the actors appropriately.

SAG has a reputation for working out other special agreements with producers operating on limited budgets. Two films, *Fresh* and *Juice,* both shot in New York and both relying heavily on minors in the cast, could not have been made under SAG jurisdiction for their respective budgets of $3 million and $5 million if SAG had not granted waivers for non-union and underage actors. SAG regulations for actors under the age of eighteen include having a guardian with the child, hiring a teacher during school hours, and limiting the number of hours per day a child is allowed to work. It is important to note that state labor laws governing the working conditions for minors vary; in some states, including California, they are more stringent than SAG regulations. You can obtain more information about all of the SAG/producer's agreements from the Screen Actors Guild at the address and phone number listed in Appendix E.

An actor's agent is not permitted to take his or her commission, usually 10 percent, from the SAG minimum-scale wage. Consequently, you must budget SAG scale plus 10 percent as a minimum wage for any actor you hire through an agent.

If you are making a non-SAG film, the actors' contracts will be customized to fit your project, and any special requirements, needs, or demands should be included in the contracts. If, for example, you are making an ultra-low-budget film and you want the actors to supply their own makeup and wardrobe, you should spell this out contractually in advance so that there are no misunderstandings on the set.

SUPPORTING PLAYERS

Your principal players will be utilized to their fullest potential only if they are surrounded by strong support people. For this reason, the philos-

ophy for hiring principal players applies to supporting players as well:
Go for the best, most experienced actors, then compromise to fit your
budget.

If you use the service offered by Breakdown Services, Ltd., as described earlier in this chapter, you will receive a multitude of submissions from which to choose your supporting players. Also, any agent
who reads your script for a particular client will invariably recommend
clients for half a dozen other roles in your film as well. The *Academy
Players Directory* will be a useful aid when casting supporting players,
but if you are working with a low or medium budget, you may have to
utilize actors who have never appeared in films and, consequently, you
won't recognize them in the directory.

Another way to find actors is through a weekly casting publication
called *Drama-Logue*. This publication is available at a limited number
of newsstands, but is read by subscribers throughout the United States
and in Europe. *Drama-Logue* routinely publishes announcements that
describe producers' casting requirements for both SAG and non-SAG
productions, and information about how actors may apply for those
roles. The ad, which runs for three weeks, costs nothing. Producers interested in placing such announcements should contact the *Drama-
Logue* office at the address and phone number listed in Appendix E.
Back Stage is a similar publication that lists casting opportunities, and is
also listed in Appendix E. Producers can also place casting announcements in industry trade papers like *Variety* and *The Hollywood Reporter,*
in local publications such as newspapers, and on the Internet. Even
without public announcements it's astonishing how fast news travels
when a producer is funded and actively casting a film.

When you are dealing with less experienced players for your supporting roles, it is important to spend extra time carefully weighing your
choices. Again, the ideal way to judge their talent is by viewing film or
videotape. If that isn't available, perhaps because the actors have had
only stage experience, and if it isn't practical to shoot screen tests for
each of them, you must judge them based on readings from the script.
The value of readings is that you have an opportunity to see and hear
candidates reading scenes from your script for the character they hope
to play in your film. Experienced actors will often come dressed appropriately for the part.

An actor who comes in to read a portion of the script for the producer, director, and perhaps the screenwriter is at something of a disadvantage. The pressures in a reading situation are quite different from
those on a working set or when performing for a screen test. The audience in a reading is not the objective eye of the camera but the collective

eyes of people who will decide whether or not to give the actor a job. It is helpful to give each candidate an opportunity to read the script in advance of the casting session, and to let the actor choose which scene or scenes to read for the audition. Appointments should be scheduled so that the various candidates are staggered over time and will have to wait no more than fifteen minutes before coming in to read.

Occasionally the actor will be required to read material he or she has never seen before. This is called a "cold" reading. Many top-name stars will readily admit that they are worthless at cold readings. Likewise, many inadequate actors who have trained specifically for interview situations are terrific at cold readings. There are entire acting courses devoted to nothing but cold readings and interview techniques. Cold readings are carried to their worst extreme in sessions called "cattle calls." A producer will have several people, sometimes as many as fifty, appear at the same time to read for the same part. The actors sit together in a lobby or waiting room. They are all there for the same job, and the atmosphere of hostile competition that pervades the room is enough to make an actor go back to waiting on tables. This method of casting is terribly destructive to the actors' feelings of self-worth and confidence and often hampers their ability to audition. The problem is compounded further when they are called in to read. They enter a room and are asked to read something they've never seen before, or have seen for only a few minutes out in the lobby, in front of a group of strange faces who've been hearing the same lines all morning. Upon completing the reading, the actor is ushered out with little or no feedback on the performance.

Since an actor's reading often takes just a few minutes, scheduling them ten or fifteen minutes apart doesn't slow the process. As I said earlier, Breakdown Services, Ltd., will not work with a producer who is unwilling to make such appointments. So avoid cattle calls. And avoid cold readings. They are an inadequate way to determine the ability of an actor. Sometimes there is no alternative, but consider the problems the situation creates for the artists and judge them accordingly.

EXTRAS

If you have signed a SAG contract, depending on your budget, you may or may not be required to use up to a certain number of nonspeaking extras from the SAG roster. The advantage of a SAG contract is that you will have available any number of professional extras on short notice, either through the guild or through an extras casting service. With the casting services you can specify not only the age and general "look" of the extras, but you can even specify their attire. One hundred people in evening clothes are yours with a phone call and a check. The drawback is that this talent can be expensive. You can obtain a copy of the SAG/producer's agreement, which lists fees and contract requirements, from the SAG offices listed in Appendix E.

If your extras requirements are small, you might be better off using your friends. You can always get a handful of people who will work for a free lunch and a chance to appear in a film. Be aware, however, that they will probably be inexperienced in front of the camera and will need a bit of "extra" guidance.

What's in a Name?

Casting choices for small independent films are often based solely on finding the best actors for the various roles, regardless of name value. But in addition to artistic considerations, a producer is generally concerned with adding at least one cast member whose name has some recognizable marquee value. This helps not only with the theatrical release but also with eventual video, television, and foreign sales. A good example is *Sling Blade,* in which Robert Duvall and J. T. Walsh appeared in small but crucial roles.

There is a small handful of actors and actresses who are considered "bankable" stars. This means that simply attaching their name to a project will guarantee financing. This may increase a picture's chances of becoming a hit, but it's no guarantee. Many name-star pictures have gone into the drink while no-name pictures sometimes rise to the top of the charts. What the bankable star *will* guarantee is a bottom-line return. Even if the picture is a flop, there are minimum guaranteed markets available simply because of its star.

Who these bankable stars are is constantly changing and depends on what part of the world you're in. There are American actors with a tremendous following in Europe but with little appeal in America. Some foreign distribution companies have been known to shuffle marquee credits if a secondary actor in the United States is more popular than the lead in a particular nation. Such actors would be of value if you're financing your picture with European money. There are also actors with a large television following. Attaching one of their names to your picture may not increase sales at the box office, but it will make an eventual sale to television more lucrative. There are a few actors who have achieved both box office drawing power *and* a high television rating. These "crossover" actors aren't usually powerful enough to be considered bankable, but they can add a great deal to a film's worth.

There are also foreign actors with significant box office drawing power both in the United States and abroad. It should be noted, however, that the United States discourages the use of actors from other countries. Foreign actors entering the United States for purposes of working on a motion picture must have an "O" visa. There is no limit to the number of actors admitted each year in this category, but the standards for admission are very high. The theory is that if the role can be played by a citizen of the United States, it should be. Basically, the law requires an alien actor to have sustained national or international acclaim, with extensive written documentation of his or her achievements in film, including awards, invitations, reviews, and recommendations from other professionals of acknowledged high standing. If you are thinking of using a foreign actor, allow your attorney ample time to complete the application and gather documentation. Submitting a complete package with your initial request will significantly improve your chances of a successful result.

Most actors whose names or faces you recognize are not bankable, either domestically or in Europe, and aren't particularly strong names on television. But that doesn't mean that they are without special value. The truth is that *any* recognizable name will add to your film's profits, but in a less obvious way than the bankable stars and television personalities. The following thoughts on the value of names are of particular importance for the producer packaging a low- or medium-budget picture.

The very first thing anyone will ask about your film, from the casual acquaintance at a cocktail party to the marketing chief of your potential distribution company, is "Who's in it?" The difference between a recognizable name and no name at all is significant. If you answer, "No one you've ever heard of," your picture will probably be treated with indifference (unless, of course, it's winning awards on the festival circuit). If you can name any actor they've heard of, your picture will be raised to a level of respectability. In addition, you and the person to whom you are speaking will have a common point of reference, a jumping-off point for further conversation.

The involvement of such an actor will also make a difference in the attitude of the rest of your cast and even in the attitude of your crew. Everyone likes to feel that his or her work is important, and everyone likes to talk about it. Nothing will contribute an air of legitimacy and importance to your project more readily than a cast name that people recognize. It costs very little to add such an actor to your cast—perhaps even just for a one-day cameo appearance—but that single element will pay off many times over in the morale and status of your production.

The Production Team

IN ADDITION TO THE PRODUCING AND DIRECTING UNITS, THE DEPART-
ments on most crews include cinematography, costumes, electrical, grip,
locations, makeup and hair, production design, props, publicity, script,
set construction, sound, special effects, stunts, and transportation. A typical crew for a medium-budget film will consist of key crew members in
each of these departments plus whatever portion of their support staffs is
appropriate to the project. The smaller the film, the smaller the crew. For
documentary films, a crew sometimes consists of only two people: a director who is also a cinematographer and a sound recordist.

The following are brief descriptions of the functions of key members
of the production team and their support staffs.

Producing Unit

No job in Hollywood is more misunderstood than that of the producer.
This is partly because the role a producer plays varies from film to film,
and because on many films there are several different producing credits,
sometimes with several names attached to each. There were ten producing credits on the film *Face/Off,* starring John Travolta and Nicolas Cage
(three *executive producers,* four *producers,* two *coproducers,* and one *associate producer*); some earned their credit, but several had no active
producing role on the picture whatsoever. This often occurs when a producer has worked for years to develop a property, and the only thing
standing in the way of production financing is giving someone (for example, an actor's manager) a producing credit. As producer Kathleen
Kennedy (*E.T., Schindler's List, The Lost World: Jurassic Park*) said,
"The producing credit is for sale." In an effort to control the proliferation
of producing credits, several major producers have established a credit
arbitration panel that would function on behalf of producers much the
way the Writers Guild Arbitration Committee functions on behalf of
writers. Unlike writers, however, producers have no collective bargaining agreement, so it may be difficult to form a united front capable of co-
ercing the studios into changing the status quo.

Executive Producer: This credit has historically been given to the person responsible for putting together the financial and/or creative package that made the movie possible. Today the title is not so clear. An executive producer may be the lead actor's associate or partner, or the owner of the production company under whose banner the film is being produced. Many executive producers are actively involved in the production process, and others have several films in production simultaneously and operate almost exclusively from behind a desk.

Producer: A creative producer (as opposed to a line producer) will be involved in all aspects of the filmmaking process, including selecting and working with the screenwriter, casting, editing, and selecting the composer. This person is often the first one on the picture and the last one off. During production, this producer is responsible for staying within the budget, is answerable to the production company and/or the studio, and acts as an interface between the production company, the studio, and the director. A creative producer supervises the line producer, who is constantly shifting money around in the budget in order to serve the picture best. It is therefore very important that the creative producer understand fully the job of the line producer.

Line Producer: On large-budget pictures, there will be both a unit production manager and a line producer, the latter being one step up from the UPM. Essentially, a line producer acts as a supervising production manager and is responsible for maximizing the available budget, which means that a good line producer will spend as much time pointing out where the budget is deficient as in pointing out places where it's over. Sometimes a single individual will be given a UPM and a line-producer credit. One value for the individual is that, unlike the UPM credit, which appears with the end credits, a line-producer credit will generally be included with the head credits and often in paid advertising such as posters and newspaper ads.

On major features, the line producer generally functions on behalf of the studio, but if a star director is attached, the line producer may be brought in as part of the director's overall deal; if that happens, the line producer will function on behalf of the director, and the studio will pay particularly close attention to who is hired as UPM. Since line producers are not involved creatively with the film, they will not attend such things as casting sessions and script meetings.

Associate Producer: This credit can mean a variety of things, but, generally, an associate producer acts as a supporting producer. In some cases, particularly in Europe, the associate producer may fulfill virtually all of the standard line-producer functions. This credit is sometimes given to a UPM or first AD for contributions that greatly exceed that person's routine duties. A production manager who supervises a project from preproduction planning through postproduction editing may receive an associate-producer credit. This type of credit offers several advantages to its recipient, as well as being a kind of "thank you" from the producer. First, the associate-producer credit usually appears with the credits at the head of the film (UPM and first AD credits are generally listed at the end of the film). Second, an associate-producer credit may be included with the principal credits in paid advertising. Third, since the credit reflects a substantial contribution to a film, a person who commands such a credit can generally command more money. A writer who is actively involved in the production process, or who simply negotiates for a producing credit as part of his or her overall deal, may be given the credit of associate producer. In television, the credit is often given to the postproduction supervisor. Other credits that are sometimes given in this way are those of the supervising producer and co-producer.

Directing Unit

Director: The director is responsible to the producer for translating the screenplay into the images and sounds of a motion picture. This includes directing the activities of the cast and crew during preproduction, production, and postproduction. The director makes most of the creative decisions throughout the filmmaking process.

First Assistant Director: The first assistant director works closely with the production manager to organize an optimum shooting schedule, is responsible to the director for the efficient execution of that schedule on the set, and assists the director in the direction of extras, crowd scenes, and special effects. The assistant director is also responsible for production paperwork, including overtime authorizations, model releases, and call sheets (see Chapter 8).

Second Assistant Director: The second assistant director supports the first assistant director. Responsibilities include managing the logistics of the set so that all members of the cast and crew arrive at the right place at the right time, assisting in the direction of extras, and distributing production paperwork.

Dialogue Director: In special circumstances, a dialogue director is hired to review lines with actors. This is sometimes done when a part requires a particular accent or dialect, in which case a dialogue director who specializes in that accent or dialect will coach the actor in the delivery of the lines. A dialogue director is most commonly used when several actors are required to speak in the same accent or dialect.

Second Unit Director: For certain shots, generally those that do not require sync sound or the use of principal actors, it is more efficient and economical to send out a small camera team called a second unit. The second unit director will be given specific instructions from the film's director as to what the second unit material will be and how to shoot it. Typical shots appropriate for a second unit include car drive-bys, establishing shots of various locations, and closeup insert shots. Sometimes a cinematographer, UPM, or first AD will function as the second unit director.

Production Management

Unit Production Manager: The UPM is responsible to the producer for preparing the budget (which may involve organizing a preliminary shooting schedule), expediting all aspects of the production, and authorizing expenditures. This person is usually engaged during preproduction and production only (see Chapter 8).

Production Coordinator: The production coordinator works in the production office to coordinate the logistics of the production. This includes such things as shipping film, receiving dailies, arranging transportation and accommodations for actors and crew, and attending to any special needs of cast and crew members such as locating a dentist in the event of a toothache.

Production Assistants: Production assistants are responsible to the producer, director, production manager, assistant director, and production coordinator. Their responsibilities include assisting in whatever manner best aids the production, such as running errands, typing production notes, carrying equipment, and making the office coffee.

Cinematography

Director of Photography: The director of photography, also called the cinematographer, is responsible to the director for achieving optimum photographic images for the film. Specific duties include selecting the camera and lighting equipment, supervising the camera and lighting crews, and determining the lighting pattern and exposure for each scene. The job includes collaborating with the director to establish a photographic style for the film, and determining ways to use the camera and lighting so that they contribute to telling the story, not simply recording it on film.

Camera Operator: The camera operator is responsible for operating the camera at all times and maintaining the compositions established by the director or, in some cases, by the director of photography.

First Camera Assistant: The first camera assistant is responsible for setting up the appropriate lenses and filters for each shot, setting the lens stop and maintaining focus for each shot. This person will also check the film gate in the camera after the completion of each scene in order to ensure that there were no hairs or dirt obstructing the image during the shot.

Second Camera Assistant (also referred to as the "loader"): The second camera assistant is responsible for loading and unloading film, setting up the camera, maintaining and cleaning all elements in the camera package, maintaining all camera department paperwork such as camera reports and shipping labels, preparing the slate for each take, and aiding the first camera assistant in whatever way is required.

Costume Department

Costume Designer: The costume designer is responsible for purchasing and/or designing and supervising the making of all costumes for the production in accordance with the overall design of the picture, which is established by the director and the production designer. The costume designer will have one or more assistants to help with the logistics of costuming the actors during production and to maintain the look and continuity of costumes on the set.

Wardrobe Supervisor: The wardrobe supervisor is responsible for the operation of the wardrobe department, which includes the efficient costuming of actors during production and the inventory and maintenance of those costumes.

Electrical Department

Gaffer: The gaffer is the chief electrician and is responsible to the director of photography for the safe and efficient execution of the lighting patterns outlined by the director of photography.

Gaffer's Best Boy: The gaffer's best boy is the first assistant electrician, and is responsible for assisting the gaffer and supervising the operation of the lighting and electrical equipment.

Electricians: Electricians are responsible to the gaffer and the gaffer's best boy for rigging and operating lighting and electrical equipment.

Generator Operator: The generator operator is responsible to the gaffer for the operation and maintenance of electrical generators.

Grip Department

Key Grip: The key grip is responsible to the director of photography for supervising all grip crews. The principal responsibilities of the grip crews are to assist the gaffer during lighting procedures and to maneuver the camera during moving shots. This includes building platforms, rigging picture vehicles, blacking out windows for night interiors shot during the day, and laying dolly track.

Dolly Grip: The dolly grip is responsible to the key grip and the director of photography for the operation and maintenance of all dolly and crane equipment. When a dolly grip is not employed, the key grip usually fulfills this function.

Grips: Grips, sometimes called "hammer grips," are responsible for performing the various functions that fall under the jurisdiction of the key grip.

Locations

Location Manager: The location manager, usually working with an assistant, is responsible for scouting locations and recommending suitable sites for production, for securing any permits and/or related paperwork necessary for the use of selected locations, for negotiating the financial and logistical arrangements for the use of various locations, for securing nearby locations in which to park production vehicles, for securing a nearby location in which to set up the catering service, and for maintaining good public relations with various persons in the community affected by the production.

Makeup Department

Key Makeup Artist: In addition to designing and applying makeup for the actors, the key makeup artist organizes and supervises the operation of all personnel in the makeup department, including body makeup artists and makeup assistants.

Assistant Makeup Artists: Assistant makeup artists assist the key makeup artist in applying and touching up actors' makeup. One of these artists will be available at all times on the set to touch up actors' makeup between takes.

Hairstylist: The hairstylist supervises one or more assistant hairdressers and is responsible for cutting, coloring, and styling actors' hair, wigs, toupees, etc. One of the hairdressers will be available at all times on the set to touch up actors' hair between takes.

Body Makeup Person: The body makeup person is responsible to the key makeup artist for applying makeup required on an actor from the neck down. An exception would be special-effects makeup such as a wound or a rash, which would probably be applied by a specialist or by the key makeup artist.

Production Design (Art Department)

Production Designer: The production designer works closely with the director and the director of photography to establish a "look" for the picture, and is responsible for planning and supervising the overall visual design of the film. This includes coordinating color schemes, designing sets, and assisting in the selection of locations. The production designer is also responsible for the artistic integration of several departments, including costumes, set construction, and props, so that each of these departments contributes to a consistent visual style established for the film (see subsequent section in this chapter titled "Production Design").

Art Director: On most pictures, a production designer will supervise an art director, whose responsibilities include both designing and executing the sets as conceived by the production designer. This requires both an artistic design sense and often a thorough knowledge of architecture. Much of this work is made easier if the art director has a working knowledge of computer-aided design programs. Occasionally the art director is in charge of the art department and there is no credit given for "production designer" (see subsequent section in this chapter titled "Production Design").

Storyboard Artists: A storyboard artist creates a multipanel pictorial representation of the film in advance of production. A detailed storyboard will have a separate panel for each camera setup and possibly several panels to indicate camera movements. The storyboard artist may function on behalf of the director to help communicate his or her vision of the film, or of specific sequences (see Chapter 15). A storyboard artist may also function on behalf of the production designer to help communicate to the director the production designer's vision of how best to utilize the sets.

Illustrators: Illustrators create detailed drawings of scenes, sets, props, vehicles, etc., in accordance with the design envisioned by the director and/or production designer. Illustrators are sometimes called "conceptual artists."

Set Designers: Set designers are responsible for executing plans and blueprints that will facilitate the work of the various art department functions, including working drawings for sets, props, and miniatures. The set designer is also responsible for designing, building, and operating all prototype models upon which the actual production models will be based, in accordance with the design established by the director and the production designer.

Special Visual Effects: The special visual effects crew is responsible for building and operating miniatures and models, sometimes initially conceived by the production designer. When visual effects crews operate independently of the production designer, they are responsible to the director for designing as well as building and operating miniatures and models. A special visual effects crew that operates in this way may have its own producer, production designer, art director, and illustrator, as well as its customary battery of visual effects technicians.

Set Decorator: The set decorator is responsible for selecting all set dressing (furniture, paintings, kitchenware, magazines, etc., which may occasionally include specific props referred to in the script) in accordance with the design established by the director and the production designer. The decorator's crew includes an on-set dresser who, in collaboration with the property master, maintains the set dressing during shooting. Also on the decorator's crew is a lead person who supervises set dressers operating in advance of the production (called the swing gang).

Greensman: The greensman is responsible to the production designer, art director, and/or the set decorator for selecting, placing, and maintaining all greenery, such as plants and flowers, necessary for the production.

Prop Department

Property Master: Props (as opposed to set dressing) refer to specific items called for in the script, perhaps a pistol, an alarm clock, or a photograph. The property master is responsible for the selection, inventory, and maintenance of all props associated with the production. In most cases the property master will provide several choices for each prop from which the director can choose. The property master will generally have one or more assistants, one of whom will be on the set all all times during production.

Prop Maker: The prop maker is responsible for designing, building, and operating any special props required for the production in accordance with the design established by the director and the production designer.

Publicity

Publicist: The publicist is responsible to the producer for preparing, arranging for, and disseminating promotional information about the production such as newspaper stories, interviews, and trade-paper announcements. When required, the publicist will also work on the set to handle the logistics of the visiting press.

Still Photographer: The still photographer is responsible to the producer and/or publicist for any still photography associated with the production.

Script

Script Supervisor: The script supervisor is responsible for taking detailed notes during production, recording on the shooting script such information as scene and take number, camera position and lens used, performance continuity, dialogue changes, and the running time of each shot. These notes will be an aid to the director and the crew during production, and to the editor during postproduction.

Set Construction

Set Construction Foreman: The set construction foreman is the key carpenter and is responsible to the production designer for supervising all set construction associated with the production.

Carpenters: Carpenters are responsible to the set construction foreman for constructing, delivering, setting up, and maintaining all construction pieces for the production.

Painters: Painters are responsible to the production designer and/or set construction foreman for any painting necessary for the production.

Scenic Artists: Scenic artists are specialists who work with paint to create specific looks, such as aging walls and doors to make a newly built house look lived in.

Drapery Crew: The drapery crew is responsible to the production designer for making (or purchasing) and installing any drapery and/or upholstery material required for the production.

Paperhanger: The paperhanger is responsible to the production designer and/or set construction foreman for applying wallpaper, tile, and other related materials to the walls, floors, and ceilings of sets.

Plasterer: The plasterer is responsible to the production designer and/or set construction foreman for any plastering required for the production.

Welder: The welder is responsible to the production designer and/or set construction foreman for any metalwork or welding required for the production.

Sound Department

Production Sound Mixer: The term "sound mixer" is used to describe both *production* sound mixers and *postproduction* sound mixers (also called rerecording engineers). The following information refers to *production* sound mixers only; the job of the postproduction mixer is different and will be discussed in Chapter 20. The production sound mixer is responsible for selecting and operating all production sound equipment, for slating each take, and for monitoring the quality of all sound recordings. In most cases the mixer will be monitoring sound recorded from a single microphone. In situations that require the use of more than one microphone, the relative levels require *mixing* (balancing level and equalization) among microphones ("level" refers to volume; "equalization" refers to the relative intensity of various frequencies). The mixer is also responsible for maintaining accurate records on the sound reports.

Boom Operator: The boom operator is responsible to the sound mixer for the placement of the microphones. Usually this requires handling a microphone boom, moving the microphone so that it is properly positioned at all times during a take. In addition to placing the microphone to achieve optimum recording quality, the boom operator must ensure that the microphone and boom do not create shadows in the shot and do not interfere with the lighting equipment, camera equipment, or actors' movements. The boom operator is also responsible for voice-slating wild sound takes (see Chapter 17 under "Production Sound").

Cable Person: The cable person's primary responsibilities include stringing and connecting all cables related to the sound recording equipment and handling these cables, if required, during shots.

Special Effects

Special Effects Coordinator: The special effects coordinator, along with his or her assistants, is responsible to the director for safely and effectively planning and executing all special effects required during production. This may include weather effects such as wind, rain, or snow; breakaway furniture for fight scenes; fire and smoke; and the like. These are sometimes referred to as "mechanical" effects.

Stunts

Stunt Coordinator: The stunt coordinator and his or her assistants are responsible to the director for safely and effectively planning and executing all stunts required for the production. This includes everything from simple fistfights to someone falling out of an airplane. Stunt coordinators often specialize in certain types of stunts, so it is worth seeking out an expert in the specific kind of stunt work your picture requires. Most stunt coordinators and stuntpersons belong to the Screen Actors Guild and are covered by the guild contract. If you are making a SAG picture that requires stunts, you must hire guild members to execute the stunts.

Transportation

Transportation Captain: The transportation captain is responsible for securing and maintaining production vehicles, including those driven by actors in the film. In the case of picture cars, the transportation captain generally will secure the availability of two vehicles of the same model, year, and color so that if the first is damaged the second can be called in. The transportation captain also supervises the drivers.

Drivers: During preproduction drivers chauffeur key production personnel to various sites during location and tech scouting and, when necessary, shuttle actors to and from rehearsal, makeup tests, wardrobe fittings, etc. During production drivers move production vehicles from location to location and, when required, shuttle actors and crew between the set and homes, hotels, parking lots, and the catering location.

Animal Specialists

Trainer: The trainer is responsible to the director for caring for, handling, transporting, and directing domestic animals and wildlife such as birds, dogs, snakes, and lions.

Wranglers: Wranglers are responsible to the trainer for caring for, handling, transporting, and directing livestock such as horses and cattle. When insects are called for, the person handling the insects is referred to as an "insect wrangler." A "kid wrangler" credit was given to a crew member working on *Welcome to the Dollhouse.*

Additional Personnel

Craft Service Person: The craft service person is responsible for providing between-meal snacks and beverages for the cast and crew during production. This person also assists in maintaining the tidiness of the area surrounding the set.

First-aid Person: The first-aid person is responsible for the immediate medical care of any person in the cast or crew requiring such attention. This person is generally a nurse or a paramedic, and their duties include everything from bandaging a small cut to life-saving CPR.

Teacher: SAG requires that a teacher be hired to teach any minors who are employed during regular school hours. State labor laws may have additional requirements. In California, for example, a teacher must be hired whenever a minor is employed, whether school is in session or not, and the teacher must have a special certification in order to function as both a teacher and a state welfare worker.

Selecting the Crew

The director, in consultation with the producer, will select the key members of the crew. These decisions will be based on artistic and technical requirements, budget, personal preference, and availability. The director will undoubtedly have a preference for certain key people, such as the director of photography and production designer, and in most cases the producer should accept those choices. If the director's choices aren't available, are too expensive, or if the director is unfamiliar with crew members in the area where the picture will be shot, the producer, unit production manager, or others will make suggestions. It is wise to check with producers, directors, and production managers who have worked with your potential key crew members previously. Try to check at least three references. Most people will not volunteer negative information, so listen for an absence of positive responses.

Once you have determined the key people, the job of crewing is over. Each of these key people will bring a support staff. The director of photography will have a favorite camera operator and camera assistants. The sound mixer will pick the boom operator, and so forth. When shooting in distant locations, key crew members will often be brought from a major film center such as Los Angeles or New York, but on low- and medium-budget pictures shooting outside major film centers, the support staffs for these key crew members will undoubtedly be hired locally. Each state has a film commissioner (discussed later in this chapter), whose job is to encourage outside producers to film in their state; in addition to helping with locations and production facilities, the film commissioner can provide valuable information about local film crews. Their offices are paid for with tax dollars so they can't recommend one person or service over another; they are obligated to represent everyone equally. However, if a producer is looking for a certain type of equipment or service, the film commissioner can be a useful source of information.

Most film commissions publish guidebooks that include lists of technical personnel available for film and video production in their jurisdiction; these books are part of the commission's promotional efforts and are available free of charge. Once information has been gathered about the availability of local talent, it is up to the director, in consultation with the producer, to select the key crew members, and it is the responsibility of the key crew members to interview and select their support staffs.

At least as important as the technical expertise of the crew is their spirit of dedication to the production. A technically qualified key grip who is accustomed to big-budget studio conditions with unlimited supplies, a leisurely shooting schedule, and lots of assistants may be a poor choice for a low-budget film. These individuals might quickly become dissatisfied and disillusioned with your project. This isn't always the case, but it's a danger worth considering.

The ideal situation for a low-budget film is to assemble key crew members who are technically brilliant in their fields but who haven't yet broken through to major-league status. For these people on the way up, each project is desperately important. If they believe in your picture they will go well beyond the call of duty to ensure that their work fully reflects their talents.

If you have special production problems such as stunts, special effects, or animals, *hire a specialist.* There are highly skilled people in virtually every specialty area, and what they can save in time, money, and anxiety is usually well worth their fee. Hiring a professional in any field is not a guarantee that nothing will go wrong, but it is added insurance that the scene will play well in the finished film, and that it will be executed with an emphasis on safety. If you can't afford to hire a professional, consider modifying or omitting the scene.

Union versus Non-Union

The terms "union" and "non-union," when applied to motion picture production, refer to whether or not a producer has signed a labor agreement governing below-the-line personnel in all categories except transportation, which is covered by the Teamsters and will be discussed later. The union governing motion picture production is the International Alliance of Theatrical Stage Employees and Moving Picture Machine Operators of the United States and Canada (IATSE and MPMO). This organization is affiliated with the AFL-CIO and is generally referred to as the IA. It began in 1893, when show business meant the stage. Today, in addition to below-the-line job categories, the IA encompasses such positions as laboratory technicians, film distributors, projectionists, motion picture mechanics, and film salespeople. There are over 800 locals throughout the United States and Canada.

It used to be that in order for a film to be projected in a theater by a union projectionist (and virtually all theaters prior to the sixties employed union projectionists), a film needed to have at the end of the tail credits the IA seal (commonly called the "the bug"), and the only way to get the bug was to hire an IA union crew for the film. Those days are gone. Today the unions are so cost prohibitive that many medium-budget films cannot afford to use them. Most independent films, and even movies-of-the-week and miniseries shot for television, use non-union or mixed crews. They have to keep a low profile in order to avoid union picket lines, but today the criterion for whether or not a film will receive distribution is the quality of the film, not the union affiliation of the crew.

A producer setting out to make a feature film must decide whether or not to use a union crew very early in the game. The principal purpose of the unions is to protect their members. There are, however, advantages to a producer who signs a union contract. First, the producer has access to any members of the union who are available within the framework of the picture's schedule and budget. Second, union members have met certain technical qualifications for membership. Pictures that are made under the jurisdiction of a union often run more smoothly than non-union pictures because the labor agreement defines an organized structure within which everyone must work.

The disadvantages to a producer who signs a labor agreement are that the production must abide by the rules and regulations set forth in the agreement and by state and federal laws governing labor contracts: often a minimum number of persons must be employed in certain categories; employees must be paid no less than the union's minimum wages and must be paid whatever overtime is provided for in the agreement; fringe benefits for health, pension, and welfare must be paid for all union employees; working conditions must meet certain standards set by the union; and there are usually hefty automatic fines if meals are late, if turnaround times between shifts are too short, or if a member works outside of his or her job category.

All of the major studios and many independent production companies have signed a long-term contract with the IA and consequently the majority of feature films are made with their crews. The IA has approximately 25,000 members on the West Coast alone and has been known to put out over a hundred complete production crews in a single day. A producer who signs an IA contract has available practically all of the top below-the-line talent in the industry. Each job category local will supply a signatory producer with a roster of available technicians from which a crew may be chosen. Locals will not recommend any one individual over another; such recommendations are generally made by key crew members or by an experienced UPM.

Members of the IA are generally highly qualified individuals with substantial track records. Many of their key crew members have come up through the ranks of apprentice and assistant positions for six years or longer. Most of those who have bypassed this traditional route established a significant reputation in their particular job category prior to joining the IA. There are, of course, a few unqualified members, but they are uncommon and they almost never work.

An individual must work for a probationary period in a particular job category on at least three IA productions before being permitted to join the union in that category. For many individuals, this presents a catch-22 situation. They can't work on an IA picture without being a member of the union, and they can't become a member of the union without working on union pictures. The break for many individuals comes during peak production seasons when all available technicians in a given category are working. Producers may then hire non-union personnel in those categories and, provided they complete the probationary requirements, they may join the union. In some cases the individual may also be required to pass a Departmental Trade Test. The process required for becoming a full-fledged member can take as long as three years. Another scenario involves a non-union or mixed crew, which the IA organizes by offering probationary entrance into the union in exchange for the crew's willingness to go on strike. This forces the producer either to replace the crew with non-union personnel or negotiate a deal with the union. While this has the appearance of hastening the probationary process, the personnel on the crew must still work on at least two additional IA productions before being fully accepted into the union.

A producer who signs with the IA is required by the union to employ a minimum number of union production personnel, usually no less than twenty-five for a feature film. Job categories for IA members are rigidly defined by the various locals, and rarely will members deviate from their specific functions. For example, a sound technician is not permitted to carry grip equipment; a camera assistant cannot touch a light. On large pictures this structure is useful and effective; on smaller pictures it is inefficient. Smaller films demand a family spirit, a team effort in which everybody is willing to lend a hand to everyone else.

Each job category within the IA has local offices throughout the country, each of which has jurisdiction over a specific geographic area. If a producer signs an agreement with the IA in Los Angeles but wishes to shoot part of the production in New York, a New York crew must be hired for that portion of the production or New York "standby" crew members must be hired for each IA person brought from Los Angeles. For example, if a producer shooting a film in Los Angeles needs to shoot some scenes in New York, the Los Angeles director of photography may be brought to New York if the producer hires a New York director of photography to stand by on the set throughout the filming period in New York.

Members of the IA are not permitted to work for producers who have not signed an IA contract (though many do), nor are producers who have signed an IA contract permitted to hire non-IA personnel in job categories over which the IA has jurisdiction. As far as the union is concerned, a picture is either 100 percent IA or it's not IA.

There are two basic IA contracts, one for the studios and one for independent companies. The IA has also established a low-budget contract (pictures made for less than $6 million) and will work with producers to accommodate their budget considerations. IATSE president Tom Short, who is actively seeking to bring independent production companies under the IA umbrella, says, "Most significantly, this agreement provides competitive wages and benefits for crews working on projects, that in the past worked non-union." In the case of *Fresh,* an IA film shot in New York, union locals agreed to defer a large chunk of their up-front payments; if the picture makes a profit, they get the rest of their money plus a bonus.

A common misconception is that a right-to-work state is a state in which there are no unions. IATSE has organized in both right-to-work and non-right-to-work states. Right-to-work simply means that the union security clause, which forces people to join the union, can't be enforced in that state. But unions often claim jurisdiction in these states because of a common contract clause called "rule of law," which places all of a producer's productions under union jurisdiction regardless of where the work is actually done.

Another common misconception is that a producer who signs an IA contract must use Teamster drivers for the production. The Teamsters are a separate union from the IA and require a separate contract. The reason most IA signatory producers also sign with the Teamsters is because most of the facilities that supply dressing rooms, honey wagons (portable toilets), camera cars and cranes, catering services, and buses for transporting the cast and crew are signatories to the Teamster contract. Consequently, it is often difficult for a producer to obtain these services without signing a Teamster contract. On a studio feature this can easily add a million dollars to the budget. Should an IA signatory producer decide against a Teamster contract, the Teamsters have no recourse except possibly to throw up a picket line at the production site, or create a racket with radios and car horns that interferes with the recording of production sound. The IA members must honor their separate contract, and will not, except in very unusual circumstances, honor such a picket line.

The advantage for a producer signing a Teamster contract is that there will be available to the production a virtually unlimited number of professional drivers under the supervision of a driver captain and cocaptain. This is particularly useful on large-budget pictures. On smaller pictures, the expense of professional drivers who contribute nothing more than moving vehicles from one place to another may be prohibitive.

When negotiating a contract with a producer, the Teamsters will push for as many driver positions as they can get. They may, for example, argue that if the maximum number of drivers you will need on a particular day of your production is twenty, you should hire twenty drivers for the entire schedule. From a producer's standpoint, it is more sensible to hire a minimum number of drivers for the duration of the schedule, and then supplement that number on days when more are needed. Another way to save money is to plan carefully which days will require a company move and hire drivers only for those days.

A third misconception is that union contracts and wage scales are written in stone, but they are in fact negotiable. Both the IA and the Teamsters are prepared to bargain, and among producers there is an unspoken understanding that it is in their collective interest not to make deals that are weighted heavily in favor of the unions. Those deals become precedents and come back to haunt all producers.

IA members are often willing to work on non-union films, but if the union discovers them doing so, the locals for those particular job categories may come to the set and request that their members leave the project. Union members will generally comply with this request. Those who don't comply face a possible fine, membership suspension, or expulsion from the union. This puts the producer of a mixed-crew film in a tough spot. If the film has been 80 percent completed using IA members in a few crucial categories such as director of photography, gaffer, and key makeup artist, the producer will either have to negotiate an agreement with the union or stop production until those individuals are replaced. This will be costly for the producer and possibly damaging to the quality of the finished film. Finding replacement crew members may take several days. Such a break in production usually has a negative effect on the morale of the crew. Furthermore, since everyone has a unique working style, the work of the new crew members may be inconsistent with that of their predecessors, and the look of the finished film may suffer.

It is not uncommon for producers to proceed with a mixed crew in spite of these dangers, especially if the film is being shot on a short schedule. The risk of discovery by the union is minimized if a producer maintains a low profile, perhaps going off to some remote location for the production. The risk is increased if large announcements are printed in trade papers and the film is shot on public streets in the heart of Manhattan. In any case, the potential danger of being shut down partway through production is worth careful consideration before proceeding with a mixed crew.

There are many qualified non-union individuals available for each below-the-line job category, but they are harder to locate and their talent is often more difficult to judge. They are not backed up by an organization that has established criteria for qualifications in each category and, in most cases, they are less experienced than their union counterparts. The best way to locate such individuals is through production managers who have had experience working on non-union pictures. Other ways include advertising in trade papers and inquiring at motion-picture-equipment rental houses. Equipment houses are often aware of which non-union people work most often.

The most important thing to avoid is hiring unskilled or unqualified labor. There are many such people who would kill for an opportunity to work on a motion picture production, but every below-the-line position, including second camera assistant, grip, best boy, electrician, and boom operator, demands a competent, experienced, highly trained individual. A producer who naively hires unqualified below-the-line technicians in an effort to save money probably will spend more money in wasted time during production and will ultimately produce an inferior film.

The question of whether to use an IA, a non-union, or a mixed crew is one that independent producers face with each new project. This information is intended to give an overview of the pros and cons of each. If it's a major studio picture or an extremely low-budget effort, the answer is obvious. For the rest it's not. The best way to determine which is most suitable for a particular project is to visit the union to discuss the project, then consult with other producers and production managers who have made similar pictures in a similar geographic region. Ultimately, the decision will be dictated by both the budget and the unique problems of each production.

A producer interested in more information regarding the minimum contract requirements and wage scales for various job categories for an IA production, as well as information about the IA low-budget agreement, can find this information in several of the publications listed in Appendix E. The IA Web site is also a valuable source of continually updated information.

Selecting a Director of Photography

Unless you are considering a cinematographer with substantial feature credits, you will probably judge candidates on the basis of sample reels. A sample film reel is not necessarily a condensation of the best work of which a cinematographer is capable. In reality, especially with beginning cinematographers, a sample reel is a compilation of the best work the cinematographer has *available*. Often the reel consists of scenes shot under limiting, low-budget conditions that represent the best the cinematographer could do under the circumstances, not the best of which he or she is capable.

Getting any scene from a film for a sample reel can be difficult. Printing small sections of a film is hard on the negative, and in order to get a two-minute scene on film, the cinematographer may have to buy an entire reel. The cost of this is often prohibitive. The cinematographer sometimes turns to the distributor and purchases used material, either an entire print or one reel at a time. When a distributor sells an old print, chances are it will be scratched or torn, perhaps in the best scenes. The cinematographer might be stuck showing second-best scenes that were shot under extreme time pressure with little lighting equipment. If the material is transferred from a release print onto video, the quality is even worse, because contrast increases in the transfer process; a special low-contrast print should be made specifically for transferring to video, which is the way commercial video releases are made, and the cost of this is usually prohibitive.

A commercial video copy, if available, is another option; this is a common way to view cinematographers' work, but it has some drawbacks. First because the quality of the image will vary depending on the television set and the way it is adjusted. Second, editing material for a sample reel using video is difficult, expensive, and results in at least one generational loss in quality. Third, the tape may be viewed anywhere, including the producer's office, with phones ringing in the background, assistants scurrying in and out, and lights glaring.

The best way to judge a sample reel, whether on film or video, is to view the material in a darkened room without distractions and to do the following:

Divorce yourself from the content. The material may be distasteful to you, or the acting may be awful, but that's not what you're judging. So don't let it interfere with your judgment of the cinematography.

Look for a style of lighting that is both consistent within the film and consistent with your vision of what your picture should look like. Pay close attention to interior lighting and exterior night scenes, which are often the most difficult to light.

Don't confuse the cinematographer's talent with the placement or movement of the camera. This will generally not be the cinematographer's responsibility. The principal function of the director of photography is to light the scene, not place the camera. A good cinematographer will make contributions to placement and movement of the camera, but this responsibility is ultimately the director's.

If you are working within a budget that requires hiring one person to work as both director of photography and camera operator, watch for sequences in which the camera moves a great deal and precise framing is done on the fly. Ideally, this will include some hand-held work, which is often the truest test of an operator's ability. Watch for smooth, steady moves. Does the operator continually overshoot and have to readjust the framing? Are there awkward jerks or bumps in the movement? These could be the fault of the dolly grip or the result of inadequate rehearsal time for the operator. Every operator makes awkward moves on occasion, and in low-budget films there often isn't time to correct them with a second take. But if the problem is repetitive, the operator is not doing an adequate job. An exception to this is when erratic movement is a stylistic choice, as in the remarkably effective documentary look of *Kids,* photographed by Eric Alan Edwards.

Be wary of flashy, tricky reels that utilize a series of fast-paced action sequences, such as car crashes or promotional trailers with wall-to-wall sound effects and bombastic music. These sequences may evoke an emotional response, but is it because of the cinematography? Or is it the editing, or the music, or the sound effects? Poor cinematography can often be masked with these tricks of the trade. Further, it is difficult to judge lighting when each scene is on the screen for only a handful of frames.

When you encounter an action reel of this kind, try viewing it a second time without the sound; silently watching it will tell you a great deal about its *visual* impact, which is what you are attempting to judge.

Production Design

Designing a production refers to the task of creating a consistent overall "look" for sets, costumes, props, special visual effects, and all other visual elements in the picture, in accordance with a visual style established by the director. The person who fulfills this function is called an art director or production designer. The title "production designer" was originally given to William Cameron Menzies for his work on *Gone With the Wind.* Not only did he fulfill all of the functions of the art director, he designed and sketched out virtually every shot in the film. He truly "designed" the production and, for many years, was the only individual in the industry who was given the title of production designer. The title was later given to art directors when, on epic pictures like *Lawrence of Arabia* and *2001: A Space Odyssey,* several art directors were employed and a title was needed for the person supervising them. Over the years, the special meaning of the title production designer has eroded and, on most films, is given to the person who functions as a traditional art director. In order for an individual to receive a production-designer credit on an IA film, the Society of Motion Picture and Television Art Directors must approve the credit. In virtually all cases this approval is given. On non-union films the approval is not necessary.

The best production designers will look for ways to use design elements to help tell the story. The way a person's home looks—the props, the furnishings, the paint or wallpaper—tells us a great deal about the character who resides there. In a more subtle way, a production designer might vary the color palette as the tone of the story shifts from light to dark and back again to light. Perhaps a specific color, say orange, will provide a consistent subliminal visual cue that something violent or dangerous is about to happen. Production designers sometimes contribute to the visual composition of specific shots in a film, much as Cameron Menzies did on *Gone With the Wind.* They may, for example, sketch compositions, consult with the director, and subsequently design sets around the visual concepts in the sketches. All of these notions center on finding the most effective way to tell the story.

When working within a limited budget, look for a production designer who understands when it is more economical and efficient to shoot on practical locations and when it is more appropriate to build sets. Sets are generally more flexible and efficient to work in but are usually more expensive than practical locations. On the other hand, if you are filming a scene in tight quarters, for example in a bathroom, you will probably save money by building the set and working with wild walls. If you elect to shoot a bathroom scene in a practical location you will use up valuable time attempting to cram actors, lights, camera gear, and crew members into an unreasonably small space. You will also compromise the quality of the finished product because working in such tight quarters has inherent limitations and causes frustrations that restrict everyone's ability to function at their peak levels. As a general rule, the smaller the space, the more you will save by building sets; the larger the space (for example, a bus station), the more money you will save by shooting on location. A production designer can save a picture additional money if locations are combined (a restaurant may be redressed to function also as a video arcade), or if several locations are found in close proximity, which minimizes or eliminates the need for company moves.

The execution of the production designer's overall plan is up to the specialists in their respective departments. The art director will supervise the building of the sets; the costume designer will select fabrics and supervise the purchase or construction of the costumes; the visual effects supervisor will decide how best to execute the effects envisioned by the director and the production designer. The function of the production designer is often to initiate concepts and to act as a central coordinator for the integration of the designs created by various departments. As a crude example, without such a person to oversee things, the costume designer may create a stunning gown for an actress only to have her appear on a set where the walls have been painted the same color as the gown.

Film Commissioners

The Association of Film Commissioners International is an organization founded in 1975 and comprised of over 250 offices around the world that function on behalf of countries, states, provinces, and cites to encourage producers to spend production dollars in their geographic locale. Their services are available to writers, producers, directors, location managers, and anyone else involved in the development and/or production of a film. The commissioner's main thrust is to attract productions from the outside, but their services are available to local production companies as well.

A common misconception is that a film commissioner is somebody's brother-in-law who's been appointed to the position. Film commissioners are trained specialists and can be an invaluable asset to a producer. The association routinely conducts seminars and workshops for its members covering such topics as location scouting, permits, pyrotechnics, special effects, how to handle emergencies, and more. Most film commissions publish a production guide that contains extensive information about local equipment houses, casting facilities, crew members living in their jurisdiction, weather data, and more. All services offered by the film commissions are provided free of charge, and they can amount to tens of thousands of dollars on a single production. If the film commissioner is successful in attracting productions, the payback for the community is significant. Not only do film-production dollars stimulate the economy, but a successful film often helps boost tourism in the area.

From a producer's point of view, the film commissioner is like a free employee and can be advantageous in two important areas: *locations* and *logistics.*

Locations are an important visual aid, and if selected carefully, they can help tell the story effectively and economically. The first step is to determine where geographically to shoot your film, and that process begins with phone calls to film commissioners in areas you feel might be appropriate for your project. Many have an 800 number, an E-mail address, and a site on the World Wide Web. A producer can make twenty phone calls and activate twenty film commissions around the country. After reading the script and, ideally, consulting with the director, the film commissioner will go to work. What you can expect to receive, in addition to the commission's production guide, are photographs and/or videotapes of potential sites for filming. These may come from a library of location information maintained by the commissioner, or they may be shot specifically for your project. The stills will be labeled and pasted into folders identified by location. In response to a single inquiry, a film commissioner might log several thousand miles scouting locations and submit $100 to $150 worth of photographs to the producer.

Many producers return the stills when they are finished with them, and this courtesy is appreciated by the film commissions. However, if there is a chance the producer will have a use for them in the future, the commissioner would often prefer that they were in the producer's hands than back in their office files. If a producer doesn't perceive any advantage in keeping the photos, they should be returned.

A film commissioner seeking locations for a producer will usually submit several potential sites. Let's say your script is set in a small town that has been dominated by a single family for generations. You will need a location with elements that visually communicate that specific history. A possible submission from a film commissioner might be a picture-perfect community with unusual objects that could have been donated by the dominant family, such as an elaborate fountain or a strange little park. Another town might be surrounded by pancake-flat topography with a single hill at the very edge of town on which is built a magnificent mansion. Images such as these say very specific things about the communities and may be visually consistent with what the director is after. If not, they will provide a jumping-off point for more discussions, after which the film commissioner will set out on a second trip and submit a second set of potential locations.

Film commissions are also actively involved in the area of image transmission via the Internet. Producers in many cases are able to connect directly to film commissioners in various jurisdictions and conduct on-line location searches using databases of still and moving images twenty-four hours a day. Eventually, this will allow nearly instantaneous preliminary location scouting throughout the world.

If a producer decides to visit the commissioner's jurisdiction, the commissioner will arrange appointments and travel with the producer to visit potential locations. The best film commissioners are highly organized and offer plenty of flexibility and contingent plans, thereby using the producer's time to maximum advantage. During the scout, and even during production, the film commissioner can also, at the producer's request, help protect the production from the media. Often producers, writers, and directors don't want anyone to know they are in the area scouting, perhaps because they are not yet ready to publicize their picture or they don't want their ideas advertised for others to exploit.

Once a producer has decided on a community in which to film, the commissioner will assist in a variety of ways. This brings us to the second principal area in which the film commissioner can be helpful: *logistics*. If the production needs to close down a highway, blow up a building, get special permission for stunts or special effects, the film commissioner knows where to go and whom to approach in order to expedite the production in the most cost-effective way for the producer.

Once a project comes into an area, a good film commissioner will stay with it until it's finished, meeting with the producer and crew members, discussing issues and concerns the commissioner may be able to fix before they become serious. The producer is usually the first person to be called in a crisis; the film commissioner is often the second.

Closely tied to logistics planning is the area of public relations. Film commissioners, though not often used for this purpose, can be an invaluable asset when it comes to establishing ties with the community. This can be especially helpful in communities that are unaccustomed to filmmaking. The film commissioner not only knows whom to approach for special favors, but also knows whom to introduce to the producer. Important figures in the community can use their influence to save a producer tens of thousands of dollars, often in exchange for nothing more than an opportunity to shake hands with an actor, or be invited to the set for lunch, or have their child appear as an extra in the film.

You can't start calling people in the community and trying to build a relationship at the eleventh hour, so some film commissioners will initiate a meeting before filming begins between members from the production (usually the producer, director, UPM, first AD, location manager, stunt coordinator, and special effects coordinator) and the town leaders (mayor, chief of police, sheriff, fire marshal, city manager, and others who will be interacting with the production). Such a meeting serves several purposes, but primarily it is to lay out exactly what the town should expect. Film production is often unpredictable, and the town should be warned to expect delays, schedule changes, last-minute permit requests to close public streets, and the like. The more the townspeople understand, the more likely they are to cooperate. It is therefore important that production companies and film commissioners be fully honest with each other. A producer who intends to shoot a major car chase with vehicles flying through store windows can't pretend that the street will only be shut down for a few hours and that the damages will be minimal. If you're going to cause explosions and possible damage to the community, you should deal with that up front. Likewise, it is not in the film commissioner's best interests to misrepresent the community in order to persuade the producer to film within the commissioner's jurisdiction. If a producer visits the area at a time of year when it rarely rains but is going to be filming months later when it may rain every day, the commissioner should convey this honestly.

I mentioned earlier that these services are offered free of charge. That's true, but there are a few things a producer can do to help support the services offered by film commissioners. Each year the commissioners must justify their existence. If the local politicians don't think they are pulling their weight, they are going to cut their budgets and thereby cut services to producers. What commissioners find helpful, after the production company has finished filming, is an approximation of how much money the production spent in their area. This information won't go to the Internal Revenue Service—it's just something the commissioner can show the boss, usually the mayor or the governor, to help justify the existence of the office. These figures can be compared to the amount of money spent in order to attract the business.

Another way a producer can help is by writing a letter of appreciation to the head of the film commissioner's jurisdiction. If it's a state, write to the governor; if it's a city, write to the mayor; if you're unsure, ask the film commissioner to whom you should write.

Promotional material from a film that was shot in the commissioner's area can be another asset for the office. A flyer, a poster, or eight-by-ten production stills of the crew working on location in the state can be used in the office as a visual statement of the office's success, and can be used in trade shows and press releases touting the accomplishments of that particular film commission.

A complete listing of film commissioners may be found in many of the publications listed in Appendix E. There is also a vast amount of information available from various film commissions on the Internet.

13

Electronic Media

FILM IS MOVING INTO A DIGITAL WORLD, ONE IN WHICH WE STORE and manipulate information in the form of numbers, at such a rapid pace that many services and facilities are continually racing to keep up. Earlier I mentioned that it is important to consider how you are going to sell your movie before you attempt to raise financing; it is equally important that you consider how you are going to edit your movie before you begin production. This chapter will explain why, and will provide information necessary to guide your decision.

It used to be that there was no choice. Films were shot, edited, and distributed on film. Films are still shot largely on film, but postproduction has become much more complex, and unless you plan for the system you are going to use in advance, you can get into serious trouble. Whatever choice you make will have ramifications from the day you begin shooting to the day you screen your final answer print. Your editing system will dictate how your film and sound dailies will be processed, transferred, and otherwise prepared for editing.

In the broadcast sense, the choices are between film and electronic editing systems. Electronic editing refers to both video and digital systems. It is no more necessary for a filmmaker to understand the inner workings of an electronic editing system than it is to understand how the gears work in a Moviola, but an overall understanding of some basic terms is important. If some of the following information seems too technical, you can skip over it and come back to it at a later time as a reference source. Most of it will be useful throughout the making of your film.

For the following discussion, I will assume that you intend to shoot your picture on film. Whether your picture is intended for theatrical release, direct-to-video, cable, or television, you will probably shoot on film. However, the information that follows applies also to pictures shot on electronic media. I will also assume that your eventual market is theatrical distribution, which requires conforming the original camera negative to match the edited material. "Original negative," "original camera negative," and "original film negative" are synonymous terms. The conformed original negative will be used to make an interpositive copy, which will be used to make an internegative copy, which will be used to make release prints for distribution to theaters. The primary reason for the interpositive-internegative process is to protect the original negative from damage. If something happens to the internegative, you can make a new one from the interpositive; in the rare event that the interpositive becomes damaged, you can make a new one from the original negative. Because contrast increases with each generation, the interpositive is a low-contrast print. Its characteristics are such that it produces a better video master than a standard low-contrast print made for that purpose. It is not often used to make video masters, however, because it is approximately three times as costly as a standard low-contrast print.

If you choose an electronic editing system and your eventual market is limited to video and/or television broadcast with no theatrical sales anywhere in the world, you may be able to avoid physically cutting your original negative since the dailies will be transferred to a master source tape such as one-inch D2, or Beta SP during the telecine process (a telecine machine is one that transfers film to magnetic tape or digital media).

With all editing systems, a copy of the original camera negative is made for editing. Depending on the system you're using, this working copy will be made on film, video, or digital media. Film editors work with film media, sprocketed magnetic tracks, tape splicers, and trim bins; they wait an average of two hours a day for assistants to locate trims from the hundreds of reels of film and sound tracks lining their shelves. Electronic systems lack the personal hands-on editing that many film editors prefer, but with these systems there is no waiting for an assistant to find trims, no scraps on the editing room floor, no tape splices, no mess of any kind. To a large degree the system used is a matter of personal preference, and many excellent editors will continue to prefer film editing using a flat bed or even an upright Moviola. Examples of editors who have continued to cut on film during the transition to digital media include Michael Kahn (*The Lost World: Jurassic Park*), Jon Gregory (*Secrets & Lies*), and Lisa Zeno Churgin and Ray Hubley (*Dead Man Walking*). There is even a statement included among the tail credits for *Dead Man Walking* that proclaims, "This film was edited using old-fashioned machines." Film editing will continue, but digital systems offer many advantages and may eventually replace film editing altogether.

Analog and Digital Information

Many important changes in technology that have taken place in the last ten years involve the shift of both audio and picture information from continuous analog form to storage in the form of numbers. This information is recorded in streams of binary numbers (zeros and ones) that *represent* the analog information. Digital techniques for recording both sound and pictures were developed at about the same time, but the advent of compact discs brought digital audio into the marketplace somewhat sooner than digitized pictures.

The sound we hear is an analog pressure wave in the air or whatever medium transmits it. Microphones respond to sound waves by generating corresponding electrical wave forms. Similarly, we perceive pictures as variations in the visual analog form of light. Human beings are incapable of observing digital information in the same way that they observe continuous analog information, so an image or sound that has been translated into digital information must be translated *back* into analog form in order for us to hear or see it.

An analog expression is a continuous and smoothly changing variable. A digital expression is a series of numerical addresses for specific points on the wave shape. When analog information is rerecorded and edited through successive generations, there are losses and distortions introduced in each recording process. A principal advantage of digital media is that each increment can be duplicated without any losses or distortion. This is because each increment has a specific, precise address; there are no approximations.

The difference between analog and digital audio is similar to the difference between a freehand drawing of a curve and the same curve drawn by connecting a series of dots with a straight line between each pair of dots. Clearly, the more dots you have, the smoother the curve will be, and the closer the digital expression will approach the analog form. If you have enough dots, the two curves will be virtually indistinguishable, but in theory a digital expression can never reach the absolutely perfect continuity of an analog expression. This is because the successive points of a digital expression never touch, but always have a space between them; the points on an analog expression are infinitely close together, which means there are actually no points at all, but rather a continuous wave. A digital expression can, however, come so close as to appear perfect to any observer.

There are many important advantages to translating sounds and pictures into numbers (digits). One primary reason is that no matter how many times they are copied and recycled, as long as the computer performs its high-speed arithmetic correctly, the sound and pictures produced by the last recording will be essentially identical to the original material. For special effects application, where multiple images are overlaid and manipulated, this advantage is especially significant. Digital optical effects are produced using a system in which the picture information is translated into numbers, then manipulated and translated back onto film. One of the important goals is to produce the effects in such a way that, from the standpoint of resolution, they are indistinguishable from the rest of the film.

Bits and Bytes

A digital system is one in which everything stored or represented in the system is in the form of binary numbers. In the language of binary arithmetic, there are only two symbols: 0 and 1. A single symbol, which can be either 0 or 1, is called a bit. A connected series of bits is called a word. Computing machine systems commonly communicate internally with eight-bit words. An eight-bit word, such as 10100100, is called a byte. The majority of binary material is presented and discussed in terms of bytes.

Sampling

Digital audio information consists of ordered sets of numbers that define analog wave forms by establishing two criteria. The first defines increments in time, called sampling. The second defines the height of the wave, called amplitude. How often a point on a wave form is represented by digital information defines the "sampling rate." This rate indicates the number of times per second that the digital recording equipment "looks" at the analog wave form of the audio signal.

Computers that translate this information assume that any point not sampled lies on a straight line between the nearest sampling points. If, for example, you provide a computer with only two points, the computer will "draw" a straight line between them and assume that the wave is flat. In order to form a reasonably smooth wave, the computer must be given a large number of sampling points. For compact-disc audio recordings, the sampling rate is 44,100 samples per second. The second criterion, amplitude, must be accurate within 1/64,000 of the maximum possible amplitude. The maximum possible amplitude will vary depending on a number of factors, but whatever the maximum amplitude is, it is divided into 64,000 increments, so the amplitude at any given point in time will be accurate to within 1/64,000 of the total. Measuring in increments of 64,000 is the meaning of the term "sixteen-bit" in computers; a sixteen-bit word has 2^{16} or 64,000 possible values (the actual figure is 65,536, but it is rounded off for convenience to 64K.) Compact-disc sound is a sixteen-bit system. Clearly, the quality increases as you reach twenty bits, twenty-four bits, thirty-two bits, and so on.

When combined, the successive numbers that represent the sampling point and amplitude (time and height) define the wave form. These numbers exist in the form of pulses and can be stored and recovered using either magnetic or optical media. On a compact disc the numbers are represented by a series of tiny bumps and pits that are read optically by a laser beam.

When shooting on film, picture information arrives at the camera lens in the form of light waves and, within the camera, forms an image on the film. After the film is processed it can be passed through equipment that translates the picture into digital information that can be stored either magnetically or optically on many different types of media, including high-density optical discs called DVDs (digital versatile disc or digital video disc), magnetic tape, and magnetic discs. Magnetic hard disks have many advantages and are the primary storage medium in digital editing equipment. Surprisingly, the criterion for high-quality reproduction of pictures is only eight bits instead of sixteen; this is because pictures do not require the same degree of resolution to look good as audio does to sound good.

When we speak of digitizing pictures, we are talking about breaking images down into tiny elements called pixels that comprise images on video, and then defining each pixel with numerical values that represent its placement in the frame, its chrominance, and its luminance. Chrominance defines the color of the pixel and luminance defines it brightness.

Linear and Nonlinear Editing

A *nonlinear* editing system for motion pictures is one in which a shot can be physically cut out and the remaining ends brought together and spliced. *Film* editing is therefore a nonlinear system.

A *linear* editing system is one in which you cannot physically cut out a shot and join the remaining ends together. *Videotape* editing is a linear system because you cannot successfully make an edit by physically cutting the tape. The system requires a continuity of the base material, the magnetic tape, so the only way to remove a shot is to erase it, leaving a blank space where the shot used to reside. The erased scene must be replaced with a new scene of the same length, or the subsequent scenes must be rerecorded so that they are moved up to begin at the point where the erased scene began.

There are several disadvantages to editing on a linear video system. One is that the quality of the image and sound suffers with each rerecording. Another is that the massive amounts of material used in making a feature film are too cumbersome for these systems to handle efficiently.

A digital editing system synthesizes the best elements from film editing and the best elements from the world of video. Like film editing, it is a nonlinear system. It requires no continuity of any base material. In digital editing, the audio and visual material is stored as numbers that are coupled together electronically.

You don't have to cut the material physically, as in film editing, nor do you rerecord the material in fixed, linear order, as in videotape editing. Rather, the system simulates the effect of the editor's decisions without actually cutting or rerecording anything; all that is stored is the list of edit decisions the computer uses to order such a simulation.

In order to edit digitally, the original camera negative must be translated into sets of numbers. The editor is then free to manipulate and modify the material endlessly without degrading or distorting the quality in any way. The system is similar to word processing with the same ease and flexibility for cutting, pasting, sequencing, and saving. Using a digital system, you can store and replay multiple versions, have instant access to the heads or tails of any shot, and substitute outtakes within moments.

Video Editing

The first application of computing machine control in the design of editing equipment evolved with videotape. The film negative was transferred to magnetic videotape and the editing accomplished with video equipment. In the early days, there were some marginally effective methods for physically cutting and splicing videotape (making it a nonlinear system), but with today's sophisticated recording systems, editing videotape by cutting and splicing is not practical.

During the mid-eighties there were efforts at making video editing systems viable by linking several tape decks together. This never worked for features because there was simply too much material for the systems to handle. The technique is primarily useful for short projects shot either on film or on videotape.

The process of manipulating picture and sound in a video format is fairly straightforward: The editor locates selected takes and edits them by rerecording selected segments onto another videotape. The edited tape may incorporate optical and audio effects, such as dissolves, fades, and altered motion. With some video systems shots can be juggled back and forth, examined, and compared in a variety of windows, an especially helpful tool for cutting scenes shot with multiple cameras.

The process is faster and in many ways smoother than film editing but even with high-speed reeling back and forth, searching for scenes on videotape and combining them is time consuming. Also, with each rerecording the working image loses quality. For television news and short films, rerecording losses are minimal and often acceptable. But the number of rerecordings required when editing a feature film are such that the losses become significant. If the original film negative will be conformed to match the edited videotape and used as the source material for making prints, the distortion of the videotape image by repetitive rerecordings will not affect the look of the finished film, but it makes it increasingly difficult to view the material during editing. Finally, these systems have been plagued with problems regarding sync, and with conforming the original negative to match the edited videotape.

Digital Editing

Virtually all studio films are edited using nonlinear digital technology, primarily Avid and Lightworks systems. There are a number of other systems on the market, and all of them have some basic elements in common. First, they are software products, not hardware, that use either IBM or Macintosh computers configured in a variety of customized hardware setups. With these systems, images and sounds are stored on hard disks; what the computer manipulates are the numbers needed to call up portions of these images and sounds in an order defined by decisions made by the editor. This list of numbers is called the edit decision list (EDL). Each edit is referred to as an "event," and each event is assigned a time code number in sequence from the beginning to the end of the film. The EDL identifies the time code on the edited film with the corresponding time code on the video and audio source tapes. The time code on the edited material is a continuous sequential time code reference from the beginning to the end of the film. The time code on each source tape, such as a production dialogue recording, is unique. The EDL tracks the relationship between the time code on the film and the time code on the source tapes, so that you can find precisely the location of the original production recording of any sound used in the edited film. The EDL will be used by sound editors when they match the original analog production recordings to the digitally edited sound tracks (see Chapter 19). If you are working in a video medium, the EDL will be used to build a video master that matches on video the edits made in the digital machine. A separate list, called a "negative cut list," will be used as an aid when conforming the original negative to the cut sequences (see Chapter 21). The term EDL is often used loosely to mean any list generated by the digital editing machine, including the negative cut list.

Digital systems generally use two monitors, one for previewing and comparing shots for the sequence being cut, and another for viewing the edited sequence. The material can be juggled back and forth, examined, edited, and compared in a variety of windows. In addition, the editor is free to manipulate and modify the picture with astonishing speed, endlessly, cutting and recutting, without degrading the quality of the picture or sound in any way.

When cutting on a digital system, you are actually logging numbers that define the sequence of events that make up your film. When you save a cut of your film to disk, you are not saving images and sounds, you are saving the numbers that the computer uses to call up the appropriate images and sounds in the right sequence. The material can be screened directly from the hard disk on one of the system monitors, or it can be transferred to video. Another option, one that allows you to screen your film in a theatrical setting, is to have a team of assistants working behind the editor to conform a film work print to the digital media as it is being edited. The quality and impact of the picture can be better evaluated when projected on the big screen using film media, but this process is expensive and done only on pictures with a sizable budget. For low-budget pictures, one of the great savings in cutting digitally is that you don't have to make a film work print, and you don't have the expense of one or more assistant editors continually reconstituting reels from trims and outs. But even on a low-budget picture it is prudent to print and screen at least a portion of the dailies on film, perhaps just the first roll, simply to ensure that the camera equipment is functioning properly.

Digital systems make it possible to save a variety of versions so that you can re-edit without the risk of losing what you've already cut. A director's cut, for example, can be saved if a producer or studio executive subsequently wants to experiment with alterations. One advantage is that the system provides a valuable training ground for assistant editors who can, on their own time, edit any scenes they want without compromising the quality or availability of material for the editor. Remember that the system does not cut anything; it manipulates numbers that represent the addresses of images and sounds, rather than the images and sounds themselves.

Digital systems have been adapted to meet the needs of film editors and are designed with digital equivalents for many traditional film editing tools, including leader, splicer, synchronizer, and rewind bench. As you edit, you see a visual representation of your film and sound tracks along the bottom of the screen, much like film going through a synchronizer on a rewind bench.

Editors using these systems have the ability to create visual effects such as fades, dissolves, altered motion, and titles that can be seen and evaluated without waiting for expensive film opticals. They can also build and mix a variety of sound tracks that can include dialogue, sound effects, and music. These tracks can incorporate segues, fades, level changes, and modifications in equilization, so that the editor can augment the picture with music and effects in a way that approximates a finished sound track. This can be especially helpful if you are screening an unfinished film for investors who might furnish completion money.

Oscar-winning editor Thelma Schoonmaker switched to a digital system when she cut *Casino* for Martin Scorcese. "Though I resisted at first, I'm quite converted. It's much faster and also has the great advantage of removing your fear to experiment because you have your original cut, which you keep." While having more choices clearly adds to the creativity of the effort, the curse is that experimenting with these choices takes time. Also, it invites the possibility of several people editing their own versions and reducing the final result to a film cut by a committee. The Directors Guild has expressed serious concerns about this issue.

For pictures on an accelerated postproduction schedule, one of the great advantages of digital editing systems is the ability for more than one system to share the same media. The special effects pictures *Dante's Peak, Independence Day,* and *Con Air* were cut in two, three, and four systems respectively, all sharing the same media. *The Fan,* for which 1.4 million feet of film was shot, utilized four editors and four systems linked in the same way.

Digital editing equipment is expensive and therefore not available to everyone. Deals can sometimes be struck with owners of digital equipment, but you may have to limit your use to odd hours and weekends. As stated earlier, money can be saved by not making a work print and transferring sound to sprocketed magnetic tape, and this may offset the expense. But chances are that you will not be able to afford the same luxury of time that you will if you are editing on film. Finally, remember that regardless of the system you are using, and regardless of whether or not you can afford a digital nonlinear system, it is the editor, not the equipment, that will determine the quality of the finished product.

Once a film is edited digitally, the original camera negative will be conformed to the digital version in order to make release prints for distribution to theaters. The ultimate goal in digital image processing is to create digital release prints that will eliminate the use of film for everything but the original material used in the camera. For a more detailed discussion of these systems, refer to Michael Rubin's book *Non-*

linear: A Guide to Digital Film and Video Editing, which is listed in Appendix E.

Compression

One of the most important contributions to the design of digital editing machines is the methods for compression that substantially reduce the storage space occupied by a given scene. Picture compression is largely based on locating redundant picture areas. The simplest example is a blank white wall. Obviously, in order to reproduce it visually, it is only necessary to store an extremely small piece of it, together with the data about its size and shape. Clear, blue skies and dark areas of night scenes lend themselves to successful compression. There are other elements that suffer from assumed redundancies that are not entirely valid, such as subtle differences in shading that the computer does not recognize but that might be important to the content of a scene. A white wire that runs down the wall to a hidden bomb might be evident on film but not when the image is translated into digital information and compressed by a computer.

Synchronization and Time Code

Techniques for coupling sound and picture began in the days of silent films, the 1920s. Theater orchestras and organists were supplied with a cue sheet that accompanied each film. The cue sheet specified musical segments selected to enhance the mood of the film, to characterize each principal actor with a musical theme, and to accent various actions with musical "strings." Most theater organists had large libraries of special music described as "Hurries," "Fights," "Love Themes," and the like, but they also did a great deal of improvising in order to match thematic musical phrases, tempos, and moods with the action.

When "talking pictures" first arrived, the sound was recorded on fifteen-inch phonograph records, played by a projectionist who constantly adjusted the speed of the record and/or the projector, trying desperately and usually with little success to keep the dialogue in sync with the picture. Then came sound on film, eliminating that problem by binding picture and sound together on the same base material. One unexpected sync problem was that movie houses were so large that the difference in the speed of light (186,000 miles per second) and sound (1,100 feet per second) made it necessary to place an extra set of loudspeakers toward the back of the theaters in order to reduce the sound delay and maintain synchronization for the audience in the back of the theater.

Techniques for recording, mixing, and replaying sound for motion pictures have become increasingly sophisticated and, along with almost everything else, are coming under the precise control of digital computing equipment. During production, film and sound elements are separate and retain code signals that will make it possible to synchronize them when they are joined together in postproduction. This means that production and postproduction equipment, including cameras, sound recorders, playback devices, and editing machines, must be capable of communicating in a code (language) that each of them understands.

The standard for maintaining sync sound during production has been, for many years, a sixty-cycle signal fed from the camera to a special track on the magnetic tape in the recorder. If the camera speed is unstable, the sixty-cycle frequency tracks the changes by shifting up or down accordingly. Later, when the sound is transferred for editing, the speed of a motor driving the playback machine for the original recording is controlled by this variable sixty-cycle signal, thus continuously adjusting the tape speed to match (synchronize with) the variations that took place in the camera. In a nutshell, the system is limited to answering a single question: How fast are we going? It is a speed-only sync code, which severely limits its use as a tool of synchronization. The sixty-cycle system, while still used, is often replaced by or coupled with a newer system called time code that answers an additional question, Where are we now?

Ever since the development of videotape recording in 1956, the television industry has been seeking a method of labeling each and every frame. The most efficient and practical way found for doing this was to use time code. SMPTE time code was established in 1969 and had its original importance in video editing. It was engineered and adopted by the Society of Motion Picture and Television Engineers in 1969. It is also termed SMPTE/EBU time code, the latter three characters referring to the European Broadcasting Union, which also adopted this code and thus made it an internationally accepted language. It is a standardized synchronizing language that utilizes a digital signal pattern of zeros and ones.

Many people ask, "What is the need for time code in film?" The primary answer is that when film is transferred to videotape or to a digital medium such as a hard disk, there are no sprocket holes or edge numbers. The complete code can include a unique numerical designation for each frame in the film, or each field (half frame) in video. The time code signal takes up only a small portion of the space between video frames, so there is plenty of room for additional information, including a coded signal representing the corresponding edge number on the original film negative. This becomes important when conforming the original negative to the edited picture (see Chapter 21, "Negative Cutting").

SMPTE time code acts as the glue that holds two or more machines in sync, just as sprockets do for film and 16mm or 35mm magnetic tracks. Based on the incoming time code, an electronic synchronizer regulates the speed of the *slave* recorder so that it always stays in perfect sync with the *master* recorder. This process is called *locking* and answers the question, How fast are we going? By numbering every frame, it gives each frame a unique address and answers the question, Where are we now? This is what makes accurate electronic editing possible. Using SMPTE time code, the master machine can find *anything* on tape or in digital storage, and all of the slave machines will chase the master to the same spot.

If you know precisely where a piece of program is and how fast it's playing, you can use this information to control other machines so that they are all in the same place at exactly the same time. In other words, SMPTE time code brings us into the realm of *position accuracy*. As an absolute timing reference that indicates both speed and position of picture and sound tracks, the system is capable of:

1. locking a variety of systems (film, videotape, audio tape, digital editing equipment, synthesizers, etc.) together with no possibility of misalignment*
2. finding a specific location on any track without the necessity of backing up and counting from the beginning
3. defining elapsed (not real) time in absolute terms, i.e., at any given point in the picture the SMPTE time code will indicate to you how much time will elapse when the film is run from the beginning to that specific point

Time code is recorded as a series of rapid-fire blips that are read by a microprocessor as binary numbers; these numbers are addresses that

---

*It should be noted that during the early days of digital editing systems, there were serious synchronization problems. To a lesser degree, they continue to plague the industry, especially when combining a variety of sync systems on a single picture. These problems are being resolved, but there are still editors who bemoan the days when film and sound were driven by sprockets.

consist of separate numbers for hours, minutes, seconds, and hundredths of a second for a twenty-four-hour time period beginning with 00:00:00:00 (this does not mean that it bears any significance with respect to the time of day; it is simply a convenient way to express this scale of digital values that represent elapsed time). Thus every hundredth of a second has a unique eight-digit number and, if the length of elapsed time is less than twenty-four hours, every frame of film will have its own unique number. In audio, this time code is invaluable in adjusting for sync because you can adjust within a hundredth of a second; since lip-sync can sometimes be off by as much as a frame or two (each frame is one-thirtieth of a second) and not be a meaningful problem, time code offers more than enough accuracy. The medium you are working in will dictate the time-code frame rate, which could be twenty-four, twenty-five, or thirty, or a variation on thirty frames per second called drop frame. These are not film frames, but tape frames. The frames-per-second rate for time code equals half of the power line frequency. In the United States, this is half of sixty cycles per second, or thirty frames per second. This is the National Television Standards Committee (NTSC) rate, which was established for black-and-white television. For a variety of technical reasons, color television has a frame rate of 29.97 frames per second and requires the use of the aforementioned drop frame.

When all the scenes have been edited, the computer compiles a "negative cut list," which will include addresses for the beginning and ending frames of each shot in the film. This will be used by the negative cutter when conforming the original negative to match the edited material.

Even with all of the advanced technology for synchronization, there are times when a filmmaker must rely on primitive methods for maintaining sync between picture and sound. Robert Rodriguez did not have sync sound capabilities when he filmed *El Mariachi,* and his Arri 16S camera was too noisy to record sound during a take, so all of the on-camera dialogue was recorded wild, after the scene was shot. There were no slates with which to sync up the sound with the picture, so Rodriguez had to do this by eye (a painstaking process; it took him two and a half weeks to sync the dailies). Because there was no system for maintaining synchronization, once he had a word at the start of a take in sync, the sound speed would drift so that a later part of the take would be out of sync. When that happened he had no choice but to cut away to something like a building or a dog, adjust the sync on the sound track, and cut back to the speaking actor. And it worked.

MIDI

Another binary code that is used in connection with motion pictures is MIDI (musical instrument digital interface). MIDI is often used in conjunction with time code and answers a third question: What do we do now? It was adopted initially in 1983 by manufacturers of electronic musical instruments (synthesizers, drum machines, etc.) as a standardized way for these instruments to send messages to each other. Its earliest application made it possible for a musician to play a variety of synthesizers simultaneously from a single keyboard.

Today MIDI codes are used in virtually every aspect of film production, including music, sound effects, electronic editing, special effects, and even lighting. Any device or machine in which the MIDI code is installed can be used to send or receive appropriate information. The MIDI pulse code language consists of lists of binary numbers, each of which have been assigned names for a wide variety of *events*. In MIDI language, the generation of a musical tone, such as middle C, is termed an event. Other events that MIDI is capable of invoking include cuing synthesized sound effects, such as traffic, rain, or footsteps; manipulating the movement of a camera on a MIDI-controlled platform; or cuing a change in a lighting pattern. Filming a model of a spaceship circling the sun may require that the light source, the camera, and the model all move in complex patterns simultaneously. These movement patterns can be recorded and manipulated using MIDI codes so that they will repeat precisely the same operations every time, or whatever variation the director, cinematographer, or special effects technicians desire. This is accomplished by the transmission of nomenclatures at 32,000 bits per second, which makes it possible to start, stop, or modify these elements with exceptional accuracy.

There is ongoing experimentation with methods for combining SMPTE time codes with MIDI codes, which adds considerably to the flexibility and application potential of each.

14

Equipment, Facilities, and Services

WHEN SELECTING AN EQUIPMENT HOUSE, A LABORATORY, OR A sound facility, lean on your specialists for guidance. The director may have preferences, but also consult with your director of photography, sound mixer, and editor. They will undoubtedly have established strong connections with certain houses, and this can be a great asset if you run into problems or require special services during production and/or post-production.

Camera and Lighting Equipment

The equipment package will be determined primarily by the requirements of the director and the director of photography. The producer and production manager will negotiate with equipment rental houses for the best price for that particular package. In addition to publishing production guides, film commissioners will be knowledgeable about the availability of local equipment houses in their areas, although because their offices are paid for with tax dollars, they can't recommend one house over another.

Generally, equipment houses will offer a three-for-seven rental price, where you pay for three days but keep the equipment for seven. This is most helpful when shooting six-day weeks. Prices are negotiable depending on the package, how long you need the equipment, and the season of the year. You will be able to negotiate for better gear at lower prices during slow production seasons. Prices will vary from house to house, depending on your particular needs. One house may have less expensive lighting gear but more expensive grip equipment. Shop around for the best price for your package.

In addition to price, consider the house's reputation for maintaining, servicing, and replacing gear quickly if something malfunctions. Find a house that offers adequate backup gear and replacement parts on short notice, ideally twenty-four hours a day. There is nothing more frustrating than a delay in production caused by equipment failure, especially if solutions are not readily available. An experienced director of photography will either know or be able to find out about a particular house's reputation in these areas. Most equipment houses will require that you provide loss and damage liability insurance or a security deposit.

A director of photography or gaffer may own some of the necessary equipment for your film. Whether this is a truckload or a small cart, it is referred to as the individual's "box" and is usually rented to the production as part of that individual's overall deal. A director of photography, for example, may own a box of filters and personalized camera attachments that will be rented to your production and used throughout principal photography. A gaffer may own a truck equipped with a complete lighting package. This can be a terrific deal, but there are two drawbacks to consider before making a decision. First, the owner of the gear may be unreasonably cautious or conservative in its use. This could cost you time during production. A gaffer who would normally support a light stand with a couple of sandbags might, if this light stand is owned by the gaffer, also nail it to the floor; on the plus side, though, self-owned equipment is usually very well maintained. Another consideration is that it becomes very difficult to fire someone if it also means replacing equipment and renegotiating for a replacement package with a rental house halfway through production. I suggest these downside considerations in order that producers entering into such arrangements do so with a full understanding of the potential problems and not simply with an eye to price. On the positive side, you can often negotiate a very good package deal and avoid purchasing loss and damage insurance by hiring crew members who own their own equipment.

Another element in the camera package is called a *video assist monitor.* This can be rented either in black and white or color. The unit is connected to the camera either by hard wire or by a remote transmitting device. It functions primarily as a way for the director, script supervisor, and others to view precisely what the camera sees. This is an extremely valuable tool, not only for setting up a shot during rehearsal but for watching the scene during filming. Its only drawback is that it sometimes distances the director from the actors. Often a director will forgo watching the monitor, especially if the camera is locked off in a static position, in order to watch the performances more intimately. Great films were made before video assist ever came into existence, so if your budget can't afford it, don't rent it. The same is true for cell phones, walkie-talkies, and a host of other conveniences that are not absolutely necessary when making a low-budget film.

Video playback is an optional piece of equipment that records what the camera sees on video so that it can be played back immediately. This can be useful for sequences that are difficult to judge during filming, such as the split-second timing of a complex stunt and scenes involving animals. Watching the scene played back on video, the director can determine which elements worked, which didn't, and whether or not to shoot another take. But the system can also be a hindrance. First, it is time consuming and expensive to stop production, rewind, and play a scene back. Second, video playback invites producers, actors, and others to watch the scene as it's played back and offer opinions about performance, camera movement, whether the scene should or should not be printed, and the like. On the set this is known as the "video village," and it can sometimes deteriorate into the nightmare of a film directed by committee.

Sound Equipment

Unlike most technicians, production sound mixers almost always bring their own gear, but this, too, is available from rental houses. The equipment usually consists of a professional sound recorder; a backup recorder; a full complement of microphones, including wireless mikes; several pairs of wireless headphones so that the director, producer, boom operator, and script supervisor can monitor the sound as it is being recorded during a take; a small television screen that picks up the signal from the video monitor so that the mixer can view what the camera sees during each take; all necessary booms, cables, connectors, etc.; and a mobile cart on which the equipment is transported and stored.

The most common technique for recording on sound stages as well as on location is by means of high-quality microphones and a professional quarter-inch tape recorder such as the Nagra. This analog recording is either transferred to sprocketed magnetic tape or is translated into digital form for editing.

Digital audio tape (DAT) recorders are commonly used to record sound effects on location (called "production effects") and are increasingly being used to record the entire spectrum of production sound, including dialogue. DAT recorders translate the analog output from microphones into binary numbers that represent the sound. Since humans can't hear sound in digital form, it must be translated back into analog form in order to be heard.

DAT units are less than half the size of the analog Nagra recorders and are much less expensive. An additional advantage to DAT recording is that it solves a problem in analog recording called "dropouts." Dropouts are the result of imperfections in the magnetic tape and mean, literally, that the sound drops out for a moment. DAT recordings are also made on magnetic tape (in DAT cassette form), but on these machines the information is recorded twice, in redundant patterns. There are a number of techniques used by these machines for observing imperfections on the track, and when these systems observe an error, such as a dropout, their circuits are capable of finding the missing information recorded redundantly elsewhere on the tape and moving it (in real time) to correct the erroneous reading. Since the chances of a dropout occurring simultaneously in the redundant recording is virtually zero, these automatic error-correction methods essentially eliminate dropouts.

A problem with DAT recordings that has not been fully resolved is the possibility that after ten years or so they may change in a way that compromises the quality of the recording. This is not a problem in most applications, but for long-term audio archiving it is best, at present, to transfer material recorded on DAT cassettes to some other medium.

There are also machines for recording digital sound directly onto a hard drive, but they have not been proven to be reliable in the field. The obvious danger with hard drives is that they can crash, potentially ruining not just the current take but all previous takes recorded on that drive. Production mixers using any kind of digital recording equipment, including DAT recorders, often operate a reel-to-reel Nagra as a backup.

Sound mixers sometimes have stereo recording equipment and wish to record production sound in stereo. Unless there is a very specific reason for doing so, this is a mistake. First of all, it is rarely practical to record two truly separate channels during production; you will almost always have some sound bleeding over from one channel to the other. If, for example, you are shooting a scene of two people conversing and you mike each person on a separate channel, you will hear both voices on each channel, with a different voice dominating on each. This creates several problems in postproduction. The sound house may inadvertently transfer one channel and not the other. The director and editor may not know why one actor sounds "muddy" and may assume that actor's lines will have to be rerecorded in a looping session (see Chapter 19). Postproduction sound mixers will have to figure out which character is speaking on which channel, and this may change from scene to scene.

Production mixers often have little experience in postproduction and are unaware of the problems stereo recordings create. Even if you intend to mix your film in stereo, record production sound in mono. A stereo effect can be created and controlled by postproduction sound mixers by panning the dialogue between right and left channels so as to place it accurately with the actor's movement on the screen.

Laboratories

Motion picture laboratories offer a variety of services, most of which are discussed in Part 5, "Distribution and Marketing." In brief, these services are:

- processing (developing) the camera negative
- making a positive film work print from the negative (this is done if you are editing on film, or if you are editing electronically but wish to conform a work print for screening purposes)
- telecine transfer to videotape, or directly into digital form, for use with electronic editing machines
- making interpositive prints from the original negative
- making internegative prints from the interpositive
- developing the optical sound track
- making color and density corrections from scene to scene within the film (called "timing")
- making release prints for distribution

In addition to the above, some laboratories have negative-cutting departments on their premises for conforming the original negative to the edited material. There are different techniques for conforming from a film work print and conforming from material that is cut digitally. The former uses key numbers and/or a machine-readable bar code printed on the edge of the original negative and updated every foot (sixteen frames) of film. This information is printed onto the edge of the work print and used for conforming. In the case of a digital edit, with no film work print, the key numbers and bar code are supplemented by a "negative cut list" that includes additional information necessary for conforming the original negative to the cut material.

Laboratories that have a reputation for handling feature films can generally be relied upon to produce quality work. There are also many smaller laboratories with less substantial reputations that are capable of handling feature films. If you are considering such a facility, it is important to scrutinize it carefully. Your director of photography will be a valuable resource for information about various laboratories. If you're unsure about a particular lab, you may request that the facility run a test. This involves giving the laboratory a sample piece of film to process and print. There is usually no charge for this. A producer, in conjunction with the director and director of photography, can often make a satisfactory judgment about a laboratory's capabilities based on such a test.

The prices for laboratory services are competitive and negotiable.

Pick the laboratory you feel is best suited for your picture, then shop around at various laboratories for the best price. Your first-choice lab will make a sincere effort to match the best price and will probably succeed. It may be worthwhile to explore more creative ways of financing lab costs, like a deferred payment in exchange for a percentage participation in the film. Du-Art Film Lab in New York, historically supportive of independent filmmakers, will often try to work out an arrangement of this kind.

Sound Facilities

Sound facilities offer a variety of services, including transferring, syncing, ADR (looping), and mixing. These services will be discussed later in this book. The prices for various services at sound facilities vary enormously and are less negotiable than the prices for laboratory services. A major sound facility might charge several times as much per hour as a smaller facility with comparable equipment and engineers. Your decision must be based on both price and reputation. A competent editor will be able to offer guidance in this area.

Full-service sound houses will often offer a deal for an entire package of services, including transfer, syncing, sound effects editing, mixing, and optical transfer. Increasingly, producers will arrive with a cut picture and production dialogue tracks and ask sound houses to compete for the entire sound "package." Like the gaffer's equipment package, this may result in an extremely good price. But, again, there are downside considerations. If you get halfway through your production and the sound facility's services deteriorate (perhaps they become overloaded with additional unexpected work), you may have a difficult time taking your film elsewhere. You will have committed yourself with a deposit and a guarantee. There are enough problems in producing a film without fighting an uphill battle for quality work at an overextended sound house. Again, this is not intended to rule out the possibility of a package deal, but simply to caution producers about potential problems.

Sound Stages versus Practical Locations

In most scripts there are choices to be made regarding shooting certain scenes on location versus building sets. Most pictures utilize a combination of sound stages and practical locations, but the smaller the budget, the more you'll be leaning toward shooting in practical locations. Nick Gomez's *Laws of Gravity* was shot almost entirely on location (mostly exteriors), but the main character's apartment was built for a cost of

$239. These choices must be based on economics, feasibility, and artistic considerations—not necessarily in that order.

In most large cities, there are stages or similar facilities available for rent. The advantages of a sound stage are that it offers flexibility and speed; rigging for lights and cable, as well as a generous supply of power, are at your fingertips; they are soundproofed, which eliminates waiting for traffic noise or airplane noise to die down before shooting a scene; and the floor surface is smooth for dolly moves. Since most sets are built with wild (movable) walls, they offer a flexibility in camera placement and movement that would not be possible on location. In some instances, especially in rural areas, a warehouse, a school gymnasium, or even a barn may serve as a stage on which to build sets, though such a location will not offer all of the advantages of a dedicated sound stage.

The drawbacks to sound stages are that you must pay for the construction of sets, you must pay for the facility during construction, you must pay for any holding time between construction and shooting, and you must pay for the time you're shooting. These prices are often negotiable, especially during a slow season. If you have shots that look out through windows or doors, you must create the exterior images. Certain moving images, such as traffic, are difficult to create when shooting through a window on a sound stage. A cityscape can be easily created using a backlit screen (called a "translight" or "chromatrans") outside the windows; having control over the "exterior" lighting in this way allows the director to film any scene on this set at any time of the day or night.

A practical location such as a working restaurant or private home that is used for only one or two days is generally rigged and shot at the same time so you will rarely pay for holding time. Exceptions are locations that require advance prep time for the art department to remove unwanted furnishings, paint walls, dress sets, etc. A practical location may offer a large window overlooking a busy street, which is difficult to duplicate on a sound stage. Practical locations will have to be rigged with power and lights, and the space must be large enough to accommodate the scene in question *and* the production crew. When scouting practical locations, look for spaces that are larger than those called for in the script. It is easy to make a room look smaller on film but extremely difficult to shoot in cramped quarters.

Consider the following carefully when shooting on practical locations: One of the most costly events is a company move from one location to another. This requires packing up all gear, moving to a new location, unpacking the gear, and resuming production. The best way to avoid this is to pick several locations in close proximity. For example, if you need to shoot in a restaurant, a pool hall, and a hair salon, look for a city block that contains all three. Or look for a pool hall with a restaurant upstairs. Or a restaurant that can be quickly redressed to look like a section of a hair salon. When you do make a company move, it is least disruptive if you schedule it at the end of the day; if you are forced to move in the middle of the day, expect to lose between two to three hours of shooting time. On a small budget, company moves should never be made in the middle of a shooting day. If there is one key to making ultra-low-budget films, it is limiting the number of locations in which the film is shot, and keeping those locations so close together that company moves, if any, are kept to a minimum. A *major* company move is when you move not just within an area, but to an entirely different geographic location, such as moving from New York City to Billings, Montana. Shooting the entire film in and around one city, even though the story takes place in two or more parts of the country, will save the production a considerable amount of money. Often a picture will require going to some distant location for production. This will be dictated by both budgetary and aesthetic considerations. It is expensive to house people in a distant location and, the farther you go from major cities, the more you will have to consider the available crew base.

On the positive side, filming in distant locations has the advantage of creating a family atmosphere among the cast and crew. Michael Apted (*Gorillas in the Mist, Nell, Incident at Oglala*) has had several positive experiences making pictures in distant and often remote locations. He observes, "You have the whole unit together, you become a kind of a family, and you get to know each other. Everybody's involved in making the film, there are no distractions. It breeds a kind of intensity which I like."

When shooting on location, you may need to obtain a permit from the city or county in which you're shooting. Often you can get away without one, but if you're uncertain, it's worth the expense to insure that your production won't be shut down. In order to purchase a permit, you will need insurance and you may need to hire one or more police officers, a medic, and/or a fireperson. For more information about permits, contact the film commissioner in the area where you will be shooting.

Film Stock

Most feature films are shot with 35mm color negative film, using an aspect ratio of 1.85:1 (*Angels & Insects, Benny & Joon, Dead Man Walking*). The aspect ratio refers to the relative size of the width and height of the projected image on the screen. A 1.85:1 aspect ratio means that the projected image is 1.85 times wider than it is high. Other 35mm formats include 1.33:1 (TV format), 1.66:1 (*Four Weddings and a Funeral, In the Soup, Indochine*), 1.75:1 (*Aladdin, The Pillow Book, Taxi Driver*), and 2.35:1 (*The Age of Innocence, Dances with Wolves, Scream*). The format for a film is generally selected by the director and director of photography in consultation with the producer.

A 2.35:1 format is almost always shot on 35mm film using anamorphic lenses. An anamorphic lens "squeezes" the image on the film so that everything appears to be stretched upward as in a carnival mirror; when shown in theaters an anamorphic lens is used on the projector to "unsqueeze" the image to produce a 2.35:1 image. The choice of format will be dictated in part by the way the director envisions composing the shots. A 2.35:1 aspect ratio provides a very wide image and is often appropriate for films requiring many outdoor panoramic scenes. Another consideration is the anticipated release format for a film. You would not, for example, shoot a film intended for a conventional video market using a 2.35:1 aspect ratio because the aspect ratio of a conventional television is 1.33:1.

Problems with the wide-screen formats occur when video copies are made and when the film is broadcast on television. Since the aspect ratio of conventional televisions is 1.33:1, the sides of the picture are cut off. One way of handling this problem is to transfer the film to video in a "letterbox" format, meaning that the entire width of the film is shown on the screen, but the top and bottom portions of the screen are left blank; these blank areas appear as black bars across the top and bottom of the screen, framing the wide-screen image. Another solution is a technique called "panning and scanning," which reframes portions of the film so that the action is more centered and appropriate for a television format. When the titles and credits on a film are too wide to be reframed by "panning and scanning," they are either "squeezed" in a way that stretches them upward or the letterbox technique is used for credits only, when the rest of the film is reframed. It sometimes surprises people to see a letterbox format appear during the credits, then vanish when the credits are over. The wide-screen television format of HDTV (high-definition television) will eliminate many of these problems.

Virtually all motion picture theaters throughout the world are equipped to project 35mm prints. Some of the larger theaters are also equipped to handle 70mm prints. This format was originally developed as a way to accommodate multiple sound tracks for theaters with multiple-channel sound systems. Today, using digital sound, 35mm prints can accommodate all of the necessary sound tracks. Seventy-millimeter prints are made either from 65mm original negative (*Far and Away, Little Buddha*, IMAX films) or blown up from 35mm original negative (*Independence Day, The Remains of the Day, Scream*). When a film is shot in 65mm, the entire picture area is used and printed onto the 70mm prints, which leaves room on the print for multichannel sound tracks. A film shot on 35mm stock with the intention of blowing up to 70mm often uses a format called "Super 35," which utilizes the optical sound track portion of the 35mm negative as part of the picture area. Blowing up from 35mm has become the more common choice because the price of film stock has risen dramatically. If a film is shot using 65mm original negative, the image must be reduced to make 35mm prints for distribution to theaters that are not equipped to handle 70mm prints. These are called "reduction prints."

Some films are shot using 16mm original negative (*The Brothers Mc-Mullen, Clerks, Laws of Gravity*), then blown up to 35mm for distribution. This is generally done when a producer has limited funds for production and cannot afford to shoot in 35mm. In addition to the cost savings, some other advantages of shooting in 16mm are that the equipment is lighter and more maneuverable and the running time for a given length of film is considerably longer than in 35mm. Both 16mm and 35mm film travel at the rate of twenty-four frames per second (called "sound speed"), but since a 16mm frame is smaller than a 35mm frame, the number of feet passing through the camera in a given span of time is smaller in 16mm. Sixteen-millimeter film travels at thirty-six feet per minute; 35mm film travels at ninety feet per minutes. Shooting in 16mm is especially advantageous to documentary filmmakers, who must move very quickly, often filming events on the spur of the moment.

Films shot in 16mm with the intention of blowing them up to 35mm are shot using a format called Super 16. The process is similar to shooting in Super 35 for the purpose of blowing up to 70mm. It was developed over twenty-five years ago in Sweden and utilizes standard 16mm film but exposes, in addition to the standard 16mm picture area, the optical sound track area on the edge of the film. Since this format closely approximates a 1.85:1 aspect ratio, there is effectively 40 percent more information on a Super-16mm frame than on a standard 16mm frame, and the result is significantly better.

The principal disadvantage of shooting in 16mm is that the quality of prints made from a blowup negative suffers, primarily from increased contrast and grain. The difference is less noticeable if your market is direct-to-video because the resolution of television screens is far less demanding than that of a screen in a movie theater. Another consideration is that when the blowup is made, the original 16mm negative is subjected to an optical printing process during which the danger of scratches and tears in the negative is increased. When you shoot in

16mm and blow up to 35mm, the amount you save in film stock, equipment, and lab costs will approximately equal what it will cost for the blowup, so if you have enough to pay for the blowup you will probably have enough to shoot in 35mm.

There are instances when the budget is so tight that there is no option but to shoot in 16mm, or a decision is made that the additional money needed to shoot in 35mm will be better spent elsewhere. There may also be aesthetic reasons for choosing Super 16mm over 35mm. Director Mike Figgis shot *Leaving Las Vegas* in Super 16mm because he wanted the film to have a distinctly unconventional documentary feel. In this instance, the increased contrast and grain of the blowup contributed to the gritty visual style that he was seeking.

If you do not have enough in the budget to shoot in 35mm, or to pay for the blowup to 35mm, you will be at a disadvantage when you show your film to distributors. Distributors have a built-in bias that favors 35mm films. This is partly because 16mm defines a film as low budget and partly because potential distributors will be facing the cost of the blowup. If a distribution deal is negotiated for a 16mm film, the cost of the blowup becomes a distribution expense that must be recouped before anyone sees a profit.

The bias against 16mm can sometimes be seen in the cast and crew. The size of the film may have little or no effect on the impact of the finished product, but some people are less enthusiastic about working on a 16mm film than on a "real movie." This attitude has become less prevalent over the years, first because the quality of both 16mm film and the blowup to 35mm has improved, and second because so many films shot in 16mm have broken through to become critical and box office successes.

Although there have been significant advancements in video and digital technology, one practice that appears not to be threatened is that of shooting the original picture on *film*. The quality of film is largely a matter of resolution and the way it responds to light. Most scientists and engineers believe it is unlikely that this will change for a very long time, if ever. Even films made exclusively for television viewing or video sales are, for the most part, shot on film. The advantages are considerably less significant for these films, largely because the resolution (lines per inch) in video transmission and reception is too low to take full advantage of the qualities of film, but there is still a significant enough difference to make shooting on film worthwhile.

Video companies are continually refining the medium so that it will simulate the look of film, but every year technicians look at side-by-side comparisons and conclude that only film looks like film. One reason is that film and video have different visual characteristics. Another reason is that with every technical development in video, there have been advances made in film stocks. Cinematographer Steven Poster, ASC, conducted in-depth experiments in an effort to see if video could be made to look like film. Speaking in an interview in *American Cinematographer* magazine, he said, "I am beginning to believe that making video look like film is not ultimately desirable—that these are two separate mediums and should be thought of as such. There is a need for both styles, and the two can definitely work side by side without one trying to dominate the other."

For a few films, such as Fred Baker's *White Trash,* which deals with the desperate lives of street hustlers and junkies, a hand-held video approach might be appropriate. *White Trash* was shot on Hi-8 video and blown up to 35mm for theatrical release. The release prints were fuzzy and grainy, but considering the subject matter, the look was fitting. It was referred to in one review as "toilet bowl realism." Unless there is a specific stylistic reason to shoot all or part of your movie on video, the only reason to do so is because you are so strapped for funds that you can't afford film stock and lab costs. The price you will pay, instead of dollars, will be the hard-to-market video look of your finished film.

A few films have been shot using a variety of film sizes and media, sometimes because the budget was so limited that the filmmaker had to take whatever free material was offered. David O. Russell initially planned to shoot *Spanking the Monkey* in 16mm, but shot on both 16mm and 35mm because much of his film stock was donated from productions shooting in different formats. There may also be artistic reasons for using various media. Spike Lee's *Girl 6* was shot on both 35mm film and high-definition video; all of the male callers were shot in high-definition video in order to achieve "a different look, different feel, different texture." Another example of a picture that utilizes both film and video effectively is *The Blair Witch Project,* in which two concurrent stories are told. The first story, shot on 16mm film, is a documentary-style telling of the search for the Blair Witch. The second story, shot on video, is a behind-the-scenes look at the filmmakers' experience while making the documentary.

Another possibility is to shoot on digital video using a digital camera, an increasingly popular tool for documentary filmmakers. HD video is a significant improvement over the current television standard called NTSC (National Television Standards Committee). NTSC scans 525 lines per frame and transmits a relatively square image (four units across by three units up). HD scans 1,125 lines and transmits a rectangular image (sixteen units across by nine units up, or 1.78 to 1), which is similar to the 1.85-to-1 aspect ratio of most motion pictures. The cameras are about the size of camcorders and are expected to dominate the camcorder market in the next few years. The image quality is similar to Super 16, but without the grain. The sound quality is comparable to a compact disc. One technical drawback to the digital camera is its tendency to create a wavy pattern, called a moiré effect, when panning or dollying past tightly patterned parallel lines, as in fences, bookshelves, and tiled surfaces. From the standpoint of resolution and sound, HD video is an entirely suitable medium for video releases. It is also possible to make 35mm theatrical release prints from this medium; the cost for a 35mm print is high, but this may be offset by the savings from shooting in video. Sony uses a process called EBR (electron beam recording) to convert HD video to 35mm film, and they say this produces an image that is indistinguishable from material that was originally shot on 35mm film. That is true of the medium's resolution but not of the way it responds to light. HD video still looks like video. It is, however, an ideal video medium for material shot originally on film and transferred to video.

John Alonzo, ASC, shot the miniseries "World War II: When Lions Roared" using the Sony HD system for NBC and concluded that HD is not a replacement for film, but another palette for his art form. "I was able to light more subtly, more boldly if you will. I discovered that I could play with color, play with shadow, at the monitors. I could fill Michael Caine's eyes by using my hat as a reflector." From a cinematographer's point of view, working in high-def also means adjusting to working with a crew comprised of engineers working in a truck and a colorist working with you on the stage.

HD is an option that should be weighed based on aesthetic and budgetary considerations. If you are seeking a video look for a feature film, it is the ideal medium. It is also useful in the area of special visual effects. John Alonzo believes that high-def "will probably make a big impact initially in the world of visual effects because it's a digital media and you can manipulate the image." There are systems that scan 2,000 or even 4,000 lines, which are the resolutions used for creating and manipulating special effects. The effects for the film *Independence Day* were made at 2,000 lines resolution. The resolution would have been improved if they had made them using 4,000 lines of resolution, but the schedule could not accommodate the added time necessary to resolve images at 4,000 lines. Resolution at 4,000 lines is so good that in the future a system for projecting such images onto the big screen will undoubtedly replace the need for release prints, perhaps transmitting films digitally via satellite directly into theaters around the world.

If you are seeking to make a theatrical film with a great many special effects but your budget is limited, HD may be your best bet. That was one of the primary reasons for choosing HD for the film *Rainbow,* the first theatrical feature made using that medium. *Rainbow* was directed by veteran actor Bob Hoskins and starred Hoskins and Dan Aykroyd. The script called for elaborate special effects on a limited $10 million budget. Dallas-based HD Vision, Inc., provided technical expertise while the Sony Picture High Definition Center (SPHDC) provided the video operations. According to Randall Paris Dark, president of HD Vision, "When you take the film into postproduction is when you begin to see the efficiencies of having everything on digital high-def tape." All postproduction, including visual effects, sound effects, editing, and scoring, for *Rainbow* was completed digitally.

Another decision you may be faced with is whether to shoot in black and white or color. Most films are shot in color but some, such as *Clerks* and *In the Soup,* are shot in black and white. It is cheaper to shoot in black and white but far more difficult to find distribution for your film. A few films, such as *Living in Oblivion,* successfully combine color with black and white, not because of the cost but in order achieve a specific effect. Unless there is a compelling financial or artistic argument for shooting in black and white, you're better off shooting in color.

Most film stock is purchased direct from the manufacturer, usually from Eastman Kodak or Fuji. If your budget is very tight, there is an option for the purchase of raw stock. Major studios purchase all of their film stock at the beginning of each production. If, when they finish the film, they have leftover, unopened cans of raw stock and/or partially used rolls (called "short ends"), they sell them at reduced prices to one of several film exchanges. The film exchanges, in turn, sell to producers for less than the manufacturer charges.

When manufacturing motion picture film, it is impossible to maintain quality control standards so exacting that there are no differences from one batch to the next. For this reason each batch is given a unique emulsion number that appears on the film. When film is purchased for a motion picture, it will all come from a single batch that contains a consistent emulsion number. You may have to sacrifice this consistent emulsion number when shooting with leftover stock and short ends, since your film may come from several different productions. If possible, avoid using bits and pieces from several productions with a variety of emulsion numbers; often you can find 100,000 feet or more of unopened 35mm negative with one consistent emulsion number that was left over from a single picture. It's wise to buy one can first and run a test to see if it's okay before committing yourself to the entire purchase. If you are buying stock from several productions, buy a test roll from each batch. There is no getting around the risks involved, even with a test roll; perhaps half of the stock was left sitting in the heat of direct sunlight for a week but your test happened to be run on one of the rolls that was kept refrigerated. Chances are, however, that if your test roll looks good, the rest is okay. Studios are pretty good about storing and handling raw stock. Two sources for short ends, recanned, and unopened stock in Los Angeles are Studio Film & Tape, Inc., and Film Stock Exchange, Inc., both listed in Appendix E.

How much film will your production require? A-list directors tend to shoot more film than ever before. It is not uncommon for a director shooting a studio feature to shoot 500,000 feet of film; for a film that runs 110 minutes, that is a shooting ratio of 50 to 1. Some films, such as *The Fan* and *Cutthroat Island,* shoot as much as 1.5 million feet of film, resulting in a shooting ratio of 150 to 1, though the studio would never allow that much in the initial budget.

On pictures in the $10 million range, the industry standard is 5,000 feet (fifty-six minutes of film) per day. Depending on the length of your finished film, this will result in a shooting ratio between 10 to 1 and 15 to 1. This is a statistical average and is meaningless with respect to a specific film or a specific shooting day. The ratio on many of Martin Ritt's pictures was 3 to 1. Sidney Lumet plans his pictures so well that he often shoots less than 3,000 feet a day. Generally, large action sequences requiring multiple cameras, and many setups require higher shooting ratios than "walk-and-talk" dialogue scenes. On low-budget pictures the amount of film stock will often be dictated by the amount you can afford. If you can afford to buy 20,000 feet of 35mm film for a ninety-minute movie (8,100 feet), your shooting ratio will be about 2.5 to 1. If you are shooting your film in fifteen days, you will need to ration your film carefully, shooting an average over the fifteen-day period of 1,300 feet per day. Some days you will shoot more, some less, but the total must be limited to what you can afford. Generally, the shorter the schedule, the more feet per day you will shoot. But remember that the key to maintaining both a high-quality film and a low shooting ratio is careful planning.

Additional information regarding equipment, facilities, and services can be found in several of the publications listed in Appendix E. Information about camera equipment, film stocks, formats, sizes, etc., may be found in the *American Cinematographer Manual,* also listed in Appendix E.

15

The Final Step

BY THIS TIME, YOUR SCRIPT SHOULD BE POLISHED TO A SPIT SHINE. You have completed casting, you have a full crew, a full complement of equipment, location and studio arrangements have been made, and your laboratory and sound houses are standing by to receive dailies. Any additional elements needed for production, such as props, special makeup, and animals, will be handled by the appropriate key people on your crew.

But the production is still not quite ready to begin. If a director intends to work efficiently, produce a quality picture, and stay on schedule, he or she must take time to rehearse with the cast and to review with the crew each scene in the film. Since every member of the cast and crew is responsible for a special part of the picture, each of them views the project from a somewhat narrow perspective. It is the director who must maintain a vision of the entire film, have a sense for the interworking of all the individual parts, direct each part toward a consistent goal, and communicate that goal to everyone else involved.

Prepping the Cast

In negotiating contracts with principal actors, it is to everyone's advantage to include time for rehearsals. This is an opportunity for the director, the actors, and the writer to discuss the script and, ideally, to arrive at a mutually understood purpose for each scene in the film. A number of directors refer to this as an opportunity to ensure that everyone is making the same movie. It is a chance to question the backgrounds and motivations of the characters, to play around with the scenes, and to work out a variety of approaches to blocking the action ("blocking" refers to how the actors will move during the scene). The time to iron out awkward scenes in the script is *before* beginning principal photography. Scenes reveal themselves much more clearly when spoken and/or acted than they do as written words on the page. You can usually negotiate for free rehearsal time from the actors, but bear in mind that you may need money to rent a space, feed the actors, and hire an assistant to handle logistics.

Initially, it is important, whenever possible, to assemble the cast (or as many as are available) around a table so that they may collectively read through the script from start to finish. The actors will read only their dialogue. The director, or an assigned reader, will fill in the connective tissue with descriptions of settings and nondialogue scenes such as car chases. While it is courteous to invite every member of the cast, it is important to have at the reading as many actors who have significant speaking parts in the film as are available. When not all of them can come to the reading, or if one or more of the roles are still not cast, you might hire one or two actors to fill in just for the read-through. It is helpful to employ a male actor to read the male parts and a female actor to read the female roles. Remember that this is just a reading, not a performance.

Hopefully the writer(s) will be available to attend the cast reading and, depending on the preference of the director, remain throughout rehearsals. Occasionally the writer will be an integral part of the filmmaking process throughout production and postproduction; this happens most commonly when the writer is also one of the film's producers. During the reading the writer will have an opportunity to hear scenes read aloud, actors will get a feel for the continuity of the story, and the director will get a sense for the interplay among the characters.

The second phase of rehearsal involves work on individual scenes. This may be done in any quiet room, though rehearsal on location or on the set is ideal. There are differing philosophies about how much rehearsal is helpful and how much becomes a hindrance, but generally it is a mistake to work on fine-tuning a performance this early in the game. Many actors feel that overrehearsing causes a performance to become stale. Other actors believe that no amount of rehearsal is too much. It is important for the director to remain sensitive to what works for the individuals.

Robert Zemeckis describes his rehearsal period as "more like putting the characters into therapy. We take the characters and we just break them down, talk about their past, about what they would do and how they would react. And I basically make sure that we're all making the same movie. That's how I want to end my rehearsal."

Nick Gomez spent four weeks rehearsing *Laws of Gravity,* and it shows in the actors' consistently remarkable performances. "We rehearsed like a band. As long as everything was in the right key, we kept going. If someone was off-key, I would tell them." They worked initially from the script, then began to improvise. Gomez incorporated the best of the improvised material into the final script. "By the time we were ready to shoot, the actors were the characters."

Mike Leigh, whose scripts evolve out of the rehearsal phase, spent five months rehearsing *Secrets & Lies*. "A lot of that time is living through the lives of the characters and building up this whole history, this back story." His rehearsals and improvisations continue through principal photography, though during that time he is limited to rehearsing at night and on days off.

Robert Rodriguez, working with nonactors for *El Mariachi,* did not want his performers to sound rehearsed, so he not only didn't rehearse them, he didn't even show them the script. "I would act out the scene for them, and give them their lines just before we shot the scene." Peter Marquardt, the mafioso character in the film, did not even speak the film's language (Spanish), so Rodriguez gave him lines, or parts of lines, phonetically. Since the film was shot without sound (the camera was too noisy), Rodriguez could feed the actors' lines to them from off camera while shooting the scene, then record the sound wild, after the scene was shot.

Michael Apted's reason for rehearsal is "a mixture of creativity and fear, basically. I hate the thought of being on the set with actors arguing about the scene and not knowing what they're doing, issues arising in front of the crew, and all that. I like to try and sort all that out beforehand—that's the fear element. And the creative element is that I think it's good to get people into it all."

I noted previously that it is ideal to rehearse on location or on the set. The principal value in doing so is to block the action (also known as "staging"). Scenes often come alive when the actors begin to move and use real props. Director George Roy Hill once said that getting the right script and the right cast is 75 percent of directing. When asked what the other 25 percent is, he said, "Staging it." If you stage a scene properly and have well-cast actors, the scene will often fall into place with no additional help.

The blocking of a scene should appear natural and comfortable. It should also contribute visually to the scene's purpose or statement. An example from *Butch Cassidy and the Sundance Kid,* which was directed by George Roy Hill, is a scene with Butch (Paul Newman), Sundance (Robert Redford), and Etta (Katharine Ross) in a three-way dialogue scene on the front porch of Etta's house. Etta was their mutual friend, but she was also Sundance's lover. Etta and Sundance were seated on the porch, but the director placed Butch inside the house, leaning out a window and overlooking the porch, for his part of the dialogue. With this simple blocking, the director created a visual image of the relationships among these characters. This was a far more interesting approach than seating all three on the porch and hoping that the words alone would carry the message. This is a simple example of good blocking. The problems become far more complex when there is movement or activity in the scene. Incidentally, crediting the director with the blocking of the above-mentioned scene is a reasonable assumption, but perhaps it was one of the actors, or the writer (William Goldman), or the cinematographer (Conrad Hall) who suggested it. Perhaps it evolved out of discussions among all of them, as so many of these choices do. But ultimately it was the director who recognized the value of the approach, approved it, and filmed the scene that way.

Blocking the action during rehearsal saves a great deal of time during production. It affords the director an opportunity to work things out with the actors, to make mistakes, to listen to suggestions. It also gives the actors an opportunity to practice and become comfortable with the moves, incorporating them into their overall performances, before going in front of the cameras.

It is not always possible during rehearsal to block a scene on location. The set on which you're going to film might not be built yet, or the practical location might not be available. In such cases it may be possible to bring in and arrange furniture in the rehearsal space in such a way as to approximate what the furniture will be like on the set. Sidney Lumet begins to block scenes during rehearsal by drawing diagrams on the floor of the rehearsal space that indicate the floor plan and furniture arrangements planned for the set; he uses these drawings to work out preliminary blocking patterns with the actors.

It is advantageous to include the director of photography during the latter stages of rehearsal. If you are blocking the action on location, you can discuss with the director of photography a style with which to approach lighting and photographing the action. How many setups will be required? Will you need a dolly, a crane, a tripod, or should the scene be hand-held? If you are unable to block the action on location, it will still be helpful to walk through the locations with the director of photography, describing the intended blocking pattern for each scene and how best to photograph it.

If you are unable to block a scene in advance, you will need to work it out during production. In such cases, having spent time in rehearsal with the writer and actors, defining the purpose of each scene, will prove invaluable.

Prepping the Crew

This is one of the most important responsibilities of the director. Prepping the crew reduces production problems, contributes to an efficient workforce, and boosts morale. It involves listening as much as speaking. A well-informed crew, to whom the director is available for consultation throughout the process, will work harder to contribute their talents than a crew that is expected simply to arrive on time and do a job. This attitude of treating the crew with respect and consideration should prevail throughout the making of the film.

In-depth discussions with the cinematographer, production designer, costume designer, property master, and so on, will establish a direction for the look of the film. Discourse of this kind, guided by the director, contributes to consistency and coordination. This process should begin with general discussions about style, mood, and approach, and evolve into concrete discussions concerning color, fabric, texture, props, sets, wardrobe, makeup, and lighting. Consider a scene in an intimate French restaurant. An attractive woman, dining alone, catches the eye of the maître d'. The director is looking for a warm, romantic, somewhat lonesome mood, perhaps the stylized feeling of the forties. Since the scene will be viewed from the point of view of the maître d', we will first see the woman in a long shot from across the restaurant where the maître d' is standing. Each of the specialists involved in the look of this scene will contribute to the director's goal. But in order to do so properly, they must coordinate their efforts. They must communicate closely with each other and proceed with a total understanding of how each of them will contribute to the scene. If, for example, the director asks the costume designer to create a red dress for the actress in a cocktail lounge, the production designer will know not to have the walls painted red, the set decorator will know not to use red tablecloths, and the cinematographer will not plan to put red gels over the lights.

The Production Meeting

An important part of prepping the crew is the *production meeting*. This is a gathering of the producer, director, production manager, first AD, and department heads. It is a customary courtesy to have an informal buffet catered for the meeting. The session begins with roundtable introductions, then proceeds with the first AD reviewing the entire script scene by scene. The AD will begin with scene one, state briefly what the scene is about (scripted dialogue is ignored), comment on any special requirements of the scene, and ask if anyone has questions. Most questions are asked of the director, though sometimes they are directed at various department heads. If rain is called for in a scene, the special effects person might ask the director how heavy the rain should be, or perhaps the location manager will be asked if a permit has been secured to block traffic so that rain towers can be erected on the street. This might trigger questions from the camera department regarding the necessity for tenting the camera in order to protect the camera gear from the rain. This might give rise to a conflict between the erection of rain towers and the transportation captain's intended site for parking the equipment trucks and trailers. The process continues, scene by scene, until everyone's questions are answered. Production meetings generally run three to four hours, though they can sometimes consume an entire day.

The Tech Scout

As the start of principal photography draws near, the director will walk through the sets and locations with all of the key crew members. This is called a tech scout. During the scout the director and director of photography will have an opportunity to discuss the look and lighting style for each location. The director may be looking for a particular quality, perhaps a glowing, bounced light effect. But what if the room is small with a low ceiling and there is no practical way to hide the lights for a bounced effect? The director of photography can communicate these difficulties and discuss alternatives. Perhaps the use of an imaginary off-camera light source, such as a window or table lamp, will be suggested to accomplish a similar effect.

A gaffer will immediately seek out the power source to determine how much power is available, how much cable will be required, the best route for stringing the cable, and whether or not a supplementary generator will be needed.

The key grip will consider problems of rigging in each location, and will make notes about such things as access to upper-story windows, width of hallways, and whether the floor is smooth enough, and quiet enough, for dolly moves.

A sound mixer will pay close attention to extraneous noise such as traffic, air conditioners, and airplanes. The mixer will work with the location manager to find solutions to problems (like locating the main air-conditioning on-off switch) or will inform the director of potential difficulties.

In this way, each key crew member will have an opportunity to make constructive suggestions for improving each scene. Each will also have an opportunity to express any problems they foresee in achieving the director's goals, and to make arrangements for any needed special equipment and/or any special logistical demands at each location.

Ideally, a tech scout will include the director, producer, and all key department heads: production manager, first AD, director of photography, gaffer, key grip, production designer, sound mixer, location manager, transportation captain, special effects and stunt coordinators. Representatives from these departments are not always necessary, nor are they always available. Sometimes it is necessary to schedule more than one scout in order to accommodate those who should be included. At a minimum, the scout should include the director, first assistant director, director of photography, gaffer, key grip, production designer, and location manager.

Occasionally during the tech scout someone will point out an unresolvable problem with a location that hadn't been previously considered, in which case the location manager will set about finding an alternate site. Whatever the outcome of the tech scout, the information gained will make a tremendous difference in the efficiency of your production, and to the cooperative atmosphere on the set. This trickles down through all levels of the various departments and is always felt by the actors. Performances are improved when actors are on a comfortable, efficient set, free from the frustrations and stress caused by inadequate planning and poor communication.

The information gained during the tech scout is invaluable for the director. It makes it possible to plan scenes more thoroughly, and to make any necessary alterations or compromises *before* beginning principal photography. Further, should the director decide to go ahead with a plan in spite of certain problems it creates for the crew, everyone will know ahead of time what they're getting into and what compromises they will have to live with. In short, there will be a minimum of surprises.

It is imperative that the director be flexible, both to take advantage of unexpected opportunities and to remain on schedule and budget, but flexibility is not an excuse for poor planning. One difference between experienced and inexperienced directors is their ability to plan. Inexperienced directors often go on a tech scout and describe how they intend to shoot a scene. Based on this, the production designer creates the look and design of the environment. Before shooting begins, the lighting crew arrives early to pre-rig the set. But when it comes time to shoot the scene, the director changes his or her mind, and everyone sits around waiting for the lighting crew to re-rig. The irony is that in most cases, the director's second approach will not improve the film in any meaningful way. Conversely, if the director is able to plan thoroughly, not only will the crews be able to do some advance rigging, but the production designer in some cases will be able to save money by painting and dressing only those areas of the set that the director knows in advance will be seen by the camera. Savings of this kind can be significant.

Storyboarding

One of the best ways for a director to organize thoughts and to communicate them to the crew is by means of a storyboard. This is a multiple-paneled pictorial representation of the film similar to a comic book. A detailed storyboard will have a separate panel for each camera setup and possibly several panels to indicate camera movements. If the camera dollies in from a long shot to a close-up in a single take, the storyboard may indicate this with two panels—one for the long-shot starting position and another for the close-up ending position. A detailed storyboard may also include color coordination and styles for costumes, sets, and props. Like everything, storyboards are subject to interpretation, but they can provide a solid basis for understanding complex visual concepts.

Robert Zemeckis uses storyboards when he needs to communicate visual ideas to several departments. "Basically, storyboards for me involve action sequences and special effects because that's where you must interpret visual ideas to second unit directors, to special effects men, to stuntmen. But I never have an artist spend hours storyboarding a scene between two actors in a room because it's just me and the cameraman that have to sort that out on the day."

There are computer programs designed specifically for the purpose of storyboarding films. They come with an array of drawing tools; a library of characters, props, and locations; frame sequencing capabilities; and text tools for adding captions. These programs are useful not only for professional artists but also for people with limited drawing abilities. An excellent resource for additional information about these programs is the Writers' Computer Store, listed in Appendix E.

A less elaborate but often satisfactory way for a director to organize camera setups is by means of a floor plan. It is common for the production designer to supply the director with floor plans of various sets and locations drawn to scale. The director can use these to sketch the position of furniture, props, the movement of the cast, the position(s) of the camera, the way the camera will move, and the order in which setups will be shot. It may also be useful to list and describe the camera setups on a separate page. This is referred to as a "shot list." The order in which these shots are listed is extremely important and is discussed in Part 3, "Production."

Production

16

Directing

Interpretation and Style

DURING PRODUCTION, THE PRINCIPAL ARTISTIC FORCE BEHIND A film is the director. Just as every director's life experience is unique, so is every director's work unique. But what makes certain directors consistently stand out in the crowd? The answer encompasses two parts: interpretation and style.

The former is a result of the unique life experience and genetic makeup of the individual. Interpretation comes alive in the director's mind when reading the script. The more the director reads and studies the script, the more a personal interpretation develops into an overall vision of the film. It is important to remember that since every director's interpretation is based on his or her unique life experiences, every director's interpretation is valid. There is, however, an invalid use of style, but this will be discussed later.

What is important initially is that the director has a sense for what the film should "feel" like, in other words, a cinematic interpretation of the material that works for the director on a personal level. If, after studying a screenplay and speaking in depth with the writer, this doesn't develop, the director has probably got the wrong screenplay. Robert Zemeckis envisioned a strong cinematic interpretation of *Forrest Gump* right from the beginning. "I visualized the movie as I was reading it the first time. I knew the screenplay was talking to me." The director must also understand the purpose of each scene. It may not be immediately apparent how to accomplish each purpose, but that's another problem. And it leads us to a discussion of style.

When I talk about "style," I am not referring to flashy stylistic techniques used to create a strong visceral experience for the audience and to cover lackluster stories. *New York Times* media columnist Bernard Weintraub said about the makers of megabudget special effects movies like *Independence Day, Twister,* and *Volcano,* "As gifted as these directors are, their skills are essentially a triumph of style over substance." When I talk about style, I am talking about the way a director uses the tools of a filmmaker to tell the story. If a style calls attention to itself, or distracts from the story, it fails. When it adds something, it succeeds. Examples of successful cinematic styles include the gritty and often crude camera work used in *Crumb;* the long, static master shots in *Sling Blade;* the lyrical images in *Enchanted April;* the kinetic frenzy created by the camera in *Trainspotting;* the dark, brooding light and constant rainfall in *Se7en.* When considering an involvement with an independent film, John Pierson says that he looks for a unique style in the work of the filmmaker. This, in combination with a strong story and characters, will more than compensate for a scarcity of dollars.

Style is the way a director translates his or her interpretation into a motion picture. It is the application and manipulation of the tools and elements that turn words on paper into the images and sounds of a movie. These include actors, words, movement, locations, color, makeup, sound effects, music, camera, lenses, light, film stock, editing, visual effects, and stunts. How a director applies a knowledge of these resources will depend on the individual's interpretation, but the more a director understands about the elements that make up a film, the more stylistic choices will be available.

Sydney Pollack, who has been called an actor's director, once said, "It's very enjoyable for me to get into the technical end of it all. I like to understand everything about how the teeth and claws work inside the camera, about the operation of the sound equipment, and I have the same curiosity concerning sets and wardrobe. I like to get into the details."

The style a director chooses will be dictated by the director's personal interpretation. Consider this scene: "A girl on a horse silhouetted against an ominous sky." If the purpose of the scene is to make the audience nervous or uncomfortable, the director may choose a staccato style, handling the scene in quick cuts back and forth between the girl and the sky, each cut moving closer to the girl's face. The director may add the neighing of the horse, a howling wind, and a background percussion track reminiscent of a quickened heart. This will result in a nervous sequence—an effective translation of the director's interpretation.

Another director may want the scene to feel tumultuous, chaotic. An appropriate style would be a hand-held camera circling the girl and horse as the horse frets and bolts. The director may add a fully orchestrated score with strings and horns that build to a crescendo as the horse suddenly bolts and lightning cracks the sky.

Another stylistic interpretation might be a strange sense of calm. The sky could be a metaphor for an intense power building in the girl. The director may choose a more lyrical style, perhaps a floating camera that gently drifts closer to the girl, settling on her fixed gaze at the darkened sky. As the first drops of rain strike the girl's face, she smiles, drops back her head, and opens her mouth to taste the rain.

It could be that a director has a "feel" for the scene but isn't certain how to achieve it on film. A number of approaches may be tried, playing with the scene, working with the girl, perhaps improvising, until the feeling begins to gel. Whatever style the director elects to use, it should both complement the overall style of the movie and support the purpose of the scene. Clearly this can only be accomplished if the director has a clear understanding not only of the film, but also of the purpose of each scene.

No scene in a film is identical to any other scene in any other film. Two scenes might be very similar, but they are never identical. Consequently, a director must evaluate each scene as a new experience. The director must develop a strong personal interpretation of the screenplay and must act on his or her convictions. This takes courage. One must avoid falling back on a formula approach simply because it's safe. A conventional approach is valid only when it effectively communicates your interpretation. Likewise, one must never use technique simply to advertise one's knowledge. An original approach is also valid only if it effectively communicates your interpretation. It is often a temptation to use a new technique simply because it's new, even if it doesn't quite fit the material. Approach each and every scene with a single-minded determination to arrive at a style that best communicates your interpretation of the story.

I believe that anyone interested in directing can learn to become a good director. Everyone can interpret the words of a screenplay in terms of his or her life experience and certainly can learn all of the techniques involved in filmmaking. But the question still remains: What makes some directors stand out as consistently great directors? Miles Davis answered this question with an excellent analogy to music. "The difference between a fair musician and a good musician is that a good musician can play anything he thinks. The difference between a good musician and a great musician is what he thinks."

Organization and Communication

The efficiency of the cast and crew during production is more closely coupled to the operation of the director than anyone else. A director must not only conceive an artistically effective approach to each scene in the film, but he or she must also organize and clearly communicate those concepts to the cast and crew. If they don't receive this information, if they don't have an understanding of what the director is after in a scene, they flounder, groping around for some direction for their work.

All too often a director will have a brilliant concept but will lack the ability to communicate it clearly. Eventually, with enough tenacity, the director may succeed, but not without a good deal of frustration and wasted time along the way. This section describes an efficient way for a director to approach any scene in any location and to communicate this approach to the cast and crew. The following is intended only as a guideline from which a director will often deviate. However, such a guideline, as a jumping-off point, can be of tremendous value to every director when planning and organizing an approach to production. For directors working within tight budget limitations, it is absolutely essential.

Prior to beginning production, the director has spent time with the cast, ironing out any difficulties in the script and in some instances blocking the action. The actors, in turn, have incorporated whatever blocking has been determined into their preparation for each scene. The director will also have spent time with the crew during the production meeting and during the tech scout, and will have discussed the work of all department heads, and their approaches to handling various scenes, one on one with those heads.

It may sound obvious that a director arriving on the set, ready to begin principal photography, should have a plan. Not all directors do. Those who take the time in advance to think through how to approach various scenes in the film will probably make a better film. They will certainly make a less expensive film. Sometimes this planning results in a shot list, either on paper or in the director's mind. Other times it will entail creating a detailed pictorial storyboard. In addition to the plan, it is essential that the director maintain a sense of improvisation and flexibility, for the following reasons: First, because filmmaking is a collaborative venture and nothing will end up exactly as it appears in the director's mind. Second, a better plan may emerge at the last minute; a cast or crew member might suggest an improvement in the dialogue, the blocking, or in the placement of the camera. Third, if the picture falls behind schedule, the director must have enough flexibility to alter plans in order to compensate for the loss of time. Also, if the director has planned well in advance and gets ahead of schedule, the cast and crew will be able to move quickly to take advantage of the available time.

Regardless of the extent of the planning, the director's first responsibility on the set is to communicate to the crew what will take place in whatever scene they are about to film. The best way to do this is to bring in the actors prior to their makeup and wardrobe calls and walk through the scene. This is not an attempt to polish the performance but rather to demonstrate the blocking and pacing to the crew. If the blocking has not been established in advance, it will be worked out now, while the crew waits in the wings. Once the blocking is set, the crew will watch a "stop-start" rehearsal, which means that the director and certain crew members may ask the actors to freeze in the middle of the scene so that technical problems can be resolved. During this rehearsal, a camera assistant will mark the actors' positions on the floor with tape or chalk; these will be used by the focus puller during the take. Assuming the actors hit their marks during filming, they will remain in focus. The director of photography and gaffer will know how to arrange the lighting specifically for the action. No one will walk into darkness unexpectedly and no one will wash out because they're too close to a light. The camera operator and camera assistants will know where to place the camera and approximately what movements will be required. The key grip will know which part of the floor will need to be smoothed and leveled, or where to lay track, for a dolly move. The boom operator will determine the ideal place to stand in order to reach the action without causing microphone shadows. The sound mixer will know in advance if the actors will be walking out of range of the boom operator and will place additional microphones to accommodate such moves. In short, there will be no surprises. Without this preliminary information, the crew would, at best, roughly approximate the setup. There would be a good deal of guesswork and, when the actors arrived on the set, the crew would take a considerable amount of time adjusting their work to accommodate the action.

A rehearsal of this kind is advantageous to the cast as well. It familiarizes the actors with the environment of the fully dressed set, so as they review the scene in their minds during makeup and wardrobe, they will be thinking about it in the context of the specific environment in which they will be performing.

The actors on a film set are referred to as the "first team." They will be watched during this "stop-start" rehearsal by stand-ins known as the "second team." The second team will "stand in" for the actors and be used as a guide for the crew after the actors are sent into makeup and wardrobe. The cinematographer will light the scene using the second team. The camera operator may use the second team to work out problems with the camera movement. All of this will be fine-tuned when the first team arrives on the set in full makeup and wardrobe, ready to shoot the scene. Because so much work is done using members of the second team, it is important that they are approximately the same build as the first-team actors; it also helps if they wear clothing that is similar in color to the actors' costumes.

Once the final blocking for a scene is set, the director and cinematographer should have a clear idea of how many setups will be required to cover it (a setup is simply a new camera position and usually requires some modification in the lighting). The order in which these setups are shot is extremely important. The most efficient ordering of shots is from largest to smallest. The reasons for starting with the largest shot are as follows: First, the largest shot establishes an overall look, or lighting pattern, for the scene. As you move in for closer shots, the basic look will already be established and the director of photography and gaffer won't have to worry about maintaining a sense of continuity to the lighting. If you begin with the close-ups and get progressively larger, the crew will have to relight for each shot, adding light after light. When you finally get to the longest shot, you'll be lucky if anyone remembers exactly what the close-ups looked like. The continuity of the lighting will therefore suffer. Second, the largest shot is usually the most time-consuming lighting job. If you can get it out of the way at the start, the lighting crew has only to make small adjustments for closer shots. In this way the crew can work with maximum efficiency as you progress from shot to shot.

Starting with the largest shot is also an advantage for the actors. The largest shot is usually the master shot and contains a complete performance. By starting with the master shot, the actors go through the entire scene prior to shooting any medium shots or close-ups, which may be just parts of the whole scene. In this way, when shooting closer shots, they have an immediate recollection of the context of each part of the scene. Consequently, their performance in each of their close-ups will be more in keeping with their performance in the master shot, and they will be better able to maintain a sense of continuity throughout their performances. Close-ups are also the most critical for an actor's performance since they will be so closely scrutinized on the screen; starting with long shots gives the actors a chance to "find the scene" and work up to the more critical demands of closer shots.

The method described herein provides a useful guide, a springboard, for thinking about any scene, at any time, in any location. In situations where this approach can be directly applied, it will prove efficient and economical. There are a multitude of considerations beyond this, however, and each scene must be approached in the manner most appropriate for that scene.

17

The Production Process

Priorities: Taking Care of Your People

THE FIRST THING THAT HAPPENS ON EVERY DAY OF EVERY PRODUC-
tion is the serving of breakfast to the cast and crew. On most productions, that is the responsibility of the catering service. At the very least,
on small-budget pictures, it means serving coffee and doughnuts. I've
never been on a set where this courtesy was overlooked, but I have seen
a production assistant arrive late with the goods. Two things happened:
First, the crew began work disgruntled. Second, when the coffee and
doughnuts finally arrived, the crew took a break from work. I'm making
a point of this in order to stress the importance of treating the cast and
crew well. It is a primary responsibility of the producer to ensure that
people are well looked after. The details of executing this responsibility
often fall on the production manager or production assistants, but in the
eyes of the cast and crew, it is the producer who is ultimately responsible for their well-being.

Taking care of your people obviously includes such things as maintaining clean rest rooms and comfortable changing facilities for the cast,
but the most obvious way to express concern for everyone's well-being
is through the quality of the food. Crew members often relate their experiences on various pictures in terms of the food more than any other
aspect of the production. One key grip, when asked if he recalled a production he had worked on in Montana, replied, "Yeah, we called it the
peanut-butter-sandwich shoot." He said it without smiling.

Some big-budget productions, aware of the importance of food as a
way to communicate respect for the cast and crew, carry this idea to another extreme. They allow enough money in the budget to have rich,
gourmet meals, complete with champagne, catered daily to the cast and
crew. That's not the most effective way to keep the cast and crew working efficiently throughout the day. In fact, these crews are noticeably
sluggish in the afternoon. Serving champagne lunches goes beyond the
point of diminishing returns.

Neither extreme—peanut butter sandwiches or champagne lunches—
will result in an efficient workforce. Lunches should be wholesome, hot

meals with a variety of beverages. They should be served with silver-ware, not plastic forks. There should be a comfortable place for people to sit during the meal. Don't expect anyone to sit on the floor. Grass, maybe, but not the floor. There should always be plenty of food for second and third helpings. There should be a selection of desserts to top off the meal. Use a catering service that appreciates the importance of appearance. Half the battle is over if your caterer makes the meal attractive and serves it with style.

Any special diet requests, such as vegetarian or salt-free meals, should be respected. The needs of such individuals should be as well served as those of the rest of the cast and crew. Occasionally, such a person may prefer not to eat from the catering truck. If so, that person should be given a cash allotment equivalent to the catered-meal allotment.

The First Assistant Director

In the same sense that the production manager runs the logistics of the production from the front office, the first assistant director runs the production on the set. The first AD is the conduit of information from the director to the crew and is responsible for the crew's efficient execution of the director's plan. Once the director has reviewed a plan of attack with the key crew members for a particular location, and once the crew has witnessed the blocking of the action for that location, it is up to the first AD, working with one or more assistants, to keep the cast and crew informed and working efficiently. The first AD is also responsible for every member of the cast and crew being in the right place at the right time. Activities will be organized so that everyone will be prepared for each shot at approximately the same time. The first AD must therefore schedule actors in makeup and wardrobe so as to ensure that the cast is fully costumed and out of Makeup in time for the first shot. This is not always a popular position. When the whip needs to be cracked, it is the first AD who does the cracking.

Although it may cost more to hire a top-notch first AD, a producer usually saves money by doing so. In a sense, the producer is buying insurance that the production will run smoothly, that all of the actors and crew members will remain on schedule, that the various production teams will be properly informed about all aspects of the shoot, and that the activities on the set will proceed quickly and efficiently. An assistant director who fails in any of these areas will cost the producer a great deal of money in delayed production time.

On low-budget films, the role of the first assistant director is no less significant than it is on a big-budget studio picture. The day-by-day expenses may be lower than on a studio picture, but the margin for error is smaller as well. Low-budget films, perhaps even more than major features, must be executed with clockwork-like precision. Without an experienced first assistant director, such precision is virtually impossible to achieve.

Occasionally, on ultra-low-budget films, one person will function as both production manager and first assistant director. It is extremely difficult for one person to function effectively in both capacities simultaneously. The producer may find it less expensive to hire one person instead of two, but neither position will receive the attention it deserves, and the overall production will suffer accordingly.

The first AD is aided by the second AD. It is usually the second AD who handles the paperwork and legwork. Since both the first and second ADs are intimately involved with the daily scheduling and operation of the cast and crew, both must have a thorough knowledge of the regulations of all guilds and unions governing the production.

Another function of the first AD, and sometimes the second AD, is the directing of extras and/or crowds. There are SAG rules that restrict a director's freedom to speak with extras, so most of that information is communicated from the director to the AD, who then relays it to the extras. Often the first or second AD will coordinate the initial staging of the extras, and then make adjustments at the request of the director.

The Call Sheet

Call sheets are made up for each day of the production by the first AD and approved by the production manager. They are usually prepared using a software program designed for that purpose, printed out, and distributed to the cast and crew each evening for the next day's work. They contain the following information: the scenes to be shot; the location(s) for the day's shooting; which cast members will be required for the day; the time each member of the cast and crew is expected to arrive (call time); any special requirements for the day such as stunt coordinators or special effects equipment; additional information such as weather forecast, time of sunrise and sunset, crew parking location, and all necessary contact information. On the back of the call sheet there is often a detailed listing of crew members and their individual call times. A sample call sheet is shown in Table 10.

TABLE 10   **Call Sheet**

Date:	Director:		Shoot Day:	of
Title:	First AD:	Phone:	Sunrise:	Sunset:
Company: Phone:	Second AD:	Phone:	Weather:	
Producer:	UPM:		Crew Parking	

SET DESCRIPTION	SCENES	CAST	D/N	PAGES	LOCATION

CAST & DAY PLAYERS	CHARACTER	M/U CALL	SET CALL	REMARKS

ATMOSPHERE & STAND-INS	NOTES AND SPECIAL INSTRUCTIONS

ADVANCE SCHEDULE					
DATE	SET DESCRIPTION	SCENES	CAST	D/N	PAGES	LOCATION

Production Reports

Daily and weekly production reports give a detailed accounting of the production status. They will include information about which scenes have been shot, how many pages those scenes cover, anticipated and actual amount of film stock used, hours each person worked, and so on. They are prepared by the UPM and distributed to the producer, director, production company, bond company, and others for whom the information is pertinent. If daily hot costs are tallied separately, they will include the five major variables when shooting a motion picture: shooting hours, film, extras, added crew, and unanticipated expenses. A sample daily production report is shown in Table 11.

Script Changes During Production

Once a script has been financed for production, revisions will usually continue. These will be the result of many factors, including changes in cast, location, and weather; budget considerations; artistic considerations; rehearsals; and an increasing understanding of the material on the part of the writer and director as the film progresses.

Once a production staff is involved, scenes are numbered, and those numbers are used and referenced by every department throughout production and postproduction (a new scene number is added in the script whenever the action changes location and/or time). Once a number is assigned to a scene, it must remain with that scene. Added scenes will therefore be given a number-letter combination. For example, if two scenes are inserted between scenes 19 and 20, they will be numbered 19A and 19B. If scene 66 is deleted, there will be a notation in the script between scenes 65 and 67 that says "66 omitted." It is standard to maintain consistent page numbers in the same manner, adding A & B pages rather than renumbering and reprinting the entire script.

In order to make it easy for everyone involved in the production to identify script changes readily, each new set of changes will be printed on a unique color of paper and each of these pages will be dated. The standard order of colors for script changes following the initial printing in white is: blue, pink, yellow, green, and goldenrod. A script that contains colored pages is referred to as a "rainbow" script. A further tool that helps everyone keep track of changes is called "X-change notation." This involves adding an X or an asterisk in the right-hand margin of the page to indicate where changes have been made. For example, if a single word in a side of dialogue (a "side" is a block of spoken text) is

TABLE 11   **Daily Production Report**

DATE:	1st Unit	2nd Unit	Travel	Holiday	Retakes	Rehearse	TOTAL	Day of Week:	
# Days Scheduled:								Weather:	
# of Days Actual:								On Schedule:	
Producer:				Director:				Behind:	Days
Exec. Producer:				Date Started:				Ahead:	Days
				Sched. Finish Date:				Crew Call:	
Shooting Day #:				Est. Finish Date:				Shooting Call:	
Sets:				Locations:				First Shot:	
								Lunch:	
								First Shot:	
								Dinner:	
								1st Shot:	
								Camera Wrap:	
								Crew Wrap:	
								Last Man Out:	

	Scenes	Pages		Minutes	Setups	Film Received		Film Stock	Film Stock
Script			Previous			Previous			
Taken Previous			Today			Rec'd Today			
Taken Today			Total			Rec'd Total			
Total to Date			Scenes:						
To Be Taken									

NOTES:

Film & Sound		Film Stock #					Film Stock #					Sound	
	Gross	Print	No Print	Waste	Ends	Gross	Print	No Print	Waste	Ends	DAT	1/4" Rolls	
Previous													
Today													
Total													

WORKED-W HOLD-H REHEARSAL-R STARTED-S TEST-T TRAVEL-Tr FINISHED-F		P A R T	W S R T	H F T Tr	M/U Call	Set Call	N D B	1st Meal		2nd Meal		Set Dismiss	M/U Dismiss	Stunt Adj.	Mileage	N O T E
CAST	CHARACTER							Out	In	Out	In					

ATMOSPHERE & STAND-INS

Number	Rate	Adjust to	O.T.	Allowances	Number	Rate	Adjust to	O.T.	Allowances

Assistant Directors: Production Manager:

modified, an X or asterisk would appear in the right-hand margin of the script opposite the line that contains that revised word. If six or more lines on a single page have been modified, the X-change may appear simply as a single X or asterisk beside the page number. When cast and crew members receive rainbow pages (they are handed out immediately to all cast members and department heads), they will insert the pages into their scripts and scan them for the location of the X-changes. If a prop is changed from a "teddy bear" to a "stuffed horse," the prop department will be able to find the change at a glance.

Occasionally, there isn't time to publish new pages with X-change notations. Actors on the set, for example, are sometimes required to speak lines they have never before seen and that they are not improvising. For example, if a scripted speech refers to a weather condition, like snow, that is not in evidence at the time the scene is being filmed, the dialogue will have to be modified in order to match the weather. Most actors will readily accommodate such necessary changes, but when a script is being rewritten routinely at the last minute and lines are continually being handed to actors just before filming, you can expect a mutiny.

The Actors in Makeup

The makeup artist can have a tremendous influence on an actor's performance. Makeup is the actor's last stop prior to going before the cameras. The better an actor feels, the more relaxed and confident, the better will be the performance. A good makeup artist understands this. In addition to a competent makeup job, a responsible makeup artist will contribute to the actors' morale and self-esteem. In order to do this, the makeup artist must feel appreciated and well cared for by the producer. Make sure that the makeup room, or trailer, is a comfortable environment to work in. Ideally, it should be a quiet place with a large sink, a large mirror, and plenty of light. Allow adequate time for the artist to do a careful job. Your efforts will evidence themselves in the quality of the makeup and in the attitude of your actors on the set.

The First Take

When the actors come out of Makeup, the crew will have completed preparations for the first shot. The actors will rehearse the scene again, now in full makeup and wardrobe, so that the crew can fine-tune their equipment. There is usually a noticeable difference in the actors when they are in full costume and makeup. The scene often becomes "real" for the first time. It may be that only one or two walk-throughs are necessary before shooting the first take. While the actors are walking through their final rehearsals, the director of photography is fine-tuning the lights, double-checking exposure, and making last-minute adjustments. The boom operator is rehearsing mike movement, and the sound mixer is adjusting levels on the recorder. The camera operator, camera assistant, and dolly grip are practicing their moves as the actors walk through the scene. In short, everyone works together to fine-tune their special areas of responsibility.

When the director feels that the actors and crew are ready, it is time to go for a take. At this point there is grave danger of the performance becoming stale if it is overrehearsed. There is a certain magic that takes over when the cameras roll, and especially when they roll for the first take. Steven Spielberg has said that he considers this magic important enough to print the first take (see "The Dailies" below for a discussion on printed takes) of every scene regardless of any problems there may have been during that take.

When everything is ready to roll, the first assistant director calls for quiet on the set, then orders, "Roll sound, roll camera." The director then calls, "Action." If the director doesn't call "Cut" before the end of the scene, the take may be good. On the other hand, the dolly might have hit a bump, or the sound mixer might have picked up a car honking in the distance, or the camera assistant might have missed a focus mark, or . . . With all of the possibilities for error, it's amazing it ever goes smoothly—even with all the specialists at work. If there are problems with the first take, shoot a second take, and a third, and a fourth, and so on until it's right. Then move on to the next setup.

A director may choose to print several takes of a given scene. Perhaps there were two or three variations in a performance and the director would like the option of choosing from among them in the cutting room. Perhaps the first half of one take was good and the second half of another was good. Perhaps the camera operator or an actor will request another take. There are many valid reasons for shooting and printing several takes. As a director, the important thing is to know what you want and to be decisive about moving on when you've got it. Knowing what you're after in a scene and knowing how to communicate it is a large part of directing; knowing when you've got it is the rest.

It is wise to schedule a simple shot as the first thing you shoot on the first day, one that you will undoubtedly be able to print on the first or second take, such as an actor sitting by a fountain or entering a building. If you print the first take and move on, you are sending a message to the crew that the first take matters, that you aren't going to shoot more than one take unless it's necessary. This helps to keep everyone on their toes.

I stressed earlier the importance of rehearsing a shot for the crew before they begin preparations for the shot. It is important to continue this process for *each setup* within a scene. The reason for this is to communicate precisely which portion of the scene will take place during the shot, and specifically how it will be filmed. It may be that only a very small segment of the scene will be covered by a particular setup and the crew will move much more efficiently if they limit their work to covering only that segment.

Follow this process, beginning with your largest setup and working down to the smallest setup until you've completed the scene. Then move on to the next scene and begin the process again. The last setup of each day is referred to as "the martini." Continue this process for each scene on each day in the schedule until you've finished the film and reached the final martini.

Slates

A slate is a small board with a clap stick across the top. Printed on the slate is information about the film and the scene about to be shot. The permanent information includes the name of the film, the director, and the director of photography. There is a box for the scene number, which changes whenever a setup for a scene is completed. For scene six you might have five setups, which would result in the following scene numbers: 6A, 6B, 6C, 6D, 6E. Another box indicates the take number. If scene 6D was shot five times, the last information on the slate for that setup would read SCENE 6D, TAKE 5.

At the start of every take, the clapper is opened and snapped shut. This provides a visual and audio reference that will be used later to put the sound track in sync with the picture. There are electronic slates that use time code in conjunction with the clap stick. Electronic slates were originally designed for music playback but have been improved for use with live-action filming. The slate shows visual time-code information that originates in a recorder equipped with a time-code generator. The numerical time-code value is recorded on the sound track as it is being filmed by the camera. This system has nothing to do with keeping the film and sound in sync during a take; it has only to do with facilitating the syncing in postproduction of the sound and picture at the point when the clapper sticks come together. The person syncing the dailies reads the time-code numbers on the clapper at the point when the sticks come together, then types the time code into a machine that causes the tape to zip down to that point in the recording. This is called "auto assembly." It is not an entirely precise system, so the sync must be fine-tuned by aligning the audible sound of the clap with the frame of picture that shows the clap sticks coming together. The material is then considered "locked" in sync. If the fine-tuning is ignored or treated casually, which it sometimes is, the sound tracks may be slightly out of sync, in which case they will cause problems throughout postproduction.

It is sometimes impractical or undesirable for a camera assistant to hold out a slate for clapping at the beginning of a take. Examples include scenes in which access to the front of the camera is unavailable, as with a scene where the shot begins with the camera positioned over the edge of a cliff; scenes involving animals that might be startled by the clap; and scenes that require an extra degree of concentration and sensitivity on the part of the actors. In such cases the clap will be done at the end of the take, and the slate will be held *upside down* to indicate visually that this is a tail slate. Just prior to clapping the slate, the camera assistant will announce "Tail sticks" so that this information is recorded on the sound track.

Pickups

Most people involved in film production are perfectionists, and directors are no exception. Budget and time limitations, however, make achieving perfection almost impossible. Most filmmaking is a series of compromises in which you do the best you can. This is especially true on a low- or medium-budget picture with a tight shooting schedule.

Sometimes it isn't important to work for perfection throughout a single take. If you're shooting a long master shot for a dialogue scene, for example, it may not be necessary to shoot it over and over until it's perfect, or even acceptable, from start to finish in a single take. Suppose you've shot the scene three times and you're pleased with the first half of the scene in all three takes, but not with the second half. Instead of starting from the top on take four, you can shoot a "pickup" beginning with the middle of the scene and running to the end. In other words, concentrate on shooting the portion of the scene that's giving you trouble. Perhaps you'll get a pickup take of the last half of the scene in which everything works except one line. You can shoot another pickup of just that one line, over and over, until it's right. It's helpful to tell the script supervisor which part of which take is acceptable immediately after the take. In this way, you won't lose track of what you've got and where it is. You also won't become confused about which pickups you need, and you won't shoot unnecessary takes.

One important consideration when shooting pickups is the effect this may have on the actors; if you break a scene into too many bits and pieces it will be difficult for the actors to maintain a sense of continuity in the performance.

In the finished film, you can't cut from one take directly to another take from the same camera position without suffering a jump in the action. Consequently, in order to utilize your pickups, you must shoot "coverage." This consists of medium shots, over-the-shoulder shots, reverse angles, close-ups, and cutaways, which can be used to cover the jump and/or pace the scene. A simple example: A man and a woman walking along the beach at water's edge. The master shot shows them walking toward the camera. The camera dollies back, keeping them both in frame. In take 1, only the first half of their dialogue is acceptable. In take 2, only the second half is acceptable. In the finished film you can't cut directly from take 1 to take 2 without causing a jump in the action. In order to make this cut, the director must shoot coverage such as a point-of-view shot (a hand-held shot that shows what the couple sees as they walk down the beach). In the finished film, the audience will see the couple in take 1 for the first half of the dialogue. The scene will then cut to the point-of-view shot, and when it cuts back to the couple for the remainder of their dialogue, the audience will be watching take 2. The jump from take 1 to take 2 will be covered by the shot of the couple's point of view. Pickups can be helpful when shooting any long takes, whether they're master shots or close-ups, but make sure they're covered with reverse angles, reaction shots, cutaways, and the like.

Contrary to what many people believe, a master shot is not necessarily one in which you see all of the actors in the frame throughout the scene, and it isn't necessarily static. A master is a shot that covers the complete scene from beginning to end. Sometimes a master will incorporate panning and/or dollying from one actor to another as the scene unfolds. Another misconception is that long-running masters are the mark of a low-budget film. The opening shot in *The Player,* directed by Robert Altman, is one of the longest-running masters in film history, and it was touted as the most effective and entertaining scene in the film. The reason people consider long-running masters the mark of a low-budget film is not because of their length or because they are a relatively inexpensive way to shoot a scene; it is because, in the hands of inexperienced directors, they are often visually boring. This is not because of their running time. It is because they are poorly executed and contain none of the pacing, either in the performance or in the movement of the camera, necessary to make them invisible to the audience. Woody Allen, speaking about the confidence he's gained over the years, said, "I practically never, *ever* shoot any coverage anymore. I work fast and rely a lot on very long masters. I shoot them because I have more confidence developed and I don't have to protect myself so much as I did when I started."

An experienced director will often know when a scene plays well from start to finish in a master, but if you're uncertain, it's wise to shoot coverage, simply as a form of insurance. This allows you the option in the editing room of selecting portions from different takes, and of manipulating the pacing of the scene if it doesn't play well in the context of the finished film. Unless you have the option of accelerating the pace in the editing room, perhaps even shortening the scene, you may be stuck with a dull scene, and you'll curse yourself for not having taken a few extra minutes during production to shoot some protection.

Production Sound

In addition to recording a clean, full dialogue track, the sound mixer must also record *room tone, production sound effects,* and *wild lines.* Room tone is the ambient, background sound of each location. Each location will have a unique tone. It will be used to fill any holes in the dialogue tracks and to smooth out differences in level and equalization between voices in the final mix.

Production sound effects are sound effects the mixer records during a take, often for scenes in which there is no dialogue. Sound effects recorded for these scenes may be used in the finished picture or used as a guide track for the sound effects editor during postproduction. In addition to sync sound effects, the mixer will record wild sound effects that can be cut to match the picture during the editing. Examples of sound effects that may be recorded wild are footsteps, dog barks, shattering glass, body hits, tire squeals, and gunshots. Sound effects recorded during production are often more effective and more economical than effects created during postproduction or taken from a library of stock sound effects.

Wild lines are short words or phrases such as "Halt," "Let's go," or "Good day," which are often recorded "wild" (that is, off camera) when the quality of the sync recording is questionable. They are easy to sync manually with the picture during postproduction (Robert Rodriguez, knowing that he would not have the necessary equipment to shoot sync sound for *El Mariachi,* wrote dialogue in short, terse phrases that would be relatively easy to record wild after each shot, and later put them into sync with the picture). Also, if a character in a film such as a skier or a bank robber wears a mask, that person's lines will often be rerecorded wild after the sync take for better intelligibility. Wild lines must also be recorded for off-camera dialogue, such as a character's rambling thoughts in a dream sequence in which we don't see the actor speaking. Often these lines can be recorded during production, saving time and money in postproduction.

If possible, sound should be recorded during every take, even if there are no dialogue and no specific sound effects in evidence. A person's POV of a mountain lake is a good example. A lake doesn't make any noise, but there is ambient sound, and the ambience will be heard and will contribute to the effectiveness of the shot. This will be most noticeable when screening dailies. A lack of sound is unsettling and distracting when viewing dailies. There is also a high probability that the ambience will be useful in the final cut. Exceptions include insert shots and cutaways that are shot on the fly and might be slowed down if sound is rolling and everyone on the set is required to cease work and remain silent during the take; second-unit work for such things as drive-bys and establishing shots, which generally do not necessitate the expense of a sound crew; and shots for which the ambient noise is inappropriate and distracting, such as the POV shot of the lake if there is an unseen construction crew working nearby with a jackhammer. Shots that are made without sound are called "MOS"; according to Hollywood lore, this stems from a German filmmaker who referred to these shots as "'mit' out sound."

The Dailies (Also Called "Rushes")

When shooting in 16mm, it is standard to print every take; when shooting in 35mm, in order to avoid the expense of printing unwanted takes, the laboratory will print selectively. At the end of each take, the director will decide whether the take is worth printing. The selected takes will be circled on the script supervisor's copy of the screenplay, on the camera reports, and on the sound reports. Selected takes are also referred to as "circled takes." In the following sample camera and sound reports (Table 12), the selected takes are scene 77: takes 1, 4, and 5; scene 77A: take 1; scene 78: takes 1 and 3; and scene 61: takes 1, 6, and 7.

At the end of each day, a production assistant will send the exposed film and a copy of the camera reports to the laboratory, and the one-quarter-inch tapes, or DAT cassettes, and a copy of the sound reports to the sound house. During the night the lab will process the film. If the film is gong to be edited on a digital editing machine, both picture and sound will be transferred to a video or digital medium in a process called "telecine." Simultaneously, and depending on the needs of the

TABLE 12   **Sample Camera and Sound Reports**

Camera Report

Date ____ Title _____
Company_____
Director _____
Cameraperson _____
Magazine 3 _____
Roll no. 16 _____
35mm color   16mm color
35mm B & W   16mm B & W
Emulsion 5247 _____
Remarks _____

Print circled takes only:

Scene no.	Takes 1/5	2/6	3/7	4/8	Remarks
77	①	2	3	④	Ext. Day
	⑤				
77A	①				Ext. Day
78	①	2	③		Ext. Day
61	①	2	3	4	Night effect
	5	⑥	⑦		

Good footage 383 _____
N.G. footage 51 _____
Waste footage 17 _____
Total footage 400

Sound Report

Date ____ Title _____
Company_____
Producer _____
Director _____
Mixer _____
Boom Person _____
Recordist_____
Recorder no. __ Mike no. __
Remarks _____
_____

Print circled takes only:

Scene no.	Take no.	Footage	Remarks
77	①		Sync
	2		
	3		
	④		
	⑤		
77A	①		
78	①		
	2		
	③		
61	①		
	2		
	3		
	4		
	5		
	⑥		
	⑦		

End of roll

production, the telecine machine may also transfer the picture and synchronized sound onto master source tapes in a video format such as one-inch, D2, or Beta SP, as well as onto one or more three-quarter-inch, Hi-8, and/or one-half-inch video formats.

Dailies for films that are going to be released in a theatrical format should ideally be viewed on the big screen. Flaws that are neither apparent nor consequential on video, such as a wide shot that is marginally out of focus or a flaw in an actor's makeup, might not be evident in a video format but be glaringly apparent on the big screen. The sooner the director knows about such problems, the more options will be available to remedy them. Directors shooting films exclusively for video or television distribution can safely view dailies on three-quarter-inch or Hi-8 video. Viewing dailies on anything with a lesser resolution, such as one-half-inch video (VHS) cassettes, or on a digital editing machine, is dangerous, since flaws that may be apparent in the final product can go unnoticed at these lower resolutions.

Producers of low-budget independent films have to consider the cost of printing film dailies. It may be that the money is better spent another way. As mentioned earlier, at least consider printing a small portion of your dailies on film, perhaps only the first interior and exterior sequences, in order to ensure that the camera equipment is functioning properly. After that you will have to screen dailies on video and rely on daily reports from the lab. Lab technicians view all the dailies, but without sound and at high speed, so only the most obvious visual flaws, such as a hair in the gate or a defective lens, will be noticed.

If you are making a film work print, either because you are cutting on film or because you intend to conform the work print to match the digitally edited picture for screening purposes, the lab will strike a positive work print, called a "daily," of the director's selected takes. Generally this will be a "one-light" print, meaning that it is made without extensive scene-to-scene color and density corrections known as "timing." A timed print is more expensive and involves the manipulation of several lights that control color balance and density. Timed prints are often ordered for specific scenes when a one-light print of those scenes raises questions about the color balance and/or exposure. Another reason for ordering a timed print is if you are experimenting with a particular visual effect, for example, an emphasis on a color such as red or blue for a surreal dream sequence.

If you are editing on film, the sound house will transfer the production recordings from the selected takes onto sprocketed magnetic tracks. This is called a "sound daily." The magnetic stock used for a 16mm magnetic track is completely coated with magnetic oxide; 35mm magnetic stock for sound dailies is coated with two stripes of oxide and is referred to as "edit stripe." The sound from the original one-quarter-inch or DAT recording will be transferred onto the wider of the two stripes. The narrow stripe is called a "balance stripe," since its purpose is to balance the thickness of the stock at both edges. If one edge were thicker than the other, the stock would have a tendency to "cone" as it's being wound onto a core or reel.

If your budget permits viewing dailies on film, an assistant editor will sync the dailies when they are returned from the lab, usually the next day, lining up the sound track with the picture for an interlock screening that evening. This is accomplished by matching the picture and sound of the clap stick closing at the beginning or end of each take. As described in Chapter 13, one of several sync signal systems will be used to ensure that both picture and sound run continuously at the same speed, so when the picture and sound of the clap stick are in sync, the rest of the take will be in sync as well.

After checking to make certain that each scene is in sync, the assistant editor working with film media will send the picture and sound track to be coded. Coding is the process of printing numbers, called "ink numbers" or "code numbers," on the edge of the picture at one-foot intervals. Identical numbers will be printed at identical intervals on the corresponding sound track. These numbers will be used as a sync reference when the picture and sound tracks are cut. In addition to syncing the dailies, the assistant editor will log each take, listing the scene and take number, the camera-roll number, the ink numbers at the beginning and end of each take, the print-through edge numbers, called "key numbers" (see Chapter 21), at the beginning and end of each take, and a brief description of each shot. A sample of this log sheet can be found in Table 13.

If you are editing digitally, the print-through edge numbers, as well as the code numbers and camera-roll numbers, will be added to a file during the telecine process, and that file will be inputted into the digital editing machine. The machine will then keep track of these numbers as the film is being cut. Ink numbers and/or key numbers will be used by assistant editors when conforming a work print to match the digital edit; ink numbers are preferable, primarily because they are larger and easier to read than key numbers. As the picture is being cut, the digital editing machine will generate a "cut list" that defines each edit by ink number and/or key number. This "cut list" is the guide that the assistant editors will use to conform the work print. The key numbers can be used as a backup in the event that there is a question about an edit based on the

TABLE 13	Sample Editing Log			

Company —————— Page number——————
Title —————— Camera roll no. ——————
Producer —————— Edge no. prefix——————
Director—————— Lab roll no. ——————
Editor —————— Order no. ——————

Code number	Key number	Sc/Tk	Description	Remarks
BD0003–040	D9x36072–109	17–1	Ms Jack in garage, Rx to Mary enters	
BD0041–086	36110–155	17–2	Same	
BD0087–103	36156–172	17A–1	Cu Mary enters garage	
BD0104–125	36173–194	17A–4	Same (slower)	Tail slate
BD0126–173	36195–242	62–1	Ms Jack in garage, gets in car, exits	
BD0174–271	36243–340	62A–1	Ls ext. garage, car exits, drives off	
BD0272–362	36341–431	62A–6	Same (better traffic)	
BD0363–387	36432–456	62B–1	Cu electric garage door device (open and close)	MOS

code number cut list. When the picture is locked, meaning that the editing is finished, the digital editing machine will generate a "negative cut list" that contains key numbers and camera-roll numbers but not ink numbers; this list will be used by the negative cutter to conform the original negative to the digitally edited film.

If you are shooting in close proximity to your lab and sound house, each day's shooting will be synced and ready for screening, either on film or video, the following evening. The first day's dailies will be screened on the second night of production, and a new set of dailies will be ready for screening every night thereafter. Deviations in this schedule occur when the production goes on distant location (it will take time to ship material to and from the lab) or switches to a nighttime shooting schedule, or when the laboratory has difficulties such as a telecine or printer breakdown. One advantage to screening dailies as quickly as possible is that if, for any reason, a scene doesn't work, it can usually be reshot with minimum effort. Even if you've moved to a different location, you may be able to rewrite the scene to fit the new location, or to fit a different location that you can work into your schedule. The sooner you know you've got a problem, the more flexibility you will have in solving it.

For the director, dailies are an opportunity to determine how the actors' performances and character interpretations translate to the screen, and how effectively the director is communicating with the production team. Dailies provide the director not only with an opportunity to judge the quality of the material, but also to begin selecting specific takes to be used in the final film. If an editor is assembling the film during production, which is the usual case, the director and editor can discuss specific ideas for cutting.

For the crew, dailies offer an opportunity to evaluate their specific areas of responsibility. The director of photography and gaffer will judge their approach to lighting and, equally important, whether the camera gear is functioning properly. The sound mixer will judge not only the original recordings, but also the quality of the transfers. The makeup artist may improve the approach to certain actors' makeup based on information gleaned from the dailies. The script supervisor will double-check continuity within each scene. In short, everyone stands to learn from the dailies and improve his or her work on the film.

Dailies are also a terrific morale booster. Film almost always looks good in daily form, sometimes deceptively so. Francis Ford Coppola once said, "A finished film never looks as good as the dailies." The daily screenings are a time for congratulations and a pat on the back for everyone. It's exciting and gratifying to sit in a screening room and

watch the previous day's work. It's usually verification that everyone
has done a good job.

The same is often true of the actors, but there is a difference. Actors
are not sitting back objectively watching their work; they are watching
themselves. For some actors this is constructive, but for others it is not.
Should an actor not like a performance in a particular scene, or an interpretation of a character, or the lighting, or the makeup, he or she may
suddenly want something changed partway through the film. Many actors are so concerned about how they look that a hair out of place or a
visible wrinkle might send them into a panic. It may be that a scene out
of context and unedited will strike a wrong note with the actor. Their
trust in the director may decline. The actor may become timid and unwilling to take chances. That same scene in the context of the finished
film, completely edited, may work magnificently, but it is often difficult
for an actor to judge a scene out of context. In a sense, it requires reading the director's mind. In his book, *Making Movies,* Sidney Lumet
says, "Looking at rushes is very, very difficult. Not many people know
how to do it or what to look for. Sometimes a take has been printed because I want one tiny moment from it. But I'm the only one who knows
that." For these reasons directors sometimes request that the cast not be
permitted to view dailies. This is often sound policy and not necessarily
a reflection on the director's sense of security about his or her work.
Many actors have no wish to see dailies, but others feel so strongly
about seeing them that they have a clause in their contract that gives
them the right to screen dailies whether the director wants them to or
not. Depending on the actor, that may be a plus. Hopefully it will contribute to his or her faith in the director and in the movie everyone is
striving to make.

Sound Decisions

Before closing this chapter, I would like to offer a few additional
thoughts about sound. Film is essentially a visual medium, and many
times it will be to the advantage of the film to compromise sound for the
sake of improving the picture, for instance, requiring the boom operator
to stand in an awkward spot in order not to interfere with the lights.

However, I have witnessed many production crews working according to an unspoken, unbendable law: "Picture at the expense of sound."
When there is a compromise to be made, the automatic assumption is
that sound comes second. I recall a scene in a florist shop in which the
air-conditioning unit on the roof created sound problems. The sound
mixer was unable to turn the unit off, so he began fastening green sound

blankets to the ceiling in order to dampen the air-conditioning noise. He had hung about three blankets when the gaffer came over and said, "You can't do that. I need the white ceiling to bounce light. Those blankets will make the lighting appear green and everyone in the scene will look sick." His assumption was that lighting took precedence over sound and that a compromise was out of the question. Fortunately, the director was more open-minded. He called the gaffer back and explained that the sound quality was important for the scene. He asked the gaffer at least to consider achieving the same lighting effect in another way, or possibly reach a compromise with the sound mixer. The minute the director opened up the possibility of an alternate solution, the gaffer had the answer. The sound mixer could put up his green sound blankets but the grips would hang a white silk cloth beneath them. The sound from the air conditioner would be dampened and the gaffer could bounce light off the white silk. This was a perfect solution without compromising either sound or picture. The gaffer had all the necessary information to solve the problem from the beginning, but his immediate assumption was "Picture at the expense of sound." It simply hadn't occurred to him to offer a compromise or an alternative.

Another problem production mixers are faced with is that many producers and directors don't know much about sound. They judge a production mixer's work in the dailies, and if it doesn't sound like a finished movie, the naive assumption is that something's wrong. A production mixer's track shouldn't sound like a finished movie. In a finished movie, the postproduction mixers take great pains to carefully equalize, filter, and otherwise adjust the production tracks for the optimum balance of sound throughout the film. What the production mixer should strive for is the cleanest, fullest track possible in order to give the postproduction mixers maximum flexibility in the final mix (see Chapter 20). It is in the final mix that the rerecording engineers carefully listen to the entire complement of sound, equalizing and balancing each track to its fullest potential. The problem is that some production mixers, knowing that their work will be evaluated in the dailies, equalize and filter the original recordings to give the impression of better sound in the dailies. Ultimately, this restricts the flexibility of the postproduction mixers, and the sound track in the finished film suffers.

When hiring a sound mixer, stress the importance of recording for the final mix, not for the dailies. If the sound mixer knows that you understand this problem, he or she will respond accordingly and you will have a better original track to work with in the final mix.

Postproduction

Introduction

POSTPRODUCTION BEGINS WITH THE EDITING OF THE PICTURE AND production sound tracks and ends with the printing of the first trial composite answer print. This is the first color-corrected print with a complete sound track. The principal steps that lead to the first trial print are picture editing, dialogue editing, sound effects editing, music scoring, music editing, the sound mix, titles and optical effects, the optical (and sometimes digital) sound track, negative cutting, and printing.

Digital editing for both picture and sound is becoming the standard in the industry, but film editing techniques are referenced throughout this chapter for three reasons. First, because film editing is still very much in use. Second, because film editing concepts are applicable to all media. Third, because many low-budget independent films cannot afford the cost of electronic editing systems.

During postproduction, independent filmmakers often have more time than money. Their films are sometimes cut on weekends and evenings over a period of months or even years. A studio picture usually has very little time and plenty of money. Twenty weeks is a normal post schedule for a studio film, but that number is shrinking all the time. *Assassins* was scheduled for an unprecedented six-week run through post to its theatrical release date. One reason for this is because digital editing systems appear to make the process go more quickly, and studios are anxious to move their pictures into theaters. In some ways digital systems do make things go more quickly, but directors and editors share a common problem: Editing isn't done by the numbers, and no matter how fast one can manipulate the material, the creative process still takes time. Director Richard Donner (*Assassins, Conspiracy Theory, Lethal Weapon*) says that he still gets the important revelation in the tenth week of postproduction, not any earlier, simply because it's digital. Editor Thelma Schoonmaker (*Kundun, GoodFellas, Raging Bull*) shares a similar sentiment: "Unfortunately, everyone got this idea that it was going to make it faster, so they've shortened and shortened [the schedule] and there's this terrible tendency to put four editors, six editors on a movie. *Heat* had four editors; *The Fugitive* had six. It makes it ten to twenty percent quicker in terms of manipulating the footage, but the time is in the creative work."

One reason studios spend incredible sums of money in overtime and other costs in order to rush a film through postproduction is because there is so much money tied up in a studio film. The quicker the studio gets the film finished, the quicker it gets a return on the investment; if there are loans involved, with interest and penalties, the incentive is even greater. For the independent filmmaker, unless you are saddled with costly editing equipment rental charges, time may be your most valuable commodity during postproduction.

18

Picture Editing

The Picture Editor

WHEN BUILDING A HOUSE, A CONSTRUCTION ENGINEER BEGINS WITH a blueprint and basic raw materials such as wood, nails, bricks, and glass. A good construction engineer will make the most out of whatever material is provided but can't miraculously turn wire and straw into a Tudor mansion. At best, wire and straw can be turned into a very good straw house. Like the construction engineer, a good film editor will make the most out of whatever material is provided, but there the similarity ends. A construction engineer can't work miracles, but a good editor often can.

I said earlier that a film often looks deceptively good in the dailies. This is because there is no story in the dailies; they are fragmented bits and pieces of random scenes. Any scene that is technically well executed will look good in the dailies. The problem for the editor is to make the most of each scene within the context of the story. That is the primary function of the editor: *to tell the story.* Technical expertise, such as matching cuts and making smooth transitions, is an assumed ability for any editor. Novice editors put tremendous emphasis on technical perfection. The best editors will throw technique out the window in favor of telling the story.

The work of editors like Stu Linder (*Quiz Show*; *Rain Man*; *Good Morning, Vietnam*), Christopher Tellefsen (*The People vs. Larry Flynt, Kids, Smoke*), and Thelma Schoonmaker transcends technique. Their editing is geared exclusively to telling the story, not to advertising their flawless cutting ability. If the pacing of the story is improved by a cut that doesn't quite match, they will suffer the imperfect cut in favor of the story. A strong, well-told story can withstand technical flaws from top to bottom, but a weak or poorly told story, no matter how technically well edited, will always be weak. An editor must think story first, technique second.

Thelma Schoonmaker describes the process as "trying to get a rhythm for the film, a flow, a structure [so that] the whole movie gets a shape." This concept is extremely important for anyone hiring an editor for a feature film. It is dangerous to hire a feature editor on the basis of a sample reel that contains only isolated scenes. It is difficult enough to judge an editor's work without knowing what raw materials were available to start with; certainly the Academy Award for best editor would be more fairly judged if the voters could screen the dailies that were available for each picture prior to editing. But assuming that an editor's sample reel contains random cuts from good raw material, the only judgment you will be able to make is whether that person is competent to make technically good cuts and smooth transitions. You may also be able to judge an editor's ability to pace an isolated scene or two, but this can be terribly misleading. An isolated scene that appears well cut and well paced in the sample reel may be ineffective in the context of the finished film. Likewise, a scene out of context that appears awkward, perhaps jarring, may be an excellent deliberate statement about a character or situation in the finished film.

Editors who can effectively execute isolated scenes are not hard to find. What matters is an editor's ability to pace a feature film in such a way as to draw an audience in at the beginning, hold them, and let them go at the end, emotionally satisfied but wanting more. Occasionally, this ability will exhibit itself in a dramatic short, but it is best if you can screen an entire feature.

Look for a style in an editor's work that is appropriate for your picture. Is there dramatic tension evident in the work? Or suspense? Or is there evidence of a sensitivity to comedy? Comedy almost more than any other genre is dependent on pacing and timing, which are determined in the cutting room. Does the editor's sensitivity mesh with that of the director? How does the editor feel about the script? These are all questions to ask when searching for the best editor for your project. But first and foremost is finding an editor who thinks in terms of *story*.

The Assistant Editor

Once you have selected an editor, it is wise to let the editor select the assistant, providing the salary demands of the assistant fall within the limitations of your budget. This is an area of the postproduction budget to which close attention should be paid. A good editor will insist on a competent, experienced assistant, and they are costly. However, an assistant who takes care of organizational details and frees the editor to concentrate on cutting the film is, from a budgetary standpoint, a producer's luxury.

Producers of low-budget films sometimes make the mistake of hiring an untrained assistant editor in order to save money, but this is a mistake that inevitably costs money. An assistant who requires on-the-job training not only chews up the editor's valuable time but also breaks the flow of the editor's concentration on the picture. A mistake by an untrained, inexperienced, or careless assistant can easily waste hours and sometimes days. If you are cutting on film and an assistant editor misfiles a trim that the editor subsequently requests, the assistant may spend hours searching for the trim. During this time, the editor will have to reorganize the cutting bench in order to move on to another scene, leaving the previous scene unfinished. Often a misfiled trim is never found, and the entire shot must be reprinted, synced, coded, and given to the editor for inclusion in the film—several days later. It often makes sense to hire an untrained *apprentice* editor who can relieve the assistant of such tasks as running errands and rewinding reels of film. Apprentice editors are less expensive and usually less experienced than assistant editors. Often the assistant can teach an untrained apprentice the basic procedures in the cutting room during postproduction without interfering with the editor's schedule.

The assistant editor's contribution varies depending on the editing system being used. In addition to the responsibilities described in the previous chapter, an assistant *film* editor must maintain throughout postproduction the organization of the editor's leftover footage (trims and outs of both film and sound tracks) from every scene in the film. At any given time the assistant should be able to locate quickly any section of film or sound the editor requests. In addition, the assistant must communicate with the laboratory, optical house, and sound facility when ordering reprints, opticals, supplies, and other necessary items.

For a picture that is being cut *digitally,* the assistant editor's job is quite different. In fact, no job has been more modified by the transition to digital media than that of the assistant editor. Some of today's highly qualified assistant editors for digital systems have never held a roll of film, never handled a plastic core, a split reel, or a tape splicer, all of which are everyday indispensable tools for assistant editors working with film.

The digital assistant editor's duties include transferring the telecine copy of the picture and sound to the digital editing machine; making backup copies of the cut material as a protection in the event that the machine crashes; maintaining all paperwork; communicating with the lab, sound, and special effects houses; and assisting the editor in the operation and maintenance of the machine. One of the primary responsibilities of an assistant editor working in a digital medium is troubleshooting, if and when the editor runs into technical problems with the system. There are various frame rates, sync problems, EDLs, time code, pull-up and pull-down references, speed conversions, and other technical issues that make these systems complex. It is very easy to make mistakes, and without a well-trained assistant editor they are inevitable and costly. You may have dialogue that's out of sync or a picture that drifts; it is not uncommon for postproduction mixers to perform audio "gear boxing," in which elements running at different rates are brought back into sync.

It used to be that a relatively untrained person could come out of college, or be related to someone, and start out working in the cutting room. In today's digital world, that is no longer true. Two-time Academy Award–winning mixer Bill Varney (*The Black Stallion, The Empire Strikes Back, Grease, Ordinary People, Raiders of the Lost Ark, Twilight Zone: The Movie*), currently working as vice president of sound operations for Universal Studios, admits that "our industry was built on nepotism, plain and simple, that's the way it was. You either knew someone or were related to someone and you moved on. That's not going to work anymore. The people who are going to emerge and keep the economies of this going are going to be very sharp technical people."

An assistant who is not technically proficient and fully familiar with the system, or who is not conversant enough to discuss difficulties and resolve problems with the technical advisers from the company that makes the system, can easily damage the digital material. One way for editorial personnel to minimize these problems and to facilitate resolving them when they arise is to connect to a user group for whichever system you're using. These are available for virtually all digital editing systems and have proved invaluable for persons who have taken advantage of them.

An exception to the statement that an assistant editor working in a digital medium needs no film experience is when a film work print has been struck from a picture that is being cut digitally. If that's the case, a film work print will be conformed to match the edited digital material for projection on a big screen. The assistant and/or apprentice editor(s) will cut the film to match the electronic digital edits so that the film can be viewed using film media on a big screen periodically as it is being cut, and during the final mix. Since electronic edits are done so much faster than the cut-and-splice technique used for film, the assistant editor is in a constant scramble to keep up. Making a film work print and paying assistant editors to chase the editor's cuts in this way is expensive and in many cases cost prohibitive. When it is not practical to do so, be prepared for subtle flaws that may not become apparent until screening a first trial print of the entire picture on the big screen. For example, if you have screened your picture only in a video format, you may realize for the first time that a shot is marginally out of focus.

Union versus Non-Union

When an IA producer settles on one or more potential editors (generally based on credits and word-of-mouth reputation), the next step will be to contact the guild for the most updated information regarding the editors' availability. Assuming that the producer's choices are available, the guild will supply the producer either with contact information for the editors or, in order to maintain the confidentiality of its members, will often contact the editors directly and give them the producer's name and phone number. It's then up to the editor to follow through. The guild maintains a partial list of members' credits and will supply this information to signatory producers. A complete list of credits may be obtained directly from the editor, from the editor's agent, or in some cases from film databases found on the Internet.

All IA editorial personnel belong to the Motion Picture Editor's Guild (it used to be called the Motion Picture *Film* Editor's Guild). The address and phone number of this guild, as well as minimum working conditions and wage scales, may be found in several of the publications listed in Appendix E.

If you are making an IA union picture, you must hire and retain a union-affiliated editorial staff from the first day of principal photography through completion of the final dub. The final dub is one of the last steps in the editorial postproduction process (see Chapter 20). The minimum editorial staff for an IA feature includes one editor and one assistant editor. There is no limit to the number of editorial personnel a producer may hire, as long as there is at least one assistant for each editor. On a major feature with a rushed postproduction schedule, half a dozen editors is not uncommon. On such pictures, a producer might have as many as fifteen people—editors, assistants, and apprentices—working simultaneously.

If your picture is non-union, you must hire either a non-union editor or an IA editor who is willing to moonlight. There is no structured organization for non-union editorial personnel. The best way to locate and evaluate them is, first, by screening non-union films and compiling a list of potential editors. Second, contact the producers and/or directors of those films and ask their opinion of the editor's talent and temperament. The producer and/or director of a particular film can often be reached through the production company that made the film or through the distribution company that released it.

Most producers and directors are happy to recommend people with whom they have had a good experience and will undoubtedly put you in touch with such people either by giving you their phone number or by contacting them on your behalf and asking them (assuming they are interested and available) to contact you.

Other ways to locate editorial personnel for non-union films are through recommendations by key members of your production crew such as the production manager and director of photography, and by placing ads in trade publications. You can also ask both union and non-union editors whose work you admire, but who are unavailable for your production, for recommendations.

Equipment and Facilities

One advantage that film editing has over digital editing is that film-editing equipment is relatively inexpensive to rent. Sometimes you can get a break on a digital system if you limit your use of the equipment to odd hours, such as at night and on weekends. Also, whether you're cutting on film or digitally, some editors have their own facilities and equipment; it is worth discussing a package deal with these editors since it is to their advantage to keep their equipment in operation. Clearly, you will need to consult with your editor to determine which systems he or she is accustomed to using. Christy's Editorial Film & Video Supply, listed in Appendix E, is an excellent resource for rentals, sales, and service of editing equipment for everything from 8mm film to digital nonlinear systems.

Unless you hire an editor who has a cutting room or you plan to set up shop in your home, you will also need to budget for the cost of renting an editing room. These are available at postproduction facilities, many of which are listed in the production guides found in Appendix E.

The Director's Role

The overall vision of the film belongs to the director, and it is ultimately that person's responsibility to ensure that the editing reflects his or her interpretation of the screenplay. Writer-director Woody Allen believes that "editing a film is making the film as much as shooting it or writing it is." Filmmaker Henry Jaglom goes even farther when he says, "Shooting the movie is like a rough draft for me; the cutting room is where I really write the movie." An editor is essential to the execution of the director's vision of the film, but a good director takes responsibility for the character of the cut.

An editor's skill will be severely restricted without a clear, open line of communication with the director. If they have worked together in the past, chances are that they will have developed a mutual respect and will communicate successfully. If not, the communication channels should be established before the cutting begins. The director must not only know what he or she is after, but also must be able to communicate that vision to the editor. The director must also be willing to listen. If a director begins working with an editor who is simply on a different wavelength, unable to comprehend and execute the director's vision of the film, the editor should be replaced. On the other hand, from the editor's point of view, there is nothing more frustrating than working with an indecisive director, trying a multitude of random combinations, hoping that one will strike a desirable note.

Probably the most difficult yet important quality for a director to maintain during postproduction is objectivity. A director working with an editor is able to view the film from a greater distance and with more objectivity than a director who attempts to cut the film on his or her own. For example, a director may be biased toward including a particular shot or sequence simply because it was excruciatingly difficult and expensive to accomplish, but the editor will carry no such bias into the cutting room.

The manner in which a director and editor work together depends on the director's relationship with the editor, the budget, the schedule, and the preferred working style of both director and editor. Some directors avoid the cutting room, while others continually stare over the editor's shoulder, commenting on every cut. Some directors will turn their picture over to the editor as it is being shot without so much as a word of discussion until production is finished and the editor completes the first cut. Others won't allow a single cut to be made until production is finished and they have had several weeks or months to decide how they would like to begin. A few filmmakers function successfully without an editor; among them is John Sayles, whose credit on *Lone Star* reads "Written, directed, and edited by . . .". There are many variations on these approaches, and no single book can cover the entire spectrum. The next section, however, does describe an efficient approach to the entire process of postproduction. A literal application of these procedures may not fit for you and your project, but it can serve as a guide for organizing a postproduction process that best fits your needs.

From Dailies to Fine-Cut

The process begins on the second night of production during the screening of the first day's dailies. The director and editor sit together in a screening room and discuss the material. Logistics of production sometimes dictate that these discussions take place over the phone. The director explains his or her intentions for each scene to the editor and selects favored takes. The following day, the editor will begin to assemble the film. This process continues throughout production. Editors will often travel to the location in order to screen dailies with the director and begin the first cut with the director close at hand.

A good editor will be able to keep pace with most directors' shooting schedules. Given a shooting ratio of approximately 10:1, it is reasonable to expect a finished first cut (sometimes called an assembly) within a week of completing principal photography. It may be three hours long, but it will all be there, roughed in with selected takes from start to finish.

During the days following principal photography, as the editor is completing the first cut, the director may go on vacation—to Hawaii, Singapore, South America, anywhere to get away. There are two advantages to this: First, the director will need to recuperate physically from the rigors of production. William Goldman once said about directing, "It's hard. I don't mean hard like it was hard for Van Gogh to fill a canvas or Kant to construct a universe. I mean hard like coal mining. Directing a film is one of the most brutally difficult occupations imaginable." At the end of production, a rest is in order. The second advantage to a hiatus for the director before viewing the first cut is to get some distance from the film, to gain some objectively. Remember that if the director cares about the film (and the good ones care desperately), he or she has been living with it seven days a week, eighteen hours a day, for several months and in some cases years and, of course, is biased in terms of the thoughts that developed during that time. It is impossible to erase this bias, but a week at the beach can contribute immeasurably to a director's objectivity when viewing the editor's cut.

This screening will be the initial opportunity to view the entire film uninterrupted, watching each scene in the context of the surrounding scenes. For the first time there will be a sense of continuity in the film. It is important for the producer to screen the editor's cut because it will contain all of the sequences and scenes the director shot, as opposed to some that may be eliminated subsequently during the director's cut. This is not the time for the producer to become involved in the editing, but when the director's cut is eventually screened for the producer, it is important that he or she is aware of what material is available, including any that the director chose not to use.

When cutting on *film,* it is best to view the completed film in an interlock screening room with changeovers. This is a screening room equipped with two projectors and two sound dubbers so that the projectionist doesn't need to stop and rethread between reels. Stopping between reels, as on a flatbed editing machine, can so disrupt the continuity of the film as to make judgments about pacing and story structure practically impossible.

When cutting on a *digital* editing machine, you can run the film directly on the machine or you can make a video copy and run it in a facility with a large monitor or with video projection capabilities. The quality of the video image will not be as sharp as film, but if you are editing digitally and saving money by not making a work print, it is your best option.

Now begins the work that will result in the "director's cut." Based on the screening of the editor's first assembly, the director will propose changes. The editor will undoubtedly offer additional suggestions. Scenes will be moved around, shortened, lengthened, added, and deleted. The first pass of the director's cut will undoubtedly run long, but it will be shorter than the editor's assembly. If the film is running short at this point, you may need to shoot additional footage, otherwise you will be faced with the problem of having to "pad" the film by extending scenes and slowing down the pace.

It is helpful to screen the work periodically during the editing process. When the editor's cut is nearing completion, invite an audience of perhaps ten or more people to a screening. The kind of audience you invite will greatly affect the value of this screening. What you will need most is objectivity, so invite an objective audience—ideally, people who know nothing about your film, nothing about making films, and nothing about you. The important thing to remember about screening for audiences is this: The degree to which you will achieve objectivity is directly proportional to the objectivity of your audience.

You are not necessarily looking to this objective audience for comments. Your film will run overlong; depending on the editing system, the picture will be viewed on a television monitor or will be a film work print (the film will be dirty, scratched, and spliced). Titles and opticals will be incomplete. You may choose to add some temporary sound effects and music. If you are cutting on film, this will mean making a temp dub in a mixing studio (see Chapter 20). For cost-saving reasons, as well as the increasing quality of digital images and sound, film is being used less and less for the preview process. One of the great advantages of working on a digital editing system is that you can make temp dubs right on the editing machine, adding and mixing dialogue, music, and sound effects.

The problem with previews of this kind is the audience expectation; the farther you remove the audience from the final theatrical experience you are working toward, the more limited will be their ability to judge the potential of the finished product. At this point, nobody except the director and sometimes the editor is in a position to fill in all the blanks. Consequently, any critical comments from the audience may have little or no meaning. Most of what you want from the audience you will glean simply by being in the room with them during the screening. What happens is a sort of magic, and until you've experienced it yourself, you will not truly understand it. You will see the film through the eyes of the audience. If your audience is comprised of cameramen, you will pay undue attention to the photography. If you screen for directors and editors, you will see the film through their biased eyes, with an emphasis on the details of techniques. But if you screen for an audience of nonfilm people who know nothing about your film, they will be essentially unbiased. The degree to which a director can achieve objectivity in this environment is truly remarkable. The director is in the unique position of simultaneously seeing the film through the eyes of an unbiased audience and of filling in all of the missing blanks. What will be seen, in the mind's eye of the director, is the polished picture with titles, opticals, and a fully mixed sound track. And it will be seen through the unbiased eyes of an audience.

Francis Ford Coppola concluded his statement "A finished film never looks as good as the dailies" with "or as bad as the first cut." If you listen to critical comments from the audience, your objectivity may be dampened as well as your spirits. All the audience sees is an incomplete skeleton of your film. Their comments will reflect this, and the words will often be painful to hear. However, in some cases, they may offer insights into problem areas. Audience comments must be carefully evaluated. Chances are that they will be vague, something like, "The ending didn't work." The audience probably won't be able to tell you why; they will simply know that for them it didn't work. It may be that a missing element such as music or an optical effect will solve the problem. Or it may be that some small change must be made clear back in reel one in order for the ending to satisfy the audience. The audience is by no means dictating the final cut. Rather, they are bringing potential problem areas to your attention. At this point it is up to you, as the director, to solve the problems.

From a practical point of view, gathering a group of totally unbiased people for your audience is difficult. When you can't succeed entirely, do the best you can. The closer you get to this ideal, the better will be your judgment of the film. Again: The degree to which a director will achieve objectivity is directly proportional to the objectivity of the audience.

Based on your experience screening with an audience, you will gain insights into how to modify and improve the picture. So it's back to the editing room for revisions. Then another audience screening. With each screening, bring in a new audience. You don't want people who are biased by the previous cut. Their view of the film will be far from objective. Continue this process of recutting and screening until your picture gels into a cohesive, well-paced structure close to your targeted final running time. Bear in mind that I'm not talking about the picture necessarily gelling at this point into a cohesive structure for the audience. It's still unfinished, with many pieces missing, and it may still be a while before it plays well for an audience. But when it gels for you while viewing the picture with an unbiased audience, filling in the missing pieces in your mind, you will know you're close to a final cut. From this point on, the picture will probably require nothing but fine-tuning. You may or may not choose to screen the film for another audience; it depends on how certain you feel about your final cut.

Once the director's cut is finished, it will be screened for the producer. Discussions, suggestions, and changes may follow this screening. Last, the film will be screened for the production company, if there is one, that financed the film. Again, discussions, suggestions, and changes may follow. One difference between independent films and many studio films is that often a director's contract with a studio is for services through the completion of the director's cut; at that point the director leaves the picture and the producer takes over. Rarely will a director of an independent film leave a picture until postproduction is completed.

When the decision has been made to stop cutting, your picture will be considered "locked." If the director has the final cut, that decision may be made very early in the game. Once the picture is locked, the postproduction work will be targeted on completing titles and optical effects, editing the sound, the sound mix, and on the first trial composite answer print.

Titles and Credits

At the head of the film are the main title and head credits; at the end of the film are the tail credits. Their size and placement, both on the film and in paid advertising, will be defined contractually in the original agreements with members of the cast and crew. Occasionally a title card will appear in the body of the film to define a location or a passage of time, e.g., *India, Six Months Later.* Titles and credits can be as simple as white letters on a black background or as elaborate as an animated television commercial. Generally, the main title and head credits are static colored words superimposed over a live-action background. End credits are usually in the form of a list of credits that moves up the screen (called a "crawl"), sometimes superimposed over a live-action background. Usually the last item in the crawl is the copyright notice (see Chapter 21).

Titles are designed and executed either by a company specializing in motion picture titles or by an optical effects house that has a title department. Most optical effects houses have such a department.

Optical, Digital, and Special Photographic Effects

Traditional optical effects (called "opticals") such as fades, dissolves, wipes, superimpositions, and split screen are made by modifying and manipulating existing images on film. This is a photochemical process that involves rephotographing portions of the film. A producer provides an optical effects house with a film image, and the optical house rephotographs the image in order to add the desired effect. Rarely will an optical house generate the original image.

Optical effects are made on a specialized camera called an "optical printer" that is designed to rephotograph images on film in such a way as to incorporate the desired effect. When the optical printing is finished, the new piece of film, which includes the original image and the optical effect, is sent to a laboratory for processing and printing. One such effect might be reframing or blowing up a shot in order to lose a microphone that drops slightly into the picture area. Laboratories are equipped to execute simple optical effects, but more creative and complex effects such as a rippling dream sequence or split screens are done by an optical house that specializes in such effects.

The problem with most traditional optical effects is that the photochemical process requires rephotographing the image at least once and often several times, which means that you are going several stages, or generations, away from the original negative; consequently the picture quality suffers, primarily with increased contrast and grain. Another problem is that your original negative for those sequences will be exposed to extra handling, dust, and printing machines. A scratch on the negative or a badly torn sprocket hole is sometimes irreparable. Taking your work to a first-rate optical house with experienced technicians will minimize, but cannot eliminate, these problems.

Digital effects are made by digitizing and manipulating an existing film image, or by creating a new image within a computer. The process for generating new images within a computer is called CGI (computer-generated imagery). Once an image is digitized, the concern about generational loss goes away (see Chapter 13); you can go a thousand generations and the last image will be the same as the first. The film *Toy Story* was created entirely using CGI, as was the alien creature in the live-action film *The Arrival.*

Digital images produce extremely large data files. A single frame of 35mm film will typically require forty megabytes of storage, and it takes 120 frames to produce just five seconds of film. CGI is a very expensive toy, but it can save you money. It may be more cost effective, for example, to create a crowd of 50,000 extras digitally than to employ this many extras on location. Two factors that limit what technicians can accomplish with CGI are computer memory and processing speeds. As these increase, and prices come down, CGI will become increasingly available to filmmakers.

There are so many advantages to creating and manipulating effects with digital media that, for many uses, they have replaced the traditional photochemical optical process. The goal in digital image processing, which usually begins by digitizing traditionally photographed film images, manipulating them in a computer, sometimes adding CGI, and putting the images back onto film, is to produce images of such high quality as to make them indistinguishable from the original film. One of the advantages of this technology is its speed. Optical effects, some of which used to take weeks to create, can now be accomplished digitally in a matter of days. Producers and directors can sit in front of a video monitor in a workstation bay and interact with artists who create effects "on the fly," almost in real time. Depending on the complexity of the effect and the sophistication of the computer equipment, the initial images may have poor resolution and may be viewed at a slower-than-normal frame rate, but often this rough approximation is enough for the filmmaker to determine whether the effect will work in the film. Visual effects artists envision the day when it will be possible to produce finished effects, no matter how complex, in this same way.

Before digital image processing, it was difficult to get mattes (layers of images shot independently and then married together optically) to match properly. This process, called green-screen or blue-screen, is one in which a portion (layer) of a scene, for instance a foreground actor, performs against a green or blue background. The background material, called a "background plate," is added behind the actor at a later time. Today these images are composited digitally, and the result is far superior to that of the earlier photochemical process.

One advantage to this kind of special effects work is that it often allows the actor to appear closer to danger than would be safe on location. One difficulty is that it creates special challenges for the director and actors: not only is a scene's timing difficult when there is nothing but a green screen with which the actors interact, but if the special effect is a living creature, there is often no eyeline for the actor to lock on to. Generally, if the background plate or an approximation of the plate is available, it can be composited on the set using a video camera, so that the director can see on a video monitor roughly how an actor's performance relates to the background images.

Because of the flexibility of digital image processing, defects such as scratches and dirt can be repaired with remarkable, though still costly, success. The same "paintbox" tools used to repair damaged footage are often used to "paint out" unwanted objects in a shot, such as a distracting billboard or the wires and rigging that support stuntpersons. It used to be that great lengths were taken to hide wires from the camera; today they are often painted orange in order to make it easy for technicians to identify and paint them out in a computer. Contemporary digital effects generators can remove an unwanted light pole, add characters and furniture to a scene, and even change the color of a car. Another popular tool afforded by digital effects systems is called "morphing," which means a metamorphosis on film. This was initially used in the film *Willow,* and has since been used so extensively that its novelty has worn thin.

Directors today consider digital effects equipment a part of the palette for all pictures, not just those dominated by special effects. One problem is that directors sometimes want to use a tool simply because it's there, which results in an inefficient use of the budget. For example, a director might prefer a shadow to fall on the left side of the building rather than the right side. When considering this, two questions must be asked: Is it worth it? and What else could that money buy that might better serve the film? Another costly scenario involves a director who designs shots without regard to distracting background images, assuming that they can and will be removed digitally during postproduction. On the other hand, there might be a case where a director designs a shot but realizes at the last minute that the equipment trucks off in the distance intrude on the frame; it may be more efficient to leave the trucks where they are, shoot the scene, and remove the trucks digitally during postproduction.

Companies that make *special photographic effects* create and film original images (almost any image the producer and director can conjure up), such as landscapes, miniatures (models of spaceships, buildings, boats, etc.), matte paintings (usually used to simulate backgrounds for live-action scenes), and animation. There is no clear distinction between these companies and companies that create optical photographic effects; often a single company will do both. Some facilities have the flexibility to produce optical effects, digital effects, special photographic effects, and computer graphics.

In the context of visual effects, animation is not limited to cartoon images. It is a process that creates the illusion of motion in a drawing, inanimate object (i.e., a model of a spaceship), or posable figure (i.e., a puppet of a dinosaur) by photographing it one frame at a time and redrawing the image, moving the model, or reposing the figure slightly between each exposure. Photographing an object *in motion* at the conventional rate of twenty-four frames per second results in a slight blur or trailing image that smooths out the movement. Traditional model animation is made up of a series of sharp still images, which often appears jerky when projected at twenty-four frames per second. In drawn animation, the artist can airbrush a trailing blur on each drawing, thereby creating an illusion of smooth motion. In traditional model animation, it is extremely difficult to create such a blur. There are some highly sophisticated computer-controlled systems, generally referred to as "motion control" systems, that make it possible to photograph model animation with the model and/or the camera actually in motion, resulting in the desired trailing image behind each photograph of the model. The frame rate during this process varies depending on the desired effect. Motion control systems are used for a variety of effects, but generally the term refers to the ability of the system to control and duplicate accurately the motion of the camera and/or the model being photographed. There are additional advantages to motion control systems that allow technicians to add a variety of special effects to an image such as a spaceship, including lights, flames, and smoke. These systems are available at many houses specializing in the production of special photographic effects. A similar system, called "go motion," is used for highly sophisticated puppet animation. With this system, a mechanical robot moves in precisely defined increments whenever the camera shutter opens, thereby creating a trailing blur behind the image. The dragon in *Dragonslayer* is an example of the lifelike movement that can be created using "go motion" photography. For *The Lost World: Jurassic Park,* monster expert Stan Winston made animatronic (a combination of the words *animation* and *electronic*) dinosaur puppets, some as tall as forty feet, which were capable of moving in real time. Technicians can get 90 percent of the way toward making a model or puppet look real by using the techniques mentioned above. The final 10 percent is attained by polishing the image digitally after it had been shot. Many of the special visual effects for *Apollo 13* and *The Lost World: Jurassic Park* were created using traditional processes and then polished digitally. On less expensive pictures, CGI is often used instead of model or puppet photography; currently, however, most images created in a computer are less effective.

Readers interested in a greater understanding of optical, digital, and special photographic effects may refer to the books *Industrial Light and Magic: Into the Digital Realm* and *The Technique of Special Effects Cinematography,* both of which are listed in Appendix E. Since the technology is constantly changing, another valuable resource is a quarterly publication called *Cinefex: The Journal of Cinematic Illusions,* also listed in Appendix E.

The specific services offered by companies specializing in titles, opticals, and special photographic effects vary enormously from house to house. Even within a particular field, such as digital effects, the services vary. A photographic effects house may specialize in miniatures, motion control, front-screen projection, rear-screen projection, matte paintings, or animation. Some effects houses maintain a demonstration reel that contains samples of their past work. When screening a sample reel, look for effects similar to those your film will require. If you're making a feature film, screen the sample reel in a projection room or movie theater. A video viewed on a television screen may distort the effects; depending on the effect, flaws may be either minimized or exaggerated. Look for an acceptable level of quality. Ask yourself if the effects are believable. Are the images sharp? Grainy? Contrasty? If there is a sound track on the reel, you might consider watching the reel a second time without the sound. In most cases a carefully made sound track can distract the viewer from flaws in the effects.

Although the world of optical, digital, and special photographic effects is highly technical, it is ultimately the artist making the effects that matters. A company may have the most sophisticated equipment in the world but unless they have seasoned professionals to operate it, the result will probably be disappointing. If a company has a demonstration reel that indicates their ability to accomplish effects similar to those your film requires, it is important to verify that the artists who made those effects are still with the company.

Occasionally, if a producer is uneasy about a company's ability to deliver a certain effect, the company will offer to make a sample test of the effect. Usually they will charge the producer only for their costs. In the case of an optical effect, the cost to the producer for the test would include the raw film stock and laboratory charges for processing and printing.

A producer or director beginning a project that requires special photographic effects should initially create storyboards (see Chapter 15) to convey the visual concepts for the film. If possible, a visual effects supervisor experienced in the kinds of effects you are seeking should be hired well in advance of beginning principal photography. The supervisor will almost certainly offer guidance that will save time and money, and that will ultimately result in superior effects. Budgets often go through the roof when a director waits until principal photography is completed before consulting an effects specialist. In such cases, the effects artists must work with footage that was shot without consideration for the effects instead of footage that was designed with the effects in mind from the start. Even something as simple as locking off the camera (meaning that the camera does not move) for certain shots that will require the addition of visual effects in postproduction (for example, adding snow to a shot of a farmhouse) can make a big difference. The visual effects supervisor will also know when to split up the effects work among several companies. Often companies will attempt to convince a producer that their approach to a particular effect is the best simply because it is the only way they are set up to do it. Another company may have a different approach that will be less expensive and result in a superior effect. Intelligently dividing the effects work can often result in considerable savings and improved results. The effects for *Independence Day,* which is considered a textbook case on how to maximize a budget when making an elaborate special effects film, were parceled out to practically every special visual effects company in the business, taking efficient advantage of each company's unique strengths. The only caution when doing this is that you hire a reputable and trustworthy supervisor, someone who does not owe favors to or receive favors from a particular effects house.

Since there is often a variety of methods by which one can obtain a desired effect, the cost and quality of the finished product will vary. Spending a lot of money won't guarantee quality effects; they can still be extremely complex, cost a lot, and look horrible. Occasionally effects artists will add unnecessary complications to a particular effect in order to make it more interesting for them to work on. Usually such complications are appreciated by other effects artists but are lost on the general public. From the producer's point of view, the simplest solution is usually the best. If you are not working with a visual effects supervisor, discuss various approaches with several companies before committing yourself to a particular one. When the effects are complex, it is especially important to discuss specifically how each company will accomplish them. Some companies can offer a variety of approaches.

Another reason for consulting specialists is that optical, digital, and special photographic effects work has evolved a language all its own. Terms include *background plate, beam splitter, r-p, d-x, split screen, slit screen, vector graphics, raster graphics, photo-repo, glass painting, matte painting, articulate matte,* and *traveling matte.* An effects artist might describe a scene as follows: "We'll use green-screen to generate an articulate matte for the spaceship miniature that will carry an 'r-p' screen to display interior action; the background plate will be a CG of the space station; then we'll 'd-x' in glows and lasers." There is so much esoteric jargon that without a specialist as a guide, a producer or director unfamiliar with this world might easily be intimidated and get lost in a labyrinth of confusion and misunderstanding.

There are several ways to find a specialist experienced in the kind of effects a particular film will require. The best way is to consult with a visual effects supervisor who knows which artists created which effects for which films. Watching for similar effects in other films and noting the effects artists who created them can be misleading because it is very difficult to decipher from the credits who was responsible for which effects. Another way is simply through word-of-mouth recommendations within the film community. A third way is to visit several effects companies and consult with the specialists working for those companies about your particular effects requirements. Contact information for special effects companies may be found in several of the publications listed in Appendix E, and in the Yellow Pages under "Motion Picture Special Effects." Also, most visual effects companies place ads in the quarterly publication *Cinefex,* which is also listed in Appendix E.

The cost for various titles, opticals, digital, and special photographic effects varies from house to house, so it's worth doing some price-comparing before settling on a particular company. Many houses provide a price list for standard effects such as fades and dissolves, but more elaborate effects require careful planning and budgeting on the part of the effects house. Occasionally an effects house will offer a reduced price for an opportunity to do something new and intriguing.

When ordering titles, opticals, and special photographic effects, spell out clearly and specifically what effects your picture will require and go for a flat, guaranteed fee in writing. Some films require only main and end titles while others require elaborate effects throughout the picture. In any event, spell out the specifics, ideally with storyboards. Some houses, even some of the best houses, will purposely underestimate the cost of your titles and effects in order to get the work and then subsequently bill you for what the estimate should have been. Optical and digital special effects work is often unpredictable, and effects houses shy away from a guaranteed fee in writing. But it becomes very difficult to budget a picture with variables that sometimes run 100 percent or more off the mark. If you can't get a guaranteed fee in writing, at least get a written estimate and insist that they inform you before incurring expenses beyond that estimate. In this way, unless you modify your requirements, you are reasonably assured of staying within your total title and effects budget. If a producer consults with a competent specialist prior to beginning principal photography and works with the title and effects houses to plan and carefully budget the work, the result stands a good chance of living up to the producer's expectations and remaining within the budget.

You can do more special effects with a small amount of money than most people realize, but for an independent producer a film that depends on visual effects should be considered only if the producer is satisfied that the director and, ideally, the production designer, are fully familiar with the kinds of effects the film requires, and are committed to doing them within the parameters of the budget. Nonetheless, it is usually a mistake to construct a low-budget screenplay that is dependent on elaborate effects. Even for a medium-budget film, elaborate special effects should be approached with caution. Films made at those budget levels can't compete with the benchmarks that have been set by films like *The Mask, Independence Day,* and *Titanic.* Not only are these effects expensive, they are unpredictable; their effectiveness can often be judged only when they are finished. You may have to modify and reorder the effects several times before they really work, and you must pay for each modification you order. Further, a tight budget often eats up the entire contingency fund during principal photography and is consequently at its tightest during postproduction. If you get into postproduction and don't have quite enough in the kitty for quality effects, your whole picture will suffer. For some films, even the price of fades and dissolves is more than the budget will allow. The reason Nick Gomez used the technique of cutting to black throughout *Laws of Gravity* was to avoid the cost of optical fades.

Stock Shots

Stock shots are silent generic images available from libraries that specialize in such material. They are the visual equivalent of library music and effects, and include such things as drive-bys, train-bys, airplanes, buildings, animals, sky scenes, landscapes, and crowds.

From an aesthetic viewpoint, stock shots are rarely satisfying, mostly because you are never working with original material but rather with a copy of the original, which means that you are at least one generation away from the original material used for the rest of your film. The result is increased contrast and grain. This will be most noticeable if the stock shot is intercut within a sequence, as in an interior airport stock shot intercut with an interior airport sequence shot specifically for your film. This rarely occurs because sequences are almost always shot in their entirely. However, that same interior sequence may require an exterior establishing shot of the airport in order to introduce it. If it was impractical to shoot the exterior during production (e.g., if the interior sequence was shot on a sound stage and a move to the airport was too expensive or if permits to shoot at the airport were unavailable), it would make sense to purchase a stock shot from a library. In such cases, material from a stock library can be cost effective and the only sensible option.

One point to consider when purchasing stock footage is that, while the stock library may own the footage, they may not own the rights to what is *shown* in the footage. For example, if you need an establishing shot of a passenger plane taking off, make sure there is nothing in the stock shot that identifies the name of the airline (unless you have the airline's written permission to associate their name with the sequence).

Stock libraries are listed in directories such as *The Pacific Coast Studio Directory, The Hollywood Reporter Blu-Book, LA 411,* and *The Producer's Masterguide,* all of which are included in Appendix E.

Reel Breaks

One thousand feet is a little over ten minutes of film. This is the approximate reel size that picture and sound editors work with during postproduction. This limitation was originally necessary because optical sound tracks (see Chapter 21) could not be made in lengths greater than 1,000 feet. Today optical tracks are commonly made in 2,000-foot lengths. The size of an editing reel has remained the same because 1,000 feet is a convenient and manageable size to work with.

A feature film that is ninety minutes or more in length is comprised of nine or more editing reels. Films are conventionally *shipped* on 2,000-foot reels, each of which holds approximately twenty minutes of film. A film that runs 100 minutes is shipped as a five-reel film. Editing reels 1 and 2 will be spliced together to form shipping reel 1, editing reels 3 and 4 will be spliced together to form shipping reel 2, and so forth. The criterion for selecting where to "break" between the *editing reels* that form the *shipping reels* is that there be no overlapping material such as a dissolve between the two reels, and that there be no continuing sound that might be jarred by a splice in the sound track. As long as it is a direct cut, usually between two distinctly separate scenes, you're safe. The two *editing reels* will be spliced together and shipped as a single *shipping reel* (shipping reels may be combined in a variety of ways, which will be discussed in Chapter 23).

All of the criteria for the break between editing reels that form the shipping reels holds true of the break between each 2,000-foot shipping reel, but in the latter case there is an additional consideration. Between shipping reels, the projectionist in many theaters operates a changeover mechanism, switching over from one projector to another. The first reel will be rewound while the second reel plays, and the next reel in the film will be loaded onto the idle projector and prepared for the next changeover. Careful observers will notice what appear to be two small circles (they are actually two series of circles on sets of consecutive frames, made by scraping off a small portion of emulsion on each of those frames) that appear in the upper right-hand corner of the screen shortly before a reel break. The first circle, often called the "motor start cue," signals the projectionist to start the motor of the incoming projector. This allows time for the incoming projector to get up to speed before the second circle, called the "changeover cue," signals the projectionist to switch from one projector to the other. Because reflex and reaction time vary with the individual operating the projectors, some extra film must be available to overlap the changeover on both the outgoing and incoming reels in order to allow for these variances. It is better to have the outgoing scene hang a little long on the screen, or the incoming scene begin a little early, than to have the screen go briefly black and silent between them.

Not every scene ending lends itself to the requirements of this less-than-precise transition. Poor choices for shots at the beginning or end of a shipping reel include those that are too short to allow for the necessary overlap or "padding," scenes that depend on the precise timing of a cut for their effectiveness, and scenes that have music running continuously.

Here is an example of an excellent transition between shipping reels: Somewhere around twenty minutes into your film there is a sequence of a farmer who steps out of his house to survey his fields; the sequence ends with a static shot of dying crops over which we hear nothing but the buzz of insects. The next scene begins with an establishing shot of a cityscape over which we hear only traffic. The exact point at which the film cuts from the fields to the city can be a few frames off without compromising the transition, and since there is no music playing, the sound cut may be a few frames off without jarring the audience.

Working Copies

Once the picture is "locked" (that is, picture editing is completed) and prior to beginning sound editing, you will need to make copies for the sound editors and the composer. They each need copies in order to work simultaneously, which is the most efficient approach to postproduction sound. If you are editing digitally, video copies with time code will be transferred from the digital editing machine and will be used by the composer and by the sound editors working at digital audio workstations.

If you are editing on film, your video copies will be made from the cut work print and will contain time code for synchronization purposes. If your sound editors and composer are equipped to work with film media, your copies will be film prints called "dirty dupes," which are simply film copies of your spliced, scratched, dirty work print. You can save the cost of one dupe if the color work print is used by one of the sound editors.

If you have edited on film, or have edited digitally and conformed a film work print, and you wish to use film media during the mix, you will not use the spliced color work print but a dupe. The reason you don't use your spliced color work print is because, during the mix, the picture will be run back and forth many times, putting great strain on the film. Weak spots, such as poor splices and torn perfs, will undoubtedly cause breaks in the film during the mix. This not only interrupts the flow of the work and the mixers' sense of continuity, but the downtime cost involved in repairing the film and getting things rolling again is high. Unlike the edited work print, the dupe contains no splices, tears, or torn perfs. It contains photographic pictures of them printed from the work print, but the film itself is mechanically flawless. If you have edited digitally and have not made and conformed a film work print, you will use a video copy with time code during the mix.

19

Postproduction Sound

ALL OF THE WORK INVOLVED IN BUILDING THE POSTPRODUCTION sound tracks for your film will be targeted on the final mix. Most of the sounds you hear in a finished film were at one time separate from one another. Mixing is the process of blending together the isolated sounds: dialogue, sound effects, and music. The process is similar to multitrack music recording, in which each instrument is recorded on a separate track. An engineer subsequently rerecords the multiple tracks, blending and equalizing the instruments. The high frequencies of the snare drum may be boosted, or selected instruments such as violins may be dialed out entirely during an organ solo. The sound mix for a film follows the same technique. Sounds are separated in order to give the mixing engineers maximum flexibility when blending them all together.

The Director's Role

Postproduction sound is divided into three categories: dialogue, sound effects, and music. The specialists responsible for the construction of these sounds are the dialogue editor, the sound effects editor, the composer, and the music editor. Each of these individuals will bring to the picture a different point of view, and each will emphasize a particular area of concern. The sound effects editor will view the picture with a prejudiced ear for sound effects; the composer will watch primarily for places where music will enhance the film. It is the responsibility of the director to maintain an overview of the entire sound structure. The specialists must be guided by the director's overall vision of the film so that their respective sounds, working together, will complement one another.

An important thing to remember about sound effects, music, and dialogue is that only one can dominate at a time; the others must be subordinate. If they are all running at full steam, the result will be confusion. If you want confusion, you can run them backward, forward, upside down, and inside out, all at full volume. But if you're going for a controlled, dramatic impact, you must decide which will dominate, and you must not make the decision arbitrarily. Let the emotion you're seeking dictate the answer. Oscar-winning rerecording mixer Richard Portman

(*The Deer Hunter, The Godfather, Body Heat, The Hand that Rocks the Cradle, The Pelican Brief*) describes the defining characteristic of an effective sound track: "It's uncluttered. Clarity. You have to hear all the words. When an idea is playing, *that* idea is playing. You can't have clarity with lots of sound."

Consider a chase sequence with several car crashes. A composer who screens this sequence without the sound effects may "hear" an entire symphony orchestra: a cacophony of sound with kettle drums, horns, strings, cymbals, and more. However, a director wishing to maintain a strong sense of reality may request that the sound effects editors create this symphony out of sound effects: tire squeals, metal ripping, people screaming, glass breaking, etc. In such a case it would be inappropriate for the music to dominate the sound effects. A more appropriate score might involve a low-end undercurrent of tension such as a synthesized bass line with a nervous, staccato, almost subliminal percussion track. Or perhaps there should be no music at all. It surprises people to learn that there is not one note of music in the epic "Battle of Stirling" sequence in the Academy Award–winning film *Braveheart*.

If the director fails to inform the composer that sound effects will dominate, the composer will very likely score the bombast of symphonic sound he or she originally "heard" and both will undoubtedly be disappointed in the mix. In order to achieve the feeling the director is after, it will be out of the question to run both the music and the sound effects at full volume. The symphony will be held down under the sound effects and its impact will be lost. It's possible that the symphony, even at low volume, will cause confusion and will finally be eliminated or rescored.

The Dialogue Editor

The original recording of the dialogue made during production will need a considerable amount of work before it is ready for the mix. The dialogue editor's objective is to construct the tracks in such a way as to give the mixers clean tracks with maximum flexibility for modifying the equalization and level of each voice individually. This work can be done by physically cutting sprocketed magnetic tracks, but more commonly it is done with the sound in a digital format on a digital audio workstation (DAW). A DAW consists of a computer, a hard drive, and a software program that causes the machine to act like a recorder and audio editing system with time code. In situations where the dialogue editors need to go back to the original production recordings, the edit decision list (EDL) generated by the digital editing machine will be used for locating and syncing the original analog production recordings with the digitally edited material (see Chapter 13). More commonly, however, when a picture is cut digitally, the sound in digital form will be used for the final mix. An early example was the production sound for Oliver Stone's *Nixon,* which was transferred to a digital editing machine, and that digital sound was used in the mix without ever returning to a magnetic analog medium. This is a more efficient approach than using the EDL and returning to the original production recordings for the mix.

You will recall in the discussion on production sound recording that the production mixer will record room tone for each location, usually thirty to sixty seconds. This will be used by the dialogue editor to replace any silence in the edited dialogue sequences or any unwanted sound between words in the dialogue, such as a distant car horn or an unwanted off-camera voice. There is no such thing as a silent location (unless you're shooting in a special anechoic chamber). Even the quietest location has some ambient sound or tone. Pure silence calls such attention to itself that it must be replaced with the correct tone for each location.

Production sound effects will be put on a separate track for the sound effects editor and replaced with room tone on the dialogue tracks. This process is called "cleaning the tracks." Finding room tone that matches precisely with the background during dialogue is sometimes difficult. Occasionally, when the match doesn't quite work, the dialogue editor will resort to using tone from dialogue outtakes, seeking quiet pauses between words to match the tone of the scene more accurately.

Once the tracks are cleaned in this way, the dialogue editor will split the voices onto separate tracks, or channels. This will allow the mixers to modify equalization and level for each voice without affecting other voices. The process involves building dialogue tracks by "checkerboarding" between the original sound track and silence. If you are cutting sprocketed magnetic tracks, the silence will be in the form of "fill," which is any sprocketed (usually nonmagnetic) film such as clear leader or salvaged prints from old films that are too badly scratched to be of use to a distributor. The latter, called "picture fill," is the most common. The important thing is that the fill contains no magnetic signal that might be picked up by a sound head. Inexpensive picture fill is available from any film salvage company.

It you are working at a digital audio workstation, the dialogue will be split onto multitrack digital cassettes. The most widely used digital recorder is the TASCAM DA-88. This machine, made by Teac, has eight digital audio tracks and uses standard 8mm "Hi-8" videocassettes. The machines can utilize SMPTE/EBU time code so that multiple units can be linked together for a virtually unlimited number of sound tracks running in perfect synchronization. A single reel of *Twister* had 600 sound tracks running simultaneously on seventy-five DA-88s, all running in absolute sync.

In principal, the checkerboard process is the same regardless of which system is used. An example for a scene involving two voices is shown in Figure 1. The two tracks will be played simultaneously on separate channels during the mix. In this way the mixer can modify one voice without affecting the other. The ideal of maximum flexibility means a separate track for each principal voice, though this extreme is not usually necessary.

If the dialogue editor foresees drastic equalization or level changes between voices, the tracks will be prepared with overlapping tone. In

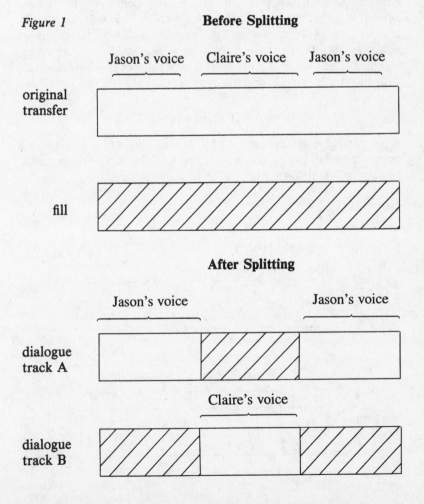

Figure 1   **Before Splitting**

Jason's voice   Claire's voice   Jason's voice

original transfer

fill

After Splitting

Jason's voice   Jason's voice

dialogue track A

Claire's voice

dialogue track B

the case of Jason and Claire, assume that Claire's volume in the original recording is much lower than Jason's. If the mixers raise the volume significantly on track B (Claire's voice), there will be a jump in the background sound whenever the voices (tracks) change. When room tone is added to overlap the background sound, the edited tracks will look as they do in Figure 2. This allows the mixers to match Claire's tone with Jason's at point 1, and gradually increase the volume of track B to optimum level for Claire's voice when she begins speaking at point 2. A gradual, overlapping change in the background tone will be far less disturbing than a direct jump from track A to track B and back again.

For additional insurance, the dialogue editor will make loops of room tone for each sequence. If the mixers need to smooth over a rough transition that isn't adequately covered with overlaps, they will run the continuous loop of tone on a separate channel, gradually increasing its volume to take out the rough transition, then gradually decreasing the volume of the loop back to zero. This process should not be confused with dialogue looping as described in the following section.

ADR (Looping)

ADR stands for "automatic dialogue replacement." It is a system for rerecording dialogue in synchronization with the picture during postproduction. This is done when the original recording is unacceptable for

Figure 2

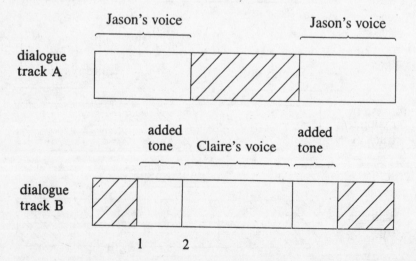

various reasons, such as a great deal of objectionable noise on the track or when the audio portion of the performance must be rerecorded for modification of an actor's delivery. It used to be that the dialogue editor would literally make a continuous-running closed loop of the picture and track for each scene in question, hence the term "looping." The ADR system plays the picture and track forward at normal speed, then zips back to the head of the scene at high speed and plays forward again. The dialogue editor marks the picture and track at the start of each ADR scene and, when rerecording is completed, the original track is replaced with the new ADR track.

Some directors, especially in Europe, rely heavily on ADR. It allows them to concentrate more fully on the visuals during production without much regard to sound quality. They then spend whatever time is required to polish the dialogue on an ADR stage during postproduction. This also gives directors the freedom to shoot in locations that would otherwise be unacceptable due to extraneous noise.

Actors' lines are cued with a series of electronic "beeps" that precede the point at which the actor should begin speaking. These beeps will be evenly spaced as a kind of countdown: "One, two, three," and when the fourth beep would occur, the actor begins speaking. When an actor has difficulty speaking in precise synchronization with the picture during an ADR recording, you may be able to utilize a software program called VocAlign, which analyzes the production track, then squeezes or stretches the ADR recording until it is running in sync with the original production recording. There are also software programs such as Sonic Solutions' No-Noise and Digidesign's DINR (Digidesign Intelligent Noises Reduction), which clean tracks in a way that sometimes eliminates the need for ADR; these programs can analyze recordings and remove much of the unwanted noise, often without an objectionable degree of signal loss.

The arguments against ADR are, first, that the quality of ADR tends to sound sterile. ADR lines lack a dimension of reality. They sound like ADR lines. This is particularly noticeable in exterior scenes. Another disadvantage to ADR is the cost. If you have to loop a line or two during postproduction, it won't break your bank, but don't rely heavily on ADR work at the tail end unless you are sure you can afford it. Also, you'll need to be sure that your actors, at least your principal actors, are contractually obligated to contribute a certain amount of time to looping during postproduction. A third disadvantage to ADR lines is that it is often difficult for an actor to match or improve upon the emotional content of the performance recorded during production. Sometimes the performance will improve during a looping session, but usually the emotional content during production is more effective. Richard Portman feels that when a line is looped, "Half the emotion is missing."

One cost saver, using contemporary technology, is the ability to connect ADR stages in different parts of the world. An actor could be on a stage in London and, using time code and fiber optics, be looping lines for a director on a stage in New York. Key characters in *Dragonheart* were looped this way. The actors were in England and the director was in a studio in Los Angeles. The actors worked with a three-quarter-inch videocassette with time code. The director communicated with the actors and they looped their lines, in real time, over ISDN (Integrated Services Digital Network) phone lines, which are used for transmitting a wide variety of digital data. This system resulted in a significant savings in travel, hotel, and per diem costs for the actors. There are also systems for sending similar digital information over the Internet.

Any non-sync lines of dialogue that the filmmaker wishes to add during postproduction, such as a line from an off-camera actor or from an actor whose back is to the camera, that will help clarify the story or a passage of time, will also be recorded on the ADR stage. Voice-over lines such as an actor's commentary, thoughts, or narration, will be recorded here as well. The ADR stage will also be used to record what's called a "loop group." This is a group of actors who will not appear on screen but whose voices will add to the atmosphere of various scenes. Loop groups are commonly used to enhance the sound for crowd scenes, parties, restaurants, and the like. They are also used more specifically. The loop group might add the sounds of a couple arguing in an adjacent room. They might be used to create the voices for a television show running in the background of a scene. Or perhaps they will contribute the voices of an angry mob in a prison. Very often, when filming crowd scenes, the background extras are told only to mime speaking so that the sound mixer can record a clean track of the actors' dialogue, and the loop group later fills in the extras' voices.

Loop groups are led by an individual who attends a "spotting session" with the director to determine where additional background voices will enhance the film. The group leader assembles a cast of appropriate actors, writes material for the actors to record, and serves as a liaison between the director and the actors during the recording session.

The Sound Effects Editor

The first step in sound effects editing is a detailed discussion called a "sound effects spotting session" among the director, producer, picture editor, and sound effects editor. The director will communicate an overall vision of the sound structure, talking first in general terms; this will evolve into discussions about the specifics of various sounds. For example, if a director asks that a ticking clock be added as ambience to a living room scene, the sound effects editor may ask if the clock should be a grandfather clock or a mantel clock and whether it should sound an occasional chime. Also discussed will be which of the production effects are acceptable and which will need to be replaced or enhanced.

A good sound effects editor approaches this work much like a composer approaches music, going beyond the obvious sound effects that the picture demands in an effort to create moods and feelings such as suspense, joy, loneliness, or terror. The sound effects will have a tremendous influence on the audience's reaction to the film. A person walking down a country road will seem lonely if the sound effects contain a quiet wind, occasional buzzing insects, and the mournful whistle of a distant train. But if the tracks consist of birds singing in the trees, a small dog yapping, and nearby traffic, the mood will shift considerably.

Sound effects, like dialogue, are constructed to give the mixers maximum flexibility for manipulating individual sounds. When cutting on sprocketed magnetic media, they are spread across a multitude of checkerboard tracks using silent fill for the spaces between sounds. Digital sound effects are checkerboarded onto multiple tracks in a digital audio workstation. The complexity of this process ranges from simple scenes requiring nothing more than a single continuous sound effect, such as background traffic, to complex action scenes requiring a hundred or more channels of effects.

In addition to cleaning and splitting the production sound effects, the sound effects editor will often embellish them. A crackling fire may need more crackle; a dull gunshot may need to be sharpened with an additional bang. These tracks will often be made up of some combination of original material recorded during postproduction, wild sound effects recorded during or after production, and sound effects taken from a stock library. They will then be checkerboarded into a complete structure. A sound effects editor often will create entire sound effects sequences from scratch. There may be a badly recorded production track that can be used as a guide (called a "scratch track"), but often the editor will be asked to work with no reference material. In such cases, all of the individual sounds needed for the sequence will be assembled or "built." The sound of the Imperial Walkers in *The Empire Strikes Back* was built from scratch and included the noise of a machinist's punch press and bicycle chains dropping on concrete.

There are many choices for each sound effect. How many ways can a gunshot sound? How many ways can crumpling paper sound? Breaking glass? Does it break on wood or on cement? Indoors or outdoors? Many of these decisions will be made by trial and error, listening to variations of a sound played in sync with the picture. More important than the realism of the sound is the psycho-acoustic experience of the audience. This is derived, in part, from audiences' experiences with film sound effects in the past. The sound of a gunshot in a movie was defined many years ago by the choice that was made for Hopalong Cassidy's gun. It defined forever what audiences expect a gunshot to sound like, and since then sound effects editors have built on that audience expectation. *The Wizard of Oz* defined the sound of a tornado. Whether a tornado really sounds that way is immaterial; what matters is the audience's psycho-acoustic experience while watching the movie. The sound of the tornado in *Twister* was made up of 120 stereo sound tracks that included real wind sounds, wind sounds created in the studio, sound effects made from tiger growls, drains sucking, stampedes, freight trains, and whistles, but the basic underlying sound was modeled after the tornado in *The Wizard of Oz*.

The sound effects editor must construct sounds that complement one another, ones that will blend together smoothly in the mix. When in doubt about a certain sound or combination of sounds, the editor will often cut one or two alternatives from which the director may choose during the mix.

The following is a simple example of sound effects construction. Imagine the inside of a dingy hotel room. A man enters, turns on the light, drops his keys on the dresser, removes his coat, revealing a splotch of blood on his shirt, tosses his coat on the chair, and flops onto the bed with a sigh. The list of sound effects needed for this scene are:

- distant city traffic
- key in lock
- doorknob turning
- door squeaking
- door closing
- light switch
- footsteps on carpet
- keys jingling
- keys hitting dresser top
- clothes rustling
- jacket dropping onto chair
- man flopping onto bed (squeaky bed springs)
- man sighing.

Depending on the mood of the scene, the sound effects editor may wish to add an angry car horn in the distance, a cat fight, a radio or television playing in the next room, a fog horn, a police siren, a train whistle, a leaky faucet, or a toilet flushing. But assume for now that we're just concerned with the basics in the list. Figure 3 shows the structure, checkerboarded across five sound effects tracks. It doesn't matter whether you are cutting on sprocketed magnetic tape or at a digital audio workstation—the principal is the same.

Each sound will be cut to synchronize precisely with the corresponding visual action in the picture. It is important to allow enough silence (or fill) between different sounds on a given track to allow the mixers enough time to make adjustments in equalization and level before each sound is played. Similar sounds are kept on one track for easy reference in the mix.

A steady "hum" sound such as a motorboat engine is treated in a slightly different way. If the picture is cutting back and forth among long shots, medium shots, and close-up shots, it would seem logical to cut the sound effects as in Figure 4.

However, the abrupt sound cuts will be too severe for the ear, and the mix will sound choppy. In order to achieve a more natural sound, the most distant sound must run continually under the closer sounds, as shown in Figure 5.

Any steady background sound such as city traffic, birds, wind, crickets, and rain may run in a continuous loop for the mixers to dial in and out whenever the picture dictates their use. This often saves a great deal of unnecessary editing, especially if such a sound is used many times throughout the film. Every mixing facility maintains a library of standard sound effects loops that are available during the mix at no extra charge. It's wise to check their library before going to the trouble of manufacturing your own loops.

Whenever a sound effect loop must begin or end abruptly on a specific cue (as opposed to being faded in or out gradually), the mixer must be given a series of cues that signal the precise point at which the sound effect should begin or end. You can provide visual cues by marking the picture with grease pencil, or electronically if you are mixing to a video image. A series of three "pluses" on the picture establishes a visual beat for the mixer's incoming cue. For an outgoing cue, the picture will be marked with "minuses" instead of pluses. Figure 6 shows an incoming picture cue for a rain loop on the left, and an outgoing cue for the loop on the right. The mixer counts silently, "One, two, three," and on "four" hits the button to begin or end the sound effect.

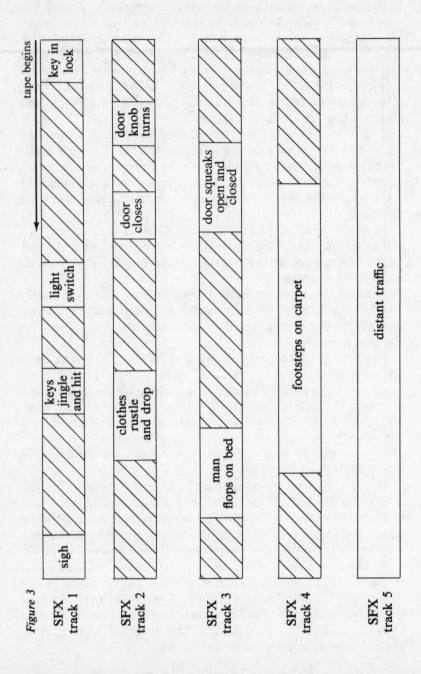

Figure 3

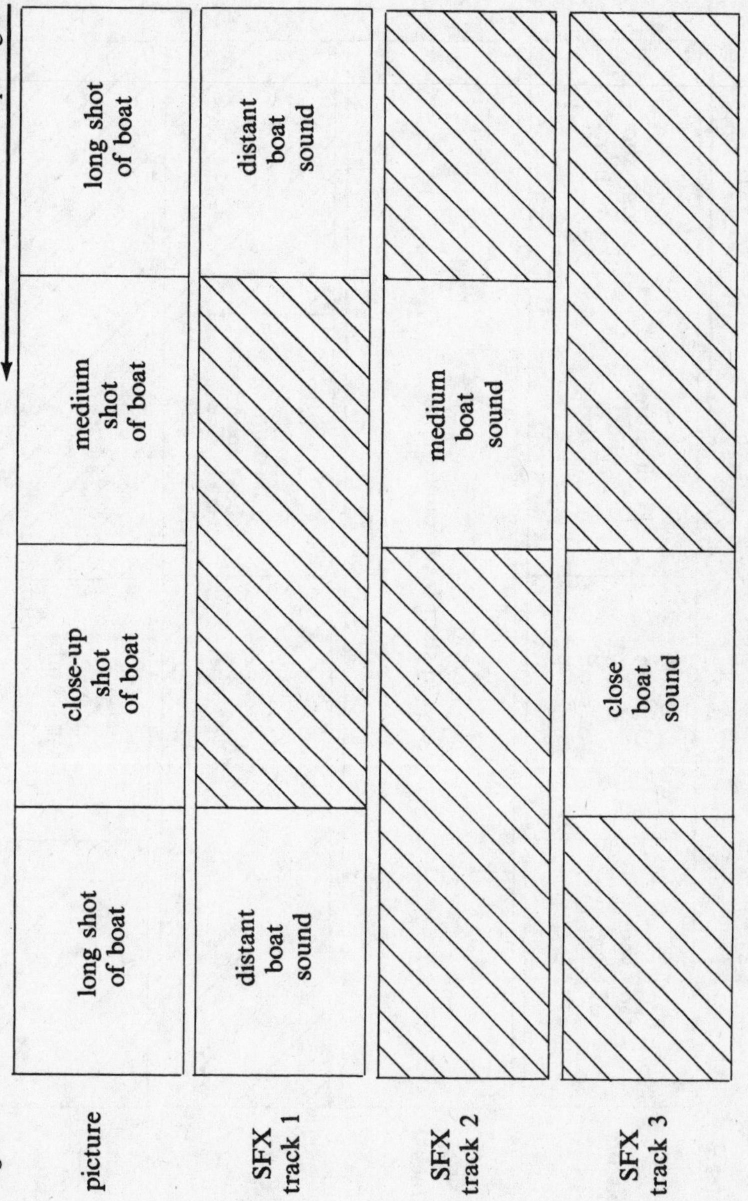

Figure 4

picture: long shot of boat | medium shot of boat | close-up shot of boat | long shot of boat

SFX track 1: distant boat sound | distant boat sound

SFX track 2: medium boat sound

SFX track 3: close boat sound

tape begins

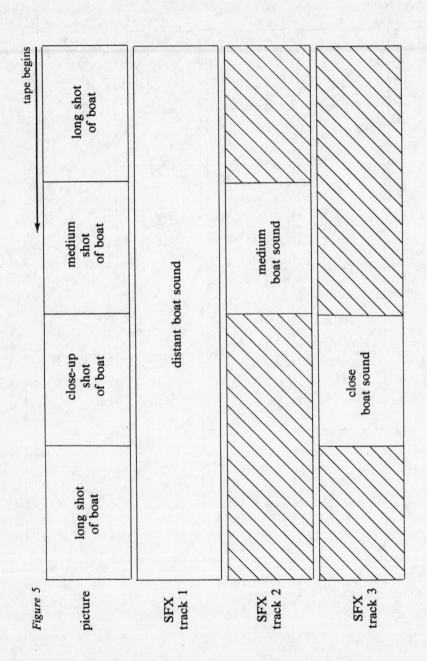

Figure 5

Figure 6

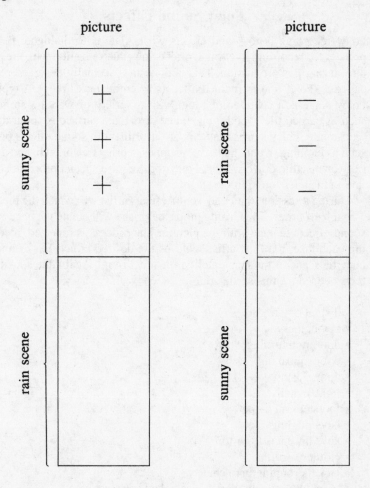

There are a variety of "plus and minus" cuing styles, but the most common begins with a two-foot line called a "streamer" drawn on the film (usually in red grease pencil), or electronically added to a video-tape, preceding the plus or minus marks on the sixth, eighth, and tenth frames before the cut. Some mixers prefer the fifth, seventh, and ninth frames. It's best to consult your mixer before cuing the picture.

Foley Sound Effects

Foley recording is to sound effects what ADR is to dialogue. It is a process for recording live sound effects in synchronization with the picture during postproduction. This is done in a specially designed room called a "Foley stage" (named after its inventor, Jack Foley). A typical Foley stage is a soundproof room with a variety of walking surfaces such as carpet, tile, wood, gravel, and dirt. Each surface is about three feet square. Foley stages maintain an assortment of sound effects props such as clothing, wooden blocks, matches, a dried tree branch, and a variety of metallic objects. Most Foley jobs require special props in addition to the ones found in the stage.

During a session, the Foley sound effects artist will watch the picture a couple of times. Then, using props, he or she will create the necessary sound effects in sync with the picture. The process is repeated, recording each take, until the artist achieves the desired effect. For example, take the scene of the man entering the hotel room. Again, the sound effects needed for this scene are:

- distant city traffic
- key in lock
- doorknob turning
- door squeaking
- door closing
- light switch
- footsteps on carpet
- keys jingling
- keys hitting dresser top
- clothes rustling
- jacket dropping onto chair
- man flopping onto bed (squeaky bed springs)
- man sighing.

Every sound on the list, with the exception of the distant city traffic and the door closing, may be recorded on a Foley stage. Unless the stage has your particular kind of door as part of their standard equipment, the door-closing sound will be impractical because a special door mounted in a frame is usually too clumsy to move onto the stage. This sound may easily be recorded wild and cut into the tracks. The props necessary to record the Foley sound effects will include keys on a key ring, a doorknob with keyhole, a squeaky hinge, a pile of clothes, a section of squeaky bed springs (perhaps four springs). A light switch will not be necessary since a similar sound effect may be created by tapping a single key on the doorknob.

The experts who specialize in Foley recording work with remarkable speed and accuracy. Often they will watch the picture only once before attempting a first take, and often the first take will be flawless.

The recording of the hotel room scene on a Foley stage might go something like this: The Foley artist will watch the picture to get a feel for the pacing. During the take the artist will stand on the carpeted floor surface, hold the keys in one hand, the doorknob in the other, and the squeaky hinge clenched between his or her teeth (the fewer times props are picked up and put down, the less chance there is for extraneous noise). When the film begins, the artist will watch the action closely. At precisely the right moment, the keys will be shaken (possibly behind the artist's back, away from the microphone, so they sound as though they're on the far side of the door as in the picture), then the key will be placed in the doorknob, the knob turned, and the artist will reach up to squeak the hinge as the door opens. As the man in the film enters the hotel room, the Foley artist will walk (often in place) on the carpeted floor surface, taking steps in sync with the man in the film. The artist will squeak the hinge as the door closes, then gently tap a single key on the doorknob to simulate the sound of the light switch. The footsteps will continue as the man in the film walks into the room and, at the right moment, the artist will shake the keys and drop them on the wooden floor surface (for the sound of the keys dropping on the dresser in the picture). The artist will then pick up the pile of clothing and rub it together as the man in the picture takes off his jacket (or perhaps the artist will remove a jacket). As the man in the film flops onto the bed, the artist may simulate the sound by dropping the clothing onto the floor (avoiding the keys that dropped earlier). When the Foley artist hits the clothing, the springs will be squeaked to match the timing of the man settling on the bed. At the proper moment, the artist may also let out a tired sigh, pause for a moment, then call "Cut."

A Foley artist can look pretty silly operating this assortment of bizarre props, moving from one floor surface to another, staring intently at the screen, glancing away only to pick up the next prop, but the results are astonishingly accurate. If the effects are complex, and depending on the Foley artist's preference, the sounds may be broken up into several groups and recorded with several passes, onto several tracks, as opposed to doing them all at once.

The advantages of a Foley recording are, first, that it is an efficient way to construct a multitude of sound effects on a single track, or multiple tracks, without editing. Further, additional time is saved in the mix since there will be fewer tracks for the postproduction mixers to deal with. The hotel room scene, instead of five edited tracks, will consist of three tracks, as shown in Figure 7. The only disadvantage to Foley recording is the cost of renting the stage and the Foley artist. You must weigh these costs against the time you will save in editing and mixing.

Small, easily controlled sounds such as walking, clothes rustling, writing, scraping, hitting, clicking, and brushing lend themselves to Foley recording. Sound effects such as traffic, cat fights, thunder, tire squeals, and airplanes lend themselves to production recording or post-production editing.

Music

A picture editor cutting a film seeks maximum visual impact, usually with little thought to the music that will eventually accompany the picture. After the picture is cut, the composer must write the music to fit the picture. The music should contribute not only to the mood of the film,

Figure 7

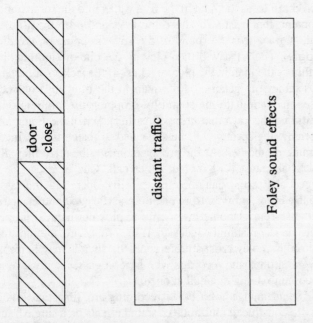

but also to telling the story. This may require writing music that plays with the scene, plays against the scene, or adds a deeper dramatic statement about the story or characters than is evident in the scene itself. The composer will often be required to write music so that it precisely accents highlights in the scene's action or dialogue. This requires a combination of creative musical talent and technical skill.

The following terminology describes the various types of music used in films: *underscoring* (dominant or subordinate); *visual vocal* (on-camera singer); *background vocal* (off-camera singer); *source music* (music coming from a specific source such as a radio, television, PA system, piano, jukebox, or the like).

It used to be that thirty to forty minutes of music was a reasonable rule of thumb for a motion picture. That guideline no longer applies. Some films play well with music running throughout, while others require almost no music at all. Producers who find themselves with a weak picture will often try to compensate by filling the sound track with wall-to-wall music. This may help disguise the problems, but it is generally an inadequate solution. It is also common for a producer to ask a composer to fix a scene that is not working. Usually the problem can be traced back to the dramatic content of the scene in the script or the failure of the director and/or actors to interpret the scene's original purpose properly. It is remarkable how often composers succeed at overcoming such deficiencies, but it is unrealistic to expect them to work miracles. As composer Bernard Herrmann (*Citizen Kane, Psycho, Taxi Driver*) said, "Composers are like morticians: We can dress it up but we can't bring it back to life."

Filmmakers often select a composer by listening to demo tapes and CDs submitted by composers and their agents. They then hire the composer whose demo music sounds most like the music the filmmaker wants for his or her movie. This is an inadequate way to choose a composer. The value of demo tapes and CDs is limited to giving filmmakers a frame of reference for a particular composer, after which the filmmaker needs to *screen the film for which the music was written.* The biggest problem with listening to demo music is that it tells you nothing about whether the music was appropriate for the film for which it was written. As an extreme example, you may hire a composer for a thriller based on brilliantly composed suspense cues heard on a demo tape, only to discover later that those cues were written for a comedy, and were entirely inappropriate for that film. A composer must not only be able to write music in a style relevant to your film, but he or she must also know when and how that style contributes to telling the story. The second problem with demo material is ascertaining whether the music was ac-

tually written by the composer submitting the demo. There are unscrupulous composers who add to their demo tapes and CDs music that
they didn't write but that they believe will appeal to a particular producer or director. The chances of this being discovered are almost zero,
and composers know it.

A producer or director who doesn't have a specific composer in mind
for a project should contact agencies that specialize in composer representation. A list of these agencies can be found in the *Hollywood Agents
and Managers Directory,* a publication of the *Hollywood Creative Directory,* which is included in Appendix E. Also, composers and agents
who represent them watch for announcements and advertisements in
trade publications such as *Variety* and *The Hollywood Reporter* alerting
them to pictures in various stages of production and postproduction.
These composers or their agents will contact the producers of these
films and offer their services. The majority of work for many composers
comes about in this way.

Often the music for low- and medium-budget films suffers because
the filmmakers hesitate to call agents who represent experienced composers, assuming that they will be too expensive. The truth is that agents
welcome calls from struggling filmmakers, even those with no money,
provided they are willing to make a sincere effort to work out an
arrangement that will benefit all parties. Composers' agents recognize
that there is often a value beyond the immediate financial remuneration
for a composer who scores the music for a worthwhile film. Also, a
composer's interest may be sparked less by money than by the content
of film, or by the opportunity to work with an interesting filmmaker. *The
Spitfire Grill* (with a budget of $6.1 million) was completed with a score
that the producers felt didn't live up to the rest of the movie. They approached composer James Horner (*Courage Under Fire, Apollo 13,
Braveheart*), who agreed to rescore the film for less than his customary
fee because he liked the movie. His score contributed immensely to the
emotional impact of the picture and to its winning the Audience Award
at the Sundance Film Festival.

Be cautious about eliminating composers from consideration simply
because they scored films you didn't like, or because they have worked
exclusively in another medium such as television or direct-to-video.
Keep open the possibility that among these individuals may be a composer who understands your film, who is thoroughly experienced and
professional, and who will pour heart and soul into providing you with
a score that will enhance your film.

When talking with agents, be prepared to discuss the music style
you're seeking and your anticipated schedule. In the 1970s, composers

were routinely given ten to twelve weeks to write a score; today the time has been cut in half. The agent will also need information about your music budget in order to recommend an appropriate composer, but it is best not to divulge the details of that budget, especially the amount allotted for the composer's fee, since that fee is open to negotiation.

Once you have selected one or more potential composers, it is crucial that you meet with them. Determining your personal and artistic compatibility with a composer requires that you spend the time necessary to discuss your project and to establish a rapport that will serve both of you in the event that you work together on the film.

Music costs for most films are between 1.5 percent and 2.5 percent of the film's total budget. Music budgets for low-budget films, those made for under $1 million, are less; they are often scored by a composer willing to work for little more than a credit on the movie. They are frequently recorded on synthesizers in a home studio, sometimes supplemented by a handful of acoustic instruments played by the composer's friends. Entire scores have been created in electronic studios using no conventional instruments whatsoever.

Agents who represent composers almost always insist that the producer pay a third or half of the composer's fee before the first note of music is written, an additional percentage on the day the music is scored, and the balance when the music is mixed onto stereo tracks. In accepting or rejecting an assignment, most composers consider not only their own fee and the approximate number of minutes of music the film will require, but also the music budget, which will determine the number of musicians and the amount of studio time available for scoring and dubbing (for a modestly budgeted film it is reasonable to anticipate scoring four minutes of music per hour of studio time). The music budget will also cover orchestrating, conducting, union fees, instrument rental, and copying fees. The music editor is a separate budget issue and will be discussed later. It may be that the composer makes a "package deal" with a producer, in which case the composer will budget and pay for the above-mentioned costs and the composer's fee will be whatever is left. Before attempting to detail these costs, the composer will consult with a music contractor, selected by the composer, who will eventually book and supervise the musicians during the scoring session. When making a package deal with a composer, the risk to the producer is that the composer will spend the money irresponsibly, perhaps taking an unreasonably high fee and hiring a smaller group of musicians than the producer expected. The risk to the composer is that the producer is expecting a full orchestra when the budget can only accommodate a small ensemble. The best protection for both parties is to communicate clearly, and to build into the written contract provisions that define within reason how the money will be spent. A provision might specify, for example, that the composer will use a minimum of ten musicians for recording a minimum of thirty minutes of music. Since package deals can be abused, it is prudent for the producer to inquire into a composer's reputation before making the deal.

Composers do not currently have a union. Back in 1953, they organized the Composers and Lyricists Guild of America, which subsequently received union status from the National Labor Relations Board. The guild negotiated a contract with studios and producers, establishing minimum wages and working conditions for composers and lyricists, but their union status lapsed in the early 1970s as a consequence of a lawsuit between the guild and major studios. Until such time as composers reestablish union status, each contract must be negotiated separately. Today composers are organized within a non-union structure called the Society of Composers and Lyricists, which is composed of nearly 600 professional composers and lyricists. Additional information regarding the society may be obtained by contacting their office at the address and phone number listed in Appendix E.

ASCAP (The American Society of Composers, Authors, and Publishers) and BMI (Broadcast Music, Incorporated) are competing societies that grant licenses and collect royalties based on their members' copyrights. They are not unions. Most composers and lyricists belong to one of these organizations, and anyone using their music must pay a licensing fee to whichever organization collects payments for the use of their music.

American Federation of Musicians

The musicians' union is called The American Federation of Musicians (AFM), and its membership includes musicians, orchestrators, conductors, arrangers, contractors, and copyists (the composer writes the entire score across long single pages; the copyist copies each instrument into its own part book). Composers frequently function as orchestrators and/or conductors, and in those capacities they are protected by the union and receive pension and health benefits. The union has various locals throughout the country, the largest of which are in Los Angeles and New York. Union music editors are not part of the AFM; they belong to the Motion Picture Editors Guild.

The musicians' union has a standard contract with producers establishing minimum wages and working conditions for their members. Since the vast majority of persons working in Los Angeles and New

York in the above-mentioned union capacities are members of the union, it is difficult for a producer to score a film in these cities without signing a union contract. For low-budget films, defined by the AFM as films costing less than $12 million, there is a separate contract that saves producers approximately 30 percent of AFM member fees. This can amount to a savings of 20 to 25 percent of the total music budget. Alternatives include using non-AFM orchestras in cities such as Salt Lake City, Seattle, and Dallas, and scoring overseas. Increasingly, films are being scored in these locations, but these alternatives (with the exception of London) have fewer first-rate musicians from which to choose and less sophisticated recording facilities for film scoring. A producer will get more musicians for a given amount of money in a non-union city, but that doesn't necessarily mean that the score will be improved. A consideration for composers who belong to the AFM is that if they function in a union capacity, such as orchestrator or conductor, they violate AFM membership rules when working with non-union musicians.

Producers sometimes shy away from the AFM contract because they fear having to make future "supplemental market" payments, which the contract requires. Supplemental markets include such things as video sales and nontheatrical distribution (see Chapter 25). The contract requires a producer to pay to the AFM 1.5 percent of the money received from a supplemental market sale, after deducting the costs of preparing the film for that market. The AFM then distributes this money to the musicians who played during the recording session. The actual cost to the producer is quite small, and in most cases not enough to be a deciding factor in choosing whether or not to use union musicians.

A producer who wishes to sign with the AFM must supply the union with pertinent information regarding the project, such as the name of the production company, the principals in that company, the type of license being applied for (motion picture or television), and the picture's music budget. In addition, the union requires a financial statement, documented by a bank, that verifies the producer's ability to pay for the costs of the music. If the union approves all of this material, it will sign a contract with the producer. The producer will then be required to post a bond equal to the amount of the total music budget for union members as a guarantee that the union members will be paid.

Preparation for Music Scoring

Before a director begins discussions with the composer, it is important for the composer to screen the film—uninterrupted from start to finish—in a screening room or in the cutting room in order to gain a sense of the overall pacing and feel of the picture. That isn't the time for a detailed spotting session; it is an opportunity for the director and the composer to begin discussions about the placement, style, and purpose of music for the film. The composer will then have time to generate ideas, perhaps listen with the director to CDs, and begin formulating a thematic approach to the score. In addition, the director and composer may wish to screen other films to examine how the music was used to enhance the story, a particular scene, a character, or a moment.

Detailed discussions about placement and style of music for your film begin in the music spotting session following a screening of the final cut. These discussions generally will take place in a cutting room, where the film can be run intermittently, stopping to examine scenes in close detail to determine the precise moments when music will begin and end. In addition to the director and composer, these session usually include the producer, film editor, and music editor.

Again, it is important for the director to communicate a concept of the overall sound structure—dialogue, sound effects, and music—to the composer. The composer is a part of the whole picture, and the director must ensure that each part complements the whole.

Each unit of music is referred to as a "cue." Within each cue there may be important moments that the music will highlight. These will be determined in the spotting session. It may take several sessions before the director and composer establish congruent thoughts about the placement and style of the music, though generally the spotting session is done in a single day. Following the spotting session, the composer will be given a copy of the film, usually on video format with time code inserted visibly along the bottom of the picture.

Spotting sessions, whether for music or sound effects, should be focused on the task at hand. If you see something in the picture you would like to change, make a note of it and save it for later. Don't stop to recut the picture during the session.

Free Timing and Click Track Recording

There are two conventional approaches to scoring music for films. The first, called *free timing,* is one in which the musicians in a scoring session play their instruments while watching the picture. This is a costly process. Running the picture involves additional studio time, and it may take several tries before the musicians record an acceptable take.

The *click track* is a more controlled approach and is usually more efficient. Click track is a type of signal used in audio recording in order to establish and maintain a beat. It is a kind of metronome. In recording studios, the individual musicians do not always play simultaneously. For example, an initial track may consist only of the rhythm section, perhaps drums, bass, and guitar. Then the sounds from a series of other instruments, playing the same piece of music, may be recorded on an adjacent track. This process is called "overdubbing." It is the way an individual musician, playing different instruments, can create multiple tracks that may later be mixed together to create the sound of a full band or orchestra. The musicians' union places some limitations on individual musicians doubling up on instruments and overdubbing in this way. The vocal track(s) is usually recorded after the instrumental tracks have been completed; the vocalist will listen to those tracks using headphones while singing the lyrics.

When a composer decides to score a cue using a click track, a digital metronome "click" speed is selected based on how the piece is paced in the composer's mind. The click track, when played over headphones to the conductor and sometimes the musicians during a recording session, establishes and maintains the beat. It also provides reference points for specific cues in the music and ensures that all of the subsequent recordings on all of the tracks are synchronized. The conductor is the only person who must hear the click. Individual musicians will often be guided solely by the visual direction of the conductor's baton.

When organizing a scoring session, the composer will begin with the most fully orchestrated cues. If the scoring session requires thirty musicians for half of the music and fifteen musicians for the rest, the composer will score all of the thirty-piece cues first. Only half of the orchestra will be kept in the studio for the remainder of the session. This avoids paying all of the musicians for the entire session.

The Music Editor

In most cases, the music editor will be selected by the composer. At the conclusion of the spotting sessions, the music editor will take a copy of the film, usually on video with time code, and time each scene that requires music. Each camera move, camera angle change, dialogue start and stop, and change in the action will be described and timed to the hundredth of a second. The starting frame for each cue will be marked with numbers that represent time code and elapsed time.

The start will be the first frame of the music cue and the end will be the last frame of the cue. If you are working with film frames instead of time code, the marked starting frame will be frame 1, and each timing in the scene will be counted in frames from that starting point. The frame counts will then be converted into seconds by dividing the number of frames by twenty-four since film travels at twenty-four frames per second. The first cue in reel one will be marked M-11, meaning: music, reel one, first cue (or 1M1, which has the same meaning). The second cue in reel one will be marked M-12 or 1M2. The first cue in reel two will be marked M-21 or 2M1, and so on throughout the picture.

Music timing sheets will be written by the music editor and will contain all of the timing information for each scene to be scored. Each timing sheet will begin with an introductory paragraph to orient the scene in the story. The director and composer will have previously determined during the spotting sessions which dialogue or actions, if any, will be highlighted or accented by the music.

For the scene in which the man enters the hotel room, as described in the previous section on sound effects, we will assume that the music will start when the door opens and we first see the man entering the room. The director and composer decide to accent, first, the moment when the man removes his jacket and reveals the blood on his shirt and, second, the moment when the man hits the bed (perhaps the music will "sigh" with him). This is a very obvious use of music (called "Mickey-Mousing"), and the example is intended only to help communicate the technical problems of the computer. Current thought in the film world tends toward a more subtle approach, such as musically emphasizing emotions rather than Mickey-Mousing the action in the picture as described here. The timing sheet for the hotel scene is shown in Table 14.

Each music cue in the film is spotted and timed in this way.

The hotel room scene is a very simple example of film scoring. You will begin to appreciate the problems of music scoring for film if you consider the complexity of scoring three minutes or more of continuous music with ten important accented moments. Imagine the problems involved in writing not only an aesthetically effective piece but also one that accents the ten musically arbitrary highlights.

While the composer is writing the score, the music editor fulfills several functions. Among them are, first, to communicate any last-minute changes in the picture to the composer; second, to lay in any prerecorded music that will not require scoring by the composer, like a live on-camera recording of a musician or library music that will be used as source from a radio or television; third, to mark the film or videotape with cues similar to the visual cues used by sound effects editors. Instead of "pluses" and "minuses," music cues are two-second lines, called "streamers," either drawn on film or electronically added to video. They serve as a cuing system for the composer during the scoring session. It is common for directors to request a long tail, or long fade,

TABLE 14   **Music Timing**

M-52 (fifth reel, second cue). The man is returning from a bar where he
was stabbed during a fight with two drunks. He ran from the bar and
we now cut to the inside of his hotel room as the door opens and . . .

SMPTE Time Code:	Real Time:	Action:
d1:04:11:04	0:00	We first see the man.
d1:04:15:03	0:03.96	Door closes.
d1:04:18:05	0:07.04	Lights on.
d1:04:24:05	0:13:04	Drops keys on dresser.
d1:04:28:07	0:17.13	Removes jacket . . .
d1:04:34:03	0:23:00	revealing blood.
d1:04:39:10	0:28.21	Drops jacket onto chair.
d1:04:43:00	0:31.88	Flops onto bed and . . .
d1:04:51:13	0:40.33	sighs. Camera slowly moves in to close-up of man's face and we cut to . . .
d1:04:59:14	0:48.38	next scene.

Note: Leave long tail on music to carry over cut to next scene.

when the music is recorded to allow leeway for a long music fade in the
final mix (see Chapter 20). Often this long tail may be used to smooth
the transition from one scene to another.

At the conclusion of a scoring session, the music editor will lay in the
completed music tracks opposite the appropriate places in the picture.
Often the music is recorded using time code, which eliminates the need
for the music editor physically to lay in the tracks in sync with the picture. Time code allows the music to be recorded onto a machine such as
a DA-88 in precisely the right spot. In this case the music editor's responsibility is limited to "cleaning the tracks," which means erasing any
unwanted sound such as a conductor's voice recorded just before or just
after recording the music.

When using prerecorded music, such as a popular song or stock library music (which is occasionally used as source music from a radio or television, or when the budget is so tight that original music is not scored), the music editor's job becomes more difficult and more creative. He or she must work with the director to select pieces of music that best approximate the desired pacing and mood of the film. Since the accents in the music will come at arbitrary points, the music editor must select the most important visual action and line up an accent in the music with that action in the picture. The piece will then be run back to the head of the cue and listened to from the beginning. Many such trial-and-error placements may be required before the most acceptable compromise is reached. Another way to deal with this problem is to select key scenes that will require music and pick the music before cutting the picture. The picture may then be cut to fit the music. This may be the most effective way to deal with certain scenes, especially montage sequences, but it is still a compromise. As a part of this process, the assistant editor may need to shorten a piece of music by cutting out a phrase, or lengthen a piece by repeating phrases or by segueing (dissolving) to another piece of music altogether. Sophisticated computer programs, such as DigiDesign ProTools and Avid Audio Vision, are designed to handle this kind of internal sound editing with excellent results. Other disadvantages of library music are the lack of a theme or musical thread throughout the picture, and the inconsistency of instrumentation. The audience will hear the change in instrumentation from piece to piece and the continuity of the film will suffer; even an untrained ear will be aware of this inconsistency. Another consideration is that library music is not yours exclusively. You may purchase the right to use a piece of music and discover later that it is associated with a product advertised in a television commercial. While the quality of library music has never been better than it is today, its only real advantage over an original score is that it's cheaper.

Temp Music

Often a music editor will cut a music temp track using cues selected by the director and composer from CDs or from music the composer has written previously. A temp track serves two purposes. First, it can be used as a way to explore by trial and error a variety of musical options. This is often an effective way for a director and composer to communicate. The second purpose of a temp track is to enhance the film when screening it for test audiences, producers, executives, or potential back-end financiers. An important caveat: Do not assemble a temp track that your composer can't reasonably approximate within your budget. If, for example, the budget for your music is $5,000, don't use the score from *Men in Black* as your temp track. At the very least, this sets up an unrealistic expectation of the finished film, and at worst it is a blatantly misleading representation of what you intend to deliver. Work closely with your composer and music editor to assemble a temp track that represents what you intend for the finished film.

Problems occur when the temp track is assembled without consulting the composer. In such cases the picture editor becomes a key player in choosing the music. Not only are most picture editors unqualified to do this, but some go so far as to use a temp music track to cover flaws in the editing. An even bigger danger is that filmmakers, producers, and executives often fall in love with the temp track. Whether it's effective or not, if you hear it often enough it may begin to sound good. In such cases the composer may be expected to copy the temp track or risk disappointing those who have fallen in love with it. The worst extreme occurs when a composer is asked to spot the picture with the temp track running. This means that the director and picture editor have scored the film before the composer has written the first note of music. This robs not only the composer of the freedom to create the score, but its robs everyone else of the opportunity to maximize the composer's potential contribution. Temp tracks are often necessary and can be used in many positive ways, but it is important to be aware of these problems.

Playback Recording

Playback recording is used primarily with on-camera musicians and singers when a live recording is impractical. For example, a location may have poor acoustics for live recording. Prior to beginning principal photography, the musicians will make a multitrack recording of the music. This will then be mixed down to a single track. The studio recording will be played back on location during each take, and the musicians will play their instruments in time to the studio recording. Given a little practice, competent musicians will be able to match their movements accurately with the studio recording during location playback. Music that is played and recorded on location is sometimes used in the final mix (see Chapter 20), but more often it is used as a "scratch track" for editing and will be replaced eventually with a studio recording.

It is crucial that each stage of recording in the playback process, including the original multitrack recording, contains a consistent time code or variable sync signal (such as the one provided by a Nagra recorder) in order to maintain synchronization with the final performance on film.

Songs

It is sometimes effective to use popular songs in a sound track, but be prepared for the expense. If you are using an unknown song by an unknown artist, the cost will be minimal, but if you are using a song from a known artist, you will probably spend at least $20,000 for the rights. When John Sayles made *Lone Star,* he discovered that he had to cut down from the twenty-seven songs he originally intended to use because the cost for songs had more than doubled since he'd made *Baby, It's You.* "Back then we could get three Motown songs for twenty-five thousand dollars. Now one Motown song will cost you twenty-five thousand dollars." A sizable portion of the film's budget went to purchasing rights to songs. Some filmmakers choose not to deal with this issue until a distribution deal is in place. Nick Gomez did not secure music rights to *Laws of Gravity,* which includes songs by six different performers, until after he had secured a distribution deal. In some cases, it is possible to obtain a relatively inexpensive "festival license" for a piece of music that allows you to use that music in your film for limited festival exhibition.

Music Clearance

Music clearance is the process of determining who owns the copyright to any given musical material, then negotiating for permission to use that material for territories and media in which exhibition or distribution is planned, in exchange for the payment of a license fee to the copyright owner. These steps should be taken before using any piece of music in order to eliminate music that is too expensive or that the copyright owners do not want used. Richard Linklater initially structured his movie *Dazed and Confused* so that it would end with the Led Zeppelin song "Rock and Roll," but discovered at the last minute that the rights were unavailable and was forced to substitute a different song.

If you use a musical composition without proper clearance, you may be held liable for copyright infringement as well as other actionable claims. You may be required to pay to the copyright owner any profits resulting from the unauthorized use of the protected material, and to pay for any damages sustained by the copyright owner as a result of its use. Even if damages or profits can't be proven, the copyright owner may still be awarded substantial statutory damages as provided by the Copyright Act. You may also face an injunction and incur costs to remove the uncleared material, which may be many times more than what the cost of the clearance and license fees would have been had they been pursued properly. Several watchdog operations have been formed to monitor use of music in all media on behalf of composers, publishers, record companies, and artists.

Attorneys who specialize in the music clearance process should always be consulted. They are fully familiar with the procedures necessary to resolve issues of ownership, licensing practices, and availability. For more information on music clearance issues, see *Clearance & Copyright* by Michael C. Donaldson, which is listed in Appendix E.

Music Rights and Sound Track Albums

Reproduction rights refer to the use of music in the film (called "synchronization" rights) and the rerecording of the music on other media such as tapes and CDs (called "mechanical" rights). In all cases, producers must obtain synchronization rights for music used in their films. If a sound track album or a song from a film becomes popular, mechanical rights may be worth a great deal, and producers should bargain for as large a percentage of these rights as possible.

Publishing rights refer to performance rights, not the printing of sheet music. Composers generally negotiate to retain music publishing rights for themselves. Half of the income from publishing royalties (principally performance rights overseas) always goes to the composer; the other half constitutes the negotiable portion. If these rights are available, most major distributors will insist on ownership. Smaller distribution companies, without ties to record and music publishing companies, will almost always agree to concede these rights entirely to the producer.

Scheduling Postproduction Sound

In the days when everyone worked in 35mm or 16mm, picture and sound matters were relatively simple. Today, with so many systems involved (film, video, digital, sprocketed mag tracks, etc.), scheduling has become more sophisticated; the ADR stage, the Foley stage, the dubbing stage, all have to be technically integrated and capable of communicating with one other. Unfortunately, postproduction sound is often not dealt with until after the film is shot, or until after the director's cut. Then the producer looks for someone to do the sound. With the digital revolution, if you wait until after the film is shot, problems can crop up. The most cost effective way to operate is to keep everything on a single system, but this is not always possible. One way to reduce this problem is to communicate with your postproduction sound house prior to beginning principal photography. In this way, you can establish technical continuity between the field and the editing room. Sound houses are becoming increasingly involved during production in order to minimize problems down the road. An added advantage to initiating a relationship with the sound house prior to beginning principal photography is that their experts will have an opportunity to come up with an overall sound design for the film, or may have ideas about using sound effects in ways not thought of by the production staff.

Given the variations in media being used for postproduction sound, it is worth discussing what materials a producer should provide to a sound facility. It used to be that a sound crew was given a 35mm dupe of the work picture and magnetic tracks. Today sound houses like to get a 35mm dupe of the conformed work print or a telecine made from a conformed work print, rather than a video copy from a digital editing machine. This eliminates any sync errors that might arise within a digital editing system. These errors can also come about because of problems in the way the telecine interacts with the EDL. Also, a telecine of a work picture looks better than one made from the digital output of a digital editing machine. A sound house would also like a track dupe from the digital editing machine that has been checked thoroughly for sync errors, a three-quarter-inch tape with time code, and several one-half-inch tapes (Super VHS works extremely well). Audio can arrive in a number of different formats, including magnetic analog and digital media, DA-88s, 35mm mag track, and DAT cassettes. The sound house will work with whatever they get, but the more you can provide to simplify their work, the less the job will eventually cost. What you provide will be what you can afford. Many low-budget films simply can't afford the luxury of printing film dailies and conforming a work print to match the digital edit. Obviously, if you cut your picture on film, that isn't an issue. You simply have the lab strike one or more dirty dupes of the work print.

You can learn more about the various systems, media, and sound facilities by participating in some of the classes offered at film schools that directly address the issues of new technology; some include field trips to various state-of-the-art facilities. Even with continuing education, it is impossible for anyone to keep up with all of the technical advances and continuing changes in technology. What is important to you as the filmmaker is finding facilities staffed with people who are knowledgeable and whom you trust. Only in that way can you concentrate on making your film. Bill Varney says that at Universal, "We find directors and producers who get so involved in the technical aspects of their movie or their television show that they lose sight of what they're really trying to do." Don't forget that what you are really trying to do, in the midst of all this technology, is tell a story.

20

The Sound Mix (Or Final Dub)

ALL OF THE POSTPRODUCTION SOUND WORK—DIALOGUE, SOUND effects, and music—culminates in the mix. It is here that the isolated sounds become blended into a finished, integrated track. There are a variety of titles used for the engineers responsible for this work; among them are "postproduction sound mixers," "rerecording engineers," "rerecording mixers," or, simply, "sound mixers." The responsibilities of the mixers are often split among two or three individuals, usually a dialogue mixer, a sound effects mixer, and a music mixer, all of which will be discussed later in this chapter.

Mixing studios (also called rerecording studios) are in a state of transition that will continue for some time. The old system of film dupes, magnetic tape, sprocketed drives, leader and splicing tape is still very much in use, though it is being overtaken by video formats and digital sound edited on digital audio workstations. One of the advantages of moving to digital media is that it allows filmmakers to make changes far more efficiently and economically than is possible with magnetic tape. Today the editor can have all of the material for a film available on the dubbing stage, including all takes, all performances, readings, sound effects, and so on. This allows not only for enormous flexibility, but it also greatly expedites last-minute changes. Picture changes can be made and all of the tracks adjusted to match, almost instantaneously. Time code is used on dubbing stages to provide an address that enables a machine to locate quickly any frame of picture or sound (the analog mag system requires cutting the picture, then running down and conforming by hand perhaps a hundred reels of 35mm magnetic track). If a sound effect doesn't work for some reason, a sound effects editor working on a hard drive in a sound house can create a new sound effect and send it over the phone lines directly to the mixing console while the mix is in progress.

This technology will continue to evolve. In the future, random-access multitrack digital storage will replace DA-88s, and sound tracks will be loaded in the form of files directly from workstations. Eventually all of the data on all of the audio workstations will be hooked up through servers directly to the digital picture editing machine. The traditional way we build sound for motion pictures will vanish. Instead, a filmmaker will walk into a very sophisticated editing room and a sound technician will "build" the sound for the movie, pooling material from a variety of workstations. Experts envision a future in which the camera negative will be processed, sent through a telecine machine directly into a digital format, and sent simultaneously, via a server, to the picture editing console, the sound editing workstation, the music editor's workstation, the ADR room, the Foley stage, and eventually to the mixing console without having been placed on any tangible media whatsoever. Richard Portman foresees a time when one person will sit in front of a workstation and put together and mix the entire spectrum of sound for a feature film. "What's going to happen is that there won't be any more people like me—we're dinosaurs. My job will be done in the editing room." There are serious union controversies going on right now over these issues. But the issue for the filmmaker is whether or not these systems will result in better sound. Richard Portman answered this quite simply: "That depends on the person sitting in front of the workstation." No matter how sophisticated the technical equipment is, it is no better than the technician who runs it. In other words, there is still no replacement for the ear of a skilled production sound mixer, the mike handling technique of an experienced boom operator, and the aesthetic sensitivity of a proficient rerecording engineer.

Selecting a Mixing Facility

A typical mixing stage (also called a dubbing stage) is about the size of a modest movie theater without the seats. At one end of the room is a projection screen and illuminated footage counter. At the other end of the room is the mixing board, or console, that looks like the control panel for a futuristic spaceship. Around the console are chairs for the mixers, director, producer, composer, picture editor, and sound editors. Between the screen and the console is an empty floor. In back of the console is another room that houses a projector, a bank of digital and analog playback machines, and the recording equipment. Personnel in this room may include a projectionist, machine operators who set up the edited sound tracks on the playback machines, and a recordist who operates the recording equipment and monitors the progress of the mix through headphones, listening for any defects in the recording.

Contemporary mixing facilities never know what format is going to come through the door, so they must be prepared to accept a variety of combinations. For a major motion picture, it is not unusual to have a thousand or more units (tracks) with 35mm sprocketed mag running for the music units, DA-88s for dialogue and sound effects, several twenty-four-track machines for Foley and ADR, and workstations feeding additional random-access sound media, all running simultaneously. The mixers may be working with film picture for one reel and video for the next. A low-budget picture may have been edited on film, but had a portion of the sound work, perhaps the sound effects, constructed on a digital audio workstation. All dubbing stages are not equipped to handle all the various media in use today, so it's important to check ahead of time to ensure that the dubbing stage you select is appropriate for the media you are working with.

Because of the time, effort, care, and expense that have gone into preparing your tracks, you will want to use a sound facility that will produce a first-rate mix. There are half a dozen studios that consistently mix major feature films. There are many others that mix smaller features, television shows, industrials, educational films, and commercials. When choosing a mixing facility, there are four important considerations: the availability of mixers, technical capabilities, reputation, and cost.

THE MIXERS

Mixers are not necessarily associated with a single mixing facility. Most facilities have staff mixers but will often bring in mixers from the outside for specific projects. The qualifications for a good mixer are technical competence, sensitivity, attitude, and experience. If you're mixing a feature, it is important to use mixers who regularly mix features. The problems involved in mixing a sixty-second commercial are very different from the problems involved in mixing a ninety-minute feature. In both cases, it's best to hire a specialist. When mixing a sixty-second commercial, the mixer will spend many hours focusing on the optimum sound for that sixty seconds. There usually isn't as much time available for mixing each minute in a feature film as there is for a sixty-second commercial. Another principal difference between mixing features and mixing almost any other type of film is that feature mixers must maintain a continuity of sound over several reels of film mixed over a period of days, weeks, or even months. This requires a special sensitivity that is developed by practice. Regardless of the facility you choose, it is best to work with mixers who regularly mix features.

Another qualification for a good mixer has to do with attitude. This varies all over the board and can be determined, first, by the mixer's reputation and, second, by meeting to discuss your project prior to committing your film to the facility. The most skillful mixer in the world, with a jaded or prima donna attitude, may be a detriment to your project. There are many top-notch mixers to choose from who will cooperate with you to achieve the best possible results within your budget. The larger mixing facilities have several staff mixers to choose from and will occasionally borrow additional mixers from other facilities. Smaller facilities have fewer on-staff choices but they, too, often borrow mixers from other studios for specific projects.

A great morale booster for mixers at every facility is a thoughtful producer who supplies an assortment of doughnuts and pastries for the mixing crew at the start of each day. Many producers do this as a matter of routine, and most mixers have come to expect it. Like the production crew during principal photography, many mixers will begin work disappointed if this simple protocol is overlooked. Some facilities keep their dubbing stages supplied with food and beverages throughout the day, in which case the producer's contribution is less important but no less appreciated.

TECHNICAL CAPABILITIES

You must find a facility capable of meeting the special requirements for your project. If your project requires a complex mix with many edited sound tracks per reel, you will need a facility with an appropriate number of playback channels. These may come from a variety of sources, including multichannel machines such as DA-88s, machines that run individual tracks of 35mm or 16mm sprocketed magnetic tape, and random-access media from digital audio workstations. Remember that you don't necessarily need to have all of your edited tracks for a given reel running simultaneously. If you have more tracks than there are channels, or than a mixer can comfortably handle at one time, the mixer will make predubs (also called premixes), discussed later in this chapter, in order to reduce the overall number of tracks. If you intend to add distortion, echo, or other special sound modifications to your original tracks, the facility must have the appropriate equipment to do so. Often there is an extra charge for the use of special equipment.

Another consideration is that, just because a facility is new, this doesn't mean it will be equipped to handle your film. Some of the new mixing facilities have no 35mm machines, except for picture (most feature producers and directors prefer film picture for the final dub). Every function on these boards is automated, and the system holds enough memory capacity so that predubs go directly onto a hard drive instead of onto magnetic tape. The engineers can edit this material on the spot, directly from the mixing console. But they can't work with sound edited on 35mm or 16mm magnetic tracks unless they have the appropriate machines.

REPUTATION AND COST

Reputation and cost considerations must be lumped together. You will ideally find a facility with a reputation for efficiently mixing feature films with consistent professional quality. Such a reputation will reflect the competence of their mixers, as well as the quality and maintenance of their equipment. The facility must also have a reputation for working with producers to stay within the production budget. It is unusual to find a mixing facility that offers a guaranteed flat fee for a mix. The reason is that it is impossible to determine in advance the complexity of the tracks and the degree of perfection that the producer and director will demand of the mixers. Every mix requires a continuous stream of compromises, but an open-ended flat fee schedule encourages producers and directors to become unreasonably demanding in their search for perfection. When the time clock is ticking away minutes and dollars, everyone is far more willing to accept reasonable compromises. If a facility does agree to a flat fee, there will almost certainly be a limit set on the maximum time allowed.

When mixing feature films, it is common to use three mixers: one for dialogue, one for sound effects, and one for music. Depending on the complexity of your mix and your budget limitation, you may wish to use only one or two mixers. Mixing studios charge an hourly rate that varies depending on the number of mixers involved. Using one mixer is not necessarily the least expensive way to mix your film. You must estimate the amount of studio time you will save by using additional mixers and weigh this against the additional cost for the added mixers.

Most feature films have enough tracks to warrant the use of three mixers. When operating on a small budget, however, it is sometimes sensible to use one or two mixers for portions of the film, bringing in a third only if necessary for the most difficult reels. If you are using union rerecording mixers, however, bear in mind that the minimum a mixer must be paid is for a full nine-hour day.

There is also a question of preference when determining the number of mixers you will use. Most directors in Los Angeles, regardless of the type of facility used, prefer to work with three mixers. A few films, including *L.A. Confidential* and *Waterworld,* have been mixed by two. Some directors, especially in New York, feel that one mixer is preferable for two reasons. First, the director has only one person with whom to communicate. Second, one mixer may be able to achieve a more consistent balance in the sound than two or three mixers. This approach to mixing is most successful in studios utilizing a computerized console, the kind of console that records into a computer memory the mix *infor-*

mation as opposed to the sound itself; this is much like the process used by digital editing machines that record binary numerical information that represents picture elements in a film rather than the images themselves. This recording is called the "program," and it includes the timing of every adjustment of every fader, every tone control and, in the case of stereo and surround sound recording, the location and speed of every sound movement, or pan. Information for any one sound in the program can be changed without affecting the information for any other sound, whereas a premix often blends sounds together.

Richard Portman, who has mixed films for such esteemed directors as Robert Altman, Arthur Penn, Hal Ashby, Mike Nichols, Sam Peckinpah, Sidney Lumet, and Martin Scorsese, prefers to work the mixing console alone. "I'm a solo mixer. I like to work by myself whenever I can. I don't have to argue with anybody when I'm doing it myself. When the music is supposed to go down under a line of dialogue, I take it down. You get a better mix—faster—with a solo mixer working with a music studio-style second engineer." He also feels that "for one person to mix by themselves, it is very necessary to have a computer."

Booking the Facility

Once you have selected a studio, estimate when you will be ready to begin your mix and book the facility for that date. You should do this early in your postproduction schedule, since the better facilities are tied up for months in advance. Also, setting a target date for the mix will give your postproduction team a specific goal. If your first-choice studio is booked so solidly that you can't get in, put your name on the waiting list in the hope that someone else cancels and book yourself into another facility for protection. Most mixing facilities won't require a holding deposit until very close to the mix date.

The saying is that a mix will expand to fill whatever time has been allotted. Depending on the complexity of the tracks, and the budget, a mix for a feature film can take a few days or a few months. The engineers who mixed *Twister* felt the schedule was tight at two months. *Waterworld* took four months. Movies made for television are generally mixed in three days. The minimum amount of time you should schedule for a low-budget film is two days. It is common for a mixing facility to schedule a minimum time with an added bumper available if necessary.

Cue Sheets

The dialogue editor, the sound effects editor, and the music editor will each prepare cue sheets for the final sound mix. The cue sheets will list each sound as it appears on each track with precise footage counts for the beginning and end of each sound. The cue sheets should be constructed as a quick-reference road map for the mixers. These sheets may be thought of as an on-paper model that parallels the construction of the edited sound tracks. A typical cue sheet, again using the hotel room sequence described previously, is shown in Table 15.

The numbers refer to footages. Head and tail footages are written for cues longer than approximately ten frames; shorter cues such as the door-closing sound at ten feet on track 2 require only the head footage. The scene ends at thirty-six feet. Compare this cue sheet with the construction of the edited tracks in Chapter 19 and you will see their parallel construction. Separate cue sheets will be written for dialogue, sound effects, and music.

Multichannel Mixing

Before the advent of stereo sound for motion pictures, films were mixed onto single rolls of full-coat magnetic stock that traveled over three separate, parallel sound heads on a single recording machine ("full-coat" is similar to 35mm edit stripe stock, only instead of two stripes, the entire surface is coated with magnetic oxide). The three sound heads recorded three parallel stripes of sound: one for dialogue, one for music, and one for sound effects. Each stripe had equalization and blending modifications built into it during the mix so that when all three stripes were played back simultaneously, they sounded like one integrated sound track. The three-stripe mix was then transferred to an optical negative (see Chapter 21), and that negative was used to print the sound tracks on release prints.

One of the principal advantages of the three-stripe system over earlier single-stripe systems, in which all sounds were blended onto a single track during the mix, was that it gave the mixers the flexibility to make changes during the mix on one stripe without affecting the other two. This saved an enormous amount of time, especially when mixing complex sequences. One mixer, perhaps the music mixer, who achieved an acceptable mix for a given portion of the film could punch out of the record mode for the music stripe while the other mixers went back to the start of the sequence and rerecorded only on the stripes that needed im-

TABLE 15 **Sample Cue Sheet**

Title _____ Mixer _____ Page ___ of ___
Production Company _____ Director _____

Track	Track	Track	Track	Track
SFX-1	SFX-2	SFX-3	SFX-4	SFX-5
				0 DISTANT
				TRAFFIC
3 KEY IN DOOR				
	5 DOORKNOB TURNING	'SQUEAKS'		
		6 DOOR OPENS		
		'SQUEAKS'		
		9 DOOR CLOSES		
	10 DOOR CLOSES		10 FOOTSTEPS ON CARPET	
12 LIGHT SWITCH				
20 KEYS JINGLE				
(HIT DRESSER)				
22	22 CLOTHES RUSTLING			
	24			
		26 MAN FLOPS ON BED	26	
		30		
32 "SIGH"				
				36

provement. For example, consider a sequence that involved three dialogue tracks, two music tracks, and eleven sound effects tracks. Assume that each of the sixteen edited sound tracks contained several tricky cues and the mixers made seven passes through the scene in an effort to get an acceptable blend. On the seventh pass, the dialogue mixer and the music mixer hit every cue flawlessly, but the sound effects mixer was still a shade off the mark. Instead of all three mixers starting again from scratch, the dialogue and music mixers could punch out of the record mode for their stripes, keeping their portions of the mix intact, while the sound effects mixer went back to the start of the sequence and continued working until an acceptable mix for the sound effects was achieved.

There were a few studios that used a four-stripe mixing system. The fourth stripe was used initially for final "sweetening" of the sound, such as a last-minute decision to boost the level of a gunshot. Rather than remixing the sound effects for the entire sequence, the louder gunshot was simply recorded onto the fourth stripe. During the early days of stereo film sound tracks, the four-stripe system was used for recording separate stereo channels. Channels are described by the location of their respective speakers in the theater: left channel, right channel, center channel, and surround channel. Surround speakers are placed along the sides and in the back of a theater, and their most important use is to enhance ambient sounds; if you are watching a scene in a rain forest with surround sound you may hear rain dripping, wind blowing, and insects buzzing all around you, immersing you in the scene. When recording music for a motion picture, an overall mike will often be placed on the scoring stage for the purpose of recording a surround music channel. Surround dialogue is less common, but in special circumstances, such as people talking and walking in an environment that produces a great deal of reverberation, perhaps a large cave, a surround dialogue channel may be used to enhance the effect of the environment. Surround dialogue also offers the mixers the flexibility to throw an off-stage voice away from the screen, either to the left or right, in order to conform to an actor's reaction to the voice or for some other dramatic purpose.

In the four-channel stereo system, the surround speakers produce a mono surround sound; six- and eight-channel digital systems, which will be discussed later, offer stereo surround sound in which the left and right channels are split down the middle of the theater so that all the surround speakers to the left of the center receive the same left-channel data, and all of the speakers to the right of center receive the same right-channel data. This will be discussed later in this chapter. Examples of early stereo films mixed with this four-stripe system include *Grease* and *More American Graffiti*.

When this system was used, dialogue, music, and effects shared the same channels. The left channel was not devoted exclusively to dialogue, music, or effects; it was devoted to the left stereo channel for all of the sounds combined. This brought the studios back to the problem that led to three-track mono recording: how to isolate dialogue, music, and effects during a stereo mix. In order to solve this, they needed to come up with a system that offered twelve stereo channels: four devoted exclusively to dialogue, four devoted exclusively to music, and four devoted exclusively to sound effects. Essentially, this meant having a three-stripe mix for each of the four channels: left, right, center, and surround. Since a single reel of full-coat mag cannot accommodate twelve tracks, the solution was to couple three four-track 35mm full-coat machines together and dedicate one machine to dialogue, one to music, and one to effects. In this way, dialogue, music, and effects each have their own four channels: left, right, center, and surround (because surround sound for dialogue is used only in special circumstances, the surround dialogue channel will often not be used). When the twelve channels (three machines) are played back simultaneously, they produce a fully integrated mix of four-track stereo dialogue, four-track stereo music, and four-track stereo effects. With this system, the mixers have all of the flexibility and advantages of three-stripe mono recording, but in four-track stereo. Some mixing facilities have systems that utilize three three-stripe machines, and eliminate the surround channel.

There is another significant advantage to multichannel mixing, whether in mono or stereo, that comes farther down the road when you sell the picture to foreign countries. If the foreign distributor wishes to rerecord the dialogue in a different language, as opposed to printing subtitles, that distributor will request a music and effects (M & E) track. This is a copy of the music and sound effects channels only. The foreign distributor records the new language and mixes it in a stereo format, but is not burdened with the cost of remixing the music and sound effects tracks as well.

Most films have some production sound effects married to the dialogue track, such as footsteps recorded during a walking dialogue sequence. Some foreign contracts require only a one-to-one M & E transfer, in which case any production sound effects on the dialogue tracks will be added by the foreign buyer. Other contracts require every sound effect to be on the M & E tracks. Often such contracts will additionally require that room tone be added to the sound effects track during dialogue sequences, which will be used as background tone for those sequences.

Temps and Trials

If the budget and time allow, it is common to make "temp" (temporary) mixes during postproduction in order to evaluate the picture more fully during screenings. Temp mixes (also referred to as predubs, but not to be confused with predubs made during the final mix), tend to have "thin" tracks, utilizing minimum sound effects and whatever prerecorded music approximates what the composer will write for the finished picture. Predubs can be made on a digital editing machine. If you are cutting on film, they can be made by editing mag tracks and taking them to a dubbing stage for a quick temporary mix.

Once all of the sound tracks are edited, it may be of value to take the picture and all of the tracks into the mixing studio for a trial run a week or so before the mix date. This will be a quick run-through, without recording, in order to gain a sense for how the tracks are fitting together. It isn't necessary to stop and start a great deal during the trial run-through, since you're not attempting to finalize the sound. You're looking only for glaring errors such as out-of-sync dialogue and ill-chosen sound effects. You may also become aware of a scene that needs a fuller track than you had originally anticipated. Perhaps a sequence for which you had intended to use nothing but music may need a few sound effects. The trial run will allow you to make any such changes before the mix.

The trial run will be of greatest value if the mixers who will do the final dub are present. This will give them an overall feeling for the flow of the film. When they begin the mix, they will have a clear understanding for where the picture is going. They will also have an opportunity to offer suggestions for improving the tracks prior to the mix.

On small-budget films, where a trial run is an unaffordable luxury, the director must spend whatever time is necessary with the sound editors discussing various selections and combinations of sounds. The more decisions that can be made during the editing, the more time will be saved in the mix. When there is doubt as to the most appropriate sound effect, or the most effective combination of sounds, a good sound editor will allow for choices in the mix, cutting more than one combination.

The Procedure

As discussed in Chapter 18, 35mm feature films are edited in reels of 1,000 feet or less. This is the way they are mixed. Consequently, a feature film is generally mixed in nine or more ten-minute reels.

Before starting the mix, the sound editors will review the cue sheets for the first reel with their respective mixers. They will synopsize the construction of the tracks and point out any special areas of concern. During this time, the machine operators in the back room will line up the edited tracks, cassettes, and other audio media for reel one on the playback equipment, the projectionist will thread reel one picture onto the projector, and the sound recordist will load reels of 35mm full-coat onto a bank of three four-stripe recorders.

The supervising mixer, most often the dialogue mixer, will sit in the center of the board with the music and sound effects mixers on either side. The dialogue mixer must listen for the blending of all the tracks, not just the dialogue. The music and sound effects mixers will be more concerned with their individual responsibilities. In addition to mixing dialogue, the dialogue mixer will operate the controls that interlock and operate all of the playback machines. At the push of a button, everything can be run simultaneously forward and backward. Each mixer will operate the buttons that determine the record and playback modes for their respective recording machines. The supervising mixer will usually have an overall control button capable of turning on or off all of the recorders simultaneously.

Once the mixers have been briefed on the content and construction of the tracks and the personnel in the back room have signaled their readiness to go, the supervising mixer hits a button and everything starts to roll. This is a very exciting moment. It is the start of the culmination of months of work.

At the beginning of the first day, the mixers will view the entire first reel, listening to all of the tracks, then return to the head of the reel and begin mixing, one sequence at a time. As the picture rolls forward on the screen, the mixers watch the action, the footage counter, the cue sheets, the level indicators, and the myriad dials, buttons, slides, and switches on the control panel. They must stay one step ahead of the picture, anticipating footage cues, listening carefully, and modifying each sound for the proper overall blend. Very few cues will sound right the first time through. It often takes several passes before the mixers find the correct level, equalization, and placement for each sound.

As in all phases of production, it is the director who must maintain an overall vision of the complete picture. The director is responsible for communicating with the mixers and guiding them through each scene. The director must also, however, listen carefully to the opinions and suggestions of the mixers before making final decisions. Each mixer is a specialist and each will bring to the film a unique experience, knowledge, and skill. If a director feels that a sound is too loud, or that the music is coming in too early, or that a voice is sounding thin, that opinion must be expressed. If there is disagreement, the director must carefully weigh the options, make a decision, and move on. The opinions in a mix are largely subjective, and ultimately one voice must make the final decisions. There is nothing more comfortable for a mixer than a single voice of authority, a director who exhibits both a respect for others' ideas and confidence in his or her final decisions. There is nothing more frustrating for a mixer than mixing by committee, when the producer, director, composer, sound editors, and mixers each express different opinions and interpretations and nobody seems able to make an intelligent final decision. The mixers need direction from a single voice of authority. The ideal situation is one in which everyone's subjective opinions are funneled through the director.

Most mixing facilities have a system of "rock and roll" mixing that allows the dialogue mixer to start the mix, stop, rock back, stop, and roll forward again. Some facilities have a high-speed backup system that runs several times faster than normal sound speed. During a take, the mixers will record onto the four-stripe mag machines until one of the mixers, say the sound effects mixer, who often has the greatest number of tracks to mix, misses a cue. Instead of going back to the beginning of the reel and remixing everything up to the missed cue, the mixers will temporarily punch out of the record mode while the dialogue mixer stops the film and tracks, rocks them back a short distance, stops again, and rolls them forward. The sound effects mixer will punch back into the record mode prior to reaching the missed cue. If the mixer hits it right this time, the others will punch back into the record mode and they will keep going. If not, they'll back up and do it again. Experienced mixers are skillful at punching in and out of the record mode without causing any observable change in the sound.

Using the hotel room scene described in Chapter 19 as an example, the mixers begin this portion of the film on the cut to the interior of the empty hotel room, waiting for the man to enter. As the scene plays, the mixers hit their cues, setting the proper level and equalization for each sound until something goes wrong. Perhaps they get to the keys falling on the dresser and it sounds more like a pail full of nuts and bolts dropping from a second-story window. The mixers stop, punch out of record, back up past the key drop, stop again, and roll forward. The sound effects mixer punches back into the record mode prior to the key drop, lowers the level for the keys, and this time it sounds like keys dropping on a dresser. The other mixers punch back into their respective record modes and they continue recording, stopping again whenever there's a problem.

It is often the dialogue mixer who determines whether to stop. If the sound effects mixer runs into a problem, as with the keys, but the dialogue mixer and music mixer are doing fine, the dialogue mixer may wish to finish out the scene, laying down the dialogue and music, then return to correct the key sound by rerecording on the sound effects stripes only.

When mixing sound from magnetic stock, such as 35mm edit stripe, the mixers can save time by adjusting levels as the sound rewinds so that they are ready for the next recording pass. One disadvantage to using digital sound is that the technology does not yet allow you to hear the sound when you rock the picture and tracks backward. This is because random-access digital sound tracks don't rewind; they offer instantaneous search capabilities. So with digital sound, when you rewind the picture, you wait.

The entire mix follows this procedure. The mixers start at the beginning of reel one and rock and roll through the film, stopping, reversing, starting, stopping again, and so forth, inching their way to the close of the final reel.

Premixes (Also Called "Predubs")

A feature film will often have more edited sound tracks per reel than the mixing facility has playback channels, or more edited tracks than the mixers can comfortably handle at one time. In these situations the mixers will select several of the edited tracks and premix them onto a single track called a "stem," combining the sounds from several edited tracks onto a single stem. They will use the premixed stems in place of the original edited tracks in the final mix. In this way they will reduce the total number of tracks to a manageable number. The tracks selected for combining into stems have usually been edited with predubs in mind.

There may be a premix stem for dialogue and another for music. Sound effects, because they are often spread out across many more tracks than dialogue or music, may require several premix stems. They will be organized in a way that keeps appropriate sounds together. For example, there may be a sound efforts stem for ambient sounds such as rain and wind, a stem for Foley effects, and another stem for the sound effects associated with a specific creature such as a horse or a giant insect.

An absolute judgment about level and equalization for most sounds can't be made until all of the sounds are heard together. The danger in premixing is that certain sounds will be blended together that you may wish to modify separately in the final mix. Consequently, premixes will often be recorded onto a multitrack machine (such as a DA-88, a 35mm six-track machine, or a twenty-four-track recorder), blending together on a single magnetic stripe only the sounds that are "safe" to combine. The mixers will separate the remaining sounds and premix them onto the other stripes. Sounds that are safe to blend onto a single stripe in the premix are those that will require identical modification in the final mix. In other words, their relative differences will be established in the premix. As a simple example, imagine a scene that takes place in downtown city traffic. A business man is screaming (dialogue) at a trio of street musicians (music). The musicians ignore him, but their dog barks back furiously (sound effects). The sequence was shot on a sound stage, so the city traffic sounds must be created with edited sound tracks. The sound effects editor has edited the following tracks: track 1, dog barking; track 2, distant city traffic; track 3, sound of cars passing close to scene; track 4, occasional car horns; track 5, distant police siren.

All of these sound effects tracks may be blended together on a single stripe in a premix except for track 1, dog barking. The modifications for tracks 2, 3, 4, and 5 will be dictated by their relative differences. If the mixers combine tracks 2, 3, 4, and 5 onto a single stripe in a premix, creating a single big-city sound effect, the overall volume of the premix may be raised and lowered accordingly in the final mix, but the relative differences between the sounds in tracks 2, 3, 4, and 5 will remain the same. Track 1, the dog barking, must remain on a separate stripe until the final mix because it will be modified to blend with the dialogue and music, not with the city traffic. If the mixers had married the dog bark to the city traffic on a single stripe in the premix and discovered in the final mix that the traffic was fine but the dog was barking much too softly to blend well with the dialogue and music, they would have been unable to increase the volume of the dog barking without also raising the volume of the traffic to an objectionable level.

If you have five dialogue tracks, eighteen sound effects tracks, and four music tracks, the mixers might choose to premix the eighteen sound effects tracks. If so, they could spread the eighteen tracks across the board, giving six to the dialogue mixer, six to the music mixer, and six to the sound effects mixer. They could then mix the tracks onto a multitrack machine, keeping certain predetermined sounds separated for individual modification during the final mix. Once they had completed the sound effects premix, they would make a final mix using the premixed sound effects, the four edited music tracks, and the five edited dialogue tracks. This brings the total number of tracks down to a more manageable number. Oscar-winning engineers Gregg Landaker, Steve Maslow, and Kevin O'Connell premixed much of the movie *Twister* despite the fact that they were working on an automated console with a 112 channels because some scenes, such as the tornado scenes, utilized many more than 100 sound elements.

Many mixing facilities use a three-quarter-inch or Betacam dupe of the film during the mix. If this type of video medium is used, it is important to remember that video runs at a different rate of speed than film. The mixing facility understands this and will do what's called an audio "pull-up" in order for the mixed tracks to run in sync with a film print. However, sync problems can and do occur, and this is your last opportunity to check sync before ordering your optical track. It is therefore a good idea, whenever possible, to screen the finished mix in sync with a film print before ordering the optical sound track.

21

The First Print

Negative Cutting (Also Called "Conforming")

THE NEGATIVE CUTTER EDITS THE ORIGINAL CAMERA NEGATIVE TO match precisely the edited work picture and line up the sound track in synchronization with the cut negative. In order to protect the irreplaceable negative, this process takes place in a dust-free, temperature- and humidity-controlled environment. The negative cutter also wears white cotton gloves when handling the negative in order to protect it further.

If you edit using a film work print, you will have numbers printed from the original negative along the edge of the film. These are called print-through edge numbers (also called key numbers), and they are built into every roll of film negative at the factory. They are spaced at one-foot intervals (sixteen frames in 35mm; twenty frames in 16mm). On 35mm film there are midfoot key numbers, distinguished by the fact that their characters are smaller than key numbers at the one-foot intervals. The negative cutter begins by locating the key numbers for the first shot on the film work print, finds the same key numbers in log sheets, locates the correct negative roll, and cuts the negative to match the work print. The work print and cut negative are kept locked together in a synchronizer, which is simply a machine with sprocketed wheels that keeps all of the elements running in absolute synchronization. If a shot is less than eight frames long and the selected frames have no numbers, the negative cutter must eyeball the photographic image on the work print and match it to the image on the original negative.

In addition to key numbers, there are several machine-readable bar-code systems used on motion picture film. They include Kodak's KeyKode and Fuji's Mr. Code ("Mr." stands for "machine readable"). With these systems, the bar-code information is spaced at half-foot intervals on 35mm film and one-foot intervals on 16m film. Among the information included in each bar code is the corresponding print-through edge number, which can be scanned by machines that generate a log. The log can either be printed or sent directly to a computer database. Bar-code information can be read and logged by telecine machines, which aids in the preparation of material for both video and digital editing systems. Other bar-code systems are Post Code, Sky Code, and Aaton Code. All of these, with the exception of Aaton Code, place the bar code on the edge of the film at the time it is manufactured. Aaton Code is a SMPTE time code recorded on the edge of the film at the time the film is being shot.

It is important to note that negative cutters use a hot splicer to couple shots together. Unlike a tape splicer, which is used to edit the film work print, or an electronic splicer in a digital editing machine, a hot splicer uses a sliver of film (less than a quarter of a frame) from the frame preceding and the frame following the first and last frames of the edited shot. It is therefore crucial that the picture editor allow for this by discarding at least one frame between cuts in every shot. For example, if you have a shot of a building that you return to more than once in your edited film, you must trim at least one frame between each section of that shot in order to accommodate the requirements of the negative cutter.

If you have cut your picture digitally, the negative cutter will use a series of numbers generated by the digital editing machine to conform the camera negative. This is called the "negative cut list." It will include edge number information, with beginning and ending frames identified for each cut. Effects such as dissolves, fades, and wipes are also identified on the list. In addition, many negative-cutting rooms are equipped with electronic synchronizers, most commonly Cinesound International's Lokbox, that use a time code system to synchronize a video playback system with a conventional mechanical synchronizer. The negative cutter can view a video copy of the film while conforming the negative to match it; this gives the negative cutter a visual reference in addition to the numbers on the negative cut list. If a film work print has been conformed during editing, that print will be used in the mechanical synchronizer.

Analog Optical Sound Track

All 35mm release prints contain an analog optical sound track. Many films also utilize sound in digital form, which will be discussed later. The analog optical track can be either mono or stereo, but feature films today are almost all released in stereo.

The analog optical track is made by translating the sound, and information about its four-channel separation, from the completed mix into an optical signal and photographing that signal along the edge of a special roll of 35mm film. This process is called the "optical transfer," and it requires the use of a special optical camera. The resulting optical negative is used to print the sound track on the release prints.

Before the days of stereo and surround recording, making an optical transfer required a simple one-to-one mono transfer: one channel of magnetic sound to one channel of optical sound. Making the optical negative from a four-channel stereo mix is not as simple. It requires a middle step called a "print master" session. During this session, the sound from the recorded mix from the three four-stripe machines is sent through a matrix that *encodes* the four-track audio and separation information onto two tracks called left total (L_t) and right total (R_t) ("matrixing" refers to the process of adding or subtracting tracks). The two-channel print master is then used to make an encoded optical negative. This can be thought of as a four-two-four process that begins with four channels that are matrixed down to two, then matrixed back to four in theaters.

The principal reason for reducing the four channels down to two is because two-channel stereo is the standard in the field. Optical cameras, for example, which are used to make the optical track, are two-channel systems. Retrofitting all of these cameras to four channels would be cost prohibitive. Another reason is because optical readers on theater projectors require precise alignment. It is difficult to maintain this alignment with two channels, but almost impossible with four.

When played back in theaters equipped with an *analog decoding* device, such as a Dolby Cinema Processor, the sound is split back into four channels or, in some cases, three channels, two channels, or even mono sound, depending on the configuration of the theater. If the encoded analog optical recording is played back in a theater that does not have a decoder, a portion of the sound will not be heard. In the case of a theater that has only left and right stereo channels, the audience will not hear the center and surround channels. This will not affect the audience's understanding of the film because all of the critical dialogue, music, and sound effects information is contained in the left and right channels; the center and surround channels provide embellishments. The same is true for videos played on home systems. If an encoded four-channel stereo video is played back on a stereo system that does not have a home version of a matrix decoder, such as Dolby's Pro Logic Surround Sound Decoder, you will hear only the left and right channels.

The optical track is an excellent medium from which sound can be reproduced, but an optical transfer is a critical process. In order to obtain maximum results, the track should be processed within hours of exposure. If you complete your mix on a Friday and the lab isn't processing optical tracks until Monday, wait until Monday to make the transfer to optical and have the track processed the same day.

A "pop" sound is built into the edited sound tracks by the sound editors at the head of each reel, opposite the number 2 on the picture academy leader, and is subsequently transferred to the optical track to be used as a sync reference for the negative cutter. When syncing an analog or digital optical sound track with picture, the negative cutter locates the "pop" sound at the head of each roll of optical sound and lines it up with the number 2 on the picture academy leader at the head of each picture roll. Actually, the negative cutter will advance the pop sound by twenty frames since the optical sound head in a projector is twenty frames ahead of the picture lens. Advancing the pop sound by twenty frames will cause the pop to pass the sound head in the projector at the same time that the number 2 on the academy leader passes the projection lens. Hence, the audible pop will be heard by the audience when number 2 of the academy leader appears on the screen. Every sound thereafter will be in sync with the picture.

Dolby Noise Reduction

The Dolby SR (spectral recording) system minimizes the noise inherent in the analog medium on which you are recording. An example is the hiss and rumble that builds up on magnetic tape as you rerecord over several generations. Not only does this system improve the quality of the mix, but the optical track is also improved, primarily because recorders used for printing Dolby optical tracks print a wider frequency response than standard optical recorders. Dolby SR works as an effective complement to several other systems.

Digital Sound Tracks

Digital sound is rapidly taking over the marketplace, and it is important to have some understanding of the systems that provide it. As noted in the previous chapter, there are mixing studios that record the *information* about sound adjustments rather than the sound itself. Once these adjustments have been finalized and recorded, they are used to encode master digital tapes for the film. These master tapes contain all of the sound for the film in digital form, with all of the adjustments that were recorded into computer memory during the mix.

One difference between analog and digital sound tracks is that the latter utilizes more channels. Most are configured with the following six channels: left, center, right, left surround, right surround, and a sub-woofer. The sub-woofer is often called the LFE, which stands for "low-frequency enhancement." The nomenclature used to describe this kind of six-channel configuration is "5.1" because the system has five full-frequency channels and one that carries only low-frequency information. Because the three four-track recording machines used for analog stereo mixes are unable to accommodate the additional channels required for digital six-channel stereo mixes, they are generally recorded onto a bank of three six-track machines. Some smaller studios utilize multitrack nonsprocketed tape machines to keep all material on one tape but still maintain the luxury of separations.

Once the mix is completed in analog form, it is converted to digital media. There are several systems for encoding digital sound, coupling the sound track to film prints, and decoding the sound back into analog form so that it can be heard in theaters. These include Dolby Digital, Digital Theater Systems (DTS), and Sony Dynamic Digital Sound (SDDS). All theatrical films that have a digital sound track, with the exception of 70mm prints using DTS, also have an analog optical sound track printed on the film; this serves both as a backup in case the digital system fails and as a way to utilize the prints in theaters that are limited to reproducing analog optical sound.

Dolby Digital is a format that prints both the analog and digital sound tracks optically on the film. The encoded analog optical track is printed along the edge of the film while the digital encoding is placed between the sprocket holes. All films released in Dolby Digital utilize SR noise reduction for the analog optical track. The encoding process for Dolby Digital does not matrix channels; it is a data compression system that compresses the audio information while maintaining the separation of each channel. In order for a theater to play a Dolby Digital sound track, it must be equipped with a *digital decoder* that decompresses the digital information. The decoder interfaces with an existing Dolby Stereo Cinema Processor, which has the ability to distribute sound to a variety of speaker configurations. Dolby Digital utilizes the standard six-channel speaker configuration described above. The Dolby Digital track contains auxiliary information that fills in missing audio data at each splice point between reels, thereby eliminating the defect caused by the splice. The auxiliary track also contains information about how far into the reel the film has run; this data may eventually be used to supplant the necessity for visual changeover cues at the end of a film reel. The first film released utilizing Dolby Digital technology was *Star Trek VI* in 1992.

DTS is a CD-Rom system that can be coupled to conventional theater projectors, thus making digital sound available to virtually any theater in the world. With this system, time code is placed on the film and read by the CD playback units; this locks the sound into absolute sync with the picture. Like Dolby digital, DTS utilizes a standard six-channel speaker configuration. The first film released using DTS technology was

Jurassic Park in 1993. One obvious advantage of this system is that you can create a variety of foreign-language sound tracks for use with a single print of the film.

SDDS, the newest of the three formats, was released in 1994. Like Dolby Digital, this system prints both the analog optical track and the digital tracks directly on the film. Unlike Dolby Digital, the digital information is printed along the outside edge of the film, not between the sprocket holes. This is an eight-channel system comprised of left, center, right, left center, right center, left surround, right surround, and subwoofer. One advantage of this system is that it will automatically interpret the number of sound channels available in a theater and convert the data so as to utilize that number of channels optimally.

These systems have redundancy checks, commonly called error correction codes, similar to those described in the section on DAT recorders. This means that flaws in the digital sound track, such as dirt and scratches, can be detected and corrected before the sound is converted back into analog form and heard by the audience.

An argument against the use of digital sound is, simply, that to some observers it doesn't sound quite as good as analog sound. Certainly to audiophiles it sounds different. This is the same kind of argument that took place when we went from tubes to transistors; many people who grew up with tubes still say that the sound reproduced by tubes is better. Part of this is a matter of adjusting to the new media, but largely it boils down to subjective evaluations for which there are no right or wrong conclusions.

One reason digital sound is different is that we are still using sixteen-bit systems (see Chapter 13). When we get past this into twenty-bit, twenty-four-bit, and faster sampling rates, the systems will improve. Digital technology at higher sampling rates will enable us to have better sounds and better silences. Aside from its benefits, this will undoubtedly emphasize one aspect of digital sound that rerecording engineers view as an increasing problem. That is the loudness of theatrical motion picture sound. Making loud sound cleaner doesn't mean that loud sound is better. Bill Varney received a round of applause at a ShowBiz Expo conference when he said, "I'm having a real serious problem dealing with the loudness of motion pictures. It makes no sense, and I don't know how we're going to stop it."

THX Sound

This system was created to complement advances in digital sound by establishing standards for motion picture audio and certifying theaters that meet those standards. The digital systems discussed previously affect the quality of the encoding of sound information onto film but not the reproduction of that sound in theaters. THX addresses this problem with a customized acoustical design for each of its nearly 1,000 certified theaters; this includes a special speaker installation method, a proprietary electronic network, and rigorous specifications for the audio equipment in the theater. It is the only program to consider all factors that affect performance in a theater, including architecture, acoustics, and equipment. The system was developed by Tomlinson Holman, Lucasfilm's corporate technical director, during the making of *Return of the Jedi* in 1983. It derives its name from two sources: George Lucas's first feature film, *THX 1138,* and an acronym for the "Tomlinson Holman experiment."

The First Trial Composite Answer Print

Once the negative has been cut and the optical track lined up accordingly, the laboratory will make a first trial composite answer print. This will be the first print that combines the fully mixed track with the first color print from your cut negative. Depending on your original negative, this may be in 16mm or 35mm.

Screening the first trial is an exciting but often disappointing experience. After all the time and effort that has gone into making the film, one enters a first trial screening hoping to see a finished, polished film. But this is an unrealistic expectation because the film is really not yet finished. The principal function of the answer print is to determine the proper color balance and density for each scene, as well as the visual continuity from scene to scene. It will also be the first time you see fades and dissolves, and hear the optical sound track. Rarely will the color and density be correct throughout the entire film on the first trial print.

A laboratory specialist in this process, called a "timer," will screen the print with the director and cinematographer to discuss the proper color balance and density for each scene. The term *timer* comes from the days when the technician controlled the look of various portions of a film by determining how long each portion should spend in the developer. Today the timer uses a machine, called a Hazeltine color analyzer, to make scene-to-scene changes in color and density wherever appropriate. The Hazeltine reverses the image on the original negative and displays it on a monitor similar to a television screen. The timer assigns each scene printer "points" for each of the three primary colors (red, green, and blue). The points range from 0 to 50, the image darkening as the number increases. Twenty-five is considered normal, though the definition of "normal" varies with the film stock and with the personal exposure preferences of the cinematographer.

It is helpful to include the director of photography in first trial screenings and discussions with the timer since this phase of production reflects directly on his or her efforts to light each scene for a particular effect. The timer's overall objective will be to maintain a pleasing visual continuity throughout the film. Often a director will wish to deviate from this continuity, and those thoughts must be communicated to the timer. This is the director's final opportunity to fine-tune the overall visual "feeling" of the picture. This can range anywhere from dark and moody with cool blue tones to bright and sunny with warm golden colors. It is crucial that within the context of the overall feeling, the scene-to-scene shifts maintain visual continuity. Once the printer lights are established for each scene, the information is stored and subsequently read by the printing machine, which makes adjustments in its "lights" during printing.

Among the problems you may encounter in first trial screenings are misaligned sound tracks and negative cutting problems, such as black leader slugs in place of scenes that the negative cutter has not yet found, or wrong scenes cut into the picture due to duplicate edge numbers on the original negative. On films where a million feet or more of original negative is shot, it is common to have a few duplicate edge numbers. Since the negative cutter depends primarily on matching edge numbers, the wrong set of matching numbers may be selected when there are duplicates to choose from. Another factor to bear in mind when screening a first trial print is that the sound is often disappointing. This is because laboratory screening rooms, where first trial prints are viewed, have notoriously poor sound systems. They are better than they used to be, but the laboratory's primary concern is with the visual image, not with the sound. The labs will go to great lengths to ensure that their projection systems are the best on the market, that the projector bulbs are accurately matched from projector to projector, that an exact sixteen footcandles falls on the screen from each projector, and so forth. But the sound system in a laboratory is given far less attention.

Mixing facilities routinely receive calls from distraught producers complaining about the drastic difference between the sound heard in the mix and the reproduction from the optical track. These calls usually follow first trial screenings. The first thing the producer will be asked is, "Where did you screen it?" If the answer is, "At the lab," the mixing facility will invite the producer to screen the print in their screening room. Nearly always, the producer is satisfied and quite astonished at the difference between sound systems. I would like to add that when screening at the sound facility, the producer may be pleased with the sound quality but disappointed in the picture quality. Similarly, the emphasis in a sound facility will be on the sound, not on the picture.

These are some of the reasons why a first trial print is often disappointing. Remember that a first trial is just a trial. Most laboratories guarantee the quality of the answer print and will retime and reprint it several times until it's right. In fact, they base the price of the answer print on the assumption that they will have to make perhaps five prints in order to get a final answer print of acceptable commercial quality. If portions of the film are acceptable, the lab may only need to retime and reprint selected reels.

Once you have worked with the laboratory to fine-tune the answer print, and once you have achieved the perfection you're after, another disappointment may come when you see the film in a movie theater. Very few theaters maintain their projection and sound systems up to industry standards. The light level in movie houses is often 20 percent below the standard sixteen foot-candles.

If you shot your picture in Super 16, you may, at this point, decide to blow it up to 35mm. Since color and density will have to be reestablished for the blowup print, you will repeat the answer-print stage in 35mm. If you have already struck a distribution deal, the cost of the blowup will undoubtedly be borne by the distributor. If you choose to blow up your 16mm film prior to striking a distribution deal, if, for example, you intend to show your film in festivals that accept only 35mm prints, you will need to allow for the cost of the blowup in the initial budget (in which case you probably could have shot the film in 35mm to begin with), obtain financing for the blowup from new investors, or strike a deferment deal with a laboratory. You should address this issue before finalizing the budget for your film. A few small distribution companies, such as Strand Releasing, distribute films theatrically in 16mm, but only a limited number of theaters can show films in this format.

Upon completion of postproduction, you will have in your possession one composite answer print made from your original negative and optical sound track. If you have made distribution arrangements prior to completing your picture, you will move right into marketing. If not, you will be in the sometimes enviable, sometimes terrifying position of a producer who has successfully financed and produced an entire motion picture without ties for distribution. Part 5, "Distribution and Marketing," discusses the pros and cons of approaching distributors during various stages of the filmmaking process and outlines the many distribution avenues available to the independent producer.

Sneak Previews

If, at some point along the way, you become involved with a studio or major production company for financing and/or distribution, your film will undoubtedly be screened for "preview audiences." These previews are different from the ones discussed in Chapter 18, and it is helpful to know what to expect. Marketing executives gather a group of people for a "research screening" or "sneak preview." The picture may be screened with temp tracks and music, or with the final music and a completed mix. Unlike the screenings described earlier, the audiences at these screenings play an active part and are encouraged after the screening to be critical. Sometimes this involves filling out questionnaires, other times it involves gathering in small groups to discuss and critique the film. A moderator may guide the discussion, probing for negative critical remarks. Television networks, when testing pilots, sometimes provide audiences with hand-held dials to turn (up as they become excited, down as they become bored). From a collective twisting of the dials, the network deduces an overall score for the film. Studios spend several hundred thousand dollars to market-research a movie, which generally includes between five and ten previews.

Filmmakers have different reactions to this preview process. Some find that it offers valuable insights, while for others the experience is a nightmare. Spike Lee, who believes that research screenings have been good for him (he's had them on all of his pictures except *She's Gotta Have It* and *Malcolm X*), says, "The thing I don't like about research screenings is the cards, when they come back with numbers: 'Spike, sixteen percent of the audience didn't like this.' I really think directors can learn from these screenings, but not the numbers. It's sitting in the audience; and you can tell if you're attuned to the audience, as all directors should be." Producer Tom Rothman, when he was head of production at Goldwyn, said, "You need to see whether the audience is with the picture, and you don't need the numbers to tell you that. You can feel it." Sidney Lumet believes that previews are necessary for comedies and for thrillers. "Barring those two things, I'd say you just have to cross your fingers."

One problem with attempting to predict a film's success with information gleaned from preview screenings is that there is no way to predict and factor in critical response, word of mouth, or the environment at the time of release.

Copyright

A motion picture is protected under the copyright laws the moment it is created. Each element in the film, including music, dialogue, photography, and performances, is covered under one motion picture copyright, though certain elements such as the screenplay and the music may require their own copyrights. Copyright protection for a motion picture covers one specific film and does not necessarily give any protection to the characters or situations portrayed, to future films in a series, or to the series as a whole (e.g., the *Back to the Future* series).

A film must be *registered* with the copyright office within ninety days of publication. Publication is defined by the copyright office as "the sale, placing on sale, or public distribution of copies. This may also include distribution to film exchanges, film distributors, exhibitors, or broadcasters under a lease or similar arrangement." An *unpublished* motion picture is also eligible for registration and should be registered for several reasons. First, you must register your film before you can file an infringement lawsuit. Second, if you win an infringement lawsuit, you may be able to recover statutory damages plus attorneys' fees if you register before the infringement occurs. Third, registration creates a public record of your copyright ownership, which will prevent anyone from claiming "innocent infringement."

U.S. Copyright Form PA (which stands for "performing arts") should be used to register a completed motion picture; this is the same form that is used to register a completed screenplay. Although it is not a requirement, it is highly recommended that a copyright notice appear on or near the last frame of every print of the film.

For more information on motion picture copyright issues, see *Clearance & Copyright* by Michael C. Donaldson or contact the U.S. Copyright Office, both of which are listed in Appendix E.

Distribution and
Marketing

Distribution Strategy

MANY INDEPENDENT FILMMAKERS, ESPECIALLY THOSE JUST START-
ing out, are intimidated by the distribution and marketing process, in
part because these aspects of the business have nothing to do with making films. Producers often imagine themselves with a finished film—a
film that represents significant investments of time, money, and effort—
knocking on distributors' doors, hat in hand, hoping not to appear too
hungry.

How many doors will you have to knock on to get someone to talk to
you, let alone look at your film? The answer, in many cases, is none.
Distributors will come to you. Every venue for motion picture marketing (domestic, international, video, and so on) has distribution companies seeking product, and every distribution company has at least one
acquisition executive whose job it is to find and acquire films. Once an
acquisition executive spots a film that he or she would like to bid on, approval must be obtained from the distribution company's sales and marketing departments, and usually from senior management, before
negotiations can begin.

The most important thing to remember is that the market for the independent producer is not the ticket-buying public, it is the acquisition
executive. If you have a known actor in your film, or if you have received recognition at festivals, acquisition executives will knock hard
and often on your door. If you have no recognizable name in your cast
and have had no festival exposure, you will need to make a considerable
effort to attract their attention. This chapter outlines a number of important ways independent producers can do this. If you follow these guidelines, acquisition executives will be alerted to the existence of your film
and, in most cases, will call to inquire about it. If you still end up knocking on doors, as many independent producers do, you won't be going in
cold.

Your first promotional task as a producer, before you begin production, is to alert acquisition executives to the existence of your project.
Each week, *Daily Variety, Weekly Variety,* and *The Hollywood Reporter*
announce "films in the future" and "films in production." Once your
film is financed and you are actively assembling your cast and crew,

contact these publications, either directly or through a publicist, and get your film listed. Ideally, this listing, which often contains nothing more than a title and the name of the producer, will appear during the final three or four weeks of preproduction, prior to the commencement of principal photography. Acquisition executives for all distribution companies pay close attention to these listings. They will contact independent producers in the hope of being first in line to determine whether your film is marketable and suitable for their company and whether to bid for distribution rights. The vast majority of independent producers are unaware of the significance of these listings.

In addition to the trade publications, it is important to get your film listed with Film Finders. This company was founded by its president, Sydney Levine (a woman with over fifteen years' experience as an acquisition executive), in 1989. Its purpose is to supply subscribers with information that tracks the development of English-language (and notable non-English-language) independent feature films. Film Finders' clients include acquisition executives for worldwide major independent and specialized film distributors, home video distributors, sales agents, entertainment attorneys, production houses, film festivals, and producer's reps (discussed later in this chapter).

Since Film Finders' publications list only films that are, or will be, available for acquisition, their tracking constitutes the basic legwork of the acquisition executive. They do not list the films of major studios, except those with coproduction deals in which some rights, such as foreign rights, are available. About half of the films listed with Film Finders are produced with no distribution attachment whatsoever, which means that all of the rights are available. About 300 international sales agents, including all AFMA (see Chapter 24) member companies' films, are listed.

When Film Finders learns of a new independent title, the film is entered into a database that tracks 15,000 titles. Approximately 2,500 new titles are added and dropped each year. The company accumulates information about projects through international and domestic trade papers, festival and market literature (often trading information with festival and market organizers), film commissions, the Independent Feature Project, and by calling producers directly for updated information. It is in the best interest of producers not to wait for Film Finders to contact them; if you have a picture that is in active development, however early, call Film Finders and alert them to your project's existence, and continue to update them on a regular basis. There is *no charge* to the producer for listing a film with Film Finders and becoming a part of their *Independent Tracking Report.* You can submit information about your project by phone or by completing the submission form available on the Internet. All necessary contact information for Film Finders can be found in Appendix E.

Films in the database can be retrieved according to genre, budget, producer, rights availability, and equity investment potential. This information forms the organization's *Independent Tracking Report,* from which the following material is compiled:

QUARTERLY REPORT: This is the master list, and it contains comprehensive reports on all films in the database that are in active development beyond the writing of the script, and that have had some activity or change in status during the previous twelve months. A published title may be a project that is ready to begin funding, that has some cast in place, possibly a director committed, or it may be a completed film that is available for distribution. There is no budget limitation for these films. A $30,000 feature shot in black and white on 16mm stock might appear in the published list alongside a $30 million epic. Titles remain in Film Finders' publications for one year after the film is finished, or one year from the time of the last activity. If, for example, a film is in the casting stage but not yet fully funded, and a year later there is no change in the film's status, it will be dropped from the published list. The report is sent out confidentially to subscribers quarterly in a two-volume set. Each volume is about the size of the Los Angeles Yellow Pages. The first is a collection of cross-referenced indexes. The first index lists films by title; the second lists films with no international agents attached; the third lists films with U.S. rights available; a fourth index lists films according to the status of the production, i.e., development, preproduction, production, postproduction, or completed (some sales agents prefer to pick up films prior to completion, during preproduction or production); a fifth index lists films by genre (action, art film, comedy, drama, horror, romance, etc.). Each list includes the title, genre, synopsis, director (with credits), producer (with credits), writer (with credits), cast (with credits), available rights, contact information, often the film's budget, and additional comments. Comments may include information about the source material on which the screenplay is based, whether the film is funded or seeking financing, the source of the picture's financing, other pictures the company has produced, and the film's anticipated start date for principal photography.

MONTHLY UPDATES: The body of the monthly publication includes the same information for indexed titles as does the quarterly report and features an index of new listings during the past month and an index of films whose status has changed since the previous monthly report. A change in status might include an MPAA rating, festival activity, funding information, or the positive tone of the film's reviews.

THE FRIDAY REPORT: A weekly faxed newsletter (forty issues per year) that contains a confidential listing of new projects with synopsis, credits, contact name, and phone number. Also included is the latest industry buzz on markets, festivals, acquisitions, and development for both domestic and international film communities. Acquisition executives who call producers most often are those who receive this weekly report.

MARKET PREMINDERS: These triannual publications are delivered to subscribers prior to the openings of five major film markets. The first preminder is for the European Film Market in Berlin and AFM (the American Film Market) in Santa Monica, California, both held in February; the second is for MIF (Marché International du Film) held in Cannes, France, in May, concurrently with the Cannes International Film Festival; the third is for the London Screenings, held in October, and MIFED (Mercato Internazionale Filme e Documentario) in Milan, Italy, also held in October. The preminders list hundreds of films with detailed information about rights availability, screening times, contact information, and more. Clients also receive special reports on major film festivals.

These publications are disseminated to a broad range of clients who pay several thousand dollars a year to receive one of several subscription options. The information is available not only in published form but on computer disk and on-line; this allows subscribers to search and retrieve data tailored to their specific needs.

At any given time, there are about 2,000 published titles in Film Finders' quarterly report, meaning that at any given time there are that many independent films that have shown some activity during the past quarter. Of these 2,000 films, about 400 are either in postproduction or have been completed. That is almost exactly the number of titles that is added and dropped from publication each month.

This service provides producers with access to potential distributors who might not be within the producer's scope of awareness. For example, the maker of an art film may seek distribution from Goldwyn, October, or New Line, but there might be an acquisition executive at RKO who, in six months, will be entering this field in a meaningful way, looking for product. Unless a producer has inside information about RKO, there would generally be no reason to pursue that company as a venue for distribution.

A listing with Film Finders is a free marketing tool that may result in a distribution deal, or in a deal with an international sales agent or with a producer's rep, or it might even garner some financing for a project; international distributors are hungry for English-language films and will sometimes invest in exchange for distribution rights in their country and possibly an equity position in the film.

An acquisition executive might use Film Finders' directory to check for films with a cast and director in place that are also in production. This means the film is at least partially financed. If it looks interesting, the executive may explore further by going into the body of the book. If there is information about the budget, it will tell the agent if it's a large film or a small film. Other notes will list the start date, the producer, the production company, and possibly how the picture was financed.

Getting your film listed in the trade papers and in Film Finders alerts acquisition executives in all media, and they will call to inquire about your film. Do not misconstrue an acquisition executive's desire to see your film as enthusiasm for your project. Acquisition executives look at everything. It's their survival, and they will call repeatedly. All they know is that you are an independent producer making a film: it might be a bomb or it might be the next break-through hit.

Though Film Finders does not require budget information, they prefer to have it; it helps distributors categorize a film, which then streamlines their decision-making process. But if your budget is very small, there is no advantage in boasting about how little it cost to make your film. It is a feather in your cap as a producer if you make a $50,000 film look like $2 million on the screen, but unlike the buying public, an acquisition executive will consider both your film *and* its budget if and when an offer is made. John Pierson, in his book *Spike, Mike, Slackers & Dykes,* says, "There are certainly repercussions from using a low budget for publicity purposes. . . . Distributors may turn the knowledge of that minimal cost against a producer when negotiating a deal." October Films president Bingham Ray says that knowing a film's ultra-low budget "would color my negotiating on the picture but wouldn't color the projections I would make on the film." Entertainment attorney Mark Litwak, a staunch advocate of independent filmmakers, says, "The most important advice I can offer to filmmakers seeking distribution is, *Don't brag about how little money you spent to make the picture* before you conclude your distribution deal."

If there are no stars attached, acquisition executives will reasonably assume that your budget isn't $20 million, but maybe it's a million and a half. And maybe it's a very good film. In the case of an ultra-low-budget film, you might simply say that it's "under a million." What matters is not so much what you spent, but how effectively your film plays for an audience, which is more a matter of content and style than production values.

Getting acquisition executives to call is easy; the trick is knowing which ones to speak with, how to deal with them, and how to make your film stand out in a crowd of films competing for their attention. The best way to gain attention is to create a mystique, or "buzz," around your film. At its most basic level, this means getting your title listed in the trades and in Film Finders. During postproduction you might make up a preliminary press kit that includes still photos from the film, a one-sheet, and a press book (see Chapter 26), and send this package to acquisition executives at distribution companies with whom you would like to discuss your film.

Another way to create a mystique is to obtain the services of a producer's rep. This term has been used to describe an individual who puts together financing for the production of independent films, but here I am referring to the more common use of the term: individuals who assist in setting up distribution for films once they are completed, and sometimes when they are only partially completed. In general, these people function as strategists, assisting producers in positioning their films at the right festivals, setting up screenings, and handling the overall marketing of the film to acquisition executives. Having a producer's rep with a solid track record attached to a film creates a mystique in and of itself. There is a little subculture of these individuals, and one way to discover who's current in the field is to contact the Independent Feature Project (East or West) and inquire about the most recently active reps. Another way is to research films of a genre similar to yours and see if anyone was connected with them in the capacity of producer's rep for financing and/or distribution.

Generally, producer's reps receive between 5 and 10 percent of the picture's revenues. If an attorney acts as a producer's rep, he or she will often charge 15 percent, but that will include legal fees. John Pierson, who has guided over a dozen low-budget independent feature films through distribution, charges 7½ percent. Because of his reputation and track record, John Pierson's attachment to a project will automatically create a buzz.

When to Screen for Distributors

The commercial success of any film is dependent upon distribution, and since many independent films never find a distributor, independent producers often feel that the risk of beginning a project without a distribution deal is simply too great. Usually this means assembling a strong package consisting of a script, director, and cast. However, independent producers commonly make distribution deals with acquisition executives at all steps in the development of their projects: concept level, preproduction packaging, midway through principal photography, rough-cut editing, and finished film.

Since many independent producers, especially beginning producers with low- or medium-budget projects, are not in a position to assemble a strong package of preproduction elements, it is often difficult for them to negotiate for distribution and/or foreign presales prior to making the film. These producers believe just as strongly as any others that their films will reap box office rewards. But a producer in this position, particularly one without a track record, is often forced either to accept unfavorable distribution terms or to finance and produce the film without a distribution deal in place. A producer who opts for proceeding without a deal in place runs the risk of never finding a distributor, but also maintains the freedom to offer a finished, or partially finished, film to several distributors. In addition—and this is a key element for many independents—creative control is retained by the filmmaker.

The kind of distribution deal you get will depend first on the film, and second on the stage of its development. Regardless of the stage of completion, remember that acquisition executives cannot afford *not* to become familiar with your film. Their business is acquiring pictures, and they need marketable products. A producer who makes a film that distributors want is in an optimum bargaining position if the film is completed independently, first because potential distributors will be able to screen a polished, finely tuned product, and second because distributors aren't being asked for money to finance the film, they are being offered an opportunity to market it. The producer's position becomes even more powerful if there are several distributors interested and the producer establishes a bidding situation among them.

An incomplete film should not be shown unless absolutely necessary. That necessity is almost always a lack of money. Distributors know this and will use it to advantage in negotiating a deal—if it ever gets that far. Selling a partially finished film in order to get completion money is not easy. One of the reasons is that a rough cut looks bad. If you are cutting on film, the picture will have scratches, dirt, splices, and often will lack titles and opticals; the sound will be incomplete, missing music and sound effects. You may choose to make a temp mix of music and sound effects, but this requires some special editing equipment, or editing sound tracks and paying for temp mix on a dubbing stage. If you are cutting digitally, you will be in a slightly better position. The quality of the picture will not be as good as film, but it will be free of dirt and scratches; it may include opticals and temporary titles and credits; and you also have the option of adding and mixing temporary music and sound effects tracts on the digital editing machine. Nonetheless, be wary of a distributor who says, "I know it's not finished, but it doesn't matter. I've seen hundreds of rough cuts." Don't be fooled: It *does* matter. An enthusiastic filmmaker sees all sorts of possibilities—and reads in all sorts of intentions—that the critical observer looking for something to sell may not understand at all.

The only people who can successfully fill in the missing blanks are the director, the editor, and sometimes the producer. A person with little or no prior knowledge of a partially completed picture, especially if he or she is unfamiliar with the script, is in no position to judge the potential impact of the completed product. This problem is compounded further if a video copy is viewed in a home or office, or if the film or video is viewed in a screening room. The immediate conditioned response to this kind of viewing environment is the expectation of seeing a completed film. No matter how many rough cuts a person has seen, a portion of their understanding for your unfinished film will vanish when he or she turns on the television, or when the lights go down in a screening room.

If, at this point, a distributor turns your picture down, chances are that the decision will be final. You probably won't be given a second chance if you finish the picture on your own and approach the acquisition executive for another screening. First impressions count for a lot, and a first impression based on a cold screening of an unfinished film is most unfair to the film. John Pierson has concluded that screening an unfinished first feature for potential distributors is almost always a pointless exercise. Personally, he is willing to see films more than once as they change and get closer to completion, but, he says, "I don't volunteer to see a movie again that's left me utterly cold."

If you must screen an unfinished version for a distributor, there is a simple way to minimize the problems: Screen it in the editing room. If you are cutting on film, screen your film in the cutting room on a flatbed editing machine such as a Kem or Steenbeck. If you are cutting digitally, you can run the picture directly from the digital editing machine. Distributors may not like the inconvenience, and maybe they will insist on a screening room or that you send them a video copy, but do your best to screen in a cutting room. There are two significant advantages to this: First, there is no conditioned "finished film" response associated with the cutting room. The environment says "work in progress." Second, you can stop the film at any point and explain how the music and sound effects will be used. You can explain missing titles and opticals. You can even high-speed through the roughest sequences. In short, you can talk your way through the film so that when it's over the acquisition executive will leave with a significant understanding of the picture's potential emotional impact. This screening may be extremely important, and you want to stack the deck as much in your favor as possible. A video copy offers the stop, start, fast-forward advantage of a cutting room but not the ambience. And if the copy is viewed in the acquisition executive's home or office, you will be robbed of the opportunity to discuss and explain what's missing.

In a cutting room setting, it is unlikely that an acquisition executive will close the door on your project. You can expect one of two reactions: "I'm unable to make a decision based on this viewing but I would like to screen the finished film" (the door's still open), or "Let's negotiate." At which point you should call your attorney.

Ideally, the picture should be completed and shown to acquisition executives on film in a comfortable film screening room with the producer present. Many acquisition executives prefer to view completed films in a screening room, but some will ask for a copy on video. This is dangerous. The copy may be viewed in an office with phones ringing and the viewer's thumb on the fast-forward button. If you have completed your film, it deserves undivided attention in a screening room. An additional consideration is that making a video copy from a film print is expensive. Contrast increases dramatically when transferring from film to video, so it is important first to make a special low-contrast print of the film from which to make the transfer. If an acquisition executive refuses to screen your finished film in a theater (or your unfinished film in a cutting room), tell him or her you'll call back; then pursue initially the ones who will take the time to see your film in an optimal setting.

If you call an acquisition executive, you may be unable to avoid an initial referral to the executive's assistant, secretary, or receptionist. Embrace this as an opportunity and make that person your biggest fan. If the assistant becomes your personal advocate, you will have paved a clear path to the executive's desk.

If you have funds to complete your picture and have followed the procedures outlined herein, acquisition executives for all media will have seen your name and your film title in the trades for about eight weeks, they will have received a press kit, and they will be anxious to screen your film. If you are a savvy producer, you will keep them politely at bay until your film is finished, and possibly until it has won a few awards and garnered some favorable reviews.

Film Festivals and Markets

A film festival is a celebration of a collection of films, usually before those films become generally available, if ever, to the movie-going public. A festival is usually geared to a specific city or town, and often includes competitions and awards in a variety of categories. Festivals that include competitions also screen films outside of competition as part of the festival program. Festivals are where filmmakers go to garner attention and create a mystique.

A market is a selling forum. This is where you go to cash in on the mystique created at festivals. Unlike festival screenings, where attendees buy tickets and generally watch entire films, market screenings are arranged for buyers who often just want to get a feeling for a film and commonly leave partway through in order to make it to another screening.

The phrase "festival route" does not mean that there is a particular route from Festival A to Festival B to Festival C and so on. It means utilizing film festivals in a variety of ways to gain exposure for your picture. There are hundreds of domestic and international film festivals each year. Virtually every state in the United States and every major city in the world has a film festival. The dates vary, so at any given time there are several to choose from. Some of the more important festivals where independent films often surface include Berlin, Cannes, Los Angeles, Lucarno, New York, Seattle, Sundance, Telluride, Toronto, and Venice. By virtue of the attention and awards garnered at these festivals, independent films often pick up distribution deals on the spot. Agents, attorneys, and bankers are all in attendance to help bring closure to these deals.

In the United States, the premiere festival for independent films is the Sundance Film Festival held in January in Park City, Utah, and sponsored by Robert Redford's Sundance Institute. It takes place over nine days, during which nearly 10,000 people screen over 100 feature films and documentaries, mostly in cramped, overheated theaters. It's not easy to get a film into one of the major festivals. Sundance screens over 1,000 submissions each year. This is an inherent limitation, and many good films are consequently overlooked. It helps if your film is finished when you submit it for entry into a festival (80 percent of the work submitted to Sundance is incomplete).

There are many sources of information about upcoming film festivals and markets. They are listed each year, including dates and contact information, in virtually every film and video publication, as well as in the trade papers. The Independent Feature Project, the Association of Independent Video and Filmmakers, and the International Documentary Association (all listed in Appendix E), are three excellent resources for information. In addition, the Internet holds a vast amount of continually updated information about festivals and markets throughout the world.

While festivals can be of great value to independent filmmakers, it is important to know how best to utilize them. Geoffrey Gilmore, program director for the Sundance Film Festival, says, "You can use a festival for a lot of different things. You can use it as a place to be discovered, to be bought. Often you're going to use it as a place to get your work showcased. If you're a distributor, you will use it as a place to launch the film, as a place to get visibility, as a place for publicity."

Tony Stafford, former program director for the U.S. Film Festival, believes that "all of these events, domestic and international, have their own personality, strategic strengths and weaknesses—all of which should be weighed for an effective sales strategy." Clearly this requires some research or a relationship with someone knowledgeable about the festival circuit. In choosing which festivals and/or markets to approach, you must weigh the value of those venues for your particular film. This assumes that you have answered a critically important question before making your film: Who is the audience? Once you have defined the audience, you have gone a long way toward selecting your festivals and/or markets. For example, if you have made an art film, or a film dealing with alternative lifestyles, you might bring your film to the Independent Feature Film Market in New York and to the European Film Market in Berlin, where films of that genre have sold well in the past. Markets you would probably avoid include the American Film Market and the Cannes Film Market, where films of that kind have not fared well. If you have made your film to appeal to a broad audience and you believe that it has a shot at winning an award at one of the top festivals, that's where you should enter it. If you are simply seeking some exposure and/or an award for publicity purposes, you should seek out more obscure festivals where you've got a shot at taking a prize. An extreme example is Joe Queenan's *12 Steps to Death*. When he completed his film, he felt that it had no chance of being accepted by *any* festival, so he started his own film festival, in his hometown, entered his film, and awarded it the top prize. This didn't help the film find distribution, but it provided additional material for Mr. Queenan's highly entertaining book, *The Unkindest Cut,* which chronicles his unfortunate experiences attempting to make an independent feature film.

There are also regional considerations when choosing among the festivals. Veteran producer Jim Stark, who chose to self-distribute his $1.4 million *Cold Fever,* premiered the film at the Edinburgh Film Festival; he did this because the film was going to open initially in the United Kingdom, and exposure at Edinburgh is important to a film's success in that territory. "Although our initial festival discussions did include speculation about the Cannes Competition, we acknowledged that ours was a small, subtle film without big stars, sex, violence, or even a dramatic story. It was beautiful, funny, and touching, but not a blockbuster or huge costume or action picture. The Cannes Competition (no less than Berlin and Venice) has a fondness for big pictures with big stars. We readily acknowledged that *Cold Fever* was not this kind of film."

Before deciding where to start on the festival circuit, it is important to consider the fact that entering and/or attending festivals can be expensive, enormously time consuming, and exhausting for the filmmakers. Also, once you have entered a festival, no matter how small or obscure, you have used up your one chance for a world premiere. All major festivals, including Sundance, prefer a film that has not had any prior public screening, even a showing at any other festival (screenings at film markets do not count since they are not "public" screenings). A prior public screening is not an issue at many of the smaller festivals, so if you are not accepted at a festival like Sundance, or if you are accepted but nothing happens, you have other places to go. You might go to the Santa Barbara Film Festival, or the Palm Springs International Film Festival, and get reviewed in *The Hollywood Reporter* or *Daily Variety,* which can be very helpful because those are reviews that acquisition executives are going to see.

In order to be considered for entry in a festival, you must ship a print to the festival committee for review. When sending a print, be prepared for your film to be tied up for as long as three months. Most festivals prefer a video copy for their initial screening, and a print subsequently, if the entry is selected for admission. There are festivals that maintain offices year round, others that open offices approximately three months in advance of the festival. Entry fees, if any, vary among festivals; some charge only enough to help defray operating costs. Most will make no contribution to shipping costs.

If your film has been seen at festivals, has garnered awards and favorable reviews, you will have created the mystique that will help you or your sales agent when your film is brought to the markets to be sold.

The Independent Feature Film Market (IFFM), sponsored by the IFP, is held in New York in the fall of each year and coincides with the New York Film Festival. During this market, members have an opportunity to screen their films for domestic and foreign buyers for both theatrical distribution and television sales. The films are divided into four categories: independent features, short films, works in progress, and completed feature screenplays. IFFM offers filmmakers the unique opportunity among film markets to screen unfinished films as "works in progress"; this is ideal for films needing completion funds. These films are often ones for which the filmmaker had start-up funds, or shelled out enough money to shoot some initial footage. If you have not yet entered the festival circuit, you may have an opportunity to do so at this market; representatives from several film festivals, including Berlin, Cannes, and Sundance, attend and select films for their festivals. This market is of increasing importance for independent films; it has resulted in a number of pictures receiving critical acclaim and obtaining both foreign and domestic distribution.

Other markets can occasionally be used for raising completion financing for films. This is especially true for films of a clearly defined genre. With a strong script and a promo reel, you may entice a sales agent to take your film on. That person may then presell enough territories to finance the film's completion. Festivals that permit screenings of works in progress, such as the Seattle Film Festival, provide similar opportunities.

As with most markets, there are many more submissions for the IFFM than there are screening slots, so the market submits the material initially to an outside jury for selection. Filmmakers whose projects are poorly conceived and/or executed are dissuaded from participating until their projects are better formulated. If a project is rejected for screening, the filmmaker may still be given a market pass so that, at the very least, he or she can bring what is ready and gain access to the buyers.

The IFFM Script Directory Program is intended to be a special opportunity for producers and filmmakers to gain exposure for unproduced scripts. Buyers may read, and consider acquisition and/or financing of, unproduced scripts. The scripts are screened to ensure that they are written in proper screenplay format, but they are not screened for artistic merit. The only exclusions are blatantly exploitative material such as pornography and slasher stories. Approximately 100 scripts are available to buyers in a library setting, but they are not allowed to be taken off the premises. Since the scripts are not prescreened, most buyers do not bother with this program. A small number will scan the first few pages in order to evaluate the writing skills; if they are interested they can find contact information in a catalog that includes the writer's name, a synopsis of the story, and any attached companies or elements.

Once you are accepted into a festival, or once you enter a market, it is helpful to hire a local publicist who will help create or continue a "buzz" about your film prior to and during a festival or market. The press won't have time to screen every film, but they are more likely to see yours if a publicist has spoken with them about it favorably. Sometimes a publicist will get your film reviewed by giving a reporter an exclusive opportunity to do so. In the absence of name stars, a publicist will help you find a unique hook for your film, something that's going to cause reporters to take notice. Even if you don't hire a publicist, you should have with you a press kit that includes publicity stills (not just of the actors, but of the director, writer, producer, and cinematographer at work on the set); a complete list of the cast and crew; bios of the producer, director, and principal actors; a summary of the story; and any anecdotes that the press might find useful.

If you do not have a sales agent for your film, consider going to film markets as part of an organization, such as the Independent Feature Project or the Independent Showcase. Producers pay a fee to these organizations in exchange for services that include representation at the organization's booth, inclusion in the organization's market brochure, and other services.

Independent Spirit Awards

The Independent Feature Project/West's Independent Spirit Awards recognize the talents and accomplishments of individuals making independent films and offer an opportunity for significant exposure for those people and their films to the entertainment industry, and to the general public. The awards ceremony is neither a film festival nor a market. It began in 1984, initially as a counterpoint to the Oscars. The first ceremony was twenty minutes long, sandwiched between two IFP/West seminars. Since then, the awards have gained national attention and caught the eye of the Hollywood elite; the biggest studios, talent agencies, and celebrities clamor to buy tickets. The ceremony has become the IFP/West's biggest source of revenue. Rules for eligibility require that a film be independently made without any studio financing whatsoever (though it can be released by a major studio). The film also must have had a paid admission through a daily screening program, which eliminates films that have been seen only in festivals. Films that have received attention at this event include *After Hours, City of Hope, Fargo, Hangin' With the Homeboys, The Grifters, Lone Star, Longtime Companion, My Own Private Idaho, Rambling Rose, Secrets & Lies, Sling Blade, Stand and Deliver, To Sleep With Anger,* and *Welcome to the Dollhouse.*

Domestic Distribution

A DOMESTIC THEATRICAL DISTRIBUTION DEAL REFERS TO THE DIS-tribution of a film to theaters in the United States. Canada is often in-cluded. In its broadest terms, the deal defines the duration of the agreement, the territories covered, and which rights are included. Do-mestic distributors range in size from divisions of huge multinational corporations such as Universal and Sony/Columbia to smaller divisions within those corporations such as Miramax (*Pulp Fiction, Kids, Trainspotting*) and Fine Line Features (*Mother Night, Feeling Min-nesota, Shine*), to midsize independent distributors like Strand Releas-ing (*Grief, A Single Girl, Totally F***ed Up*) and Trimark Pictures (*Nothing Personal, Ripe, Swimming with the Sharks*), to small storefront operations like Greycat Films (*Fun, Henry: Portrait of a Serial Killer, Meet the Feebles*), which is operated by David and Suzanne Whitten out of their garage in Las Vegas. These options will be explored later in this chapter, as will other possibilities for distribution, but first an overview of domestic distribution.

When motion pictures were first shown in theaters, they were distrib-uted exclusively to persons holding licenses to use a patented machine called a "projector"; these licensed individuals had an absolute lock on the film distribution business. As the business grew and became more or-ganized, the United States was divided into thirty-two territories, which were called exchanges (the Chicago exchange, the New England ex-change, the Dallas/Fort Worth exchange, and so on), and major distribu-tors maintained sales offices in each of these exchanges. Today they maintain offices only in the principal exchanges. In the remaining territo-ries, they operate subdepots that function simply as shipping offices for their films and related promotional material. Because of the advances in communication and shipping technology over the past ten years, main-taining offices in various exchanges is much less important than it used to be.

Back in the days when independent films were limited to art films, noncommercial experimental works, and B movies, the majors had no in-terest in them. When it became apparent that independent films were growing in size and popularity and that they were beginning to compete with the major studio releases both commercially and critically, the studios got involved in a big way. The majors now own some of the most successful distributors of independent films in the country, among them Goldwyn, Gramercy, Miramax, New Line, October, and Searchlight (Sony Classics is not owned by Sony, but has a unique financing arrangement with the studio). These companies handle the lion's share of independent releases that compete both critically and commercially with films marketed by the studios. They are equipped to finance and/or distribute films both domestically and overseas, to mount a national advertising campaign, and to open their films nationwide. Clearly, the line between the majors and the independent distributors has blurred significantly.

Independents without studio affiliation include First Look Pictures, Strand Releasing, Taurus Entertainment, and Trimark Pictures. These companies compete for the distribution rights to the same films as the studio-affiliated independents. They handle less product and generally market their films on a more limited basis.

Two other options that will be explored later in this chapter are "four-walling" and "rent-a-system." For now, you need only to understand that four-walling is a technique by which the producer pays all distribution costs and rents theaters for a flat weekly fee; the producer does this without support from a distributor. With the "rent-a-system" approach, a producer pays all distribution costs but utilizes a distributor's in-place distribution and collection system; in exchange, the producer gives the distributor a small percentage of the income generated by the film.

When evaluating these four approaches—majors, independents, four-walling, and rent-a-system—it is important to bear in mind that every distributor, from the corporate conglomerate major to the smallest independent, competes for the same theaters. This used to be a terrible disadvantage for the independent distributors when it came to booking the "best" theaters. But now, with the advent of the multiplex and the mall theaters, the notion of the "best" theaters has been substantially modified. Certain showcase theaters remain available primarily to the major distributors, and occasionally to the larger independents, because only major films can fill those houses on a regular and predictable basis. At the other end of the spectrum, small art house theaters are still of little interest to the majors. Most theaters fall somewhere in between, and those exhibitors will generally keep a film in the largest room the film will support, for as long as it will support it. If a major studio release is playing in the same multiplex as a smaller independent film but the independent is selling more tickets than the major release, the theater owner will often move the independent picture to the larger theater and shift the major release to the smaller theater. This practice is frowned upon by the majors, and in some cases they attempt contractually to pre-

vent it from happening. As a practical matter, this process of "natural selection" in the marketplace works out to everyone's advantage.

The Majors

Major distributors pick up from independents nearly as many theatrical
and direct-to-video films as they produce in-house. This combined total
hovers around 150 films per year. However, because promotional budgets are so high and competition so fierce, major studios seek primarily
to distribute what are called "event" pictures. An "event" is something
that becomes bigger than the film itself; it's what people talk about all
over the country or around the world, often influencing speech patterns
and popular culture. Films that didn't start out as events but grew into
them include *Forrest Gump* and *Schindler's List.* Films that studios set
out to create as events include *Jurassic Park, Twister,* and *Independence
Day.* One reason for this trend is the competition motion pictures face
from other sources of entertainment, including home computers, cable
TV, and video rentals. Another reason is because Hollywood is living
increasingly on Wall Street. Studios are owned by conglomerates. If a
movie opens well, the stock goes up. Opening weekend grosses have
become so important that unless the picture opens well it is considered
a failure. Paramount executive John Goldwyn says of the studios, "We
all know we can pretty much determine what your picture will do overall based on your opening weekend." William Mechanic, chairman of
Fox Filmed Entertainment, went a step farther: "Unfortunately, it's
reached a point where your fate is written after the first matinee in New
York." The public has bought into this "opening weekend" mentality in
a big way, in part because the press calls such attention to the top-ten
box office grosses. These figures are published in over three hundred
newspapers and broadcast on radio and television news. Many people
decide what movie to see based on the box office top ten, which has
nothing to do with whether or not the movie is any good, or even if
people like it. The press has become so enamored with the numbers that
they fail to mention, or even consider, what they really mean. If the
number-one box office gross is a film playing in 4,000 theaters, each of
which is only a quarter full, and the number-twelve film is playing to
sell-out crowds in only three hundred theaters, the latter is clearly doing
better business and is more favored by the public. It would help if this
information were included with the reported box office totals so that
people could better interpret the numbers. Some publications, such as
The New York Times, include per-screen averages but not the number of
seats per screen. Studios contribute to the problem by misleading, and

in some cases lying to, the public about the cost of a movie, inflating the budget because audiences have been conditioned to believe that the cost of a movie is somehow related to its quality. Individuals susceptible to this stratagem are more likely to pay to see an expensive picture than an inexpensive one.

The majors handle virtually all of the blockbuster films and consequently wield the greatest financial power. They command the best theaters at the best times of year. They also wield the greatest collection power. If an exhibitor is slow in paying, a major distributor can put a sizable dent in the exhibitor's business by withholding product.

There are a little over 25,000 screens in this country. When the studios release an "event" film, they open it on as many as 6,000 screens simultaneously. Some multiplexes will devote half their screens to a single "event" picture. *The Lost World: Jurassic Park* opened on 6,000 screens in a little over 3,000 theaters. Exhibitors will sometimes try to "burn off" smaller pictures by July so that they are prepared for the influx of summer "events" from the majors.

An exhibitor will be allowed to book a film on as many screens as he or she wants, provided the distributor feels that the picture will be a hit; if the distributor feels less secure about a film, the prints available to the exhibitor will be limited. The reason for this is that the more prints an exhibitor uses, the less film rental the distributor receives. This is because the distributor not only pays for a portion of every added screen, but also pays for making the additional release print.

Major distributors offer the most clout for an independent producer, but not necessarily the most profit. They are certainly strong enough financially to offer a large advance and to mount an impressive national advertising campaign. The advance will be paid back, generally with interest, to the distributor out of the producer's share of profits. The standard division of receipts a producer can expect from a major distributor for theatrical distribution in the United States and Canada is between 60 and 70 percent to the producer, and between 30 and 40 percent to the distributor.

On the surface, a 70/30 split in favor of the producer sounds terrific. But what this actually means is that the distributor will take 30 cents off the top of every dollar that comes in, and then deduct the distribution expenses from the remaining 70 cents. If anything is left over, it will go to the producer. Since all of the expenses are deducted from the producer's share, there is often nothing left for the producer. Consequently, knowledgeable producers negotiate primarily for the largest advance they can get. They believe it's all they will ever see. Even if the picture is a blockbuster, they question whether they will ever see a share of the film's revenues, and they question this with good reason (see the *Batman* accounting sheet in Chapter 1).

The ideal film from the studio perspective is an action movie with big stars that is relatively easy to market and promote in the United States, and that will attract an audience abroad. The machinery in place is simply too large to handle films that are not obvious commercial pictures. Exceptions clearly exist, such as the brilliantly marketed *A River Runs Through It.* Robert Redford made the film with outside financing and cast Brad Pitt in a leading role before anyone knew who Brad Pitt was. At one point, North American distribution rights (including video, cable, and pay TV) were offered to distributors for $7 million, but there was enormous reluctance among the studios to gamble on such an unusual picture. Sony, however, loved the film, and cautiously acquired the domestic rights. I say "cautiously" because rather than opening the film nationwide, they opened on twelve screens in five major cities. If the film didn't perform well they could pull the plug and cut their losses. They marketed the picture carefully and honestly, offering audiences an epic life experience rather than an "event." Audiences responded enthusiastically, word of mouth was excellent, and the picture rapidly built up steam. By the second week it was playing in twenty-five theaters, by the third week it was up to 130, by the fourth week the number of screens was 795, and it kept expanding until it was showing on over 1,000 screens nationwide. Opening a picture in selected theaters in selected markets then broadening out as it becomes successful is called a "platform" release.

Another example is *Leaving Las Vegas,* which was acquired by MGM. It opened in limited markets with a little over 200 prints, then broadened out as it became successful. The film became a contender in the Oscars and won for its star, Nicolas Cage, the Academy Award for Best Actor. These films are special cases, and their success is certainly not something an independent producer can count on.

Remember that the majors are not interested in simply making a profit: They are interested in making an enormous profit. From the producer's point of view, a low- or medium-budget film needs only to gross a fraction of what a studio needs in order to return a reasonable profit to the investors. The standard industry rule of thumb says that a film must gross three to four times its negative cost to break even. This means that for a $1 million film, everything over $3 or $4 million gross will pay profits. Revenues for Henry Jaglom's pictures (*Always, Can She Bake a Cherry Pie?, Eating, New Years Day*), each made for under $1 million, range from $5 to $10 million per picture. The figures look terrific to the low-budget producer, but to the major distributors they mean almost nothing. Notable low-budget exceptions include *El Mariachi,* which was distributed by Columbia, and *Roger & Me,* which was distributed by Warner Bros. But for the most part, there is little meeting ground for major distributors and independent filmmakers, especially those making low-budget films.

Should you go with a major, be prepared to lose control of your picture. The marketing department will determine how the picture will be sold, including the concept for the campaign and the marketing strategy for where and when to open the picture. They will probably listen to your opinion on these matters, but the final decisions will rest with them.

The Independents

This is the marketplace for most independent pictures. Independent distributors release each year approximately the same number of films as the majors, and the average cost of these films is far below the average cost of films produced by the major studios. Independent distributors generally offer smaller advances, less promotional capital, and have less clout with exhibitors than the majors. But they are willing to take on pictures that will make money on a smaller scale.

These companies range in size from large operations owned by the studios to small storefront family businesses. They are all more approachable and more interested in small independent pictures than the major distributors. And they offer more flexibility in structuring the deal. The extent to which the producer can negotiate will depend entirely on the distributor's enthusiasm for the picture.

An independent domestic distribution deal is often a 50/50 split between the producer and the distributor. The principal difference between this split and the majors' 70/30 split is that expenses come off the top and the balance is split 50/50. In other words, the distributor and producer share equally in distribution expenses such as prints and advertising, whereas the major distributor generally takes 30 percent off the top as profit and deducts distribution expenses entirely out of the producer's 70 percent share.

Another possible variation, although it is very hard to get, is a sliding scale whereby the distributor pays for all promotional costs and receives 70 percent from the first million, 60 percent from the second million, and 50 percent thereafter. The argument in favor of the sliding scale is that the majority of the distributor's expenses for prints and advertising is incurred during the initial opening of the film. These costs are usually covered during the first million dollars of gross receipts. Promotional costs are reduced during the second and third million dollars of gross receipts.

Some producers, when dealing with independent distributors, may elect to give up their advance in favor of a greater percentage of the profits. This leaves the distributor with more cash on hand to spend promoting the film. However, many producers believe that the more a distributor is at risk (i.e., the greater the advance paid to the producer and the commitment to prints and advertising), the harder the distributor will work; they view a large financial commitment as insurance against the distributor dropping a picture before it has a chance to prove itself. Whether you choose to negotiate for a large advance or a large percentage of the profits, or some meeting ground in between, will depend on many things, including your faith in the picture, your personal financial situation, investor and creditor pressures bearing down on you, the general climate of the marketplace, and the definition of profits in your distribution agreement.

Independent distributors have less product than the majors and can therefore give more personal attention to each film. They are also smaller and less bureaucratic. An independent producer will probably find independent distributors reasonably receptive to opinions about the campaign concept and marketing strategy. All of this is attractive to the producer since independent films generally need special handling. Bear in mind that although these distributors may listen to a filmmaker's marketing ideas, they will not give up control over the campaign. They know that filmmakers are often highly opinionated about how their films should be handled, and that many of those filmmakers know nothing about the world of marketing.

The downside, at least with the smaller independent distributors, is that they have less promotional capital available to launch a film than their larger counterparts. A national campaign is often out of the question. Instead they will strike a minimum number of prints and open the picture in one region at a time. This is often the most effective strategy since each market can be carefully monitored and, in some cases, customized for that particular area.

There are many theories about the best marketing strategy when playing one territory at a time. Some films perform best when they begin in major cities and branch out from there. Others are better off starting in smaller communities, allowing the picture to build up steam gradually before hitting major markets such as New York, Chicago, and Los Angeles. Sometimes it is best to start out in the locale where the film was shot or where the story in the film takes place. The strategy will vary depending on the marketplace orientation of the film, the distributor's promotional budget, the time of year, and the distributor's intuitive sense for the most effective approach. But the most important consideration is that the film be launched where and when it has the best chance of success. Similar strategies are used by the majors; the opening of *Twister,* for example, was scheduled to coincide with the tornado season.

Timing a picture's release is critical. Pictures like *Titanic* and *Godzilla,* for example, must open during a peak movie-going season in order to offset their enormous production and marketing costs with the maximum number of potential ticket buyers. It is almost impossible to open a small independent film during a peak season, such as in July or on Thanksgiving weekend, because so many of the major releases will be competing for the same screens. More than 100 films, at least six a week, are released during the summer season from May to September. Opening in a good theater during a statistically slow season is an advantage since there will be fewer major releases opening at the same time. There may be fewer people going to the movies, but there are fewer movies to choose from. This strategy was used by New Line to open a picture that many people thought was unmarketable. The film was *Se7en,* and the distributor went to great expense to move the picture's opening up to September 22, and to open it nationwide, in order to get a jump on the fall competition.

Often independent distributors who seek to open a film in the best theaters must initially settle for whatever times those theaters become available. This lack of booking clout takes considerable marketing control away from the distributor. Only if the film becomes a hit will the distributor gain power for negotiating competitive playdates. In addition to having less booking power than the majors, independent distributors have less collection power. If a theater is late in paying, there is often little the independent distributor can do. A threat to withhold a low-budget picture is far less powerful than a major distributor's threat to withhold a multimillion-dollar all-star Christmas show.

How to Choose

There is no film that is right for all distributors, and no distributor that is right for all films. The trick is finding the right match. There are several ways for an independent producer to determine which distribution pattern, and specifically which distributors, are suitable for a particular film. The first is to seek the advice of an entertainment attorney experienced in motion picture distribution. This person may be able to offer suggestions regarding appropriate distributors, and in some cases may act as a direct contact with those distributors. There are some entertainment attorneys who function as producer's reps by contacting distributors, arranging screenings of films, and negotiating contracts. Such attorneys may be found either through word-of-mouth recommendations within the film community or by following the procedure outlined in Chapter 1.

Another approach is for the producer to make a list of films that have successfully reached the producer's intended market and to approach the distribution companies that handled those films. This involves:

1. screening those films, generally available on video
2. taking a close look at their advertising campaigns, much of which can be found in film libraries that maintain such records
3. checking the box office results (described in Chapter 2)

It is also wise to check with the producer to see how much money actually came back to the production company (entertainment attorneys experienced in independent filmmaking often have this information at their fingertips). When speaking with producers, inquire about the extent to which the distributor listened to their suggestions, and how much personal attention was given to their films. Producers may be contacted through the distribution companies that handled their films, the Producers Guild of America, or the companies for whom they work. Several publications listed in Appendix E contain contact information for producers; many are also listed in the Yellow Pages under "Motion Picture Producers, Production Companies, and Studios."

Should you find yourself in the enviable position of choosing among several interested distributors, your decision will undoubtedly be based on which distributor you feel will return the greatest profit to your investors. This by no means suggests an automatic decision to choose a major over an independent. The company with a solid reputation, a sensible marketing strategy, and obvious enthusiasm for your picture will be your best choice. As with every step in the process of distribution, an experienced attorney will be your most effective guide in evaluating the pros and cons of various offers.

The Independent Feature Project

The country's largest organization devoted to supporting independent filmmakers, and a prime resource for information about distribution, is the Independent Feature Project. It is headquartered in New York City (IFP/East) and Los Angeles (IFP/West) with a network of affiliated IFP organizations throughout the country, each of which functions independently. They are IFP/Midwest in Chicago, IFP/North in Minneapolis St. Paul, and IFP/South in Miami. The IFP was founded in New York in 1979 around the Independent Feature Film Market. The western branch was founded a year later. It is a nonprofit membership organization comprised of filmmakers, festival programmers, distributors, and other industry professionals dedicated to the support, promotion, and production of American independent films. The principal purpose of the organization is to pool together information and resources for the mutual benefit of its members.

In addition to its many benefits and programs, the organization offers members a variety of resources that help facilitate financing and distribution of independent films. Their quarterly publication, *Filmmaker: The Magazine of Independent Film*, is an ongoing source of information for independent filmmakers. Contact information for the IFP is included in Appendix E.

The Distribution Deal

Writing a thorough document on distribution deals is an impossible task, since each agreement is tailored to fit the specific requirements of each project. Therefore I have written this part as an overview of distribution, not as a guide for negotiating deals. The first and most important rule for an independent producer is to involve legal and accounting counsel *experienced* in motion picture contracts prior to entering into discussions with distributors.

In addition to many legal provisions applicable to all contracts, the guts of a standard distribution deal usually include:

- a nonrefundable advance and/or guarantee to the producer by the distributor in exchange for the right to distribute the film. This advance and/or guarantee will be deducted from the producer's profit participation in the film. There are also distribution agreements in which the producer receives no advance or guarantee.
- a complete definition of how the box office receipts will be disbursed
- a commitment by the distributor to spend a specified minimum amount of money on prints and advertising
- a definition of the territories covered by the agreement
- certain minimum sales figures for the territories covered by the agreement (foreign distribution only)
- a schedule for the delivery of material from the producer to the distributor (negative, optical track, stills, etc.)
- the distributor's fee for the services being rendered (generally 30 to 35 percent for domestic theatrical; 25 percent for foreign sales; 25 to 35 percent for home video, pay cable, and syndication sales)

• sometimes a producer can negotiate for a "bump" in the producer's share if the film's grosses exceed a predetermined figure

The Worst Deal

The worst deal is not getting a deal at all. The second worst deal, from the producer's point of view, is when a film is completed and a distributor takes it on with reluctance. In such cases the producer will get little or no advance, little or no guarantees, and a small or vague commitment to prints and advertising. The distributor will send the picture out with little support and if it doesn't perform, will pull the picture and call it quits. Occasionally the distribution agreement will provide the producer with an option to regain control of the picture if the distributor puts it on the shelf. Remember that unless there is a reasonable certainty that a picture will perform well at the box office, a distributor will not commit large sums to advances, guarantees, prints, and advertising. Only if the picture proves itself at the box office will the distributor begin to push it. Consequently, the picture is forced to prove itself to the distributor without the benefit of a reasonable advertising campaign. This process is self-defeating, since even the best pictures will rarely perform well in the first two weeks without a strong campaign. For any film in any location, the box office receipts for the first two weeks are almost entirely a matter of the advertising and have little to do with the film itself. A worse-deal situation occurs only when a producer is desperate and willing to accept minimum terms. The distributor has almost nothing at stake, which makes it very easy to pull the picture and quit trying.

Another potentially dangerous distribution deal is one in which the producer is offered a modest advance and an enormous profit participation, but little commitment to guarantees or prints and ads. It's a "trust me" deal and one the producer should be wary of. Chances are that the distributor will contractually commit to nothing more than a "reasonable efforts" clause in the distribution agreement that gives far greater leeway than a "best efforts" clause. If, for example, the distributor spends $50,000 to open the film in three cities, recoups only $40,000, and shelves the film, one can argue that this was a reasonable effort, perhaps not a best effort, but a reasonable effort to market the film. Again, your best protection is to obtain substantially experienced legal counsel prior to entering into negotiations with a distributor.

If you don't get a domestic theatrical release, there are still several avenues worth pursuing; these include foreign markets, television sales, cable outlets, and video distribution (Appendix D includes a breakdown of the relative values of domestic venues for motion pictures). Bear in mind, however, that a domestic theatrical release increases your bargaining power when negotiating for any of these markets.

The Best Deal

The scenario that producers hope for is that an acquisition executive will pick up the rights to his or her film for domestic theatrical release with a sizable advance for the producer, a substantial commitment to prints and advertising, strong guarantees, and a reasonable percentage profit participation. If this happens, and it sometimes does, you will need to engage an experienced attorney to negotiate the deal.

The best distribution deal is one in which the distributor is enthusiastic about the film, has a clear idea of how to promote it, and is willing to make a substantial commitment to its marketing. This is a deal where the distributor has a lot at stake and will suffer a sizable loss if the picture dies. This was the case with *The Spitfire Grill,* a $6.1 million film financed by a Mississippi-based Catholic charity. The film was purchased by Castle Rock for $10 million at the Sundance Film Festival, where it got standing ovations and won the coveted Audience Award. That $10 million was triple the amount ever paid for an independent film at Sundance. According to Castle Rock president Martin Shafer, "We love the movie, and we would not have been able to have made it for as little as $10 million." Castle Rock spent an additional $15 million to promote the film, opened it in fifteen cities to a per-screen weekend average of $8,826. This was initially encouraging, but ultimately the film did not perform up to expectations. Nonetheless, from the producer's point of view, the advance paid for the rights, as well as the exposure for the film, and made this a very good distribution deal.

The advantage of a large advance, in addition to money in the producer's pocket, is that the distributor has a vested interest in the film's success. The marketing department must push the picture by developing a strong campaign, and the distributor must open the picture with a large enough advertising budget to (hopefully) draw people in for the first two weeks. From then on, if the picture clicks with the public, the distributor can cut back on the advertising and let word of mouth carry the film.

Money Coming Back

A motion picture goes from the producer to the distributor to theaters. The box office receipts generated by the film travel this same route in reverse. The exhibitor takes a cut from the gross box office receipts and sends the balance, called film rental, to the distributor, who takes a cut and sends the balance, less expenses, to the producer. The inequity in this system is that the investors, who have had their money at risk for the longest time, are at the bottom of the food chain; the only money that passes through their hands has first passed through the hands of everyone else in the chain.

Fortunately, stealing, once a big problem in the distribution business, has been greatly minimized. At its worst, the process went something like this: The theater reported only 80 percent of sales to the subdistributor; the subdistributor in turn skimmed a little off the top before reporting to the distributor; and the distributor did the same before reporting to the producer. Distributors used to keep two separate books of account, one for the producer to examine and one for themselves. The producer's set was adjusted dishonestly to hide a portion of the film's profits. This rarely happens today because the exhibition business, for the most part, is controlled by large companies that have systems in place to prevent theft. One of the principal safeguards is electronic ticketing. There are also companies that specialize in attendance-checking services for producers and distributors. In addition, producers negotiate for a contractual right to audit distributors' books of account.

Even with these safeguards, problems still exist. Major distributors have a reputation for inflating expenses and minimizing income. This often goes unchecked because it is difficult for a producer to track box office figures accurately, even more difficult to track video sales, and it is almost impossible to obtain verification of television sales figures. Independent distributors are less prone to manipulating figures and contract provisions, but it sometimes happens. One way to protect yourself from becoming involved with an unscrupulous distribution company is to speak with the people who made films previously released by a distributor you are considering. You can also check the court records in the city where a distribution company is headquartered to find out if the company has been sued in the past.

Independent filmmakers who do end up with a dishonest distributor often don't have the funds to mount a lawsuit. As a protection, they should insist on an arbitration clause in the contract that binds both the filmmaker and the distributor to agree to settle disputes through arbitration rather than through litigation. AFMA offers an arbitration service for both members and nonmembers, provided that AFMA is identified in the contracts as the arbitration service of choice, or that the parties submit a separate written agreement requesting that their dispute be resolved through AFMA arbitration. AFMA is not the only option for alternative dispute resolution (ADR), but it is the best choice for filmmakers because its panel of arbiters is fully familiar with the world of independent film. One alternative to AFMA is the American Arbitration Association. For information on this and other options in your area, contact your state or country bar association; in California contact California Lawyers for the Arts. Mediation, another form of ADR that can help filmmakers, is offered by the World Intellectual Property Organization (WIPO). See Appendix E for information about contacting AFMA and the WIPO.

Remember that you can lay a strong foundation for protection against stealing and deception in the initial distribution agreement. Experienced legal and accounting counsel are essential when negotiating for safeguards.

Four-Wall Distribution

This technique involves renting theaters for a flat weekly fee. A producer does this without the aid of a distributor. The rental fee for the theater includes the theater staff (manager, projectionist, ticket and concession-counter salespeople). The entire box office income is paid to the producer, and anything beyond the rental fee and advertising expenses is profit. Some exhibitors are more receptive to four-wall distribution than others. The Laemmle chain, for example, is more likely than a large multiplex operation, such as Cineplex Odeon, to accept a four-wall film.

Filmmakers Joe Berlinger and Bruce Sinofsky successfully self-distributed their $100,000 documentary, *Brother's Keeper,* in this way. The film captures the real-life story of sixty-year-old Delbert Ward, an illiterate dairy farmer (his IQ is not much greater than his age), accused of suffocating his brother. Ultimately, with the support of his surviving brothers and the local community, he was acquitted. Despite the success of the film on the festival circuit, they failed to get a distribution offer. So they took the film on the road and learned as they went along. Berlinger did the promotional work and marketing while Sinofsky booked the film into theaters and shipped prints. They spent $15,000 to open in New York and San Francisco, passed out flyers at rival theaters, stood in lines at those theaters and talked up their film, and made personal appearances at screenings to answer questions and to plead with audiences to spread the word. They also reached out to organizations that might have an interest in the subject matter, including bar associations, organizations devoted to rural issues and the rights of the elderly, and film clubs. They hired an assistant who researched colleges in areas where the film was playing, identifying department heads and professors in sociology, law, American studies, anthropology, and agriculture. The filmmakers phoned them and suggested that viewing the film might be a worthwhile homework assignment.

They devoted a year to the distribution effort, receiving additional distribution support from American Playhouse. They spent around $250,000 on prints (twenty-eight of them) and advertising for their $100,000 movie, but the film has grossed over $1.5 million in domestic theatrical release, another $900,000 in worldwide television sales, $80,000 in video sales, and additional money through a sound track deal and various merchandising items such as T-shirts and buttons for a total of $2.6 million.

Writer/director Dan Mirvish did not receive any meaningful distribution offers for his film *Omaha: The Movie,* so he decided to distribute it himself. He made the trailer, posters, and ads, and opened the film in Nebraska. The film did well but not well enough to convince distributors to make the deal he wanted. So he used the revenue from the opening in Omaha to take three prints to another city, and used that money to continue on. He went city by city, carefully selecting his markets. In Phoenix he timed the opening to coincide with the week the University of Nebraska was playing in the Fiesta Bowl. He placed sandwich boards outside the stadium and handed out flyers to 15,000 Nebraska fans. The film ran for seven days in Phoenix, and he moved on.

Four-wall distribution on a larger scale is a difficult and risky proposition. However, it has been demonstrated that this can result in a sizable profit. In order to initiate a large-scale four-wall operation, a producer must have an advertising campaign (see Chapter 26), a thorough knowledge of the value of various theaters at different times of the year, and a substantial amount of money to spend on promotion. Many of the family "adventure/wilderness" films have been successfully distributed using the four-wall technique. The producer will enter a territory, rent many theaters in neighborhoods throughout the area, then saturate the territory with television advertising. The films are often made for very little money and may not be very interesting, but they contain enough exciting highlights to make an effective television advertising campaign. Since each television ad reaches all of the neighborhoods where the film is playing, the cost of the television time is amortized among all of the theaters playing the film, thus greatly reducing the advertising cost per theater. Sometimes the producer will spend much more on the saturation television campaigns than was spent to make the film.

If the films themselves fail to live up to audience expectations, they will get poor word of mouth and die after a week or two. But that's often expected. The producer relies on an expensive saturation campaign to draw large enough crowds in the first two weeks to return a profit. Rarely will the film stay for a third week. It's a hit-and-run technique that is sometimes profitable, sometimes not, but always risky.

Other films that are sometimes distributed in this way include those financed by religious groups, and films dealing with specific social issues. A film focused on a particular religious or philosophical group might take a different marketing approach, such as intensive direct-mail advertising or leaflets handed out at meetings attended by the target audience. These campaigns go virtually unnoticed by the general public, and the films usually play at off times such as weekend mornings or matinees.

Rent-a-System

Between turning your film over to a distributor and taking on the burdens of four-walling, there is another option sometimes referred to as rent-a-system. This is a technique whereby a producer puts up all the money for prints and advertising, and rents a distributor's in-place distribution and collection system. The fee a producer can expect to pay for such a system generally ranges between 12½ to 17½ percent of gross film rental (the percentage of the box office gross received by the distributor), which is far less than a producer gives up when a distributor risks money on advances, guarantees, and the cost of an advertising campaign.

With this method, the producer retains control over the marketing and advertising campaign. The distribution company provides its internal system, which includes in-house bookers to book the film into theaters; a shipping room to order, prepare, and send out publicity material and prints; a bookkeeping system to keep track of money and materials; and its in-house collection system to follow up on receivables. This approach works best when no one except the producer and the distribution company knows this is anything other than a standard distribution deal. The advantage of having Fox or Universal call for overdue accounts is obvious, but theater owners know that the studio's collections staff will be less aggressive if the system has been rented and the percentage to be collected for the distributor is relatively small.

Rent-a-system has been the savior of several films, among them *Twice in a Lifetime,* directed by Bud Yorkin and starring Gene Hackman. It is a great deal of work, with considerable financial risk, though not as arduous a burden as four-walling.

Prints and Advertising (P & A) Funds

A key element to the success of four-walling and rent-a-system techniques is access to a source of funds for prints and advertising, the so-called P & A funds. Even if you do not plan to four-wall or rent-a-system, you gain great advantage when negotiating with a distributor if you can bring P & A funds to the table.

Basically, the funds are put up for the purpose of financing the purchase of prints, which cost about $1,250 each, and the advertising campaign, which can be anything from a hundred thousand dollars to millions of dollars. They amount to some of the safest investments in the motion picture industry for the following three reasons:

1. The fund is repaid either immediately before or immediately after the distributor is paid, depending upon the relative strengths of those two parties when negotiating the deal;
2. When a producer contributes P & A funds, the distributor has less at risk and receives a proportionately lower distribution fee;
3. The repayment will be fully collateralized not only by the distribution efforts being funded, but also by income from video, television sales, cable sales, foreign sales, and all other revenues generated by the film.

There are many sources for this money, most of which are private investment funds. These funds come and go rather rapidly, so you will need a well-connected entertainment attorney or accounting firm to assist in locating them. It is unusual for a producer to give up equity positions in exchange for P & A fund investments because the risk is relatively low.

Release Prints

Upon completion of distribution negotiations and the signing of a distribution agreement, the producer will turn over to the distributor, or provide access to, among other things, all materials necessary for making release prints (see Appendix F). These elements will be defined in a laboratory access letter called a "lab letter" and will include the conformed original negative and the optical sound track. The distributor will then order from the laboratory an interpositive (IP) from which an internegative will be made. The internegative will be used to make the release prints. The purpose of the IP/internegative process is to protect the original negative from wear and tear during release printing. For very small print orders, or for special engagements, release prints may be struck directly from the original camera negative. The interneg will be timed (see Chapter 21) and, like the first print from the original negative, will be called a first trial "check print" or "answer print." The purpose of the check print is to ensure that the scene-to-scene color and density are correct, and that all of the visual and sound elements are lined up correctly. When the laboratory produces an acceptable first trial from the internegative, the distributor will order release prints for distribution to theaters.

As explained in Chapter 18, release prints are generally shipped on 2,000-foot reels. Automated cinemas use a "platter" system for which the individual 2,000-foot shipping reels are spliced together by the projectionist into one giant reel. The platter is a large plate-like device that holds the entire film. In theaters with multiple screens, this permits a single projectionist to operate the equipment for several screens simultaneously. Single-screen theaters are often equipped to show films on extended-length reels (ELRs), which hold up to 6,800 feet of standard triacetate film stock (or 8,000 feet of the thinner polyester stock). For these theaters, the contents of three 2,000-foot reels will be spliced together and shipped as a single reel. It is not uncommon for films to be shipped on both the standard 2,000-foot reels and also on ELRs. Shipping on ELRs reduces the time it takes to break down and build up reels and reduces the handling damage to the film in theaters that have a platter system and those with projectors that can accommodate ELRs.

If the distributor intends to open the picture in a small way, perhaps on a territory-by-territory basis, the order may be only fifty release prints. Four-walling may require only one. A national distribution pattern, however, will require several hundred prints; in the case of the largest releases, between 3,000 and 6,000 prints will be released simultaneously.

As noted earlier in the text, there is talk about eliminating or cutting down on the need for release prints in the future and replacing them with digital images; these would be sent via satellite and projected in theaters on a large-screen equivalent of HDTV. In addition to savings in print costs and shipping, this system will eliminate dirt, scratches, and other wear-and-tear damage that occurs with film prints.

Foreign Distribution

OVER HALF OF ALL FILM REVENUE ($4.9 BILLION A YEAR) COMES from abroad, which puts the motion picture industry second only to the aerospace industry in contributing to a positive balance of trade in the United States. Jack Valenti, president of the MPAA, believes that the foreign market is the "locomotive" that will carry the movie industry into the next decade. The building boom of showcase theaters and theater complexes abroad will undoubtedly contribute to this trend. More than ever before, studios and filmmakers are thinking globally right from the beginning. Many executives within the industry view the foreign market as the bridge that will carry the studios from the video boom of the 1980s to the widely anticipated pay-per-view boom of the new millennium.

A sales agent is more likely to secure a foreign distribution deal for a film if there is already a domestic deal in place, but a domestic theatrical release is not necessarily an indicator of a film's eventual success overseas. An example is Wayne Wang's award-winning *Smoke,* a $5 million film starring Harvey Keitel, William Hurt, and Stockard Channing. The film's domestic box office was only $8 million, but its eventual revenue from all other theatrical markets was $30 million.

Historically, the films most likely to find distribution in the foreign market have been visually oriented films shot with American backdrops and American actors. A studio action film will earn more than half its money from foreign sales. Studio comedies do not have the same appeal overseas, and films that are dialogue oriented are not generally as popular worldwide as they are domestically. That isn't to say that the foreign market is limited to action or horror films. Many producers are finding that the foreign market is becoming more director driven and story driven than ever before, and that foreign audiences are often more sophisticated than their domestic counterpart.

It is common for a producer to make distribution deals with separate distributors for domestic and foreign release. Foreign distribution, sometimes referred to as "worldwide" or "international" distribution, covers all territories outside the United States and Canada. A *foreign distributor* is someone who buys the rights to market and distribute films in a specific foreign country or territory such as Italy, Germany, India, Japan, the former Yugoslavia, or the Philippines (see Appendix D for a list of the relative values of foreign markets available to independent producers). In order to reach these distributors, a producer needs a *foreign sales agent* (there are approximately 200) who sells films to foreign distributors in territories throughout the world. This person will cart films and promotional materials to film markets in an effort to generate sales.

More and more commonly, foreign sales agents are making permanent deals with foreign distributors for all their pictures in certain territories, creating a network of distribution partnerships throughout the world. Once you strike a deal with a foreign sales agent, your film, video copies, one-sheets, still photographs, and other promotional material will be taken to film markets and exhibited for foreign buyers (distributors). The worst-case scenario for a film that gets picked up by a foreign agent is that it doesn't sell. If it does, money will probably trickle in over several years, almost exclusively from advances; rarely will a producer see any profits from foreign sales beyond the initial advance from the foreign distributor.

A few producers, such as Jim Stark, producer of the Jim Jarmusch films, sell foreign rights directly to distributors. Stark, Jarmusch, and attorney Richard Heller hammer out their deals at the film markets that include the following guarantees: ownership of the negative; direct supervision of subtitling (Jarmusch does not permit his pictures to be dubbed), marketing, and distribution in every territory; rights reversions within seven to ten years; the option to split off ancillary sales; and video release in the letterbox format (meaning that it will be shown with black bars across the top and bottom in order to retain the wider aspect ratio of the theatrical release).

Sales to foreign countries center around the big three international markets: the American Film Market (AFM) held in Santa Monica, California, in February; the MIF (Marché International du Film) held in Cannes, France (concurrently with the Cannes International Film Festival), in May; and MIFED (Mercato Internazionale Filme e Documentario) held in Milan, Italy, in October. Distributors come to these markets from around the world to view films. In addition to finished films, foreign distributors evaluate preproduction packages for possible foreign presales.

About sixty foreign agents participate in all three major film markets. Those are the agents to focus on because they offer maximum exposure at the markets. This isn't easy because the lists at Cannes and MIFED are incomplete and hopelessly disorganized. The AFM, which is run by an association of producers and distributors called AFMA (formerly called the American Film Marketing Association), is the most organized and offers the most complete information to producers. AFMA was started in 1980 by thirteen independent producers and distributors for the purpose of establishing a film market in Los Angeles that would facilitate the international licensing of their films abroad. It has since grown to over 130 member companies that develop, finance, produce, and/or distribute worldwide English-language motion pictures and television programming, while retaining control of the films' rights. The organization seeks to advance and protect the interests of independents throughout the world, serving its members much as the MPAA serves the major studios.

AFM is the largest motion picture trade event in the world. It is held in late February and runs for ten days. Over 200 independent motion picture and television production and distribution companies (exhibitors) license feature films and television programs to 850 buying companies from 65 countries. The AFM market directory offers a fairly complete list of foreign sales agents for independent films, along with addresses, phone numbers, fax numbers, and more. All AFMA member companies sell films abroad; some of these companies also distribute theatrically in the United States and Canada. Those are the ones for the producer with both domestic and foreign rights available to focus on. AFMA will not provide a list of foreign buyers (distributors), only the member sellers (sales agents). All of the productions of AFMA member companies are listed with Film Finders (see Chapter 22). There are some excellent agents who choose not to belong to AFMA, opting to work as off-market sellers; these may be found through their ads in the trade papers during the market season.

During AFM there is a massive influx of buyers from around the world. Sellers screen their films during a ten-day period. Some of these films are in postproduction. Some are screened in offices in a video format. Participating companies range in size from large companies like Miramax to small companies with only two or three films to sell. While AFM is available to independent producers who are not members of AFMA, the market suggests that nonmember producers exhibit and sell their film(s) through an AFMA-member company. Virtually all of these companies are available to act as a rep for an independent producer's film. Even New Line and Miramax will take a picture and rep it at AFM.

A deal with a foreign agent must be carefully structured with the aid of an experienced entertainment attorney. Ideally, it will rule out such things as cross-collateralizing or packaging a film with several others that might not sell on their own merit. If packaging is allowed, it is important to spell out the allocation formula. For example, if five films are sold in a package and one of those films is especially strong (sometimes called an "engine"), it would be unfair to allocate 20 percent of the producers' share to each of the five films. One option is to prenegotiate a formula for the films in the package; this formula might be based on previous domestic box office revenues or on video sales. If you believe that you have an engine, you should avoid a package deal. But even if your contract stipulates that your film cannot be part of a package, it will be difficult to police that provision. A sales agent might, for example, make a package sale but draw up five separate contracts and allocate the lion's share of the money to a film for which the agent had the most expenses. Remember that the buyer of the package, the distributor, doesn't care how the money is allocated, only that the five films are delivered. A similar deception involves allocating 20 percent to the engine in a package and less than 20 percent, say 10 percent, to each of the weaker films. This leaves 40 percent of the producer's advance sitting in the agent's pocket.

An agreement with a foreign sales agent does not always involve an advance; often it will merely define the relationship between the producer and the agent if and when the agent is successful in selling the film to foreign distributors. In such a case the agent will take a film for a specified period of time, do his or her utmost to sell it for exhibition in territories around the world, and split the sales with the producer. If the sales agent gives the producer an advance, that advance will be recouped with interest by the agent before the producer sees any additional money. The foreign agent's fee is negotiable but is generally between 20 and 30 percent. Major distributors will usually charge a 35 to 40 percent distribution fee for distribution in foreign countries. Independent distributors' fees are more negotiable and hover around 25 percent.

Sales to foreign *distributors* usually involve an advance against a percentage from the territory for which the sale is made. In other words, a foreign buyer (distributor) will pay an advance to the sales agent on behalf of the producer that will be paid back out of the producer's percentage participation in the film's profits in that country. It is extremely rare for an independent producer to realize foreign profits beyond the initial advance in any given territory. Even when a film performs significantly at the foreign box office, keeping track of box office receipts abroad is virtually impossible.

A portion of the producer's advance, usually 20 percent, will be paid upon signing the agreement, and the balance of 80 percent upon receipt by the foreign distributor of documents that make available for delivery to the distributor all materials necessary to make prints and promotional materials. These materials (referred to as "deliverables") are not usually turned over to the *distributor* until all the money has been paid, but foreign sales agents usually require the producer to make full delivery to the agent prior to initiating the sales effort. This is because many independent producers are unaware of the materials foreign distributors require and often slow down or abort sales because the materials are unavailable. It is extremely important to pay attention to these needs, and to allow for them in your budget prior to beginning principal photography. Sales agents have checklists for the materials they require, some of which are the picture negative, music and effects (M & E) track for subsequent dubbing in another language (described in Chapter 20), a copy of the "errors and omissions" insurance policy, and a set of advertising materials that includes still photographs, posters, and trailers, also with M & E tracks. Once the materials have been delivered to the foreign buyer(s), the costs of making release prints for foreign versions of a film, as well as foreign-language dubbing or subtitling, are generally the responsibility of the foreign buyer for each country.

Foreign advances for a motion picture with an all-star cast may be worth many millions of dollars, even before the film is shot. A leading authority in this arena is Jake Eberts, a Montreal-born financier who has shepherded the financing of such critical and commercial successes as *Chariots of Fire, City of Joy, Dances With Wolves, Driving Miss Daisy, Gandhi,* and *The Killing Fields.* Despite the refusal by Hollywood studios to finance these films, Eberts raised money through the presale of distribution rights to foreign countries. In the case of *Driving Miss Daisy,* which was turned down by every major studio in spite of the heavyweight producing team of Richard and Lili Zanuck, Eberts presold the distribution rights to several European countries, thereby raising $3.2 million of the $7.75 million budget; the balance of the budget was then supplied by Warner Bros. in exchange for domestic distribution rights. For *Dances With Wolves,* which was also turned down by every major studio in Hollywood, Eberts was able to raise a considerable portion of the budget during preproduction from Japan, where Kevin Costner is a huge draw. Both films went on to win Academy Awards for "Best Picture of the Year."

Henry Jaglom finances his $1 million budgets by preselling distribution rights to four or five countries in Europe. He gets around $200,000 per country, thereby raising enough to make his film. He retains ownership of the negative and domestic distribution rights. In addition to theatrical distribution, his films are strong contenders in the video market. Paramount Pictures has the video rights to his films and has paid more money for those rights than some of the movies cost to make.

Jim Jarmusch, together with associates Jim Stark and Richard Heller, financed nearly the entire $1.1 million budget for *Down by Law* by pre-selling rights to all English-speaking territories to Island Pictures. His $2.8 million budget for *Mystery Train* came from Japanese hardware giant JVC in exchange for distribution rights in Japan; Jarmusch and company retained the right to handle all sales outside Japan. Jarmusch's *Dead Man,* produced by Demetra J. MacBride for a cost of $10 million, was financed almost entirely with European and Japanese money.

The foreign advance is the money that the foreign sales agent sees. After deducting the agent's fee plus expenses, the balance goes to the producer. Assuming a foreign agent is successful in selling a film to foreign distributors, money will trickle in over several years. If the agent picks up a film but is unable to sell it in a single territory, the producer must wait until the term of the agreement with the sales agent runs out before the rights return to the filmmaker. For this reason, many filmmakers negotiate a reversion of rights if certain thresholds are not met.

Additional Markets

Home Video

IN THE EARLY 1980S, ABOUT 30,000 LITTLE STOREFRONT VIDEO outlets popped up in the United States and Canada. The owners needed an inventory of titles but knew little about films. If an independent producer sent them a flyer for a film, chances are they'd buy two copies at $79.95 each for subsequent rental. This was true even for small pictures made for $200,000 or $300,000. Roughly speaking, that's 60,000 copies x $80.00 = $4.8 million. This happened for the first year or two after these stores opened because there were so many outlets and so little product: They all started from scratch. Some of these video companies also financed independent productions.

Video distributors subsequently emerged and began offering advances for the video rights to independent films. The market peaked in 1986, when the festival hit *My Beautiful Laundrette,* made by Film Four International for British Television, at a cost of $850,000, garnered millions of dollars in revenues, both theatrically and in the home video market. This raised the price tag for home video distribution advances for independent films toward the $1 million mark. The end of the boom came abruptly the following year, when another festival hit, *Wish You Were Here,* also made by Film Four International, at a cost of nearly $1.5 million, was sold for domestic theatrical distribution to Atlantic Releasing for $1 million, and subsequently for video distribution to Fries Home Video for $1.3 million. The film was a commercial disappointment, and the price tag for domestic video distribution of independent films dropped to between $250,000 and $350,000. Prices are climbing again, but it is doubtful that they will ever reach the figure for small independent films that existed for that brief time when video distribution was still feeling its way in the marketplace and was hungry for product.

Today home video is Hollywood's number-one source of revenue. A highly successful film will ship several hundred thousand units. Half a million units were shipped for *Scream* in its initial video release. Video rentals total about $9 billion annually, and video sales about $8 billion.

According to the Video Software Dealers Association (VSDA), a trade group that monitors the home video market, total video revenues are expected to top $25 billion by the end of the millennium. There are about 40,000 well-stocked video outlets in the United States and Canada; their inventories include new films as well as back titles accumulated over the years. These stores are primarily oriented toward "A" titles, meaning films that have had significant exposure during a theatrical release. Buyers for video stores will also look at what they call "A minus," "B," and "B minus" films.

Direct-to-video films are generally made for between $250,000 and $2 million. Running times are sometimes less than ninety minutes, even as short as sixty minutes. Consequently, you don't necessarily need a feature-length script when shooting for this market. Marketing usually centers around a solid cast and a strong story line, or some clearly defined exploitation niche. The movies are not limited to any specific genre; projects can range from children's films to psychological thrillers to romantic comedies to science fiction and horror films.

Charles Band's company, Full Moon Entertainment, which he started in the late 1980s, makes and self-distributes six to eight films per year, budgeted between $1 and $2 million, for the direct-to-video market. The projects are low-budget fantasy, science fiction, and horror films with titles like *Doctor Mordrid, Dollman vs. Demonic Toys, Femalian Fantasy, Oblivion, Puppet Master, Seedpeople, Trancers,* and *The Vampire Journals.* Several of his films have spawned one or more sequels. "We're making feature films that several years ago would have played theatrically, but today's theatrical market is so unforgiving that if you bomb, that could be the end of the company. So, in my opinion, there is no shame in releasing a film in a premiere situation directly to home video." Competition in this market is fierce, with retailers choosing from over 200 titles each month. "With the exception of a few big titles," says Band, "the B-movie caldron includes everything from twenty-to-thirty-million-dollar major films that didn't make the grade theatrically all the way to some guy who, for a hundred thousand dollars on sixteen-millimeter, whipped out a slasher movie." Additional revenue from these films, plus a handful of similar films Full Moon acquires for distribution each year, comes from international sales, which are also handled by the company's in-house sales team.

Companies such as Vidmark, the home video label for Trimark Pictures, and Saban will consider any type of film. Saban will sometimes provide up to $2 million in production funding. Vidmark will fund up to $1 million and suggests that filmmakers of live-action pictures submit a demo tape of what they intend to produce. Other companies prefer to see a treatment and a short list of suggested talent so that the company can provide input regarding the packaging and marketing of the film during its development.

Some video distribution companies are experimenting with positioning independent films theatrically in the United States for a brief time in order to enhance their value in video stores (the standard lag time between theatrical and video release dates is five to six months). They are paying between $400,000 and $700,000 for the rights, plus investing an additional $200,000 for limited theatrical exposure. At the top end, this is beginning to approach the $1 million investment mark for the video distributor. The gamble they are taking is whether or not the film's limited theatrical exposure will pay off in subsequent video sales and rentals, even if the film bombs at the box office. At the major studios, the video divisions bring in three times the revenues of their theatrical counterparts, which helps to bail out many of their box office failures.

Films marketed to home video without prior domestic theatrical distribution are principally those made for the foreign market. Often they have some name value but no box office stars. In the mid- to late-eighties, Columbia-Tristar Home Video, owned by Sony (back then it was called RCA/Columbia), was funding twenty-four independent films a year intended for foreign theatrical release with subsequent worldwide video distribution. Today that number has been cut in half. The budgets are between $1 million and $3 million.

A select few direct-to-video titles are strong enough to play competitively in theaters domestically which boosts their value enormously in the video market. An early example was *sex, lies, & videotape,* which was given domestic distribution only after its glowing success on the festival circuit, particularly at the Sundance Film Festival. A different route was followed by *A Weekend in the Country,* an independent feature made for $2.5 million by Rita Rudner and Martin Bregman. The cast included Rudner, Jack Lemmon, Christine Lahti, Dudley Moore, and John Shea. The film was shown at the American Film Market but failed to sell as a theatrical release. It was subsequently sold to cable's USA Network and, following the cable airing, was distributed on video.

The largest video distributors, the ones with the highest overhead and promotional budgets, seek films that they believe will sell at least 50,000 units. Smaller video distributors can make a profit with 20,000 to 30,000 units. And about thirty video distributors keep marketing and overhead costs so low that they can make a profit by selling just 5,000 to 10,000 units. A small film without marketable elements associated with it, either in the form of recognizable cast names or favorable attention on the festival circuit, that sells between 5,000 and 10,000 units can be expected to earn for the distributor (after deducting promotional costs) around $125,000.

The best way to locate appropriate video distributors for a particular film is to check similar video releases and note their distributors. A list of video titles and their distributors may be obtained through video reference books available in bookstores, film libraries, and public libraries; you can also check the distributor's name on the packaging of similar films in video stores. But remember that if you profile your film correctly, as discussed in Chapter 22, they will call you. Acquisition executives for video distribution companies are seeking the same marketable elements as are acquisition executives for film distributors. At the studios and many independent distribution companies, the same executives acquire films for both theatrical and video markets. Generally they look for films that have recognizable names in the cast or films that have garnered considerable attention at festivals. These are key elements because they rely on the advertising on the box to sell the product, not word of mouth. The expectation is that these films sell at least 20,000 units in video.

Video distributors generally offer producers an advance against royalties, which are usually 20 percent of the wholesale price of the videos. The advance is recouped by the distributor from the producer's 20 percent share before the producer is paid any additional money. If a video deal is tied to a domestic theatrical release, the advance a producer receives from video distribution will often be paid through the film distributor, who may withhold these funds temporarily to help handle the cash flow problems involved in paying the substantial costs of marketing the film. Occasionally separate deals will be made for film and video rights within the domestic market, but such deals are always made in conjunction with the film distributor. You may see a different distribution label on the video release, but the deal will be tied together by an agreement that includes the producer, the film distributor, and the video company. It is rare to split film and video rights within the foreign market.

Digital Video Discs

Digital video discs, also known as digital versatile discs or DVDs, are high-density optical discs that will play on a DVD movie player. A DVD holds twenty times more data than a CD-Rom and is used for recording and playing digital information for a variety of media, including music, movies, videos, computer programs, and computer games. DVD will eventually replace videocassettes the way CDs replaced vinyl records. DVD recorders that behave like VCRs, meaning that they are erasable and are capable of recording entire movies in real time, are currently being developed, but the recordable DVD systems needed to create the compressed video found on a DVD are expensive and time consuming; it takes several hours and multiple passes to compress a single movie.

Because of its large storage size (nearly nine gigabytes in a dual-layer format), a DVD is capable of holding multiple versions of a film (for example, PG, R-rated, or "director's cut"), multiple sound tracks (as for a variety of foreign-language versions), subtitles in several languages, as well as associated media such as a computer game or a documentary about the making of the movie.

While DVD far surpasses the resolution of videotape and conventional television sets, it cannot currently deliver HDTV-quality images. Within the next few years the systems will improve and are likely to become what might be called HDVD, with a high enough quality to take full advantage of the resolution offered by HDTV.

Cable and Other Television Sales

Television sales include cable TV, pay TV, network showings, syndication, and other new technologies that are currently in development and may soon provide additional outlets. These rights, together with video rights, are generally granted to larger distributors as part of the initial distribution agreement. They should not, however, be given away lightly; they are negotiable and should be used to advantage. Many of the smaller independent distributors don't have facilities to handle sales to television and video outlets, and in such cases the producer may bargain for retaining these rights. The distributor, however, will request a contractual restriction, called a "holdback," in the distribution agreement that prevents the producer from exercising television and video rights for a given period of time. Thus the film will not be shown in these markets before the distributor has had time to give the film thorough theatrical exposure. As stated earlier, the standard lag time between theatrical and video release dates is five to six months; video dealers generally get exclusive use of a movie for thirty to sixty days (called a "window") before the film is allowed to be shown on cable.

There are three avenues for cable sales: pay cable, basic cable, and pay-per-view. *Pay cable* includes several potential major buyers of movies: Bravo, Disney, Encore, HBO, Playboy, and Showtime. HBO and Showtime, when they were first starting out, learned quickly that they lost subscribers when they aired a picture that had not had prior theatrical exposure. Today they will rarely air a film that has not been distributed theatrically. Occasionally a film will air on one of the premium cable channels before its theatrical release. This was the case with *Freeway,* which aired initially on Showtime, and two films directed by John Dahl, *Red Rock West* and *The Last Seduction,* each of which aired initially on HBO. Exceptions also include the feature documentaries *Hearts of Darkness* and *Paradise Lost: The Child Murders at Robin Hood Hills* (originally intended as an hour-long episode of HBO's "America Undercover"). Cinemax and The Movie Channel are owned by HBO and Showtime respectively, and their buying policies are similar. Regardless of a film's prior exposure, these companies prefer to buy *packages* of films from distributors, or from strong producers who can supply several films a year. Figures are not attributed to individual films in the package until the distributor does the accounting to the producer. Bravo, Disney, and Playboy will consider showing a small independent film, but the revenues from these sales are nominal. A standard distribution fee for a sale to a pay cable channel is 10 to 20 percent.

Basic cable includes Arts & Entertainment, Discovery Channel, Lifetime, USA Network, TBS, and TNT. These companies buy original films that have not been distributed theatrically. They pay very little, sometimes under $50,000, for which they obtain the right to show the film an unlimited number of times for a fixed number of days. Although the money isn't very good, the exposure for the filmmaker can be significant. Two other cable venues that offer exposure for independent filmmakers are the Sundance Channel and Bravo's Independent Film Channel (IFC). Both are committed to supporting independent features, documentaries, shorts, and animation. Each has its own requirements for acquisition and airing. Contact information for the Sundance Channel and IFC can be found in Appendix E.

There are around 5,000 *pay-per-view* cable systems in America. Currently they are oriented toward concerts and sporting events. The films they offer are often ones that will soon appear on HBO or Showtime, and will also appear within a few weeks in video stores. They announce their events to subscribers, who phone in and order what they wish to see. The viewer is then billed either directly or on the viewer's phone bill. There is a high likelihood that pay-per-view will eventually make a significant dent in the video store market. The customer will be able to order by phone any film in the catalog of the company's library, and that film will be transmitted (most likely via the phone lines) at a time specified by the consumer. Drawbacks include the inability to stop, start, pause, and rewind. It is possible that pay-per-view will also replace a theatrical release for some films; however, a film will still need a large marketing budget with massive publicity in order to make it a "buying event" on pay-per-view television.

The most significant television money is paid for prime-time network showings, and the bulk of this money goes to the major studio releases. The record television sale of Steven Spielberg's *The Lost World: Jurassic Park* to Fox was reported to be $80 million. In order for a low-budget independent film to gain clout in television negotiations, it must first prove itself at the box office. Independent films like *The English Patient* that have broken out to become hits command major release status in a television sale.

Films are often shown on television within two years of their initial release, although the sale may be made much earlier. The key, of course, is the network's perception of the film's tune-in value. One of the essential factors in determining a film's worth on television is its theatrical box office gross. One theory is that the sale price should be 20 to 25 percent of that gross for two prime-time network showings, with a maximum ceiling and a bottom-line figure of around $250,000. Even a particularly hot film will not rise above the ceiling because there is a limited number of advertising minutes (usually thirty-two) available for any two-hour film on television.

Most films that have received theatrical distribution, whether or not they are picked up by the networks for prime-time showing, are sold for non–prime time showing, as well as to smaller cable outlets, other forms of pay TV, and syndication. These often prove to be lucrative markets even for low-budget films, with a bottom-line figure for all these rights being around $250,000. A distributor will generally take 30 percent of this figure.

If your picture contains scenes that may not pass the standards and practices of the television networks, such as those involving nudity, excessive violence, or unacceptable language, it is important to shoot television "cover" shots during production. This means that after you've shot the theatrical version of such a scene, modify it to comply with television censorship and shoot it again. This involves such things as covering nudity, deleting expletives, and minimizing gore. When you make your sale to television, simply replace the objectionable scenes with your cover shots.

Nontheatrical Distribution Rights

These rights refer to distribution in which the film is shown to audiences as groups, but not in conventional theaters. This includes distribution to ships, airlines, and trains that depart from territories covered in the distribution agreement; hotel movies; U.S. military installations through-out the world; the Red Cross; colleges; clubs; and religious groups. In-dependent producers, as well as many of the smaller distributors, allow millions of dollars in potential revenues to go uncollected in the U.S. market each year because they lack the expertise to take proper advan-tage of the nontheatrical market. It is often wise for a producer to retain control of nontheatrical rights, and to negotiate a separate contact with a distributor who specializes in nontheatrical sales. An experienced enter-tainment attorney will be able to guide you in the selection of the best nontheatrical distributor for your film.

Ancillary Rights

This is a catch-all phrase that can be defined as all subsidiary rights to the film, including sound track recording rights, music publishing rights, merchandising rights, literary publishing rights (including novel-ization or publication of the screenplay), commercial tie-in rights, live television rights, radio rights, the right to produce a remake, sequel, television series, stage play, or interactive CD, and additional motion picture rights.

Ancillary rights are potentially worth a great deal of money, and dis-tributors will generally attempt to negotiate for their ownership. They can take many forms in a distribution agreement, some of which will be discussed below. They may also be frozen, with neither the producer nor the distributor free to exercise them without the consent of the other party.

Merchandising Rights

Characters and events in films often lend themselves to exploitation be-yond the motion picture market. Books, posters, jewelry, games, dolls, toys, and T-shirts can reap enormous royalty profits. For the most part, these merchandising rights are valuable only for major films with name-star casts and large promotional budgets. Usually these pictures are based on an existing franchise such as known comic book characters like Batman and Dick Tracy, but created characters such as those in *Wayne's World* sometimes garner huge merchandising profits. The most successful example of an *independent* picture reaping rewards in this arena is *Teenage Mutant Ninja Turtles,* based on characters that were es-tablished in comic books before the film was made.

Marketing

The Importance of the Campaign

As PRODUCTION COSTS HAVE RISEN, SO HAVE MARKETING COSTS, and today more money is being spent on prints and ads than ever before. A turning point took place in 1989, when the summer season included an extraordinary number of hits: *Batman, Ghostbusters II, Honey, I Shrunk the Kids,* and *Indiana Jones and the Last Crusade.* As a result, the studios felt compelled to spend more and more in order to compete. According to the MPAA, studios' marketing costs average close to $20 million per movie. A portion of that goes for prints of the film; the rest is spent on advertisements and promotions, which cover everything from TV and newspaper ads to premiere parties. Promotional costs for *The Rock,* which included a premiere party on Alcatraz Island, came to nearly $50 million.

When you have $40 million in production costs and $20 million in a domestic marketing campaign (double those figures for the biggest studio blockbusters), you're in trouble if you don't get the money back quickly with large opening grosses. Conversely, if you don't score at the box office, you bottom out in a bigger way than ever before. The studios have so much at risk that they care about nothing so much as a film's opening weekend. This pressures studios to be ever more creative and experimental in their efforts to entice large numbers of people to be among the first to see a particular film.

The marketing department for these films may get involved during development, meaning before the studio decides to spend the money to make the movie. Robert G. Griedman, marketing chief of Warner Bros., said in *The New York Times,* "Selling movies is like a volcanic eruption. You have to build as much pressure as you can on opening weekend so everyone pours out to see that particular movie. You start at a foundation base of title and star. Then there's the trailer exposure and general buzz—and you hope that buzz is building. Then you have the advertising—the TV, the newspapers, outdoor ads, big publicity campaigns. The pressure builds and you hope it bursts on opening weekend. You hope."

Many producers find this opening-weekend mentality antithetical to the making of motion pictures. In another article in *The New York Times* titled "Why Hollywood Makes Movies by the Numbers," director Edward Zwick questioned how this attitude affects the choices of films that top Hollywood filmmakers decide to make. "Is it just a coincidence that many of those same directors who so galvanized me in my student days now share another common bond: in recent times they have all directed movies based on the same kind of high-concept best-seller whose most distinctive quality seems to be the guarantee of a strong opening weekend." In other words, when each film is a $60 million to $120 million start-up business that can fail in a single weekend, the question isn't the quality of the film, but how much it earns. Scott Rudin, one of the most prolific producers in Hollywood *(Mother, Clueless, The Firm, Sister Act, The Addams Family),* feels that the choice in producing movies increasingly comes down to making either a relatively small film or a high-concept, big-star movie in the range of $90 million to $100 million. "Anything in the thirty-million-dollar to seventy-five-million-dollar range is going to be wiped out."

This is good news for independent filmmakers because it means that studios are finding it more and more difficult to make and market films that depend on finely woven stories and rich characterizations. Those are the kinds of movies that require the personal attention and commitment of a filmmaker who is more concerned with telling a good story than with the opening-weekend grosses. However, with so much money being spent on the studio megahits, the smaller distributors have been forced to spend more simply in order to maintain a share of the marketplace. New Line spent $21 million each on marketing *Se7en* and *Dumb and Dumber,* which covered the estimated twelve-week runs of both movies.

A successful film is ultimately sold by word of mouth, but word of mouth can only be generated if the campaign has enticed the initial audience into the theater. One reason why awards and favorable reviews are such an important part of a film's campaign is because they *are* word of mouth. They are an individual or a judging panel who has seen the film and given it a favorable nod. If you have a strong campaign that includes either or both of these elements, you will have begun your word-of-mouth campaign before the film even opens. And you or your distributor will not have to spend nearly the amount of money necessary to start generating good word of mouth from scratch.

If you don't have reviews or awards to include in your campaign, the initial box office will be the result of the campaign exclusively. It will have nothing to do with the movie. Frank Price, independent producer and former head of Columbia Pictures, says, "Research screenings only tell you how the audience in the theater is reacting to your movie. They don't tell you how to get the audience *into* the theater." If your campaign succeeds in getting substantial initial audiences into theaters and they say good things about the film, their friends will come to see it and they will tell *their* friends about it, and their friends will tell their friends, and so on. This kind of snowballing effect takes at least two weeks to get rolling. Consequently, the campaign must be strong enough on its own to draw people for the first two weeks. Often this requires substantial and costly promotion during this time. But if the film clicks with the public and word-of-mouth comment is strong, the expense is worthwhile.

By the third week, the promotional budget may be cut back, letting word-of-mouth advertising carry the film into its fourth, fifth, or sixth week, or even longer. A film that generates its own audience by word-of-mouth advertising, maintaining a strong box office over several weeks or months, is said to have "legs."

The experts who conduct market research and preview screenings for films say that the rule of thumb is that if a film is good, a good campaign will enhance its earnings by 15 to 20 percent. If the film is bad, a good campaign is even more important because at least you get the audience into the theaters before they find out how bad it is. If a picture is perceived as having little potential for positive word of mouth, the distributor and exhibitors will try to get people in fast, using whatever tricks they can pull out of the hat, before word gets out. The initial launch of a picture is the time when the distributor spends the most money, but it is also during those first opening weeks that the distributor receives the highest percentage of the box office from the exhibitors.

Unless a producer is four-walling a picture or renting a distribution system, the film's advertising and marketing campaign will be in the hands of a distributor. One hopes that the distributor will listen to the opinions of the producer when assembling the elements for the campaign, but it is important to recognize that the distributor is experienced in these matters, is paying for the campaign, and consequently has the final say. Remember this when selecting a distributor for your film. Settle on one who understands your film and whom you trust to make sound marketing decisions. A few filmmakers, like Jim Jarmusch, are able to negotiate for control over the marketing and promotion of their films, but this is very rare and virtually unheard of for a filmmaker without a substantial track record.

The more you understand about the distributor's task, the more helpful and supportive you can be during distribution. The problems for a distributor involve more than just selling tickets to the public. Exhibitors must be sold on showing the picture in the first place. Exhibitors know how important the campaign is to the success of a film, and they will sometimes pay more attention to the campaign than they will to the film. Sales to theaters are often made solely on the strength of the campaign. That is why many experienced producers create a one-sheet before they shoot one foot of film: They want to know going in that they are creating a picture that can readily be sold. Once a picture has established a good box office track record in any one territory, those box office figures can be used to sell exhibitors in other territories. Until that time, the distributor must rely on the film's campaign, awards, and favorable critical reviews.

The exhibition of a film will usually follow one of three patterns. First, a film that opens weak at the box office will probably stay weak. The distributor should consider changing the campaign. Second, if a film opens strong but the audience drops rapidly after the second week, the campaign is succeeding in drawing the initial crowd but the film isn't generating positive word of mouth. It may be that the campaign is misleading the public and drawing in the wrong initial audience. For example, if a sophisticated psychological drama is sold to the public as an action exploitation picture, the campaign may draw a large number of thrill-seekers in the initial audience. But these people are expecting something they're not going to get and will probably be disappointed. The result will be poor word of mouth. Another audience for the same film, if it's sold as a psychological drama, may leave entirely satisfied and their praise for the film will generate subsequent audiences. A person's expectation upon entering a theater greatly influences the response to the film. This challenges distributors to create an innovative campaign that reasonably represents the film, and also succeeds in drawing a strong initial audience during the first two weeks. An example was the marketing challenge faced by New Line for the film *Se7en.* This is a very dark picture, all rain, not a moment of sunshine, with a series of macabre violent crimes. It stars Brad Pitt and Morgan Freeman, but the largest fan base for those actors is younger and older women, not necessarily the audience for *Se7en.* The opening weekend was critical to the success of the film, but if they hadn't prepared the audience for what they would see, it might have been a disaster. This is especially true for a film like *Se7en* that breaks so many commercial rules. So they not only marketed their stars, they marketed the crimes with the lead line "Seven deadly sins, seven ways to die." The crimes got equal billing with the stars. On opening weekend over half the ticket buyers were women, but they were prepared for what they were going to see. The $30 million film that many people felt was unmarketable has earned $400 million worldwide. As with everything, there are exceptions, and, on rare occasions, it works to mislead the public in order to draw an initial crowd into the theater. The initial public impression of the drama *Dead Poets Society,* starring Robin Williams, was that it was a comedy. It was marketed that way because the distributor believed that the initial audience had to be drawn in by hook or by crook, or the film would have died. Because the film was so thoroughly satisfying for the audience, positive word of mouth spread, and the picture was a hit.

A third pattern that a film may follow at the box office is a strong opening and healthy legs. If this happens, you've got a good campaign and a successful film. It is important to add that simply because a film doesn't have legs, this doesn't mean it's a bad film. It may be a good film that is not commercially successful. An example is Steven Zaillian's brilliant film, *Searching for Bobby Fischer.* Audiences loved it, talked about it, and recommended it to their friends, but it was a commercial disappointment. Scott Rudin said that of all the films he has produced, this film was his favorite, and is "the only movie that should have worked but didn't." The box office success of a film relies on many things that are entirely out of the producer's hands, including public taste at the time of release, what other films are running concurrently, the political and economic climate of the country, and unpredictable critical reviews. All of these greatly affect a film's chances at the box office and may have nothing to do with whether the film is good or bad.

MPAA Ratings

If a producer complies with the voluntary rating system of the MPAA (Motion Picture Association of America), which virtually all producers do, the film and *each of the campaign elements* must be rated. NATO (The National Association of Theater Owners) estimates that 85 percent of theater owners in the nation adhere to the rating system. This same rating system is used as a guideline for home videos, and the VSDA (Video Software Dealers Association), which is the major trade association for video retailers in the United States, strongly endorses its observance by video retailers. The MPAA rating board does not rate movies based on quality or lack of quality, nor do they rate movies based on what is imagined or thought. They determine the ratings solely by what is seen or heard, making their judgments based on such things as theme, violence, language, nudity, sensuality, drug abuse, etc. The MPAA Classification and Rating Administration offers the following five ratings:

G: *"General Audience." All ages admitted.*
PG: *"Parental Guidance Suggested." Some material may not be suitable for children.*
PG-13: *"Parents strongly cautioned." Some material may be inappropriate for children under 13.*
R: *"Restricted" Under 17 requires accompanying parent or adult guardian (age varies in some jurisdictions).*
NC-17: *"No children under 17 admitted" (age varies in some jurisdictions).*

MPAA film ratings are set by a group of parents whose identities are kept confidential. This panel makes a highly subjective judgment about the suitability of material for children of various ages. They will not tell you specifically what to cut to achieve a more favorable rating—that's up to you. They will only tell you generally (e.g., language, sex, violence) what they feel is excessive. In most cases, the producer knows ahead of time where the problems lie, but it may take several tries to get the desired rating. It took Roger Avary six months to get the "R" rating he wanted for *Killing Zoe.* If you do not feel that the MPAA rating accurately reflects the content of your film, you may appeal the decision. The Rating Appeals Board sits as the final arbiter.

All advertising for rated motion pictures must be submitted to the MPAA Advertising Administration for approval prior to its release to the public. This includes print ads, radio and TV spots, press books, video packaging, and theatrical and home video trailers. This material is evaluated by the Advertising Administration, not by the parental panel.

While there is no legal requirement to rate a film in this way, most distribution contracts require delivery of a specific MPAA rating, and most theater owners require a film to be rated by the MPAA. If you decide to have your film rated, contact the MPAA well in advance to find out how much lead time they need in order to screen your film and determine its rating. You may also choose to wait until you have a distribution deal before having your film rated, in which case the responsibility for applying for, and paying for, the rating will probably rest with the distributor. The MPAA charges on a sliding scale between $2,000 and $15,000 to rate a film. Films budgeted at less than $150,000 are charged the minimum; films budgeted at over $50 million are charged the maximum.

A more detailed explanation of the entire rating system can be found in a brochure titled "The Voluntary Movie Rating System" obtainable from the MPAA. Contact information for the MPAA Classification and Rating Administration is included in Appendix E.

The Elements of the Campaign

The campaign package may be used initially to convince exhibitors to handle the film, and subsequently to draw movie-goers into the theaters. This section describes the standard elements in a motion picture advertising campaign.

The *press book* is a folder that contains all of the promotional print material for the film, including newspaper ads, interviews with stars and filmmakers, and newsworthy insights into the making of the film. It also contains a synopsis of the story, the film's running time, a complete list of the cast and crew, any awards, and possibly quotes from critical reviews. This not only gives exhibitors a feeling for what the film is about, it also provides them with information that reporters and critics may ask for. *Electronic press books* include promotional spots, taped interviews, and newsworthy material for radio and television.

The *one-sheet* is a standard-size color poster for display in front of theaters. The one-sheet usually contains the basic elements from which the newspaper ads are made (called the "key art"). These elements include a graphic design such as a photograph or drawing, a custom title treatment, which often becomes a logo for the film, a lead line to accompany the title, credits for principal cast and crew (usually contractual), and, finally, any outstanding quotes from reviews.

Examples of lead lines include those for *Fargo:* "A lot can happen in the middle of nowhere." *Smoke:* "Where there's smoke . . . there's laughter." *I Shot Andy Warhol:* "You only get one shot at fame." *Welcome to the Dollhouse:* "Not all girls want to play with dolls." *Ripe:* "No one stays innocent forever." *Anaconda:* "It will take your breath away." And one of the most memorable from a Dutch horror film called *The Lift:* "For God's sake, take the stairs!"

The *trailer* is a short promotional film exhibited in theaters as a preview of coming attractions prior to a film's exhibition. A trailer usually contains highlights from the film, although special material such as interviews with the cast and director may be used as well. Trailers generally run less than three minutes. For trailers, the MPAA offers only two ratings: "all audiences," which means they can be shown with *all* feature films, or "restricted audiences," which means they can be shown only with films rated R or NC-17. The reasons for this have to do with the difficulty of keeping track of which trailer is playing with which films. Each trailer carries at the front a tag that tells two things: the audience for which the trailer has been approved, and the rating of the *motion picture* being advertised by the trailer. The background for the "all audience" tag is green, while the background for the "restricted audience" tag is red; this helps guard against a projectionist combining films and trailers inappropriately, e.g., showing a "restricted audience" trailer with a film rated G, PG, or PG-13.

Since the majority of films are rated PG or PG-13, it is wise for a producer with an R-rated film to make a "general audience" trailer, in addition to a "restricted audience" trailer, thereby reaching the maximum number of movie-goers prior to the film's opening. This presents quite a challenge to the trailer maker: The goal is for a trailer to achieve maximum impact yet be "soft" enough to be suitable for five-year-olds watching a G-rated family film.

It is advisable to screen a trailer for the MPAA in rough-cut interlock form prior to mixing the sound and cutting the original negative. There are specific guidelines that the MPAA follows when rating trailers, and they will tell you at this stage whether your material conforms to them. The MPAA Advertising Administration is most cooperative in helping producers get their advertising materials cleared through the rating system.

Teaser trailers are rarely used to promote independent films. They are reserved for approximately 20 percent of studio films and generally run about ninety seconds or less. They are shown well in advance of the film's trailer. A teaser might be nothing more than a logo, such as for *Batman,* or a familiar musical theme, such as for *The Addams Family* or *Mission: Impossible.* Six months before the release of *Independence Day,* the studio ran a forty-five-second theatrical teaser that showed off the film's awesome special effects; an additional million dollars was spent to run a similar teaser during the Super Bowl.

Television ads are similar to trailers, only shorter. The most common running time for a television spot is thirty seconds. Release prints for television spots are distributed on video, as opposed to the theatrical 35mm format of the trailer. In order to minimize the expense involved in making television spots, the trailer may be constructed in a modular format so that entire sections may be removed intact, providing ready-made television spots.

Producing an effective *radio spot* presents a somewhat different problem from producing a trailer or television spot. On radio, you are selling a motion picture without the pictures. If you're lucky, the same audio elements used in the trailer will work effectively on radio. But there's a good chance they won't work without visual support. It is not uncommon to start entirely from scratch in an effort to produce an effective radio campaign. Running times for radio spots are usually ten, thirty, and sixty seconds. They are sent to exhibitors on cassette as part of the initial sales package.

Half a dozen carefully chosen eight-by-ten *production stills* (still photographs) will go a long way toward stimulating interest from exhibitors. They will also be used in front of the theater to attract the attention of pedestrian traffic. Foreign distributors often request many more stills than are used for domestic distribution. It is wise to prepare for this and have an assortment of at least twenty-five different black-and-white stills and twenty-five different color stills available upon request. These usually must be delivered, along with certain other elements stipulated in the distribution agreement, just after the agreement is signed.

In addition to the basic campaign package, a distributor may include an *alternate campaign.* This will be used to spur new interest and give the film a fresh look in its sixth or seventh week at one location. An alternate campaign often appeals to a different market from the primary campaign. Another reason for an alternate campaign is if the primary campaign contains a graphic image (say, one that includes partial nudity or the depiction of extreme violence) that may be censored by newspapers in certain territories. The alternate campaign will utilize a more conservative graphic design in order to provide exhibitors everywhere with an acceptable newspaper ad.

Web sites are commonly used to promote films. This can be an effective and relatively inexpensive way to gain exposure. The site can be simple text, or it can include graphics, stills, interviews, E-mail, trailer, portions of the sound track, and video clips.

The Promotional Concept

The term "high concept" is used by the studios to label film ideas that contain clearly marketable concepts. Examples of such films are *Con Air, Indecent Proposal, Jurassic Park,* and *Twister.* In the studio system, a high concept may get you a development deal, but it will not get you a green light for production. For that, you will also need a screenplay and probably a star. In the world of independent production, especially low-budget filmmaking, a high concept may be all you need to raise money for production, but if you rely too heavily on the concept to carry the show, you will rarely recoup the investment. In order to succeed, you must develop the story and characters carefully and ensure that your production is well executed. A concept is often the brainchild of a producer, but the responsibility for constructing the story and developing the characters rests with the screenwriter. After that it is up to the interpretive artists, principally the director, performers, cinematographer, production designer, and editor, to ensure that the integrity of the story and characters is not lost in the labyrinth of obstacles inherent in the production of every feature film. Once a picture is finished, it is time to return to the concept that sparked the process in the first place, and use it to draw the initial audiences into theaters.

Most films contain a multitude of potentially commercial elements, and it's easy for an ambitious producer, anxious to sell tickets, to get bogged down trying to devise a campaign that contains "something for everyone." A far more effective approach is to define the audience for your film narrowly and tailor the campaign to appeal to that audience.

Analogies can be found in the automobile industry. The Ford Motor Company once designed a car based on the concept that if no one would find anything to dislike about it, the car would please everyone. This was the concept that produced the Edsel. On the other hand, prior to launching the most successful campaign in American automotive history, the same company defined the potential buyer in great personal detail. The resulting campaign lifted Ford into the black and made their Mustang the number-one-selling car in America.

It is important to define your audience as specifically as possible. Don't be afraid of controversy and don't be afraid to take a stand. You can't possibly please everyone, and if you try, you'll fail. Without a strong, definite position, chances are you will get no one into the theater, but with a well-defined approach, you stand a good chance of drawing a specific, well-defined audience. If the film satisfies their expectations, word of mouth will carry it from there.

Conclusion

IF YOU HAVE READ THIS BOOK FROM COVER TO COVER, YOU HAVE experienced, vicariously, the entire process of independent feature production from concept through distribution. Norman Mailer once described this process as "a cross between a circus, a military campaign, a nightmare, an orgy, and a high." Certainly no one who successfully completes an independent feature looks back over the experience and says it was easy.

Every filmmaker enters into production with the hope that his or her film will become a success and maybe even a hit. In striving for that goal, all filmmakers do the best they can. Those who succeed deserve congratulations and every bit of praise they receive. But those whose films, for whatever reasons, are not accepted by distributors or by the movie-going public also deserve recognition. They have taken a risk for something they believed in and they did the best they could. The variables involved in the success of a feature film are so tenuous and unpredictable that no filmmaker can guarantee success from the start. The history of the industry is filled with examples of films made by seasoned professionals for budgets of $50 million or more that were not accepted by the public, and other small independent films that achieved outstanding success.

If there is a single theme that resonates throughout this book, it is the importance of setting one's sights high and firmly sticking to one's convictions. In the introduction I mentioned several successful independent feature films that achieved great success. In every case, at some point along the way, the people responsible for those films were faced with awesome challenges. Had they lacked the strength to meet those challenges, their films would be nothing more than unrealized dreams. But each went on to achieve great success because they had the courage and stamina to pursue their goals with unrelenting vigor. Even a brilliant filmmaker with a thorough knowledge of the filmmaking process will not succeed without the ability to face disappointment, discouragement, and rejection with strength, fortitude, and courage. The ones who successfully realize their dreams are those who cling tenaciously to their convictions and simply refuse to accept defeat.

What I have provided in this book is the information necessary to guide a picture through the entire process of feature production from concept to distribution. What no book can provide is the courage and tenacity in the soul of the filmmaker. That part is up to you.

Sample Limited
Partnership Agreement

This Agreement of Limited Partnership, dated _____, is made and entered into by _____, a California _____, as general partner (the "General Partner"), and the parties named as limited partners on the final page of this document (the "Limited Partners").

1. FORMATION

This Limited Partnership (the "Partnership") is organized pursuant to the provisions of the California Revised Limited Partnership Act (the "Act") upon the terms and conditions herein provided. The parties shall execute all certificates and documents, and do all other acts as are required or, in the judgment of the General Partner, may be appropriate to comply with all requirements of the Act.

2. NAME

The name of the Partnership shall be _____, a California Limited Partnership.

3. DEFINITIONS

The defined terms in this Agreement shall have the following meanings:

3.1 "Agreement" shall mean this Agreement of Limited Partnership, as amended, modified, or supplemented from time to time.

3.2 "Ancillary Rights" for purposes of the business of the Partnership, ancillary rights in connection with the exploitation of the Motion Picture shall include, without limitation, sound track recording rights, merchandising rights, i.e., the merchandising of products, including T-shirts, dolls, toys, posters, and the like, literary publishing rights, i.e., novelization of the motion picture, live television rights, radio rights, legitimate stage rights, remake rights, sequel rights, and additional motion picture rights.

3.3 "Capital Account" shall mean an account established and maintained throughout the full term of the Partnership for each Partner in accordance with the following rules set forth in Treasury Regulation Section 1.704-1(b)(2)(iv):

3.3.1 Each Partner's Capital Account shall be increased by (i) the amount of money contributed by such Partner to the Partnership, (ii) the fair market value of property contributed by such Partner to the Partnership (as such fair market value shall be mutually agreed upon by the Partners and net of liabilities secured by such contributed property that the Partnership is considered to assume or take subject to under Internal Revenue Code ("Code") Section 752), and (iii) allocations to such Partner of Partnership Net Income (defined below) and gain of all types.

    3.3.2   Each Partner's Capital Account shall be decreased by (i) the amount of money distributed to such Partner by the Partnership, (ii) the fair market value of property distributed to such Partner by the Partnership (as such, fair market value shall be mutually agreed upon by the Partners, net of liabilities secured by such distributed property that such Partner is considered to assume or take subject to under Code Section 752), (iii) allocations to such Partner of expenditures of the Partnership described in Code Section 705(a)(2)(B) and (iv) allocations to such Partner of Partnership Net Loss (defined below) and deduction.

    3.3.3   The initial Capital Account of each Partner shall be described in Schedule "A" hereto. Such amounts shall consist solely of the cash capital contributions made by the Limited Partners.

    3.4   "Capital Contribution Accounts" shall mean, from time to time, with respect to each Limited Partner, (a) the sum of (i) its initial capital contribution and (ii) the total of all additional capital contributions made by such Limited Partner, in cash, if any, less (b) the sum of all distributions made to such Limited Partner pursuant to Section 9.2 and 9.3 hereof.

    3.5   "Capital Event" shall mean a Sale of the Play or other disposition, hypothecation, mortgaging, or transfer of other Partnership assets.

    3.6   "Cash Flow" shall mean all cash received by the Partnership from any source (other than Sale Proceeds or Net Capital Proceeds, as defined herein), less (i) such Partnership working capital or reserves as the General Partner deems advisable to retain, and (ii) all cash expenditures paid or incurred by the Partnership, including without limitation all principal and interest payments on any indebtedness of the Partnership, all payments on account of participation in the gross collections or net profits from the Play, and all compensation and fees payable to the General Partner, if any, for services rendered to the Partnership.

    3.7   "Code" shall mean the Internal Revenue Code of 1986, as amended, and corresponding provisions of subsequent revenue laws, together with Treasury Regulations and Revenue Rulings promulgated thereunder.

    3.8   "Effective Date" shall mean the date a Certificate of Limited Partnership for the Partnership is filed in the office of the Secretary of State of California.

    3.9   "General Partner" shall mean _____, a California _____, and any persons succeeding as general partner pursuant to the provisions of this Agreement. The General Partner was organized by its principal shareholders, _____, _____, _____, _____, and _____ (the "Principals"), in _____, 19__. The aforementioned shareholders may hereinafter sometimes be referred to as the "Principals."

    3.10   "Interest Ratio" shall mean the ratio which the capital contribution of a particular Limited Partner bears to the aggregate capital contributions of all Limited Partners of the same class.

    3.11   "Interim Capital Event" shall mean a Capital Event not associated with the termination and liquidation of the Partnership.

    3.12   "Limited Partners, shall mean the parties listed on the signature page as Limited Partners, and any person who becomes a Limited Partner by substitution after receiving an assignment from a Limited Partner and the consent of the General Partner and any Substituted Limited Partner.

    3.13   "Majority Vote of the Limited Partners" shall mean the vote of Limited Partners who together hold more than 50% of the total Partnership interests of all

Limited Partners. Those Limited Partners who together represent such a majority vote may be referred to as a "Majority in Interest of the Limited Partners."

3.14   "Memorandum" shall mean the Confidential Private Placement Memorandum to which this Exhibit "A" is attached.

3.15   "Motion Picture" shall mean the prospective feature-length motion picture to be produced by the Partnership currently entitled "_____."

3.16   "Offering" shall mean the "mini-maxi" offering of a minimum of _____ and a maximum of _____ Units at a price of $_____ per Unit, with a minimum required purchase of 1 Unit, for gross offering proceeds of a minimum of $_____ and a maximum of $_____, as described in the Memorandum. No Units will be sold unless at least the minimum number of Units are subscribed and the subscriptions are accepted by the General Partner by the termination of the Offering.

3.17   "Partners" means the General Partner and all Limited Partners, collectively, where no distinction is required by the context in which the term is used herein.

3.18   "Sale" shall mean a sale or other disposition, whether by operation of law or otherwise, of all or substantially all of the Partnership's title in and to the Motion Picture; but such term shall not include any arrangement whereby the Partnership grants rights (including but not limited to a license) to a third party to exploit the Motion Picture in any medium, whether or not such right or rights are exclusive or nonexclusive and limited or unlimited as to time or geographical area.

3.19   "Sale Proceeds and Net Capital Proceeds" shall mean all proceeds from a Capital Event, less all necessary reserves and amounts needed to pay current obligations of the Partnership and closing costs and other fees associated with a Sale.

3.20   "Substituted Limited Partner" shall mean a Transferee of a Unit who is admitted as a Limited Partner in place of a Limited Partner Transferor pursuant to the provisions of this Agreement.

3.21   "Terminating Capital Event" shall mean a Capital Event incident to the termination and liquidation of the Partnership.

3.22   "Transfer" shall mean a sale, transfer, assignment, hypothecation, or other disposition of Units or General Partner's interests.

3.23   "Unit" means a limited partnership interest in the Partnership resulting from a contribution of capital to the Partnership of $_____.

4. PURPOSE

The purpose of the Partnership is to engage in the development and production of the Motion Picture and to exploit all rights therein, including, but not limited to, theatrical, television, and home video rights and all Ancillary Rights related thereto, and to engage in any lawful business activities reasonably related to any of the foregoing.

5. TERM

The term of the Partnership shall commence on the Effective Date and shall continue until the date of the first of the following events:

5.1   The expiration of fifty (50) years from the Effective Date; or

5.2   The dissolution of the Partnership pursuant to the terms of this Agreement.

6. PRINCIPAL EXECUTIVE OFFICE

The principal executive office of the Partnership shall be located at _____

_____. The General Partner may from time to time change the principal executive office. In such event, the General Partner shall notify the Limited Partners in writing of such change. The General Partner may, in its discretion, establish additional places of business for the Partnership, within and without the State of California.

7. CAPITAL AND CONTRIBUTIONS

7.1   The General Partner shall not be required to contribute to the capital of the Partnership. Notwithstanding the foregoing, the General Partner may, from time to time, advance sums to the Partnership which shall be deemed loans to the Partnership and which shall be repaid as such, with interest at the then prime rate. The General Partner may also become a Limited Partner or Substituted Limited Partner to the extent the General Partner has contributed capital to the Partnership, either in cash or by promissory note, and upon any such contribution of capital the General Partner will become a Limited Partner in, as well as the General Partner of, the Partnership, with all rights, powers, and privileges of a Limited Partner with respect to the Units held as a consequence thereof; except, however, the foregoing right may only be exercised to the extent of the maximum Units currently available; no further dilution will be permissible unless upon the prior written consent of all of the Limited Partners.

7.2   Each Limited Partner shall contribute to the capital of the Partnership, in cash, or in the sole discretion of the General Partner, a combination of cash and instruments acceptable to the General Partner, the sums set forth opposite such Limited Partner's name on the signature page hereto. Any interest earned on subscriptions deposited in trust as described in the Memorandum shall be deemed to be income earned by the Partnership and shall not be deemed a capital contribution of the Limited Partners. If the Offering is terminated and the cumulative subscription is for less than the minimum number Units, said interest shall be returned to subscribers along with their contributions.

7.3   An individual Capital Account shall be maintained for each Partner.

8. ALLOCATIONS OF PROFITS AND LOSSES

8.1   "Net Income" or "Net Loss" shall mean the taxable income or gain and taxable loss of the Partnership as determined in accordance with accounting methods followed by the Partnership for Federal Income tax reporting purposes.

8.1.1   "Net Income from Operations" and "Net Loss from Operations" shall mean the Net Income and Net Loss, respectively, from the day-to-day operation of the Partnership.

8.1.2   "Net Income and Net Loss from Capital Events" shall mean the Net Income and Net Loss, respectively, of the Partnership from sources other than the day-to-day operation of the Partnership, including, without limitation, Net Income and Net Loss from the sale or other disposition of Partnership assets.

8.2   After the close of each fiscal year of the Partnership, the Partnership's Net Income or Net Loss shall be determined.

8.2.1   Net Income and Net Loss from Operations of the Partnership for each fiscal year shall be allocated as follows:

8.2.1.1   First, Net Income in the same ratio and up to the same amount as cash is distributed to the Partners pursuant to Section 9.2.1 hereof.

8.2.1.2   Any remaining Net Income shall be allocated fifty percent (50%) to the Limited Partners and fifty percent (50%) to the General Partner.

8.2.1.3   Net Loss shall, subject to Section 8.3, be allocated ninety-nine percent (99%) to the Limited Partners and one percent (1%) to the General Partner, until the balances of the Limited Partners' Capital Accounts are reduced to zero. Thereafter, all Net Loss shall, subject to Section 8.3, be allocated fifty percent (50%) to the Limited Partners and fifty percent (50%) to the General Partner.

8.2.2   All Net Income from a Capital Event shall be allocated as follows:

8.2.2.1   First, to each of the Partners, in proportion to, and to the extent of any deficit in, such Partner's Capital Account;

8.2.2.2   Second, ninety-nine percent (99%) to the Limited Partners and one percent (1%) to the General Partner, to the extent necessary to cause the positive balance of each of the Limited Partner's Capital Accounts to equal the then balance of their Capital Contribution Accounts;

8.2.2.3   Thereafter, all remaining Net Income shall be allocated fifty percent (50%) to the Limited Partners and fifty percent (50%) to the General Partner.

8.2.3   All Net Loss from a Capital Event shall, subject to Section 8.3, be allocated ninety-nine percent (99%) to the Limited Partners and one percent (1%) to the General Partner, until the balance of the Limited Partners' Capital Accounts are reduced to zero. Thereafter, all Net Loss shall, subject to Section 8.3, be allocated fifty percent (50%) to the Limited Partners and fifty percent (50%) to the General Partner.

8.3   Notwithstanding the foregoing provisions of this Article 8; the losses allocated under Sections 8.2.1 and 8.2.3 to any Partner shall not exceed the maximum amount of losses that can be so allocated without causing such Partner to have an Adjusted Capital Account Deficit (as defined below) at the end of any fiscal year. If some but not all of the Partners would have Adjusted Capital Account Deficits as a consequence of an allocation of losses pursuant to Sections 8.2.1 and 8.2.3, the limitation set forth in this Section 8.3 shall be applied so as to allocate the maximum permissible loss to each Partner under the preceding sentence and Treasury Regulation Section 1.704-1(b)2(ii)(d). Any losses that cannot be allocated to a Partner under the first sentence of this Section 8.3 shall be allocated to the remaining Partners in proportion to their respective Interest Ratios.

8.3.1   Notwithstanding The preceding provisions of this Article 8, Partner Nonrecourse Deductions (as defined below) shall be allocated among the Partners as required in Temporary Treasury Regulation Section 1.704-1T(b)(4)(iv)(h)(2), in accordance with the manner in which the Partner or Partners bear the economic risk of loss for the Partner Nonrecourse Debt corresponding to the Partner Nonrecourse Deductions, and if more than one Partner bears such economic risk of loss for a Partner Nonrecourse Debt, the corresponding Partner Nonrecourse Deductions shall be allocated among such Partners in accordance with the ratios in which the Partners share the economic risk of loss for the Partner Nonrecourse Debt.

8.3.2   Except as provided in Section 8.3.3 hereof, if any Partner unexpectedly receives any adjustments, allocations, or distributions described in Treasury Regulation Sections 1.704-1(b)(2)(ii)(d)(4), (5) or (6), items of Partnership income and gain shall be allocated, in accordance with, and to the extent required by Treasury Regulation Section 1.704-1(b)(2)(ii)(d), to each such Partner in an amount and manner sufficient to eliminate the Adjusted Capital Account Deficit of such Partner as quickly as possible. It is intended that this Section 8.3.2 constitute a "qualified income offset" within the meaning of Treasury Regulation Section 1.704-1(b)(2)(ii)(d).

8.3.3   Notwithstanding Sections 8.3, 8.3.1, and 8.3.2, if there is a net decrease in Partnership Minimum Gain (as defined below) during any fiscal year, each Partner that would otherwise have an Adjusted Capital Account Deficit at the end of such year shall be allocated, in accordance with Treasury Regulation Section 1.704-1(b)(4)(iv)(e), items of Partnership income and gain for such year (and, if necessary, subsequent years) in the amount and manner sufficient to eliminate such Adjusted Capital Account Deficit as quickly as possible. It is intended that this Section 8.3.3 constitute a "minimum gain chargeback" within the meaning of Treasury Regulation Section 1.704-1T(b)(4)(iv).

8.3.4   In the event that there is a net decrease in the Minimum Gain Attributable to a Partner Nonrecourse Debt of the Partnership during a Partnership taxable year, after the allocation required by Section 8.3.3, but prior to any other allocation for the year, each Partner with a share of the Minimum Gain Attributable to the Partner Nonrecourse Debt at the beginning of the taxable year shall be allocated income and gain for the year (and, if necessary subsequent years) in accordance with Temporary Treasury Regulation Section 1.704-1T(b)(4)(if)(h)(4). Each such Partner shall be allocated income and gain for that taxable year (and, if necessary, subsequent years) in proportion to, and to the extent of, an amount equal to the greater of (i) the portion of the Partner's share of the net decrease in Minimum Gain Attributable to this Partner Nonrecourse Debt that is allocable to the disposition of Partnership property subject to this Partner Nonrecourse Debt, and (ii) the Adjusted Capital Account Deficit at the end of this year.

8.3.5   As used herein, the following terms shall have the meanings associated with them:

8.3.5.1   The term "Adjusted Capital Account Deficit" shall mean, with respect to any Partner, the deficit balance, if any, in such Partner's Capital Account as of the end of the relevant fiscal year, after giving effect to the following adjustments:

8.3.5.1.1   Allocations of loss and deduction that, as of the end of any fiscal year of the Partnership, are reasonably expected to be made to such Partner under Code Section 704(e)(2), Code Section 706(d) and Treasury Regulation Section 1.751-1(b)(2)(ii);

8.3.5.1.2   Distributions that, as of the end of any fiscal year of the Partnership, are reasonably expected to be made to such Partner to the extent they exceed offsetting increases to such Partner's Capital Account which are reasonably expected to occur during (or prior to) the fiscal year in which such distributions are reasonably expected to be made (other than increases under Section 8.3.3 and 8.3.4);

8.3.5.1.3 Each Partner's Capital Account shall, for purposes of this Section 8.3.5.1, be credited with such Partner's share of Partnership Minimum Gain, as described in Section 1.704-1(b)(4)(iv)(f) and any deficit balance that the Partner is obligated to restore; and

8.3.5.1.4 The term "Partnership Minimum Gain" shall have the meaning set forth in Treasury Regulation Section 1.704-1(b)(4)(iv)(c).

8.3.5.2 The term "Partnership Nonrecourse Debt" shall mean the "nonrecourse debt" of the Partnership for which any Partner bears the "economic risk of loss as defined in Temporary Treasury Regulations Section 1.752-1T(d)(3). For this purpose, "nonrecourse debt" means any Partnership liability that is considered nonrecourse for purposes of Treasury Regulations Section 1.1001-2 and any Partnership liability for which the creditor's right to repayment is limited to one or more assets of the Partnership.

8.3.5.3 The term "Partner Nonrecourse Deductions" shall mean, with respect to any Partnership taxable year, the Partnership deductions that are characterized as "partner nonrecourse deductions" under Temporary Treasury Regulation Section 1.704-1T(b)(4)(iv)(h)(2) and (3). The amount of Partner Nonrecourse Deductions with respect to a Partner Nonrecourse Debt for a Partnership taxable year shall mean the excess, if any, of (i) the net increase in the Minimum Gain Attributable to the Partner Nonrecourse Debt during such year, over (ii) the aggregate amount of any distribution during the taxable year to the Partner that bears the economic risk of loss for the Partner Nonrecourse Debt of proceeds of the Partner Nonrecourse Debt that are allocable to an increase in the Minimum Gain Attributable to the Partner Nonrecourse Debt. The determination of which items of Partnership loss, deduction, and Code Section 705(a)(2)(B) expenditure constitute Partner Nonrecourse Deductions for a Partnership taxable year shall be made before the determination of which items constitute Nonrecourse Deductions.

8.3.5.4 The term "Nonrecourse Deductions" shall mean the Partnership deductions that are characterized as "nonrecourse deductions" under Temporary Treasury Regulations Section 1.704-1T(b)(4)(iv)(b). The amount of Nonrecourse Deductions for the Partnership taxable year shall mean the excess, if any, of (i) the net increase in the amount of Minimum Gain during the year, over (ii) the aggregate amount of any distributions during the taxable year of proceeds of a Nonrecourse Liability that are allocable to an increase in Minimum Gain. Any item of loss deduction, and Code Section 705(a)(2)(B) expenditure for a taxable year that is treated as a Partner Nonrecourse Deduction shall be excluded in determining Nonrecourse Deductions.

8.3.5.5 The term "Minimum Gain Attributable to Partner Nonrecourse Debt" shall mean, with respect to any taxable year of the Partnership, the amount of taxable income or gain that would be realized by the Partnership if the Partnership disposed of the Partnership assets subject to the Partner Nonrecourse Debt in full satisfaction of that Partner Nonrecourse Debt (and for no other consideration).

8.3.6 In accordance with Section 704(c) of the Code and the Treasury Regulations promulgated thereunder, income, gain, loss, and deduction with respect to any asset contributed to the capital of the Partnership shall, solely for tax purposes, be allocated among the Partners as provided in Section 704(c) of the Code so as to take account of any variation between the adjusted basis of such asset to the Partnership for Federal income tax purposes and its initial value.

9. CASH DISTRIBUTIONS

9.1   The General Partner may make distributions to the Partners at such time and in such amounts as the General Partner deems advisable. Such distributions may include withdrawals or reductions of capital of the Partners, and all Partners hereby consent thereto.

9.2   When and to the extent Cash Flow is distributed, it shall be distributed in the following manner:

9.2.1   First, it shall be distributed ninety-nine percent (99%) to the Limited Partners (pro rata in accordance with their respective Interest Ratios) and one percent (1%) to the General Partner, until the balances of the Limited Partners' Capital Contribution Accounts are reduced to zero.

9.2.2   Thereafter, it shall be distributed fifty percent (50%) to the Limited Partners (pro rata in accordance with their respective Interest Ratios) and fifty percent (50%) to the General Partner.

9.3   All Sale Proceeds and Net Capital Proceeds from an Interim Capital Event shall be distributed to the General Partner as soon as practicable following receipt by the Partnership in the following order of priority:

9.3.1   First, it shall be distributed ninety-nine percent (99%) to the Limited Partners (pro rata in accordance with their respective Interest Ratios) and one percent (1%) to the General Partner, until the balances of the Limited Partners' Capital Contribution Accounts are reduced to zero.

9.3.2   Thereafter, it shall be distributed fifty percent (50%) to the Limited Partners (pro rata in accordance with their respective Interest Ratios) and fifty percent (50%) to the General Partner.

9.4   All distributions from the Partnership upon the liquidation and termination of the Partnership or attributable to a Terminating Capital Event shall be governed by Section 18.2 hereof.

9.5   All Partners will be required to return pro rata to the Partnership any distribution to the extent that, immediately after giving effect to the distribution, the liabilities of the Partnership exceed the fair value of the Partnership assets in violation of California Corporations Code Section 15666.

10. FEES PAYABLE TO GENERAL PARTNER; EXPENSES

10.1   The General Partner shall not be entitled to receive compensation for services rendered to the Partnership.

10.2   General Partner shall be entitled to be reimbursed by the Partnership for (i) Offering and Organizational Expenses incurred by it in connection with the Offering and (ii) Development Expenses incurred by it in connection with the development of the Motion Picture, immediately upon completion of the Offering and the funding of the Partnership, as described in the Memorandum. The General Partner shall not be entitled to interest on these expenses.

10.3   The General Partner shall be entitled to an annual Administrative and Overhead Fee in connection with the business of the Partnership, as described in the Memorandum, in consideration of the furnishing by the General Partner of office facilities, which shall include office space (which may also be used by other productions), telephones, fax machines, photocopiers and like facilities.

10.4   Neither the Partnership, the General Partner, nor any person selling Units on behalf of the Partnership shall pay directly or indirectly, an award, finder's fees, commission, or other compensation to any person engaged for investment advice by a potential Limited Partner.

10.5   The Partnership shall pay all of its own operating expenses directly.

11. MANAGEMENT OF PARTNERSHIP

11.1   The General Partner shall have the sole and exclusive control of the management of the business and affairs of the Partnership to the extent allowed by law. The Principals of the General Partner shall consult with each other regarding the exercise of said control, including, without limitation, all creative, business, administrative, financial, and legal matters in connection with the Partnership. Without limiting the generality of the foregoing, the General Partner shall have the authority and right:

11.1.1   To do all acts and things which are in the General Partner's judgment necessary or desirable to operate the business of the Partnership including, without limitation, enabling the Motion Picture to be developed, produced, and exploited in the markets and media as described in the Memorandum; to borrow money, whether on a secured or unsecured basis, from any source; to deal in or with any Partnership assets, including, but not limited to, the rights to purchase or acquire title, sell or convey title, pledge or otherwise encumber, and grant options and licenses respecting all or any portion of such assets, including the Motion Picture; to obtain refinancing of any indebtedness of the Partnership or to prepay the same in whole or in part; to loan funds of the Partnership; to invest funds of the Partnership in securities of any nature; and to make or revoke any election permitted the Partnership by any taxing authority;

11.1.2   To employ from time to time, on behalf of the Partnership, such persons, firms, or corporations as, in the General Partner's sole judgment, the General Partner shall deem advisable for the operation of the Partnership's business on such terms and for such compensation including, but not limited to, compensation based on a participation in the gross proceeds or net profits from the Motion Picture as the General Partner, in the General Partner's sole judgment, shall determine; and

11.1.3   To execute, acknowledge, and deliver any and all instruments to effectuate the foregoing.

11.2   The General Partner shall devote only such time and effort to the business and affairs of the Partnership as the General Partner shall deem necessary or appropriate.

11.3   The Limited Partners shall not participate in the control or the management of the business and affairs of the Partnership and shall have no authority to transact business on behalf or in the name of the Partnership, or have any authority to bind or obligate the Partnership.

11.4   The Partnership shall indemnify and hold harmless the General Partner, its shareholders, officers, and agents, from any loss, cost (including actual attorneys' fees), damage, expense, liability, or claim incurred by or asserted against the General Partner, its shareholders, officers, and agents, and/or the Partnership arising out of any act or omission performed or omitted by General Partner, its shareholders, officers, and agents, in connection with the Partnership business unless the loss, liability, or damage was caused by gross negligence, fraud, recklessness, criminal act, or civil regulatory violation.

11.5   Any of the Partners, or the Principals' General Partner, may engage in or possess an interest in other business ventures of every nature and description (whether or not competitive with the business of the Partnership) independently or with others, including but not limited to the creation, production, and exploitation of motion pictures, without first offering the Partnership the opportunity to participate in such business ventures.

11.6   The General Partner, on behalf of the Partnership, may enter into agreements (except with respect to investment of Partnership funds) with itself, related entities, or its Principals, provided that such agreements are made on terms which are competitive with those typically found in the entertainment and motion picture industry for works and services similar to those being rendered to the Partnership in connection with the Motion Picture.

11.7   The General Partner shall open and maintain a separate bank account or accounts in the name of the Partnership into which all Partnership funds from any source shall be deposited. Personal funds belonging to any Partner or anyone else shall not be deposited into said bank account or accounts.

12. RIGHTS AND OBLIGATIONS OF LIMITED PARTNERS

12.1   *Voting Rights.* Limited Partners have the right to vote only upon the following matters affecting the basic structure of the Partnership. Except as herein specifically set forth to the contrary, each such matter shall be approved or disapproved by a Majority in Interest of the Limited Partners, but action thereon shall remain subject to approval by the General Partner when allowable by law:

12.1.1   Any action to amend this Agreement which would adversely affect the rights of the Limited Partners.

12.1.2   Approval or disapproval of the sale of all or substantially all of the assets of the Partnership; provided, however the granting or licensing of rights concerning the Motion Picture shall not constitute a sale of assets under this clause.

12.1.3   Any other matter for which voting rights have been expressly provided to the Limited Partners hereunder.

12.2   *No Personal Liability*: No Limited Partner as such shall have any personal liability whatever, whether to the Partnership, to any of the Partners, or to the creditors of the Partnership, for the debts of the Partnership or any of its losses beyond (i) the amount of the Limited Partner's contribution to the Partnership, (ii) the Limited Partner's share of any undistributed assets of the Partnership and (iii) to the extent and for the period required by applicable law, of the amount of the Limited Partner's capital in the Partnership returned to the Limited Partner. Each Unit, upon issuance, shall be fully paid and nonassessable. No Limited Partner shall be required to lend any funds to the Partnership or, after the original capital contribution has been paid, to make any further capital contribution to the Partnership.

13. ASSIGNMENT OF GENERAL PARTNER'S INTEREST

The General Partner shall not assign, pledge, encumber, sell or otherwise dispose of the General Partner's interest as General Partner in the Partnership, except that the General Partner may assign, pledge, encumber, sell or otherwise dispose of the General Partner's interest in the Cash Distributions of the Partnership.

14. TRANSFER AND ASSIGNMENT

14.1   Except to the extent expressly permitted herein, no Limited Partner shall have the right to Transfer all or any portion of the Limited Partner's Units in the Partnership, including the right to receive a return of capital or share of profits. Any attempt to Transfer and any offer to Transfer which is not permitted shall be null and void *ab initio.*

14.2   No Limited Partner shall have the right to Transfer any Units to any minor or to any person who, for any reason, lacks the capacity to contract for such Limited Partner's Unit(s) under the applicable law.

14.3   Any Limited Partner desiring to transfer or encumber all or any part of the Limited Partner's interest in the Partnership pursuant to a bona fide offer shall deliver notice to all the other Partners offering such interest to them on the same terms contained in such bona fide offer. If any part of the consideration to be received by such transferring Limited Partner consists of property or services, such property or services will be considered the equivalent of the cash value of such property or services. Within twenty (20) days after receipt of such notice of offer each other Partner may elect to accept all or any part of such tendered interest.

14.3.1   If the sum of all the percentages stated in all such notices of acceptance totals 100% or more, each accepting Partner will accept that portion of the total tendered interest and pay that portion of the total consideration which the percentage stated in such Partner's notice of acceptance bears to the total of the percentages stated in all the notices of acceptance. Promptly thereafter the transferring Limited Partner and all the accepting Partners will execute all documents and do all acts necessary or convenient to effect:

14.3.1.1   the transfer or encumbrance to each accepting Partner in that Partner's individual capacity of that Partner's portion of such tendered interest as of the close of business on the last day of the calendar month in which falls the final day on which any Partner may serve a notice of acceptance; and

14.3.1.2   the payment to the transferring Limited Partner by each accepting Partner, severally, in that Partner's individual capacity, of that Partner's same portion of such consideration upon the same terms stated in the notice of offer.

14.3.2   If the sum of all the percentages stated in all such notices of acceptance does not total at least 100%, such transferring Limited Partner may, for a period of sixty (60) days following the expiration of such twenty (20) day period, effect such transfer or encumbrance to any one for the same consideration and upon the same terms stated in the notice of offer. After the expiration of such sixty (60) days such transferring Limited Partner will again offer such interest to all the other Partners in the manner stated above prior to any transfer or encumbrance.

14.4   Unless and until a Transferee has become a Substituted Limited Partner under the provisions of Article 15 hereof, a Transferee shall be deemed to be a Transferee only of the right of his/her/its Transferor to receive distributions and shall have no right to experience any rights of a Limited Partner. The Partnership shall recognize the Transfer not later than the first day of the fiscal quarter following the date a notice of assignment and other required documentation is received and accepted by the General Partner.

14.5   The profits and losses of the Partnership attributable to any Unit acquired by reason of a Transfer shall be allocated to the Transferor for the period during the fiscal year prior to the date the Transfer is recognized and to the Transferee for the remainder of the fiscal year. Any distribution of Distributable Cash made with respect to any Unit acquired by reason of a Transfer shall be made to the holder of the Unit recognized by the Partnership on the date of distribution.

14.6   Subject to all the above subsections, a Limited Partner may Transfer the Limited Partner's entire interest in any Units:

14.6.1   To the Limited Partner's spouse or to any of the Limited Partner's descendants, if the Transfer is without consideration; or

14.6.2   To any person, firm, or corporation if:

14.6.2.1   Such Transfer is consented to, in writing, by the General Partner, in the General Partner's absolute discretion and no refusal to so consent may be challenged on any ground.

14.6.2.2   Such Transfer does not result in the Partnership being treated, for federal income tax purposes, as having been terminated pursuant to Section 708 of the Internal Revenue Code of 1954, as amended or state law;

14.6.2.3   The General Partner shall have received an opinion of counsel, satisfactory to the General Partner, to the effect that the proposed Transfer will not be in violation of the Securities Act of 1933, as amended, or of applicable provisions of any state securities or blue sky laws, or of the rules and regulations under any such laws. All costs of any such opinion shall be borne by the Limited Partner; and

14.6.2.4   The instruments of Transfer shall be in the form and substance satisfactory to the General Partner, and the General Partner shall have been paid such reasonable transfer fee (not in excess of $50.00) as the General Partners shall determine.

15. SUBSTITUTED LIMITED PARTNERS

Subject to the prior written consent of the General Partner, which may be withheld in the General Partner's sole and complete discretion, a transferee shall have the right to become a Substituted Limited Partner, conditioned on:

15.1   The Transferor and Transferee executing and acknowledging such other instrument or instruments as the General Partner may deem necessary or desirable to effectuate such admission;

15.2   The Transferee accepting and adopting all of the terms and provisions of this Agreement, as the same may have been amended; and

15.3   The Transferee paying or obligating the Transferee to pay, as the General Partner may determine, all reasonable expenses connected with such admission, including, but not limited to, the cost of preparing any amendment of this Agreement or Certificate of Limited Partnership to effectuate such admission.

16. WITHDRAWAL OF LIMITED PARTNER

In no event shall any Limited Partner be entitled to withdraw or retire from the Partnership or demand the right to return of capital before dissolution of the Partnership without full compliance with Article 15 hereof to admit the Transferee as a Substituted Limited Partner.

17. DISSOLUTION AND LIQUIDATION

17.1   The Partnership shall be dissolved upon the happening of any of the following events:

17.1.1   The expiration of the Partnership's term pursuant to the provisions of this Agreement.

17.1.2   The General Partner ceases to be general partner (other than by removal) under Section 15642 of the CRLPA or any successor statute (unless all Partners agree in writing to continue the business of the Partnership and to admit one or more general partners) for whatever reason, including the following circumstances:

17.1.2.1   The General Partner withdraws from the Partnership.

17.1.2.2   An Order of Relief against the General Partner is entered under Chapter 7 of the federal bankruptcy law, or the General Partner: (1) makes a general assignment for the benefit of creditors, (2) files a voluntary petition under the federal bankruptcy law, (3) files a petition or answer seeking for the General Partner, any arrangement, composition, readjustment, liquidation, or similar relief under any statute, law, or regulation, (4) files an answer or other pleading admitting or failing to contest the material allegations of a petition filed against the partner in any proceeding of this nature or (5) seeks, consents to, or acquiesces in the appointment of a trustee, receiver, or liquidator of the General Partner or of all or any substantial part of the General Partner's properties.

17.1.2.3   If, sixty (60) days after the commencement of any proceeding against the General Partner seeking arrangement, composition, readjustment, liquidation, or similar relief under any statute, law, or regulation, the proceeding has not been dismissed or, if within sixty (60) days after the appointment without the General Partner's consent or acquiescence of a trustee, receiver, or liquidator of the General Partner or of all or any substantial part of the General Partner's properties, the appointment is not vacated or stayed, or within sixty (60) days after the expiration of any such stay, the appointment is not vacated.

17.1.3   The entry of a decree of judicial dissolution under Section 15682 of the Act of any successor statute.

17.1.4   The decision of the General Partner to dissolve and wind up the affairs of the Partnership; or

17.1.5   The sale of all or substantially all of the Partnership's assets.

17.2   Upon dissolution or termination of the Partnership, either by voluntary agreement or for any other reason, the General Partner or, if none, such persons as may be assigned by a Majority in Interest of the Limited Partners, shall wind up and terminate the affairs of the Partnership, liquidate the assets of the Partnership, provide the Limited Partners with a current statement of the assets and liabilities of the Partnership, establish any reserves deemed reasonably necessary for any contingent or unforeseen liabilities or obligations of the Partnership, and distribute the assets of the Partnership. Such assets shall be distributed in the following manner:

17.2.1   First, to creditors, including Partners who are creditors to the extent permitted by law; and

17.2.2   Second, to the Partners in accordance with the positive balances if their respective Capital Accounts.

17.3   In the event that upon dissolution or termination of the Partnership there is no General Partner, a Majority in Interest of the Limited Partners may appoint a trustee or other representative to wind up and terminate the affairs of the Partnership.

17.4   Each Limited Partner shall look solely to the assets of the Partnership for all distributions with respect to the Partnership and such Limited Partner's capital contribution and share of Net Income or Net Loss thereof, and shall have no recourse thereof (upon dissolution or otherwise) against the General Partner or any other Limited Partner. Holders of the Units shall have no right to demand or receive property other than cash upon dissolution and termination of the Partnership.

18. BOOKS, RECORDS, AND REPORTS

18.1   At all times during the continuance of the Partnership, the General Partner shall keep or cause to be kept, full and true books of account in accordance with the methods used for reporting of Federal Income Taxes. The General Partner may make such elections for federal and state income tax purposes as it deems appropriate. The Partnership will file a federal partnership return of income (Form 1065) and related statements with the IRS for each calendar year.

18.2   All of said documents shall at all times be maintained at the principal executive office of the Partnership or at the office of the Partnership's accountant and shall be open during reasonable business hours for the reasonable inspection and examination by the Limited Partners or their representatives upon reasonable notice. The Limited Partners or their representatives shall have the right to make copies thereof at their own expense. A reasonable charge for copying may be charged to the requesting Limited Partner.

18.3   The fiscal year of the Partnership shall be the calendar year.

18.4   The General Partner shall cause to be prepared, in accordance with the methods used by the Partnership to determine income tax liability, and distributed to the Partners the following reports:

18.4.1   Not later than seventy-five (75) days following the end of each fiscal year of the Partnership, a report containing all information necessary for the preparation of each individual Partner's federal income tax returns and a Schedule K-1 indicating the distributive share of the Partnership's taxable income or loss allocable to each Limited Partner for the taxable year;

18.4.2   Within one hundred twenty (120) days following the end of each fiscal year of the Partnership, an annual report (which may be combined, if timely, with the report described in subparagraph 18.4.1 above) containing (i) a balance sheet as of the end of such fiscal year and statements of income, Partners' equity and changes in financial position for such fiscal year, (ii) a brief summary of the activities of the Partnership during the period covered by the report; and (iii) a schedule of all distributions to the Partners for the period covered thereby identifying the source of such distributions.

19. ADDITIONAL DOCUMENTS/SPECIAL POWER OF ATTORNEY

19.1   Each Limited Partner agrees to execute, acknowledge, and deliver, or cause to be executed, acknowledged, and delivered, to the General Partner any further documents or instruments that may be reasonably necessary, proper or expedient in the creation of the Partnership and the achievement of its purpose, which shall include, without limitation, the following:

19.1.1   The certificates of limited partnership, and any amendment(s) to the certificate, which under the laws of the State of California or the laws of any other state, are required to be filed or which the General Partner elect to file;

19.1.2   Any other instrument or document required to be filed by the Partnership under the laws of any state or by any governmental agency, or which the General Partner elect to file;

19.1.3   Any instrument or document that may be required to effect the continuation of the Partnership, the admission of an additional or substituted Limited Partner, or the dissolution and termination of the Partnership, or to reflect any reduction in amount of the Partner's Invested Capital or reduction in the Partner's Capital Accounts, if in accordance with the terms of this Agreement.

19.2   If any Limited Partner shall fail, refuse, or neglect to so execute and deliver, or cause to be so executed and delivered, any such documents or instruments, within ten (10) calendar days after such documents are delivered to such Limited Partner, the General Partner shall be deemed to be, and such Limited Partner irrevocably appoints the General Partner, the true and lawful attorney-in-fact of such Limited Partner, to execute, acknowledge, deliver and/or register any and all such documents or instruments in the name of such Limited Partner and on behalf of such Limited Partner, which right is coupled with an interest.

20. MISCELLANEOUS PROVISIONS

20.1   All notices under this Agreement shall be in writing and shall be given to the parties at the addresses set forth herein and to the Partnership c/o _____, Esq., Dern & Donaldson, 1901 Avenue of the Stars, Suite 400, Los Angeles, California 90067, fax no. (213) 286-9660, with a copy to its principal executive office or at such other address as any of the parties may hereafter specify in the same manner. Notices shall be deemed duly given five (5) days after their deposit, postage prepaid, in the United States mails.

Sample Budget
for a $500,000 Film

Note: Every film budget is unique and must be written for the specific requirements of each project. This budget is for a film using SAG actors. Fringes and taxes are included in the totals. There is no allowance for a completion bond because bond companies generally will not bond a film costing less than $1 million.

Budget Top Sheet

Title_____ Production company_____

Above-the-line

100 Screenplay	$16,000	
200 Producer	17,000	
300 Director	12,500	
400 Cast	55,000	$100,500

Below-the-line
Production

500 Production staff	20,700	
600 Extras	6,000	
700 Set operations	34,800	
800 Sets	17,000	
900 Props	10,600	
1000 Costumes	6,900	
1100 Makeup and hairdressing	7,000	
1200 Production equipment	21,000	
1300 Locations/studio	12,800	
1400 Laboratory and film	39,000	
1500 Tests	500	
1600 Production miscellaneous	16,500	192,800

Postproduction

1700 Editing	46,000	

	1800 Sound	14,500	
	1900 Music	26,000	
	2000 Titles and opticals	5,000	
	2100 Laboratory	12,800	
	2200 Sound mix	11,800	116,100

Other costs

	2300 Insurance	$20,000	
	2400 Miscellaneous	25,100	45,100
	Total		454,500
	10% Contingency		45,500
	Grand total		$500,000

Budget Detail

100 Screenplay

	101 Story rights	$ __	
	102 Writer, screenplay	15,500	
	103 Research and travel	__	
	104 Mimeograph	120	
	105 WGA registration	20	
	106 Script timing	350	$16,000

200 Producer

	201 Executive producer	__	
	202 Producer	15,000	
	203 Associate producer	__	
	204 Secretary	2,000	
	205 Assistants	__	17,000

300 Director

| | 301 Director | 12,500 | |
| | 303 Secretary | __ | 12,500 |

400 Cast

	401 Lead players	35,000	
	402 Supporting players	15,000	
	403 Stuntpersons	3,000	
	404 Looping allowance	2,000	55,000

500 Production staff

	501 Production manager	8,500	
	502 First assistant director	4,000	
	503 Second assistant director	2,000	

	504 Script supervisor	2,800	
	505 Technical advisers	—	
	506 Production assistants	1,200	
	507 Secretary	2,000	20,700

600 Extras

	601 Extras	5,000	
	602 Stand-ins	1,000	6,000

700 Set operations

	701 Director of photography	4,800	
	702 Camera operator	—	
	703 First camera assistant	3,000	
	704 Second camera assistant	2,000	
	705 Sound mixer	4,000	
	706 Boom operator	3,000	
	707 Gaffer	3,000	
	708 Best boy	2,000	
	709 Generator operator	—	
	710 Electrician	2,000	
	711 Key grip	3,000	
	712 Set grips	6,000	
	713 Dolly grip	—	
	714 Wranglers	—	
	715 Still photographer	1,000	
	716 Special effects supervisor	1,000	
	717 Welfare worker	—	
	718 Guards	—	34,800

800 Sets

	801 Art director	4,000	
	802 Construction crew	8,000	
	803 Construction costs	5,000	17,000

900 Props

	901 Property master	2,500	
	902 Assistant	1,600	
	903 Props purchase	2,000	
	904 Props rental	3,000	
	905 Prop truck	1,500	10,600

1000 Costumes

	1001 Wardrobe supervisor	2,500	
	1002 Assistant	1,600	

1003 Wardrobe purchase	1,500	
1004 Wardrobe rental	500	
1005 Cleaning	700	
1006 Miscellaneous supplies	100	6,900

1100 Makeup and hairdressing

1101 Makeup person	4,000	
1102 Hairstylist	3,000	
1103 Assistants	—	
1104 Body makeup	—	
1105 Supplies purchase	—	
1106 Supplies rental	—	7,000

1200 Production equipment

1201 Camera package	11,000	
1202 Sound package	2,000	
1203 Lighting package	3,000	
1204 Grip package	3,000	
1205 Generator	—	
1206 Vehicles	2,000	
1207 Miscellaneous	—	21,000

1300 Locations/studio

1301 Location manager	4,000	
1302 Location rental	5,500	
1303 Permits	600	
1304 Police and firemen	200	
1305 Studio rental	1,000	
1306 Studio personnel	800	
1307 Dressing rooms	—	
1308 Portable rest rooms	1,000	12,800

1400 Laboratory and film

1401 Negative film stock	15,000	
1402 Developing negative	8,000	
1403 Daily printing	15,000	
1404 Still film and printing	1,000	39,000

1500 Tests

1501 Makeup tests	500	
1502 Screen tests	—	500

1600 Production miscellaneous

1601 Animals	—	
1602 Telephone	2,000	

1603 Catering	7,000	
1604 Mileage	6,000	
1605 Shipping	1,500	16,500

1700 Editing

1701 Editor	18,000	
1702 Assistant editor	9,000	
1703 Apprentice editor	4,000	
1704 Editing facility rental	7,000	
1705 Editing equipment rental	4,000	
1706 Supplies purchase	800	
1707 Coding	3,000	
1708 Preview screenings	200	46,000

1800 Postproduction Sound

1801 Sound transfer	4,000	
1802 Dialogue editing	3,000	
1803 ADR costs	2,000	
1804 Sound effects editor	3,000	
1805 Sound effects costs	2,000	
1806 Foley recording	500	14,500

1900 Music

1901 Composer	10,000	
1902 Conductor	—	
1903 Musicians and singers	10,500	
1904 Arranger	—	
1905 Copyist	1,000	
1906 Recording facility	2,500	
1907 Instrument rental and cartage	500	
1908 Miscellaneous supplies	500	
1909 Music rights	—	
1910 Music editor	1,000	26,000

2000 Titles and opticals

2001 Main and end titles	4,000	
2002 Optical effects	1,000	5,000

2100 Laboratory

2101 Postproduction lab (film and video dupes)	1,000	
2102 Reprints	—	
2103 Stock footage	—	
2104 Optical sound track developed	800	

2105 Answer print	8,000		
2108 Miscellaneous laboratory costs	500		
2109 Negative cutting	2,500	12,800	

2200 Sound mix

2201 Mixing facility	10,000	
2202 Magnetic stock	1,100	
2203 Optical transfer	500	
2204 ¼" protection copy	200	11,800

2300 Insurance

2301 Negative insurance	—	
2302 Errors and omissions	—	
2303 Workers' compensation	—	
2304 Cast insurance	—	allow
2305 Other	—	20,000

2400 Miscellaneous

2401 Business license	600	
2402 Accounting	3,000	
2403 Legal	10,000	
2404 Miscellaneous supplies	2,500	
2405 Office and phone	6,000	
2406 Postage	500	
2407 Promo	2,500	25,100
Subtotal		454,500
10% Contingency		45,500
Grand total		$500,000

Sample Budget
for a $4.6 Million Film

Note: Every film budget is unique and must be written for the specific requirements of each project. This budget is for a film shot on location in Wilmington, North Carolina, using several actors and key crew members from Los Angeles. It is governed by SAG, WGA, and DGA, but otherwise it is a non-union film.

Title

EXEC PRODUCER: PRINCIPAL PHOTOGRAPHY: 20 DAYS
PRODUCER: IN & AROUND WILMINGTON, NC
DIRECTOR: 12 HR DYS/5 DY WK * 2ND CAMERA=2 DYS
PROD MANAGER: WGA/DGA/SAG   NON-UNION CREW
PROD ACCOUNTANT: 35MM- DIGITAL POSTPRODUCTION

Acct #	Description	Page #			Total
1100	Script	1			181,500
1200	Producers' Unit	2			259,142
1300	Direction	3			83,119
1400	Cast	4			822,764
1800	A-T-L Fringe	5			92,819
	TOTAL ABOVE-THE-LINE	5			1,439,344
2000	Production Staff	5			158,395
2100	Extra Talent	7			24,400
2200	Set Design	7			22,500
2300	Set Construction	8			62,550
2400	Set Dressing	8			88,096
2500	Property	9			28,050
2600	Special Equip. & Animals	10			13,700
2700	Wardrobe	10			68,983
2800	Makeup and Hair	10			28,950
2900	Set Operations	12			67,001
3000	Electrical	14			67,820
3100	Camera	15			96,676
3200	Production Sound	16			26,330
3300	Special Effects	17			2,000
3400	Location Expenses	17			261,695
3600	Location Transportation	20			172,634
3700	Overtime	23			79,000
3800	Production Film	23			52,718
4800	Production Fringe	23			112,634
	TOTAL PRODUCTION	23			1,434,132
5000	Editorial	23			206,750
5100	Music	24			140,000
5200	Postproduction Sound	24			150,000
5300	Film Library	25			5,500
5400	Film/Audio/Video Stock	25			15,500
5600	Film Laboratory	25			128,957
5700	Video Post	25			34,000
5800	Postproduction Fringe	26			44,880
	TOTAL POSTPRODUCTION	26			725,587
7000	Administrative Expenses	26			226,790
	TOTAL OTHER	27			226,790
	TOTAL ABOVE-THE-LINE				1,439,344
	TOTAL BELOW-THE-LINE				2,159,719
	ABOVE- & BELOW-THE-LINE				3,599,063
	TOTAL FRINGES				250,330
	SUBTOTAL				4,076,183
	CONTINGENCY		10%		407,618
	COMPLETION BOND		5%		203,809
	(2 % refund if not used)				
	GRAND TOTAL				4,687,610

Title

EXEC PRODUCER:
PRODUCER:
DIRECTOR:
PROD MANAGER:
PROD ACCOUNTANT:

PRINCIPAL PHOTOGRAPHY: 20 DAYS
IN & AROUND WILMINGTON, NC
12 HR DYS/5 DY WK * 2ND CAMERA=2 DYS
WGA/DGA/SAG   NON-UNION CREW
35MM- DIGITAL POSTPRODUCTION

Acct #	Description	Amount	Units	X	Rate	Subtotal	Total
1100	SCRIPT						
1101	WRITER'S SALARIES						
			Allow		105,000	105,000	
							105,000
1103	RESEARCH						
	Writer/Producer research trips		Allow		12,500	12,500	
	Airfare, hotel, taxi, legal research, car rentals consultations, shipping						
	clearances		Allow		500	500	13,000
1104	STORY RIGHTS/ COPYRIGHTS						
			Allow		54,500	54,500	
			Allow		5,000	5,000	59,500
1106	SCRIPT SUPERVISION						
			Allow		4,000	4,000	
	expenses during development regarding script						4,000
					Total for 1100		181,500
1200	PRODUCERS' UNIT						
1201	EXECUTIVE PRODUCER						
			Allow		100,00	100,000	100,000
1202	COPRODUCER						
			Allow		37,500	37,500	
							37,500
1203	PRODUCER						
			Allow		55,000	55,000	
							55,000

Acct #	Description	Amount	Units	X	Rate	Subtotal	Total
1200	PRODUCERS' UNIT (Cont'd)						
1203	PRODUCER (Cont'd)						
	Unit Production						
	Manager						
	PREP	1	Week		5,500	5,500	
	PREP	3	Weeks		1,563	4,689	
	SHOOT	4	Weeks		835	3,340	
	WRAP	1	Week		1,563	1,563	70,092
1204	ASSOCIATE						
	PRODUCER						
			Allow		25,000	25,000	25,000
1240	TRAVEL						
	L.A./Wilmington/L.A.						
	Executive Producer	1	FC/RT		1,550	1,550	
	Producer	2	Coach		550	1,100	
	Coproducer	1	Coach		564	564	
	Associate Producer	1	Coach		564	564	
	Producer's Assistant	1	Coach		562	562	
	Producer's Assistant	1	Coach		563	563	
	Transport to/	5	TRIPS		150	750	5,733
	from airport						
1241	HOTEL COSTS						
	Executive Producer	50	Nights		76	3,800	
	Producer	50	Nights		66	3,300	
	Coproducer	5	Nights		56	280	
	Associate Producer	5	Nights		56	280	
	Producer's Assistant	5	Nights		87	435	
	Producer's Assistant	43	Nights		22	946	
	Cleaning/utilities		Allow		1,000	1,000	
	*tax included						10,041
1242	PER DIEM						
	Executive Producer	51	Days		75	3,825	
	Producer	51	Days		75	3,825	
	Coproducer	5	Days		40	200	
	Associate Producer	5	Days		40	200	
	Producer's Assistant	5	Days		75	375	
	Producer's Assistant						
	PREP	15	Days		25	375	
	SHOOT	20	Days		15	300	
	WEEKENDS	7	Days		25	175	9,275
1280	MISCELLANEOUS						
	Videotape rentals/		Allow		1,500	1,500	
	casting meetings/						
	research						
							1,500
					Total for 1200		259,142

Acct #	Description	Amount	Units	X	Rate	Subtotal	Total
1300	DIRECTION						
1301	DIRECTOR						
			Allow		70,899	70,899	70,899
1340	TRAVEL						
	L.A./Wilmington/L.A.	2	FC/RT		1,530	3,060	
	Trips to/from airport	2	Trips		150	300	3,360
1341	HOTEL COSTS						
		51	Nights		60	3,060	
	Cleaning/utilities		Allow		700	700	
	*tax included						3,760
1342	PER DIEM						
		51	Days		100	5,100	5,100
					Total for 1300		83,119
1400	CAST						
1401	PRINCIPAL CAST						
	Jerry Halloran		Allow		303,000	303,000	
	Detective Thiele		Allow		50,000	50,000	
	Claire Roscher		Allow		300,000	300,000	
	Marty Halloran		Allow		13,750	13,750	
	*overtime		Allow		2,750	2,750	669,500
1403	SUPPORTING CAST						
	Jerry's Mother		Allow		9,000	9,000	
	Dennis Urman		Allow		15,000	15,000	
	Officer Balder		Allow		1,200	1,200	
	Officer LeSalle		Allow		4,500	4,500	
	Patty Miles		Allow		2,405	2,405	
	Patty's brother	2	Days		575	1,150	
	Giles		Allow		5,000	5,000	
	OVERTIME	0.20	%		38,255	7,651	45,906
1404	DAY PLAYERS						
	Local hires:						
	Billy		Allow		2,875	2,875	
	Peggy		Allow		2,875	2,875	
	Wart	1	Day		575	575	
	Billy's friend	1	Day		575	575	
	Cab driver	1	Day		600	600	
	Dr. Williamson	1	Day		575	575	
	Undercover cop	1	Day		575	575	
	Nurse	1	Day		600	600	
	Clerk	1	Day		575	575	
	Hairdresser	1	Day		575	575	
	OVERTIME	0.20	%		10,400	2,080	12,480

Acct #	Description	Amount	Units	X	Rate	Subtotal	Total
1400	CAST (Cont'd)						
1411	STUNTS AND ADJUSTMENTS						
			Allow		522	522	522
1414	LOOPING						
			Allow		4,200	4,200	4,200
1420	CASTING DIRECTOR						
	Los Angeles:						
			Allow		25,000	25,000	
	WILMINGTON:						
			Allow		5,000	5,000	
							30,000
1421	CASTING DIRECTOR EXPENSES						
	L.A. expenses		Allow		500	500	
	Wilmington expenses		Allow		500	500	1,000
1440	TRAVEL						
	L.A./Wilmington/L.A.						
	Jerry Halloran	3	FC/RT		1,530	4,590	
	Detective Thiele	2	FC/RT		1,530	3,060	
	Claire Roscher	2	FC/RT		1,530	3,060	
	Marty Halloran	1	FC/RT		670	670	
	Jerry's Mother	1	Coach		475	475	
	Dennis Urman	1	FC/RT		1,530	1,530	
	Officer Balder	2	FC/RT		1,530	3,060	
	Officer LaSalle	1	Coach		575	575	
	Local Hire Travel		Allow		2,500	2,500	
	Trans to/from Airport		Allow		1,000	1,000	20,520
1441	HOTEL COSTS						
	Jerry Halloran	33	Nights		97	3,201	
	Detective Thiele	33	Nights		97	3,201	
	Claire Roscher	33	Nights		60	1,980	
	Marty Halloran	1	Mos		1,541	1,541	
	Jerry's Mother	2	Nights		97	194	
	Dennis Urman		Allow		1,000	1,000	
	Officer Balder	3	Nights		97	291	
	Local hire hotel	75	Nights		60	4,500	
	Cleaning/utilities		Allow		4,000	4,000	
	*tax included						19,908

Acct #	Description	Amount	Units	X	Rate	Subtotal	Total
1400	CAST (Cont'd)						
1442	PER DIEM						
	Jerry Halloran	33	Days		100	3,300	
	Detective Thiele	33	Days		75	2,475	
	Claire Roscher	33	Days		100	3,300	
	Marty Halloran	33	Days		75	2,475	
	Jerry's Mother	26	Days		53	1,378	
	Dennis Urman	2	Days		75	150	
	Officer Balder	16	Days		75	1,200	
	Local hire per diem	50	Days		53	2,650	16,928
1480	MISCELLANEOUS						
	Misc. Cast expenses,		Allow		1,800	1,800	
	rehearsal/read-						
	through exp.						1,800
						Total for 1400	822,764
1800	A-T-L FRINGE						
1899	Fringes						
	WGA-PBW	12.50	%		77,500	9,688	
	DIRECTOR-PBW	12.50	%		70,899	8,862	
	SAG-PBW	13.30	%		199,608	26,548	
	CA. TAXES	15	%		30,106	4,516	
	N. CAROLINA	15	%		37,094	5,564	
	N.Y.	16	%		15,000	2,400	
	FICA DIS	6.20	%		395,100	24,496	
	FICA MED	1.45	%		459,899	6,669	
	FUI	0.80	%		65,750	526	
	SUI	5.40	%		65,750	3,551	92,820
						Total for 1800	92,820
	TOTAL ABOVE-THE-LINE						1,439,344

2000	PRODUCTION STAFF						
2002	UNIT PRODUCTION						
	MANAGER						
	TRAVEL/PREP	3	Weeks		3,937	11,811	
	SHOOT	4	Weeks		4,665	18,660	
	WRAP/TRAVEL	1	Week		3,937	3,937	
	COMPLETION	1	Week		4,665	4,665	39,073
2003	1ST ASSISTANT						
	DIRECTOR						
	Local hire:						
	Scale:						
	PREP	3	Weeks		2,672	8,016	
	SHOOT	4	Weeks		2,672	10,688	
	COMPLETION	1	Week		2,672	2,672	

Acct #	Description	Amount	Units	X	Rate	Subtotal	Total
2000	PRODUCTION STAFF (Cont'd)						
2011	1ST ASSISTANT DIRECTOR (Cont'd)						
	Over scale+prod. Fee						
	PREP	3	Weeks		1,328	3,984	
	SHOOT	4	Weeks		1,328	5,312	
	COMPLETION	1	Week		1,328	1,328	
	*salary is $4,000.						
	p&w on scale portion						32,000
2004	KEY 2ND ASS'T DIRECTOR						
	Local hire:						
	Scale+$378 prod. fee						
	PREP	1.40	Weeks		1,791	2,507	
	SHOOT	4	Weeks		2,169	8,676	
	OVERTIME	10	Days	0.50	359	1,795	
	COMPLETION	1	Week		1,791	1,791	14,769
2007	SCRIPT SUPERVISOR						
	PREP	5	Days		300	1,500	
	SHOOT	20	Days		300	6,000	
	2ND CAMERA	2	Days		40	80	
	TRAVEL	1	Day		150	150	7,730
2010	PRODUCTION COORDINATOR						
	L.A. hire:						
	TRAVEL/PREP	16	Days		240	3,840	
	SHOOT/HOLIDAY	21	Days		240	5,040	
	WRAP/TRAVEL	11	Days		240	2,640	
	SATURDAY	1	Day		360	360	11,880
2011	ASST PROD. CO-ORDINATOR						
	Local hire:						
	PREP	15	Days		150	2,250	
	SHOOT	20	Days		150	3,000	
	WRAP	5	Days		150	750	
							6,000
2012	PRODUCTION ASSISTANTS						
	OFFICE P.A.						
	PREP	15	Days		125	1,875	
	SHOOT	20	Days		125	2,500	
	WRAP	10	Days		125	1,250	
	#1 KEY SET P.A.						
	PREP	2	Days		125	250	
	SHOOT	20	Days		125	2,500	
	#2 SET P.A.						
	SHOOT	20	Days		125	2,500	
	add'l Set P.A.		Allow		1,000	1,000	11,875

Acct #	Description	Amount	Units	X	Rate	Subtotal	Total
2000	PRODUCTION STAFF (Cont'd)						
2018	PRODUCTION						
	ACCOUNTANT						
	L.A. hire:						
	TRAVEL/PREP	3	Weeks		1,900	5,700	
	SHOOT	4	Weeks		1,900	7,600	
	WRAP/TRAVEL	2	Weeks		1,900	3,800	
	WRAP/L.A.	2	Weeks		1,584	3,168	20,268
2019	ASST PROD.						
	ACCOUNTANT						
	L.A. hire:						
	TRAVEL/PREP	3	Weeks		1,200	3,600	
	SHOOT	4	Weeks		1,200	4,800	
	WRAP/TRAVEL	2	Weeks		1,200	2,400	
	WRAP/L.A.	2	Weeks		1,000	2,000	12,800
2080	MISCELLANEOUS						
	Prod. Accountant	11	Weeks		100	1,100	
	Prod. Coordinator	9	Weeks		100	900	2,000
						Total for 2000	158,395
2100	EXTRA TALENT						
2101	STAND-INS						
		80	Man-days		75	6,000	6,000
2102	EXTRAS						
		300	Man-days		40	12,000	
	OVERTIME		Allow		3,500	3,500	
	Adjustments		Allow		250	250	
	Cars		Allow		250	250	16,000
2110	CASTING FEE						
	Commission is based						
	on 15% of the gross		Allow		2,400	2,400	2,400
						Total for 2100	24,400
2200	SET DESIGN						
2201	PRODUCTION						
	DESIGNER						
	L.A. hire:						
	TRAVEL/PREP	2	Weeks		2,500	5,000	
	SHOOT	4	Weeks		2,500	10,000	
	SATURDAY	1	Day		150	150	
	WRAP/TRAVEL	2	Days		375	750	15,900
2203	ART DEPT.						
	COORDINATOR						
	Local hire:						
	PREP	2.60	Weeks		750	1,950	
	SHOOT	4	Weeks		750	3,000	
	WRAP	1	Week		750	750	5,700

Acct #	Description	Amount	Units	X	Rate	Subtotal	Total
2200	SET DESIGN (Cont'd)						
2210	RESEARCH COSTS						
	Magazines/books/						
	videos		Allow		250	250	250
2211	BLUEPRINTS, ETC.						
	Color copying		Allow		250	250	250
2215	EXPENDABLES						
			Allow		400	400	400
					Total for 2200		22,500
2300	SET CONSTRUCTION						
2301	CONSTRUCTION						
	CO-ORDINATOR						
		6	Weeks		1,250	7,500	7,500
2303	CONSTRUCTION						
	LABOR		Allow		28,380	28,380	28,380
2315	EXPENDABLES/						
	PURCHASES		Allow		19,920	19,920	19,920
2317	RENTALS						
	Equipment		Allow		2,500	2,500	
	Shop space		Allow		1,250	1,250	3,750
2378	BOX RENTALS						
	Constr. Coord.	6	Weeks		350	2,100	2,100
2379	CAR ALLOWANCE						
	Const. Coord.	6	Weeks		150	900	900
					Total for 2300		62,550
2400	SET DRESSING						
2401	SET DECORATOR						
	PREP	15	Days		400	6,000	
	SHOOT	20	Days		400	8,000	
	SUNDAY		Allow		600	600	
	WRAP	5	Days		400	2,000	
	TRAVEL	2	Days		250	500	17,100
2402	LEAD MAN						
	Local hire:						
	PREP	10	Days		250	2,500	
	SHOOT	20	Days		250	5,000	
	WRAP	5	Days		250	1,250	
	SATURDAY	1	Day		321	321	9,071
2403	SWING GANG						
	Local hires:						

Acct #	Description	Amount	Units	X	Rate	Subtotal	Total
2400	SET DRESSING (Cont'd)						
2403	SWING GANG (Cont'd)						
	BUYER						
	PREP	10	Days		175	1,750	
	SHOOT	20	Days		175	3,500	
	WRAP	2	Days		175	350	
	SATURDAY	2	Days		225	450	
	#1:						
	PREP	10	Days		175	1,750	
	SHOOT	20	Days		175	3,500	
	WRAP	5	Days		175	875	
	SATURDAY	1	Day		225	225	
	#2:						
	PREP	8	Days		175	1,400	
	SHOOT	20	Days		175	3,500	
	WRAP	5	Days		175	875	
	#3:						
	PREP	7	Days		175	1,225	
	SHOOT	20	Days		175	3,500	
	WRAP	5	Days		175	875	
	#4 ON-SET						
	DRESSER						
	PREP	4	Days		200	800	
	SHOOT	20	Days		200	4,000	
	ADD'L MAN-DAYS	10	Days		175	1,750	30,325
2415	EXPENDABLES						
			Allow		1,000	1,000	1,000
2416	PURCHASES						
	All sets		Allow		14,150	14,150	14,150
2417	RENTALS						
	All sets		Allow		14,150	14,150	14,150
2418	PRODUCTION						
	RENTALS						
	Storage area		Allow		1,250	1,250	1,250
2478	BOX RENTAL						
	Leadman	7	Weeks		150	1,050	1,050
					Total for 2400		88,096
2500	PROPERTY						
2501	PROPERTY MASTER						
	Local hire:						
	PREP	15	Days		300	4,500	
	SHOOT	20	Days		300	6,000	
	WRAP	3	Days		300	900	11,400

Acct #	Description	Amount	Units	X	Rate	Subtotal	Total
2500	PROPERTY (Cont'd)						
2502	ASSISTANT						
	PROPERTY						
	MASTER						
	Local hire:						
	PREP	10	Days		200	2,000	
	SHOOT	20	Days		200	4,000	
	WRAP	3	Days		200	600	
	ADD'L MAN-DAYS	3	Days		100	300	6,900
2515	EXPENDABLES						
			Allow		1,000	1,000	1,000
2516	PURCHASES						
			Allow		3,250	3,250	3,250
2517	RENTALS						
	includes E-FAN		Allow		3,850	3,850	3,850
2578	BOX RENTALS						
	Propmaster	4	Weeks		300	1,200	1,200
2579	CAR ALLOWANCE						
	Propmaster	3.60	Weeks		125	450	
	*prep/wrap only						450
					Total for 2500		28,050
2600	SPECIAL EQUIP. & ANIMALS						
2602	LEAD WRANGLER						
		2	Weeks		1,800	3,600	3,600
2604	ANIMALS						
	Live Birds		Allow		1,900	1,900	1,900
2605	MANUFACTURE						
	ANIMALS						
	Mechanical Birds		Allow		2,000	2,000	2,000
2609	PICTURE CARS						
	Includes modification		Allow		6,200	6,200	6,200
					Total for 2600		13,700
2700	WARDROBE						
2701	COSTUME DESIGNER						
	L.A. hire:						
	PREP	15	Days		375	5,625	
	SHOOT	20	Days		375	7,500	
	SATURDAY	2	Days	1.50	375	1,125	
	TRAVEL	1	Day		400	400	14,650

Acct #	Description	Amount	Units	X	Rate	Subtotal	Total
2700	WARDROBE (Cont'd)						
2702	COSTUME SUPERVISOR						
	Local hire:						
	PREP	10	Days		270	2,700	
	SHOOT	20	Days		270	5,400	
	SATURDAY	2	Days		150	300	
	WRAP	3	Days		270	810	
	L.A. ASS'T FOR SHOPPING	6	Days		133	798	10,008
2703	ON-SET LABOR						
	Local hire:						
	PREP	5	Days		200	1,000	
	SHOOT	20	Days		200	4,000	
	WRAP	3	Days		200	600	5,600
2704	CUSTOMER						
	Local hire:						
	PREP	7	Days		150	1,050	
	SHOOT	20	Days		150	3,000	
	WRAP	3	Days		150	450	4,500
2708	ALTERATIONS & MANUFACTURE		Allow		2,500	2,500	2,500
2715	EXPENDABLES		Allow		500	500	500
2716	PURCHASES		Allow		19,000	19,000	19,000
2717	RENTALS		Allow		8,000	8,000	8,000
2725	CLEANING AND DYEING		Allow		1,500	1,500	1,500
2778	BOX RENTAL						
	Costume Designer	7	Weeks		125	875	
	Costume Supervisor	4	Weeks		100	400	
	Costumer	5	Weeks		125	625	
	Add'l box rentals		Allow		450	450	2,350
2779	CAR ALLOWANCE						
	Costume Designer in L.A.	3	Weeks		125	375	375
					Total for 2700		68,983
2800	MAKEUP AND HAIR						
2801	KEY MAKEUP ARTIST						
	Local hire:						

Acct #	Description	Amount	Units	X	Rate	Subtotal	Total
2800	MAKEUP AND HAIR (Cont'd)						
	PREP	4	Days		375	1,500	
	SHOOT	20	Days		375	7,500	9,000
2802	ADDITIONAL MAKEUP						
	Local hire:						
	SUNDAY		Allow		150	150	
	SHOOT	1	Day		200	200	
	SHOOT	19	Day		250	4,750	5,100
2803	KEY HAIR ARTIST						
	Local hire:						
	SHOOT	20	Days		300	6,000	
	TEST/PREP	2	Days		300	600	6,600
2804	ADDITIONAL HAIR						
	Local hire:						
	SHOOT	20	Days		200	4,000	
	TEST/PREP	1.50	Days		200	300	4,300
2815	EXPENDABLES						
	Makeup/Hair supplies		Allow		2,000	2,000	
	*special products						
							2,000
2816	PURCHASES						
			Allow		500	500	500
2878	KIT RENTAL						
	Key Makeup	20	Days		25	500	
	Key Hair	20	Days		25	500	
	Add'l Makeup	20	Days		10	200	
	Add'l Hair	20	Days		10	200	
	TEST/PREP	2	Days		25	50	1,450
					Total for 2800		28,950
2900	SET OPERATIONS						
2901	KEY GRIP:						
	Local hire:						
	PREP	5	Days		300	1,500	
	SHOOT	20	Days		300	6,000	
	WRAP	2	Days		300	600	8,100
2902	GRIP BEST BOY						
	Local hire:						
	PREP	5	Days		250	1,250	
	SHOOT	20	Days		250	5,000	
	WRAP	2	Days		250	500	6,750

Acct #	Description	Amount	Units	X	Rate	Subtotal	Total
2900	SET OPERATIONS (Cont'd)						
2903	GRIPS						
	Local hires:						
	#1:						
	PREP	2	Days		225	450	
	SHOOT	20	Days		225	4,500	
	WRAP	2	Days		225	450	
	#2:						
	PREP	1	Day		225	225	
	SHOOT	20	Days		225	4,500	
	ADD'L MAN-DAYS	15.50	Days		225	3,488	13,613
2904	BOOM/DOLLY GRIP						
	Local hire:						
	PREP	1	Day		250	250	
	SHOOT	20	Days		250	5,000	
	WRAP	1	Day		250	250	5,500
2908	CRAFT SERVICE/ MEDIC						
	Local hire:						
	PREP	1	Day		240	240	
	SHOOT	20	Days		240	4,800	
	WRAP	1	Day		240	240	
	ADD'L MAN-DAYS	6	Days		125	750	6,030
2915	EXPENDABLES						
	Gels, tape, etc.		Allow		2,500	2,500	2,500
2916	PURCHASES						
	Shelving, floor, etc.		Allow		1,500	1,500	1,500
2917	RENTALS						
	GRIP PACKAGE	4	Weeks		1,350	5,400	
	Add'l equipment		Allow		300	300	5,700
2920	CAMERA DOLLIES						
	Dollies	4	Weeks		1,370	5,480	
	Giraffe crane	3	Days		606	1,818	7,298
2925	CRAFT SERVICE EXPENSES						
	Food/Beverage	20	Days		250	5,000	
	Food for Extras		Allow		1,500	1,500	6,500
2978	BOX RENTAL						
	Key Grip	5	Weeks		350	1,750	1,750
2980	MISCELLANEOUS						
	Craft svs. equip./Truck	21	Days		60	1,260	
	Medical supplies/Box	20	Days		25	500	1,760
					Total for 2900		67,001

Acct #	Description	Amount	Units	X	Rate	Subtotal	Total
3000	ELECTRICAL						
3001	GAFFER						
	PREP/TRAVEL	6	Days		375	2,250	
	SHOOT	20	Days		375	7,500	
	TRAVEL	1	Day		375	375	10,125
3002	BEST BOY						
	Local hire:						
	PREP	5	Days		250	1,250	
	SHOOT	20	Days		250	5,000	
	WRAP	2	Days		250	500	6,750
3003	LAMP OPERATORS						
	Local hires:						
	#1: PREP	2	Days		225	450	
	SHOOT	20	Days		225	4,500	
	WRAP	2	Days		225	450	
	#2:						
	PREP	2	Days		225	450	
	SHOOT	20	Days		225	4,500	
	WRAP	2	Days		225	450	
	#3 SHOOT	20	Days		225	4,500	
	ADD'L MAN-DAYS	17	Days		225	3,825	19,125
3015	EXPENDABLES						
	Gels, etc.		Allow		3,500	3,500	3,500
3017	RENTALS						
	ELECTRIC PACKAGE	4	Weeks		3,930	15,720	
	Add'l equipment		Allow		2,500	2,500	
	Condor/Scissor lift		Allow		2,500	2,500	
	Lightning	1	Day	2	300	600	21,320
3018	GENERATOR RENTAL						
		4	Weeks		800	3,200	
	Lightning gennie	1	Day		450	450	
	Base camp gennie		Allow		600	600	
	Gennie for camera truck	4	Weeks		25	100	4,350
3019	BURNOUTS						
	Globes		Allow		500	500	500
3078	BOX RENTAL						
	Gaffer	4	Weeks		100	400	
	BB Elec	5	Weeks		350	1,750	2,150
						Total for 3000	67,820

Acct #	Description	Amount	Units	X	Rate	Subtotal	Total
3100	CAMERA						
3101	DIRECTOR OF PHOTOGRAPHY Local hire:						
	PREP/TRAVEL	7	Days		1,000	7,000	
	SHOOT	20	Days		1,000	20,000	
	SATURDAY	1	Day		500	500	
	TRAVEL	1	Day		1,000	1,000	28,500
3102	CAMERA OPERATOR						
	Local hire:						
		20	Days		400	8,000	8,000
3103	EXTRA CAMERA OPERATOR						
	SHOOT	1	Day		450	450	
	Power Pod Tech	3	Days		250	750	1,200
3104	1ST ASSISTANT CAMERA						
	Local hire:						
	PREP	2	Days		300	600	
	SHOOT	20	Days		300	6,000	
	WRAP	1	Day		300	300	
	TEST	1	Day		300	300	7,200
3105	EXTRA 1ST ASSISTANT CAM. SHOOT	3	Days		300	900	900
3106	2ND ASSISTANT CAMERA						
	Local hire:						
	PREP	2	Days		250	500	
	SHOOT	20	Days		250	5,000	
	TEST	1	Day		250	250	5,750
3107	LOADER						
	Local hire:						
	PREP	1	Day		150	150	
	SHOOT	20	Days		150	3,000	
	Camera bump	2	Days		75	150	3,300
3115	EXPENDABLES						
	Pens, tape, markers, etc.		Allow		1,000	1,000	1,000
3117	RENTALS (Cameras)						
	CAMERA PACKAGE	4	Weeks		4,900	19,600	
	Add'l equipment		Allow		600	600	20,200

Acct #	Description	Amount	Units	X	Rate	Subtotal	Total
3100	CAMERA (Cont'd)						
3118	RENTALS						
	(Special Equip)						
	Steadicam (camera)	3	Weeks		1,672	5,016	
	Steadicam (harness)	8	Days		750	6,000	
	Power Pod	2	Days		775	1,550	12,566
3178	BOX RENTAL						
	Director of						
	Photography						
	Filters, lenses, gels,	4	Weeks		300	1,200	
	special equipment, etc.	28	Days		200	5,600	
	1st A.C. box	4.20	Weeks		300	1,260	8,060
					Total for 3100		96,676
3200	PRODUCTION SOUND						
3201	SOUND MIXER						
	Local hire:						
	PREP	1	Day		300	300	
	SHOOT	20	Days		300	6,000	
	WRAP	1	Day		300	300	6,600
3202	BOOM OPERATOR						
	Local hire:						
	SHOOT:	20	Days		250	5,000	5,000
3203	CABLEMAN						
	Local hire:						
	SHOOT	20	Days		100	2,000	2,000
3215	EXPENDABLES						
	Batteries, etc.		Allow		750	750	750
3217	RENTALS (SOUND						
	PKG.)						
	SOUND PACKAGE						
	Includes radio mikes	4	Weeks		1,500	6,000	6,000
3218	RENTALS (OTHER)						
	Walkie-talkies+access.	20	Days	25	2.50	1,250	
	Add'l Radios		Allow		100	100	
	Repeater		Allow		230	230	1,580
3219	VIDEO RENTAL						
	(SYNC PLYBK)						
	AND TRANSFER		Allow		3,500	3,500	3,500
3220	1/4" AUDIOTAPE						
	3 roll/day @ $15	20	Days	3	15	900	900
	per roll						
					Total for 3200		26,330

Acct #	Description	Amount	Units	X	Rate	Subtotal	Total
3300	SPECIAL EFFECTS						
3317	RENTALS		Allow		2,000	2,000	2,000
					Total for 3300		2,000
3400	LOCATION EXPENSES						
3401	LOCATION MANAGER						
	Local hire:						
	PREP	5	Weeks		1,500	7,500	
	SHOOT	3.80	Weeks		1,500	5,700	
	SATURDAY	1	Day	1.50	300	450	
	SATURDAY	2	Days	0.50	300	300	
	WRAP	1	Week		1,500	1,500	
	ASSIST LOC. MGR.						
	PREP	1.40	Weeks		1,000	1,400	
	PREP	1	Week		850	850	
	SHOOT	4	Weeks		850	3,400	
	WRAP	1	Week		850	850	21,950
3402	LOCATION SURVEY		Allow		3,000	3,000	3,000
	EXPENSE						
3403	GRATUITIES						
			Allow		200	200	200
3405	POLICE		Allow		7,100	7,100	7,100
3407	WATCHMAN						
			Allow		4,200	4,200	4,200
3410	CATERING SERVICE						
	Crew lunches	20	Days	70	12.50	17,500	
	Add'l lunches		Allow		1,000	1,000	
	2nd meals	14	Days		250	3,500	
	Swing/constr lunches	20	Days	7	10	1,400	
	Standins/Extras	380	Meals		12.50	4,750	
	Coffee/tea/soup/chili/ ice	20	Days		75	1,500	
	*includes tax						29, 650
3411	SITE RENTALS/						
	PERMITS/FEES						
	LOCATION SITES		Allow		53,650	53,650	
	Includes:						
	Crew/extras parking						
	Catering/holding tents						
	Changing areas						
	Air-conditioning						53,650
3415	EXPENDABLES						
	OFFICE SUPPLIES	10	Weeks		900	9,000	

Acct #	Description	Amount	Units	X	Rate	Subtotal	Total
3400	LOCATION EXPENSES (Cont'd)						
	Includes Xerox paper,						
	service calls, supplies						
	OFFICE						
	REFRESHMENTS	10	Weeks		250	2,500	6,500
3416	PURCHASES						
	Office/household items						
	nonexpendable for						
	location setup/						
	condos		Allow		1,000	1,000	1,000
3417	RENTALS						
	Plain paper	2	Mos		180	360	
	Photocopier	2	Mos		505	1,010	
	add'l copy coverage		Allow		500	500	
	Typewriters	2	Mos	2	132	528	
	Prod office laser						
	printer	2	Mos	2	127	508	
	Laser printer/Director	2	Mos		152	304	
	Accounting safe						
	(Del/Pkp)	2	Mos		105	210	
	Water/Coffee dispenser	2	Mos		75	150	
	VCR rentals		Allow		500	500	
	Microwave/misc		Allow		800	800	4,870
3419	RENTALS (OFFICE						
	SPACE)						
	PRODUCTION						
	OFFICES		Allow		18,000	18,000	18,000
3430	TELEPHONE EQUIP. &						
	INSTALL						
	OFFICE PHONES		Allow		2,100	2,100	
	PAGERS	6	Weeks	20	16	1,920	
	Connection fee		Allow		200	200	4,220
3431	TELEPHONE USAGE						
	Calls only	2	Mos		4,000	8,000	
	CELLULAR						
	Calls and equipment		Allow		5,000	5,000	13,000
3435	SHIPPING (airfreight						
	etc)						
	FedEx equip, kits,						
	dailies		Allow		12,000	12,000	
	postage						12,000
3440	FARES (TO/FROM						
	LOCATION)						
	Unit Production						
	Manager	1	FC/RT		1,671	1,671	
	Prod. Coordinator	1	Coach		556	556	
	Prod. Accountant	2	Coach		600	1,200	
	Assist. Accountant	1	Coach		652	652	
	Prod. Designer	1	FC/RT		1,550	1,550	

Acct #	Description	Amount	Units	X	Rate	Subtotal	Total
3400	LOCATION EXPENSES (Cont'd)						
3440	FARES TO/FROM LOC. (Cont'd)						
	Costume Designer	1	Coach		580	580	
	Costume Supervisor	1	Coach		575	575	
	Director of Photography	1	FC/RT		1,550	1,550	
	Gaffer	1	Coach		607	607	
	Script Supervisor	1	Coach		575	575	
	Hairdresser	1	Coach		1,425	1,425	10,941
3441	HOTEL COSTS						
	Unit Production Manager	2	Mos		1,900	3,800	
	Prod. Coordinator	2	Mos		1,671	3,342	
	Prod. Accountant	2	Mos		1,600	3,200	
	Assist. Accountant	2	Mos		1,600	3,200	
	Prod. Designer	2	Mos		1,175	2,350	
	Costume Designer	5	Weeks		371	1,855	
	Costume Supervisor	3	Nights		54	162	
	Director of Photography	40	Nights		58	2,320	
	Gaffer	5	Weeks		396	1,980	
	Set Decorator	3	Days		76	228	
			Allow		2,000	2,000	
	Honeywagon Driver	30	Weeks		53	1,590	
	Insert Car Driver	3	Days		53	159	
	Script Supervisor	1	Mos		1,162	1,162	
	Hairdresser	1	Mos		875	875	
	Cleaning/utilities		Allow		2,000	2,000	
	*tax included						30,223
3442	PER DIEM						
	Unit Production Manager	56	Allow		65	3,640	
	Prod. Coordinator	63	Days		40	2,520	
	Prod. Accountant	63	Days		40	2,520	
	Assist. Accountant	63	Days		40	2,520	
	Prod. Designer	51	Days		50	2,550	
	Costume Designer	43	Days		50	2,150	
	Director of Photography	36	Days		50	1,800	
	Gaffer	36	Days		40	1,440	
	Set Decorator		Allow		2,000	2,000	
	Honeywagon Driver	4	Weeks		225	900	
	Insert Car Driver		Allow		136	136	
	Script Supervisor		Allow		350	350	
	Hairdresser	26	Days		40	1,040	23,566
3478	BOX RENTAL						
	Location Mgr. box	4	Weeks		50	200	200
3479	CAR ALLOWANCE						
	Location Manager	9.50	Weeks		150	1,425	
	Assist. Loc. Mgr.	8	Weeks		125	1,000	2,425

Acct #	Description	Amount	Units	X	Rate	Subtotal	Total
3480	MISCELLANEOUS						
	Polaroid/35mm film		Allow		10,000	10,000	
	Process all depts.						10,000
					Total for 3400		261,695
3600	LOCATION TRANSPORTATION						
3601	TRANS. COORDINATOR						
	Local hire:						
	PREP	15	Days		300	4,500	
	SHOOT	20	Days		300	6,000	
	WRAP	5	Days		300	1,500	
	SUBURBAN/SINGLE #1						12,000
3602	TRANSPORTATION						
	CAPTAIN						
	Local hire:						
	PREP	5	Days		225	1,125	
	SHOOT	20	Days		225	4,500	
	WRAP	3	Days		225	675	
	OVERTIME	20	Days		20	400	
	CAMERA TRUCK						6,700
3603	DRIVERS						
	14-hour day/17						
	payhours						
	GRIP TRUCK						
	SHOOT	20	Days		200	4,000	
	ELECTRIC TRUCK						
	SHOOT	20	Days		200	4,000	
	PROP TRUCK						
	See on set-dresser						
	HONEYWAGON						
	SHOOT	20	Days		300	6,000	
	STAKEBED #1						
	Dressing rooms						
	SHOOT	20	Days		200	4,000	
	STAKEBED #2						
	SHOOT	20	Days		200	4,000	
	WARDROBE/MKP/						
	HAIR COMBO						
	SHOOT	20	Days		225	4,500	
	REFUELER						
	SHOOT	20	Days		200	4,000	
	GENNIE BUMP	3	Days		20	60	
	MAXIVAN SHOOT	20	Days		170	3,400	

Acct #	Description	Amount	Units	X	Rate	Subtotal	Total
3600	LOCATION TRANSPORTATION (Cont'd)						
3603	DRIVERS (Cont'd)						
	CATERER						
	PREP	2	Days		300	600	
	SHOOT	20	Days		300	6,000	
	WRAP	1	Day		300	300	
	CATERING HELPER						
	PREP	2	Days		200	400	
	SHOOT	20	Days		200	4,000	
	WRAP	1	Days		200	200	
	ADDITIONAL						
	CATERING HELP	1	Day		150	150	
	INSERT CAR	3	Days		300	900	
	ALL DRIVERS: PREP/						
	WRAP						
	PREP (P.A. Driver)	9	Days		100	900	
	PREP	4	Man-Days		150	750	
	WRAP	5	Man-Days		150	750	
	PREP/WRAP (ward/						
	mkp/hr	2	Days		225	450	
	PREP/WRAP (honey-						
	wagon)	3	Day		300	900	
	OVERTIME	0.12	%		50,260	6,031	
							56,291
3615	EXPENDABLES						
	Small Purchases		Allow		4,000	4,000	
	Honeywagon supplies		Allow		1,500	1,500	5,500
3617	PRODUCTION						
	VEHICLES						
	01 Coord Suburb/						
	Single #1	8	Weeks		270	2,160	
	02 Camera Truck	5	Weeks		486	2,430	
	03 Grip Trk. *include						
	in pkg.		Allow		0	0	
	04 Elec Trk. *include						
	in pkg.		Allow		0	0	
	05 Prop Truck	5.40	Weeks		525	2,835	
	06 Set Dressing 5-ton	6	Weeks		420	2,520	
	07 Set Dressing Cube						
	#1	6	Weeks		315	1,890	
	add'l day in prep	2	Days		75	150	
	08 Honeywagon	4	Weeks		1,575	6,300	
	09 Stakebed #1/Two						
	Hole	4	Weeks		420	1,680	
	10 Stakebed #2/Single						
	#2	4	Weeks		420	1,680	
	11 Wardrobe/Mkp/Hair	5.60	Weeks		1,549	8,674	
	hydraulic mkp.						

Acct #	Description	Amount	Units	X	Rate	Subtotal	Total
3600	LOCATION TRANSPORTATION (Cont'd)						
3617	PRODUCTION VEHICLES (Cont'd)						
	chairs		Allow		100	100	
	12 Refueler/Single #3	5	Weeks		486	2,430	
	13 Insert Car		Allow		2,000	2,000	
	14 Maxivan	5	Weeks		324	1,620	
	15 Minivan #1	9	Weeks		216	1,944	
	16 Minivan #2	4	Weeks		200	800	
	17 Two-Hole	4	Weeks		840	3,360	
	18 Single Dressing						
	Rooms	4	Weeks	3	500	6,000	
	19 Cargo vans/Grip/						
	Elec		Allow	2	1,350	2,700	
	20 Pick-up Truck/P.A.	3	Weeks		162	486	
	21 Insert Car	1	Week		1,360	1,360	
	22 Cargo van/Caterer	5	Weeks		227	1,135	
	*includes tax						
							54,254
3625	SELF-DRIVE VEHICLES						
	01 Executive Producer	7	Weeks		152	1,064	
	02 Producer	7	Weeks		152	1,064	
	03 Co. Producer	1	Week		152	152	
	04 Assoc. Producer						
	*see Co-Producer						
	05 Production Manager	8	Weeks		135	1,000	
	06 Prod. Office						
	Explorer	7	Weeks		216	1,512	
	07 Accounting cars	9	Weeks	2	135	2,430	
	08 Production						
	Designer	6	Weeks		152	912	
	09 Dir. of Photog-						
	raphy	5.60	Weeks		135	756	
	10 Costume Designer	5.60	Weeks		227	1,271	
	11 Cast Cars	4.80	Weeks	2	135	1,296	
	12 Cast Cars	4.80	Weeks		152	1,459	
	13 Director	7	Weeks		152	1,064	
	14 Gaffer	5	Weeks		135	675	
	15 Minivan #3/Buyer	7	Weeks		216	1,512	
	16 Cargo Van/Leadman	6	Weeks		150	900	
	17 Exec Producer asst.	6	Weeks		135	810	
	18 Set Decorator	2	Weeks		135	270	
	Minivan #4	6	Weeks		216	1,296	
	To/Fr Wilm.	2	Days		144	288	
	19 Hairdresser	4	Weeks		135	540	
	20 Cast	2.50	Weeks		135	338	
	*includes tax						
							20,689
3627	DRIVE-TO MILEAGE						
	EXPENSE						
			Allow		1,500	1,500	1,500

22

Acct #	Description	Amount	Units	X	Rate	Subtotal	Total
3600	LOCATION TRANSPORTATION (Cont'd)						
3629	ROAD PERMITS/						
	CABS/PARKING						
	Truck permits		Allow		1,200	1,200	
	B-T-L cabs to/fr.						
	airport		Allow		1,000	1,000	
	Parking, meters, etc.		Allow		500	500	2,700
3630	GAS AND OIL						
	AND WASH		Allow		12,000	12,000	12,000
3635	MAINTENANCE						
	Flats, batteries, etc.		Allow		1,000	1,000	1,000
						Total for 3600	172,634
3700	OVERTIME						
3701	B-T-L CREW						
	OVERTIME						
	BEYOND 12 HOURS		Allow		79,000	79,000	
	*includes swing						
	*excludes drivers						79,000
						Total for 3700	79,000
3800	PRODUCTION FILM						
3801	NEGATIVE RAW-						
	STOCK						
	35mm						
	SHOOT	5,000	Feet	20	0.4971	49,710	
	EXTRA CAMERA	2,500	Feet	2	0.4971	2,486	
	SALES TAX	0.01	%		52,196	522	
	105,000' TOTAL						
	FOOTAGE						52,718
						Total for 3800	52,718
4800	PRODUCTION FRINGE						
4899	Fringes						
	DGA-BTL	20.719	%		75,218	15,584	
	CA. TAXES	15	%		94,068	14,110	
	W/COMP	0.90	%		178,323	1,605	
	N. CAROLINA	15	%		494,922	74,238	
	EXTRAS	17.50	%		22,00	3,850	
	N.Y.	16	%		20,268	3,243	112,630
						Total for 4800	112,630
	TOTAL PRODUCTION						1,333,132
5000	EDITORIAL						
5001	EDITOR						
		4	Weeks		4,000	16,000	
		12	Weeks		4,000	48,800	64,000

Acct #	Description	Amount	Units	X	Rate	Subtotal	Total
5000	EDITORIAL						
	(Cont'd)						
5002	ASSISTANT EDITOR						
		16	Weeks		2,000	32,000	
	2ND ASST. EDITOR	16	Weeks		2,000	32,000	
	OVERTIME		Allow		8,000	8,000	72,000
5015	EXPENDABLES		Allow		250	250	250
5016	PURCHASES		Allow		250	250	250
5017	RENTALS						
	(EQUIPMENT)						
	Avid	10	Weeks		1,900	19,000	19,000
5019	CUTTING ROOM						
	RENTAL	10	Weeks		250	2,500	2,500
5020	ON-LINE EDITING						
	Conform		Allow		8,000	8,000	8,000
5025	SOUND EFFECTS						
	EDITING						
	Contract		Allow		30,000	30,000	30,000
5030	MUSIC EDITOR						
	Package		Allow		6,500	6,500	6,500
5031	MUSIC CONTINUITY						
			Allow		750	750	750
5035	MESSENGERS/FILM						
	SHIPPING						
	Post Production		Allow		3,500	3,500	3,500
					Total for 5000		206,750
5100	MUSIC						
5101	COMPOSER/						
	ORCHEST./						
	CONDUCT.						
			Allow		140,000	140,000	140,000
					Total for 5100		140,000
5200	POSTPRODUCTION						
	SOUND						
	Postsound pkg. to						
	include Foley, ADR,						
	2 predubs, final dub,						
	layback, laydown,						
	transfers, stock, etc.		Allow		150,000	150,000	150,000
					Total for 5200		150,000

Acct #	Description	Amount	Units	X	Rate	Subtotal	Total
5300	FILM LIBRARY						
5317	STOCK SHOT RENTAL		Allow		5,500	5,500	5,500
					Total for 5,300		5,500
5400	FILM/AUDIO/VIDEO STOCK						
5422	VIDEO STOCK						
	Allowance for entire account:						
	1",3/4",1/2" Video stock						
	1/2" Audio stock		Allow		15,500	15,500	15,500
					Total for 5400		15,500
5600	FILM LABORATORY						
5601	DEVELOP NEGATIVE						
	90% of 105,000' 35mm	105,000	Feet	0.90	0.117	11,057	11,057
5602	REPRINTS		Allow			10,000	10,000
5603	DEV. OPTICAL SOUNDTRACK	9,000	Feet	.10		900	900
5604	TITLES		Allow			30,000	30,000
5605	OPTICAL EFFECTS		Allow			10,000	10,000
5606	CUT NEGATIVE	9	Reels	500		45,000	45,000
5607	TIMING		Allow			8,000	8,000
5608	ANSWER PRINT	9,000	Feet	1		9,000	9,000
5609	MISC.		Allow			5,000	5,000
					Total for 5600		128,957
5700	VIDEO POST						
5701	TRANS DAILIES (NEG TO 1")						
	Neg. to tape transfer		Allow		20,000	20,000	
	3/4" copies of dailies		Allow		2,000	2,000	
	1/2" copies of dailies		Allow		4,000	4,000	26,000
5705	DUB 3/4" VHS (VIEWING)						
	VHS/Beta cassettes and backup cartridges		Allow		4,000	4,000	4,000
5715	ELECTRONIC ASSEMBLY		Allow		4,000	4,000	4,000
					Total for 5700		34,000

Acct #	Description	Amount	Units	X	Rate	Subtotal	Total
5800	POST PRODUCTION						
5899	Fringes						
	EDITORIAL	18	%			24,480	
	CA. TAXES	15	%			20,400	44,880
						Total for 5800	44,880
	TOTAL POSTPRODUCTION						285,723

Acct #	Description	Amount	Units	X	Rate	Subtotal	Total
7000	ADMINISTRATIVE EXPENSES						
7001	AUDITOR/						
	ACCOUNTANT						
	Accountant clean-up						
	through delivery						
	including fringe	8	Weeks		400	3,200	3,200
7002	LEGAL		Allow		175,000	175,000	175,000
7005	COMPUTER						
	PROGRAM FEE		Allow		1,000	1,000	1,000
7006	PUBLICITY/						
	ADVERTISING		Allow		1,000	1,000	1,000
	0						
7009	MESSENGER (not						
	script/post)						
	L.A. messengers/						
	runners		Allow		500	500	500
7015	EXPENDABLES						
	Prep through delivery		Allow		1,000	1,000	1,000
7016	PURCHASES		Allow		3,177	3,177	3,177
7017	RENTALS (office						
	equip.)		Allow		1,000	1,000	1,000
7019	RENTALS (office						
	space)						
			Allow		3,750	3,750	3,750
7020	MPAA RATING		Allow		5,000	5,000	5,000
7030	TELEPHONE EQUIP/						
	INSTALL		Allow		500	500	500
7031	TELEPHONE USAGE						
	L.A. calls, etc.	4	Mos		1,000	4,000	4,000
7035	SHIPPING (airfreight,						
	FedEx)		Allow		200	200	200

Acct #	Description	Amount	Units	X	Rate	Subtotal	Total
7000	ADMINISTRATIVE EXPENSES (Cont'd)						
7042	POSTAGE						
	Prep, shoot, postprod.		Allow		1,500	1,500	1,500
7044	INSURANCE						
	Premium ($17,730 + 25%)		Allow		22,163	22,163	
	Medical exams	6	Exams		50	300	
	(director and 5 cast)						22,463
7050	WRAP PARTY						
			Allow		3,500	3,500	3,500
					Total for 7000		226,790
	TOTAL OTHER						226,790
	TOTAL ABOVE-THE-LINE						1,439,344
	TOTAL BELOW-THE-LINE						2,159,719
	ABOVE & BELOW-THE-LINE						3,599,063
	TOTAL FRINGES						250,330
	SUBTOTAL						4,076,183
	CONTINGENCY				10%		407,618
	COMPLETION BOND						
	(2% refund if not used)				5%		203,809
	GRAND TOTAL						4,687,610

Relative Values of Domestic and International Markets

The following is a breakdown of average domestic and foreign revenues generated by motion pictures. Though these numbers often shift, domestic distribution is currently worth about 60 percent of the total world market.

Domestic Theatrical 18%
Domestic Video 30%
Domestic Cable 09%
Domestic Syndication & Network 05%
        Total Domestic 62%

Foreign Theatrical 13%
Foreign Video 18%
Foreign TV 07%
        Total Foreign 38%

The following principal foreign territories are listed with an approximate percentage of their combined value for theatrical, TV/cable, and video distribution in the foreign market:

Europe ....65% of foreign market
Far East ....19% of foreign market
Latin America ....06% of foreign market
Other countries ....10% of foreign market

The following is a more detailed breakdown of each territory:

Europe:
        United Kingdom..........................25% of European market
        France.................................18% of European market
        Germany/Austria.........................19% of European market
        Italy..................................16% of European market
        Scandinavia.............................05% of European market
        Spain..................................10% of European market
        Other countries........................07% of European market

According to Film Finders, Germany, France, Italy, Spain, the United Kingdom, and Sweden collectively represent about 80 percent of the European box office.

Far East:
Hong Kong .... .02% of Far Eastern market
Japan .... .60% of Far Eastern market
Korea .... .21% of Far Eastern market
Philippines .... .02% of Far Eastern market
Taiwan .... .11% of Far Eastern market
Other countries .... .04% of Far Eastern market

Latin America:
Argentina .... .19% of Latin American market
Brazil .... .24% of Latin American market
Mexico .... .25% of Latin American market
Venezuela .... .12% of Latin American market
Other countries .... .20% of Latin American market

Other countries:
Australia/New Zealand .... .51% of remaining markets
South Africa .... .08% of remaining markets
USSR/Eastern Europe .... .11% of remaining markets
Other countries .... .30% of remaining markets

These figures can be deceptive to an independent producer since they represent across-the-board average values. The relative worth of each territory will vary enormously from picture to picture. A star, for example, who has significant box office clout in the Far East but little appeal in Europe may skew these numbers in a completely different direction. Likewise, pictures of a particular genre (action, comedy, drama) may be more valuable in certain territories than others.

References and Sources
for Additional Information

BOOKS AND PUBLICATIONS

American Cinematographer Manual
-Rod Ryan
-ASC Holding
-reference text with data, tables, charts, formulas, and other information related
-to cinematography

American Cinematographer Video Manual
-Frank Beacham
-ASC Holding
-reference text with data, tables, charts, formulas, and other information related
to video photography

The Art of Dramatic Writing: Its Basis in the Creative Interpretation of Human Nature
-by Lajos Egri
-Simon and Schuster
-Originally published in 1942 as *How to Write a Play,* this book has become a
bible for many screenwriters.

Art Murphy's Box Office Register
P.O. Box 3786
Hollywood, CA 90078
-domestic theatrical box office figures and statistics from 1982 to the present
-series of calendar-year summaries of domestic theatrical film box office performance as reported publicly by film distributors
-listings are alphabetical, numerical, and weekly (1–52)

Back Stage
1515 Broadway, 12th Floor
New York, NY 10036
(212) 764-7300

Big Screen Book
-Jonathan H. Banner
-Homily Press

-directory of contacts at independent production companies, independent distributors, and studios; each listing includes credits, address, phone and fax numbers

By Design: Interviews with Film Production Designers
-Vincent LoBrutto
-Praeger
-interviews with a wide range of designers, old timers as well as contemporary

Cinefex: The Journal of Cinematic Illusions
P.O. Box 20027
Riverside, CA 92516
fax (800) 434-3339
-quarterly publication that features the season's top effects films and major effects companies

Clearance & Copyright: Everything the Independent Filmmaker Needs to Know
-Michael C. Donaldson
-Silman-James Press
-excellent resource for information on all aspects of motion picture clearance and copyright issues

Complete Guide to Standard Script Formats
-Hillis R. Cole and Judith H. Haag
-CMC Publishing

Contracts for the Film and Television Industry
-Mark Litwak
-Silman-James Press
-collection of sample film production contracts

Dealmaking in the Film and Television Industry: From Negotiations Through Final Contracts
-Mark Litwak
-Silman-James Press
-a layman's guide to standard practices in entertainment law

Drama-Logue, Inc.
P.O. Box 38771
Los Angeles, CA 90038-0771
(213) 464-5079

Film & Video on the Internet: The Top 500 Sites
-Bert Deivert and Dan Harries
-Michael Wiese Publications
-book and diskette

Film Budgeting: Or How Much Will It Cost to Shoot Your Movie
-Ralph Singleton and Robert Koster
-Lone Eagle Publishing Company

Film Finance & Distribution—A Dictionary of Terms
   -Silman-James Press
   -definitions of some 3,600 terms used in the film industry in the finance and distribution of feature films

Film Scheduling: Or How Long Will It Take to Shoot Your Movie
   -Ralph Singleton
   -Lone Eagle Publishing Company

Get the Money and Shoot: The DRI Guide to Funding Documentary Films
   -Bruce Jackson and Diane Christian
   -Documentary Research, Inc.
   -covers how to find out about money, get a sponsor, prepare your budget and proposal

Getting the Best Score for your Film: A Filmmakers' Guide to Music Scoring
   -David Bell
   -Silman-James Press

Grants for Film, Media and Communications
   -The Foundation Center
   -covers grants to nonprofit organizations in the United States and abroad for film, video, documentaries, radio, television, printing, and publishing
   -lists 2,167 grants of $10,000 or more with a total value of $420,122,881 made by 539 foundations

Hollywood Agents and Managers Directory
   3000 W. Olympic Blvd., Suite 2525
   Santa Monica, CA 90404-5041
      (800) 815-0503
      (310) 315-4815
   -160-page publication of the *Hollywood Creative Directory* that lists addresses, and phone and fax numbers for 1,025 talent and literary agencies and managers coast to coast, 475 casting directors and talent executives, and over 3,000 staff names cross-referenced by company type and affiliation. The book includes representatives of actors, comedians, dancers, voice-over artists, models, composers, songwriters, directors, producers, writers, below-the-line talent, and photographers. Published biannually.
   -also available to subscribers as a searchable on-line database

Hollywood Creative Directory
   3000 W. Olympic Blvd., Suite 2525
   Santa Monica, CA 90404-5041
      (800) 815-0503
      (310) 315-4815
      http://www.hollyvision.com
   -listing of over 1,650 production companies, studios and networks, and over 5,750 names and titles of producers, studio and network executives, development executives, story editors, and their staffs. Includes companies with studio deals. Published triannually.
   -also available to subscribers as a searchable on-line database

Hollywood Distributors Directory
    3000 W. Olympic Blvd., Suite 2525
    Santa Monica, CA 90404-5041
        (800) 815-0503
        (310) 315-4815
    -125-page publication of the *Hollywood Creative Directory* that lists addresses, phone and fax numbers, and recent releases of over 550 domestic and foreign distributors. Includes over 2,360 cross-referenced names and titles of corporate, sales, acquisitions, publicity, and marketing staffs. Also includes public relations companies. Published annually.
    -also available to subscribers as a searchable on-line database

Hollywood Financial Directory
    3000 W. Olympic Blvd., Suite 2525
    Santa Monica, CA 90404-5041
        (800) 815-0503
        (310) 315-4815
    -100-page publication of the listing of the *Hollywood Creative Directory* that includes financial players in the film and television industry. Includes business and legal affairs executives for over 600 companies. Also contains information on production financing, entertainment law, insurance, and entertainment banking. Published annually.

Hollywood Movie Music Directory
    3000 W. Olympic Blvd., Suite 2525
    Santa Monica, CA 90404-5041
        (800) 815-0503
        (310) 315-4815
    -a publication of the *Hollywood Creative Directory* that lists over 875 companies involved with the licensing, production, clearance, publishing, and scoring of movie and television music and their staffs. Includes studio and network music executives, songwriters, composers, music supervisors, and performance rights organizations. Published annually.

The Hollywood Reporter
    5055 Wilshire Blvd.
    Los Angeles, CA 90036-4396
        (213) 525-2000
        fax (213) 525-2377
        http://www.hollywoodreporter.com
    -daily industry trade paper

Hollywood Reporter Blu-Book
    c/o *The Hollywood Reporter*
    5055 Wilshire Blvd., 6th Floor
    Los Angeles, CA 90036
        (213) 525-2000
        fax (213) 525-2377
    -over 30,000 listings in over 250 categories, including producers and production companies; financial, legal, and office services; production equipment and facil-

ities; location, transportation, and travel; cameras, lighting, and sound equipment; special effects; postproduction; distribution and marketing; crew, talent, and executive rosters

Industrial Light and Magic: Into the Digital Realm
-Mark Cotta Vaz and Patricia Rose Duignan
-Ballantine Books
-a beautifully illustrated book describing the visual effects created by George Lucas's company, Industrial Light and Magic

Industry Labor Guide
-Industry Labor Guide Publishing Company
14806 Weddington St.
Sherman Oaks, CA 91411
  (800) 820-7601
  (818) 995-4008
  http://www.laborguide.com
-labor rates and working conditions for all union/guild agreements, including IATSE, SAG, DGA, and WGA
-includes fringe benefits, insurance rates, and the going rates for "below-the-line" professionals in major metropolitan areas
-all low-budget and interactive agreements
-rules and regulations relating to the hiring of minors
-overview of production insurance requirements
-available in book form, as a computer database on disk or CD-Rom, and on the Internet

The International Motion Picture Almanac
-Quigley Publishing Company, Inc.
159 West 53rd St.
New York, NY 10019
  (212) 247-3100
-annual publication that includes historical and contemporary statistical data on motion pictures

Kemps Film TV & Video Handbook
-Reed Information Services
-comprehensive international production guide to the film, television, and video industries in fifty-three countries
-updated annually

LA 411
-LA 411 Publishing Company
611 N. Larchmont Blvd., Suite 201
Los Angeles, CA 90004
-includes information on production companies, agencies, crew and union regulations, sets and stages, location services and equipment, support services, camera and sound equipment, grip and lighting equipment, transportation, props and wardrobe, postproduction

Making Films Your Business
   -Mollie Gregory
   -Schocken Books
   -covers writing proposals to foundations, using foundations as sources of support, and an appendix listing foundations with an interest in funding films

Making Movies
   -Sidney Lumet
   -Random House
   -a personal journey through the movie-making process

The National Directory of Grants and Aid to Individuals in the Arts
   -Nancy A. Fandel
   -Allied Business Consultants, Inc.
   -lists most grants, prizes, and awards for professional work in the United States and abroad, and information about universities and schools that offer special aid to students

Negotiating for Dummies
   -Michael C. Donaldson and Mimi Donaldson
   -IDG Books Worldwide
   919 E. Hillsdale Blvd., Suite 400
   Foster City, CA 94404-9691
      (800) 762-2974
   -an excellent primer on negotiating skills and techniques, all of which are applicable to the motion picture industry

New York Production Guide (NYPG)
   150 5th Ave., #221
   New York, NY 10011
      (212) 243-0404
   -annually updated listing of products, services, facilities, and crew members for film and video in New York City

Nonlinear: A Guide to Digital Film and Video Editing
   -Michael Rubin
   -Triad Publishing Company

Pacific Coast Studio Directory
   P.O. Box V
   Pine Mountain, CA 93222-4921
      (805) 242-2722
      fax (805) 242-2724
   -oldest motion picture publication on the West Coast (since 1919)
   -published three times a year (January 1, May 1, and September 1)
   -each issue consists of a Wall Chart and an Index & Supplement Book with more than 5,000 advertisers and companies pertaining to the motion picture and television business
   -production services and supplies; advertising agencies; artists', and writers' representatives; casting; distributors and exchanges; film commissions; govern-

ment offices; guilds and unions, organizations and associations; production companies; publications; publicity; studios; television stations

The Producer's Masterguide
  -NY Production Manual, Inc.
    60 E. 8th St., 34th floor
    New York, NY 10003
    (212) 777-4002
    fax (212) 777-4101
    http://www.producers.masterguide.com
  -annually updated international directory of information on financing, contracts, unions, insurance, facilities, equipment, permits, festivals, markets, and distribution

Production Weekly
    P.O. Box 15052
    Beverly Hills, CA 90209
    fax (213) 651-1916
  -a weekly breakdown of projects in preproduction, preparation, and development for film, television, music videos, commercials, etc. Covering all of the major markets from Los Angeles to New York and all points in between, as well as Canada

Scenario, The Magazine of Screenwriting Art
    3200 Tower Oaks Blvd.
    Rockville, MD 20852
    (800) 222-2654
    fax (301) 984-3203
  -publishes four complete screenplays plus interviews with screenwriters, original artwork, and essays
  -published quarterly

Screen International: The International Film & Television Directory
  -Emap Media Information
  -three-volume publication listing international production services, companies, festivals, markets, film commissions, and more
  -updated annually

Screenplay: the Foundations of Screenwriting
  -Syd Field
  -Delta Books

Spike, Mike, Slackers & Dykes: A Guided Tour Across a Decade of American Independent Cinema
  -John Pierson
  -Miramax Books

The Technique of Special Effects Cinematography
  -by Raymond Fielding
  -Focal Press

Variety and *Daily Variety*
   5700 Wilshire Blvd., Suite 120
   Los Angeles, CA 90036
     (213) 857-6600
     http://www.variety.com
   -weekly and daily industry trade papers

Variety International Film Guide
   -Focal Press
   -a guide to film festivals, film schools, major awards, films produced in some sixty countries, plus box office information for each country's top-ten grossing films
   -updated annually

What an Art Director Does
   -Ward Preston
   -Silman-James Press
   -an introduction to motion picture production design
   -a good, practical how-to book on the film art department
   -subject matter doesn't cover design in the artistic sense

Working Cinema: Learning from the Masters
   -Roy Paul Marsden
   -Wadsworth
   -a textbook that includes an excellent section on production design with designer Dean Tavoularis

INTERNET SITES

Ain't It Cool News
   http://www.aint-it-cool-news.com
   -operated by Harry Knowles in Austin, Texas, this site provides film news, reviews, rumors, and gossip, much of which is not available elsewhere
   -includes an interactive forum and links to other film sites

Baseline on the Web
   Los Angeles
     (310) 789-2030
     (800) 858-3669
   New York
     (212) 254-8235
     (800) CHAPLIN
     http://www.pkbaseline.com
   -BASELINE verifies and maintains data on Paul Kagan film revenue and cost estimates, film and TV credits, film and TV projects in production, celebrity and industry contacts, TV episodic credits, domestic and international box office figures, bios, Paul Kagan box office analysis, and more. BASELINE maintains a database from Paul Kagan Associates, Inc., that includes the negative cost, prints and ads, domestic theatrical box office and rentals, domestic video revenues and the number of units shipped, and international theatrical rentals for

over 2,500 film titles. These films may be searched for by title, genre, or distributor.

Cinemedia
http://www.afionline.org/CINEMEDIA/CineMedia.home
-directory with listings covering radio, television, cinema, and new media

Cinema-Sites
http://www.cinema-sites.com
-Internet links to festivals, film schools, guilds, production resources, screenwriting sites, studios, and more

eMoon Online Production Resource Guide
http://www.emoon.com
(213) 876-8193
(outside California) (800) 550-6342
fax (213) 876-6410
E-mail: nme@emoon.com
-This guide is divided into three sections, each of which is broken down geographically:
   -Vendors Unlimited, which lists production vendors
   -Entertainment Services, which lists production resources
   -Crew Up on the Web, which lists production personnel

Entertainment Law Resources for Film, TV and Multimedia Producers
http://www.laig.com/law/entlaw
-Web site provided by entertainment attorney and producer's rep Mark Litwak
-valuable information on the legal aspects of film production and distribution

Film Festivals Server
http://www.filmfestivals.com
-updates on film festivals around the world
-includes interviews, news updates, film synopsis, and photos
-also offers information on film markets

Hollywired
http://www.hollywoodwired.com
-on-line production research tool for products, services, locations, film commissions talent, and more
-One of their offerings is Location Online, which will search a database for location images based on criteria that you supply, (e.g., a front exterior view of a Victorian home in Chicago with a lake view).

Hollywood Law CyberCenter
http://www.hollywoodnetwork.com/Law/Cones
-Hosted by entertainment attorney John W. Cones, this site contains information on legal and financing aspects of independent filmmaking, distribution, clearance procedures, and links to other motion picture sites on the Internet.

Internet Movie Database (IMDb)
> http://www.us.imdb.com
> -free source of information covering tens of thousands of movies, from the earliest silent films to films still in production
> -includes biographies and filmographies of writers, directors, producers, actors, and technicians
> -information is cross-indexed by title, production company, individuals, and more

Money for Film and Video Artists
> http://www.artsusa.org
> -American Council for the Arts
> -information on over 200 organizations that provide grants, awards, fellowships, residencies; also covers equipment access, legal assistance, loan programs, and technical assistance

Movienet Links
> http://www.movienet.com/movienet/linkshp.html
> -Internet links to box office reports, databases, distributors, festivals, studios, and more

WebMovie: The Producer's Guide to the Web
> http://www.webmovie.com/guide.htm
> -host for over 1,500 domestic and international production facilities and services
> -hotlinks to hundreds more information sources, including distributors, producers, festivals, markets, financing, packaging, archives, entertainment law, special effects, unions and guilds, and film schools

COMPANIES, FACILITIES AND SERVICES

Baseline Los Angeles
> 1925 Century Park East, Suite 250
> Los Angeles, CA 90067-2703
> > (310) 789-2030
> > fax (310) 789-2031
> Call (800) 858-3669 for off-line research services (see Baseline on the Web above)

Breakdown Services, Ltd.
> 1120 S. Robertson Blvd., 3rd Floor
> Los Angeles, CA 90035
> > (310) 276-9166
> > fax (310) 276-8829
> > Los Angeles (310) 276-9166
> > New York (212) 869-2003
> > Toronto (416) 323-0723
> > Vancouver (604) 684-4525
> > London (01) 459-2781
> > www.breakdownservices.com

-In addition to the publications referenced in Chapter 11, Breakdown Services publishes a booklet called *The Agency Directory*. This is an alphabetical listing of all agencies in the Southern California area, along with the names of each agent, the areas that each agent specializes in, and contact information.

Christy's Editorial Film & Video Supply
135 North Victory Blvd.
Burbank, CA 91502
  (818) 845-1755
-editing equipment and supplies
-rentals, sales, and service
-everything from 8mm to digital nonlinear systems

Enterprise Printers and Stationers
7401 Sunset Blvd.
Los Angeles, CA 90046
  (213) 876-3530 or 876-3533
  E-mail: enterprise@loop.com
-complete source for motion picture forms, budgets, lists, reports, breakdown sheets, contracts, productions boards and strips, call sheets, and more

Entertainment Data, Inc.
8350 Wilshire Blvd., Suite 210
Beverly Hills, CA 90211
  (213) 658-8300
  fax (213) 658-6650
  E-mail info@entdata.com
  http://www.entdata.com
-offices in Beverly Hills, London, Munich, and Madrid
-hard copy and on-line data access

Film Finders
Los Angeles Office
718 Westbourne Dr.
West Hollywood, CA 90069-5104
  (310) 657-6397
  fax: (310) 657-6608
  E-mail: 76015 1377@compuserve.com
  http://www.movienet.com
Paris Office
21, Avenue Montaigne
75008 Paris France
Tel: (011-33-1) 49-52-83-45
Fax: (011 33 1) 49-52-05-80
EMBALM: 101233 2314@compuserve.com
Internet site http://www.movienet.com

Film Stock Exchange, Inc.
1041 N. Formosa Ave.
Santa Monica West, Bldg. #15-D

Los Angeles, CA 90046
(213) 850-2800
fax (213) 850-2840
-short ends, recanned and unopened film stock

Focal Press
313 Washington St.
Newton, MA 02158-1626
  (800) 366-2665
  (617) 928-2500
  fax (800) 466-6520
  fax (617) 928-2620
  http://www.bh.com/bh/fp/
-extensive list of books covering all aspects of film and video production

The Hollywood Book & Poster Co.
6562 Hollywood Blvd.
Hollywood, CA 90028
  (213) 465-8764
-books, stills, posters, and scripts for motion picture and television productions

Hollywood Film Institute
P.O. Box 481252
Los Angeles, CA 90048

5225 Wilshire Blvd., Suite 414
Los Angeles, CA 90036
  (800) 366-3456
  (213) 933-3456
  fax (213) 933-1464
  http://HollywoodU.com
-offers classes on screenwriting, producing and directing, as well as a two-day crash course that covers the start-to-finish process of making an independent feature film
-two-day seminar on the nuts and bolts of filmmaking
  -the course assumes that you have the money and are ready to start. Day one is devoted to making of the film. Day is devoted to marketing. The course is conducted with humor and insight, and is a valuable experience for anyone considering independent production.

Hollywood Collectables
120 South San Fernando Blvd., #446
Burbank, CA 91502
  (818) 845-5450
  fax (818) 845-5422
-wide selection of scripts, treatments, and storyboards for movies, movies-of-the-week, miniseries, and television series

Independent Film Channel (IFC)
http://www.ifctv.com

-cable television channel dedicated to independent film presented twenty-four hours a day
-uncut and commercial free
-reaches 8 million homes
-Bravo/IFC
   150 Crossways Park West
   Woodbury, NY 11797

Larry Edmunds Bookshop, Inc.
   6644 Hollywood Blvd.
   Hollywood, CA 90028
      (213) 463-3273
      fax (213) 463-4245
-specializes in books and memorabilia on cinema and theater

Opamp Technical Books
   1033 N. Sycamore Ave.
   Los Angeles, CA 90038
      (213) 464-4322
      (800) 468-4322
      fax (213) 464-0977
      http://computer-hardware-books.opamp.com
-comprehensive technical bookstore with a section devoted to film and television

Paul Kagan Associates
   126 Clock Tower Place
   Carmel, CA 93923
      (408) 624-1536
-maintains extensive data on the motion picture industry (see Baseline on the Web in this appendix under "Internet Sites")

Script City
   8033 Sunset Blvd., #1500
   Hollywood, CA 90046
      (213) 871-0707
-books, stills, posters, and scripts for motion picture and television productions

Studio Film & Tape, Inc.
   1215 N. Highland Ave.
   Hollywood, CA 90038
   (800) 824-3130
-short ends, recanned and unopened film stock

Sundance Channel
   http://www.sundancechannel.com
-offers the full spectrum of independent films, including feature films, documentaries, shorts, and animation
-uncut and commercial free

Truman Van Dyke Company
     6290 Sunset Boulevard, Suite 1800
     Hollywood, CA 90028
          (213) 462-3300
          (415) 386-8956
          fax (213) 462-4857
     -insurance brokers to the entertainment industry

U.S. Copyright Office
     Register of Copyrights
     Library of Congress
     Washington, D.C. 20559-6000
          (800) 726-4995
          (202) 707-3000
          (202) 707-9100 to order application forms
          http://lcweb.loc.gov/copyright
     -form PA (which stands for "performing arts") is the correct form for the registration of a published of unpublished script, treatment, or script outline

Writers' Computer Store
     11317 Santa Monica Blvd.
     Los Angeles, CA 90025-3118
          (310) 479-7774
          fax (310) 477-5314
          (800) 272-8927
          E-mail: writerscom@aol.com
          http://writerscomputer.com
     -a comprehensive source for software and books on screenplay, novel, dramatic, and fiction writing
     -They also carry an extensive inventory of books and software on film, TV and multimedia budgeting, scheduling, and storyboarding.

ORGANIZATIONS

The Academy of Motion Picture Arts & Sciences (AMPAS)
     8949 Wilshire Blvd.
     Beverly Hills, CA 90211
     (310) 247-3000

AFMA (formerly called the American Film Marketing Association)
     12424 Wilshire Blvd., Suite 600
     Los Angeles, CA 90025
          (310) 446-1000
          http://www.afma.com

-nonprofit trade association that seeks to advance and protect the interests of the independents throughout the world, serving its members as the MPAA serves major studios

Alliance of Motion Picture and Television Producers (AMPTP)
    15503 Ventura Blvd.
    Encino, CA 91436
        (818) 995-3600

American Federation of Musicians
    1501 Broadway
    New York, NY 10036
    (212) 869-1330

The American Film Institute (AFI)
    2021 N. Western Avenue
    Los Angeles, CA 90027
        (213) 856-7600
        fax (213) 467-4578

American Society of Cinematographers
    1782 N. Orange Dr.
    Hollywood, CA 90028
        (213) 876-5080
        fax (213) 882-6391

Arts Resource Consortium Library at the American Council for the Arts
    -hot line (212) 223-2787, ext. 223
    -referral hot line for visual artists regarding such issues as funding, insurance, health, and law

Association of Film Commissioners International
    7060 Hollywood Blvd., Suite 614
    Los Angeles, CA 90028
        (213) 462-6092
        fax (213) 462-6091
        http://www.afciweb.org

Association of Independent Video & Filmmakers/Foundation for Independent Video & Film (AIVF/FIVF)
    304 Hudson St., 6th Floor
    New York, NY 10013
        (212) 807-1400
        fax (212) 463-8519
        E-mail: aivffivf@aol.com
        http://www.virtualfilm.com/AIVF

Directors Guild of America
  7920 Sunset Blvd.
  Los Angeles, CA 90046
    (310) 289-2000
    fax (310) 289-2029

  400 N. Michigan Ave., Suite 307
  Chicago, IL 60611
    (312) 644-5050
    fax (312) 644-5776

  110 West 57th St.
  New York, NY 10019
    (212) 581-0370
    fax (212) 581-1441
  http://www.dga.org

Film & Video Arts, Inc.
  817 Broadway
  New York, NY 10003
    (212) 673-9361

The Filmmakers Foundation
  5858 Wilshire Blvd., Suite 205
  Los Angeles, CA 90036
    (213) 937-5505
    fax (213) 937-7772
    www.filmfound.org
  -nonprofit organization founded in 1994 that operates as a networking structure
  connecting people, programs, information, and resources to help filmmakers
  launch and sustain careers in the motion picture and television industries
  -offers educational and training programs for filmmakers
  -runs the Los Angeles Independent Film Festival

Independent Feature Project/East
  104 W. 29th St., 12th Floor
  New York, NY 10001
    (212) 243-7777
  -a nonprofit membership organization devoted to nurturing emerging and established talent, promoting independent filmmaking within the industry and to the
  general public, and recognizing exceptional efforts. Services include seminars,
  workshops, screenings, advice, and referrals.

Independent Feature Project/West
  1625 Olympic Blvd.
  Santa Monica, CA 90404
  (310) 392-8832
  fax (310) 392-6792

Independent Feature Project/Midwest
676 N. LaSalle, 4th Floor
Chicago, IL 60610
   (312) 587-1818
   fax (312) 587-9630

Independent Feature Project/North
401 N. 3rd St., #450
Minneapolis, MN 55401
   (612) 338-0871
   fax (612) 338-4747

Independent Feature Project/South
P.O. Box 145246
Coral Gables, FL 33114
(305) 461-3544
fax (305) 446-5168

International Alliance of Theatrical Stage Employees (IATSE)
1515 Broadway, Suite 601
New York, NY 10036
   (212) 730-1770

13949 Ventura Blvd.
Sherman Oaks, CA 91423
   (818) 905-8999

International Brotherhood of Teamsters
1 Hollow Ln.
Lake Success, NY 11042
   (516) 365-3470

International Documentary Association
1551 So. Robertson Blvd.
Los Angeles, CA 90035
   (310) 284-8422
   fax (310) 785-9334
   http://www.ida@netcom.com
-a nonprofit association founded in 1982 to promote nonfiction film and video,
to support the efforts of documentary film and video makers around the world,
and to increase public appreciation and demand for documentary films and television programs

International Film Financing Conference (IFFCON)
360 Ritch St.
San Francisco, CA 94107
   (415) 281-9777
   http://www.iffcon.com

-"Linking independent producers with international dollars"
-international market for North American films in development
-intensive three-day gathering in San Francisco where independent producers gain access to foreign financiers, buyers, and coproducers
-attended by leading independent producers and industry executives from around the globe

Motion Picture Association of America (MPAA)
  1600 Eye St., NW
  Washington, DC 20006
    (202) 293-1966

  15503 Ventura Blvd.
  Encino, CA 91436
    (818) 995-6600
-The MPAA Classification and Rating Administration can be contacted at the California address and phone number.

Motion Picture Editors Guild
  7715 Sunset Blvd.
  Hollywood, CA 90046
    (213) 876-4770

Producers Guild of America
  400 S. Beverly Dr.
  Beverly Hills, CA 90212
    (310) 557-0807

Screen Actors Guild
  5757 Wilshire Blvd.
  Los Angeles, CA 90036
    (213) 954-1600

The Society of Composers and Lyricists
  400 S. Beverly Dr., Suite 214
  Beverly Hills, CA 90212
    (310) 281-2812
    FAX (818) 990-0601
    E-mail: SCL ADMIN@aol.com

Society of Motion Picture and Television Engineers (SMPTE)
  595 W. Hartsdale Ave.
  White Plains, NY 10607-1824
    (914) 761-1100
    fax (914) 761-3115
    (818) 846-3102
    http://www.smpte.org

Society of Motion Picture Art Directors
  11365 Ventura Blvd.
  Studio City, CA 91604
    (818) 762-9995

The Sundance Institute
  P.O. Box 16450
  Salt Lake City, Utah 84116
    (801) 328-3456
    fax (801) 575-5175
    E-mail: sundance@mission.com
    http://www.sundance.net

  225 Santa Monica Blvd., 8th Floor
  Santa Monica, CA 90401
    (310) 394-4662
    fax (310) 394-8353
    E-mail: sundance@deltanet.com

Writers Guild of America, East
  555 W. 57th St.
  New York, NY 10019
    (212) 767-7800

Writers Guild of America, West
  7000 W. 3rd St.
  Los Angeles, CA 90048-4329
    (213) 951-4000
    fax (213) 782-4800
    http://www.wga.org
  Script Registration:
    (213) 782-4540
    fax (213) 782-4803

World Intellectual Property Organization (WIPO)
  P.O. Box 18
  CH-1211
  Geneva, 20
  Switzerland
    41-22 338-9111
    http://www.wipo.INT

  U.S. Office:
  2 United Nations Plaza, Room 560
  New York, NY 10017
    (212) 963-6813
    fax (212) 963-4801
  E-mail:
    General: WIPO.mail@wipo.INT
    Arbitration and mediation: ARBITER.mail@wipo.INT
    Copyright: COPYRIGHT.mail@wipo.INT

Sample Domestic Distribution Delivery Requirements

QUALITY CONTROL REQUIREMENTS:

Distributor shall, at its own cost, perform one quality-control test on each element supplied by Licensor. Licensor shall be liable for the cost of all quality control tests after the initial quality-control test of all elements replaced because of failure to conform to Distributor's technical quality requirements.

ASPECT RATIOS:

The Picture shall not be in an aspect ratio other than the standard theatrical 1:85 to 1 without Distributor's prior written consent. No elements shall be "letter boxed" without Distributor's prior written consent.

A. Delivery Location:

(Distributor's address).

B. FILM MATERIALS:

1. <u>Original Negative</u>: The original 35mm picture negative (without scratches or defects) conformed to the American National Standards Institute catalogue reference ANSI/SMPTE S9-1989 "35mm Motion Picture Camera Aperture Images," fully cut, edited, and assembled complete with credits and main, narrative (if any), end, and all descriptive titles, and conforming to the final edited version of the action work print of the Picture approved by Distributor and in all respects ready and suitable for the manufacture of protection interpositive.

2. <u>Optical Sound Track Negative</u>: One (1) fully mixed and recorded original 35mm optical sound track negative of the Picture, of technically acceptable quality prepared for printing in perfect synchronization with the Action Negative and conforming in all respects to the Answer Print approved by Distributor. Note: If the original sound track was manufactured as an optical stereo

mix, a list of facilities for which the stereo optical sound track has been cross-modulated must be supplied.

3. 35mm 3-Track Master: One (1) 35mm 3-track stereo magnetic master of the dubbed sound track of the Picture on 1,000' reels from which the Optical Sound Track Negative has been made.

4. Answer Print: One (1) first-class sample composite 35mm positive print of the Picture fully timed or color corrected, manufactured from Action Negative and Sound Track Negative, fully titled, with the sound track printed thereon in perfect synchronization with photographic action and conformed to the final edited version of the action work print of the Picture approved by Distributor and in all respects ready and suitable for distribution and exhibition.

5. Color Interpositive Protection Master: If the Picture is in color, one (1) color-corrected and complete interpositive master of the Picture, conformed in all respects to the Answer Print for protection purposes without scratches or defects. If the Picture is in black and white, one (1) graded or timed protection master of the Picture, conformed in all respects to the Answer Print for protection purposes.

6. Color Internegative/Dupe Negative: One (1) 35mm Internegative manufactured from the color interpositive protection master conformed in all respects to the delivered and accepted Answer Print without scratches or defects.

7. 35mm Low-Contrast Print: One (1) first-class 35mm composite low-contrast print fully timed and color corrected, manufactured from the original action negative and final sound track, fully titled, conformed, and synchronized to the final edited version of the Picture.

8. Titles/Textless Background: One (1) original 35mm textless (i.e., without any superimposed lettering) main and end title background negative, and one (1) 35mm textless (i.e., without any superimposed lettering) main and end title background interpositive protection master and one (1) interpositive protective master of the credits and main, narrative (if any), end, and all descriptive titles conformed in all respects to the background of the Action Negative.

9. Sound Tracks: The separate dialogue tracks, sound effects tracks, and music tracks, each recorded on 35mm magnetic tracks from which the original Magnetic Sound Track was made. A separate dialogue track recorded on 35mm magnetic track for each language into which the Picture has been dubbed by Producer or will be dubbed by Producer.

10. Spanish Dialogue Track: One (1) 35mm magnetic Spanish dialogue track in perfect synchronization with the music and effects track of the feature.

11. <u>M&E Track</u>: One (1) 35mm state-of-the-art magnetic sound track master, including the music track and the 100% fully filled effects track on separate channels where the effect track contains all effects, including any effects recorded on the dialogue track. This M&E track shall also include a third separate dialogue guide track with no English dialogue in the M&E tracks. If the Picture is to be released with stereophonic sound, Licensor shall deliver an additional 35mm stereophonic dubbing four-channel magnetic sound track minus any English dialogue or narration, for use as a M&E track with surrounds if surrounds were recorded and in Dolby if the picture is in Dolby or in Ultra-Stereo if the picture is in Ultra-Stereo.

12. <u>Trims and Outs</u>: Irrevocable access to all 35mm picture negative and positive cutouts, trims, second takes plus matching 35mm sound track cutouts, and trims (including "dailies," looped dialogue, wild tracks, sound effects tracks, music tracks, and all takes made for the purpose of making the Picture suitable for television exhibition) with an inventory specifying the number of the container in which each take is located, including a list of cuts and trims suitable for use as stock footage. (Deliver laboratory letter).

13. <u>Closed-Captioned Version</u>: All closed-captioned elements.

14. <u>Televisoin "Cover Shots"</u>: All television elements, including "cover shots" and dialogue coverage to enable the Picture to be exhibited for U.S. network television release. (Deliver laboratory letter).

C. VIDEOTAPE ITEMS:

1. <u>Digital Video Masters</u>: One (1) D1 or D3 individually manufactured (conversions not acceptable) video master in the NTSC format (panned and scanned if the Picture is in 1.85 ratio or in anamorphic) made from the interpositive of the feature or low-contrast print on unspliced stock. Transfer master required with stereo audio if stereo elements exist (if not, then mono elements) and SMPTE non-drop frame time code on channel 3.

   (a) The transfer process from film to videotape shall not cause any coloration when a pure white, gray, or black scene is reproduced.

   (b) All transfers done from widescreen or anamorphic film elements to tape must be panned and scanned so as to make them acceptable for television framing. In the case of 1.85:1 or 1.66:1 elements, framelines in the picture (letterboxing) are not acceptable except in the case of titles. If necessary, for title safety, the main and/or end title sequences may be transferred in the letterbox format so long as the framelines are wiped with a complementary color to the picture behind the credits. (White or colored titles in a black field need not be wiped).

2. <u>Digital Television Master</u>: One (1) D1 or D3 individually manufactured (conversion not acceptable) video master in the NTSC format (panned and scanned if the Picture is in 1.85 ratio or in anamorphic) made from the in-

ternegative of the television version of the Picture with a running time of no less than 95 minutes and no greater than 98 minutes.

(a) The transfer process from film to videotape shall not cause any coloration when a pure white, gray, or black scene is reproduced.

(b) All transfers done from widescreen or anamorphic film elements to tape must be panned and scanned so as to make them acceptable for television framing. In the case of 1.85:1 or 1.66:1 elements, framelines in the picture (letterboxing) are not acceptable except in the case of titles. If necessary, for title safety, the main and/or end title sequences may be transferred in the letterbox format so long as the framelines are wiped with a complementary color to the picture behind the credits. (White or colored titles in a black field need not be wiped).

3. <u>Digital Trailer Video Masters</u>: One (1) D1 or D3 individually manufactured (conversions not acceptable) Trailer Video Master in the NTSC format (panned and scanned if the Picture is in 1.85 ratio or in scope) made from the interpositive of the feature. Composite audio, music, and effects on channel 1, and music and effects on channel 2.

4. <u>Digital Unrated Masters</u>: One (1) D1 or D3 individually manufactured (conversions not acceptable) video master in the NTSC format (panned and scanned if the Picture is in 1.85 ratio or in anamorphic) made from the interpositive of the feature or low-contrast print on unspliced stock and containing such outtakes, scenes, and footage as specified by Distributor that would result in a rating of "NC-17" if the Picture were rated by the M.P.A.A. Transfer master required with stereo audio if stereo elements exist (if not, then mono elements) and SMPTE nondrop frame time code on channel 3.

(a) The transfer process from film to videotape shall not cause any coloration when a pure white, gray, or black scene is reproduced.

(b) All transfers done from widescreen or anamorphic film elements to tape must be panned and scanned so as to make them acceptable for television framing. In the case of 1.85:1 or 1.66:1 elements, framelines in the picture (letterboxing) are not acceptable except in the case of titles. If necessary, for title safety, the main and/or end title sequences may be transferred in the letterbox format so long as the framelines are wiped with a complementary color to the picture behind the credits. (White or colored titles in a black field need not be wiped).

D. PUBLICITY MATERIALS:

1. <u>B&W stills</u>: 200 production B&W shots (8×10 B&W stills and 8×10 B&W negatives) depicting scenes in the Picture with members of the cast (including principals) appearing therein.

2. <u>Color Stills</u>: 200 production color shots (8×10 color stills and 8×10 color negative) depicting scenes in the Picture with members of the cast (including principals) appearing therein.

3. <u>Color Slides</u>: 300 production color slides (35mm color transparencies) depicting scenes in the Picture with members of the cast (including principals) appearing therein.

4. <u>Advertising Materials</u>: One (1) copy of all advertisements, paper accessories, and other advertising materials, if any, prepared by Producer or by any other party in connection with the Picture, including samples of one-sheet posters and individual advertising art elements and transparencies necessary to make proofs thereof.

5. <u>Electronic Press Kit</u>: One (1) Electronic Press Kit ("EPK") created using 35mm film or broadcast quality videotape suitable in all respects for network broadcast. The EPK shall have a running time of no less than ten (10) minutes and no more than thirty (30) minutes. The EPK shall contain interviews with the principal cast, the director, and producer as well as behind-the-scenes footage and production footage. The EPK shall have four-track discrete audio with the voice-over and/or narration on one track, the dialogue on a separate track, the music on a separate track, and the effects on a separate track.

E. LEGAL AND PUBLICITY DOCUMENTS:

1. <u>Laboratory Access Letter</u>: One (1) Laboratory Access Letter, giving irrevocable access for the period of this agreement to all preprint and video materials being held, said letter to be countersigned by laboratory.

2. <u>Sound Laboratory Access Letter:</u> One (1) letter of access to the Sound Service House, giving irrevocable access to all preprint and video materials being held.

3. <u>Pressbooks</u>: Five (5) Pressbooks, including biographies (one to three typewritten pages in length) of key members of cast, individual producer, director, cinematographer, and screenwriter.

4. <u>Production Notes</u>: Copy of the production notes of the Picture prepared by the Unit Publicist, including items relating to: underlying work (original screenplay, book, etc.), places where the Picture was photographed, anecdotes about the production of background of the Picture.

5. <u>Feature Dialogue Continuity and Spotting List</u>: Two (2) copies in the English language of a detailed, final dialogue and action continuity, in an acceptable format, of the completed Picture and two (2) copies in the English language of a detailed, final spotting list, in an acceptable format, of the Picture.

6. <u>Trailer Dialogue Continuity and Spotting List</u>: Two (2) copies in the English language of a detailed, final dialogue and action continuity, in an acceptable format, of the completed Trailer and two (2) copies in the English language of a detailed, final spotting list, in an acceptable format, of the Trailer.

7. <u>Synopsis</u>: Three (3) copies of a brief synopsis in English language (one typewritten page in length) of the Picture and three (3) copies of a synopsis in the English language (three typewritten pages in length) of the story of the Picture. (Deliver to "Director of Worldwide Services.")

8. <u>Technical Crew</u>: One (1) copy of a list of all technical personnel (including their title or assignment) involved in the production of the Picture.

9. <u>Screen Credit Obligations</u>: Three (3) copies of the Screen Credit Obligations for all individuals and entities affiliated with the Picture.

10. <u>Paid Ad Credit Obligations</u>: Three (3) copies of the Paid Advertising Credit Obligations for all individuals and entities affiliated with the Picture.

11. <u>Billing Block</u>: Three (3) copies of the approved credit block to be used in paid advertising of the Picture.

12. <u>Name and Likeness Restrictions</u>: Three (3) copies of all name and likeness restrictions and/or obligations pertaining to all individuals and entities affiliated with the Picture.

13. <u>Talent Agreements</u>: All contracts of the cast, director, cinematographer, screenwriter(s), producer(s), and author (or other owners of the underlying material, if applicable), including their respective Agents' names and phone numbers.

14. <u>Music Cue Sheets</u>: Two (2) Music Cue Sheets of the Picture.

15. <u>Certificate of Origin</u>: Ten (10) original notarized Certificates of Origin of the Picture.

16. <u>Notarized Assignment of Rights</u>: Ten (10) original notarized Assignment of all rights in the Picture from Producer to Distributor.

17. <u>Copyright Certificate</u>: Two (2) U.S. Copyright Registration Certificates (stamped by the Library of Congress). If the copyright application has not yet been received from the Library of Congress, then Licensor shall deliver a copy of the Application PA Form, along with a copy of the cover letter and check that accompanied the PA Form. Licensor agrees to deliver two (2) copies of the Copyright Certificate to Distributor when received from the Library of Congress.

18. <u>Producer's Errors and Omissions Insurance</u>: One (1) copy of the policy and one (1) Certificate of Errors & Omissions Insurance naming Purchaser as

additional insured for a minimum coverage of One Million Dollars ($1,000,000) for a single occurrence and Three Million ($3,000,000) for aggregate claims with a minimum term of three (3) years from the Delivery Date.

19. <u>Music Licenses and Composer Agreement</u>: Copies of Music Licenses (synchronization and mechanical) and composer's agreement.

20. <u>Chain of Title</u>: Complete Chain of Title documentation.

21. <u>UCC Search</u>: One current UCC search from the following states:

(i) California
(ii) the state of Licensor's principal place of business
(iii) the state of producer's principal place of business

Each search report must show that the Picture is free and clear of any and all liens.

22. <u>MPAA Certificate</u>: (i) MPAA certificate of Approval and rating with a receipt for the Payment of the fee. In addition, if a third party is distributing the Picture theatrically, then Licensor must deliver in writing such distributor's name, address, and telephone number.

OR

(ii) Licensor must acknowledge that it has not released and has no intention to release the Picture theatrically. Licensor must deliver to Distributor an MPAA Classification and Rating Administration Theatrical Distribution Rights Form—Part I and, if required, Part II. These forms must be accurately completed with original signatures; photocopies and faxes are not acceptable. Licensor shall be responsible for the cost of rating the Picture.

23. <u>Title Report</u>: One current (no more than 60 days old) title report showing that the title of the Picture is available for use without infringing any other person's or entity's rights.

24. <u>Copyright Report</u>: One current (no more than 60 days old) copyright report showing that Licensor has good clear title to the picture and all underlying rights.

25. <u>Copyright Mortgage</u>: Three (3) original copyright mortgages, fully executed and notarized by Licensor granting Distributor a security interest in and to all rights in the Picture.

26. <u>UCC Financing Statement</u>: One (1) California UCC-1 financing statement, fully executed by Licensor granting Distributor a first position security interest in and to all rights in the Picture.

F. COMPLETE TRAILER MATERIALS:

1. <u>Trailer Picture Negative</u>: One (1) 35mm negative (without scratches or defects), fully cut, edited, and assembled, of the completed trailer.

2. <u>Trailer Optical Sound Track Negative</u>: One (1) fully mixed and recorded original 35mm optical sound track negative of the Completed Trailer prepared for printing in perfect synchronization with the Trailer Picture negative.

3. <u>Trailer Magnetic Sound Track</u>: One (1) 35mm original magnetic three-track, consisting of separate dialogue, music, and 100% filled sound effects, fully recorded and equalized in perfect synchronization with the Trailer Picture Negative.

4. <u>Trailer Answer Print</u>: One (1) first-class sample composite 35mm positive print of the Completed Trailer, fully timed and color corrected, manufactured from the Trailer Picture Negative and Trailer Sound Track Negative, with the sound track printed thereon in perfect synchronization with photographic action and with Distributor identification symbols as Distributor shall determine, in all respects ready and suitable for distribution and exhibition.

5. <u>Trailer Overlay Text</u>: One (1) 35mm negative of the text used for superimposing the lettering of the Completed Trailer fully cut to match the trailer picture negative.

6. <u>Trailer Sound Track</u>: The separate dialogue tracks, sound effect tracks, narration tracks, and music tracks, each in 35mm magnetic tracks from which the original Trailer Magnetic Sound Track was made.

7. <u>Trailer Textless Background</u>: One (1) 35mm textless (i.e., without any superimposed lettering) background negative of the Completed Trailer conformed in all respects to the background of the Trailer Negative.

Index

About the Author

GREGORY GOODELL is an award-winning writer-producer-director whose credits include independent features, documentaries, television movies, and mini-series. He has lectured and taught at the American Film Institute and other organizations. Mr. Goodell lives on the West Coast with his wife and two daughters.